# SYNTAX and SEMANTICS

VOLUME 8

# SYNTAX and SEMANTICS

## VOLUME 8
**Grammatical Relations**

**Edited by**

*PETER COLE*

*University of Illinois*
*Urbana, Illinois*

*JERROLD M. SADOCK*

*University of Chicago*
*Chicago, Illinois*

**ACADEMIC PRESS**     *New York  San Francisco  London*

*A Subsidiary of Harcourt Brace Jovanovich, Publishers*

ACADEMIC PRESS, INC.
111 Fifth Avenue, New York, New York 10003


United Kingdom Edition published by
ACADEMIC PRESS, INC. (LONDON) LTD.
24/28 Oval Road, London NW1


LIBRARY OF CONGRESS CATALOG CARD NUMBER: 72–9423

ISBN 0–12–613508–8

PRINTED IN THE UNITED STATES OF AMERICA

80 81 82    9 8 7 6 5 4 3 2

# CONTENTS

# LIST OF CONTRIBUTORS

*Numbers in parentheses indicate the pages on which the authors' contributions begin.*

MOHAMMAD IMAM ABASHEIKH (179), *Department of Linguistics, University of Illinois, Urbana, Illinois*

STEPHEN R. ANDERSON (1), *Department of Linguistics, University of California, Los Angeles, Los Angeles, California*

SANDRA CHUNG (1), *Department of Linguistics, University of California, San Diego, La Jolla, California*

PETER COLE (27), *Department of Linguistics, University of Illinois, Urbana, Illinois*

BERNARD COMRIE (47), *Department of Linguistics, University of Cambridge, Cambridge, England*

CHARLES J. FILLMORE (59), *Department of Linguistics, University of California, Berkeley, Berkeley, California*

JUDITH OLMSTED GARY (83), *Department of Linguistics, University of California, Los Angeles, Los Angeles, California*

WAYNE HARBERT (27, 121), *Department of Linguistics, University of Illinois, Urbana, Illinois*

SACHIKO HASHIMOTO (27), *Department of Linguistics, University of Illinois, Urbana, Illinois*

DAVID E. JOHNSON (151), *Mathematical Sciences Department, IBM Thomas J. Watson Research Center, Yorktown Heights, New York*

EDWARD LOUIS KEENAN (83), *Department of Linguistics, University of California, Los Angeles, Los Angeles, California*

CHARLES W. KISSEBERTH (179), *Department of Linguistics, University of Illinois, Urbana, Illinois*

JOHN M. LAWLER (219), *Department of Linguistics, University of Michigan, Ann Arbor, Michigan*

CECIL NELSON (27), *Department of Linguistics, University of Illinois, Urbana, Illinois*

GEOFFREY K. PULLUM (249), *Linguistics Section, University College London, London, England*

PAUL SCHACHTER (279), *Department of Linguistics, University of California, Los Angeles, Los Angeles, California*

DIANE SMIETANA (27), *Department of Linguistics, University of Illinois, Urbana, Illinois*

SHIKARIPUR SRIDHAR (27), *Department of Linguistics, University of Illinois, Urbana, Illinois*

ANTHONY C. WOODBURY (307), *Department of Linguistics, University of California, Berkeley, Berkeley, California*

# PREFACE

Dissatisfaction with the existing generative-transformational model of syntactic description has given rise to several new, closely related models. The new models differ from the earlier theory in that grammatical relations, such as subject and object, are treated as primitives, and are not, as in other theories, notions derived from structural primitives such as precedence and dominance. For purposes of this preface, we shall term all such theories RELATIONAL GRAMMAR.

There are two main reasons for the rapid growth of interest in Relational Grammar. First of all, the theory is intuitively attractive: It agrees better with the insights of traditional grammar than does tne ordinary transformational model. Second, it allows the direct statement of many striking, cross-linguistic generalizations that are impossible to capture in a straightforward way in the older framework. For example, a universal statement of passivization as a process that makes direct objects into subjects is possible in relational terms whereas the statement of passive in the classical transformational model will differ from language to language depending on word order and details of morphology.

As yet, little on the topic of Relational Grammar has been published. The literature that exists is widely sought after but is mainly available only through underground channels. The present volume seeks to remedy this deficiency by gathering together several of the most original and insightful examples of work within the relational framework. There is considerable divergence of opinion in the field, and this is reflected in the selections in the volume. Because of the newness of Relational Grammar, several of the contributors take pains to explain their assumptions and terminology carefully enough so that the book can be used as an introduction to this branch of grammatical theory.

David Johnson sketches some principal assumptions of Relational Grammar, defines terms, and provides a list of laws that make the theory empirically testable. His aim is to characterize one of the central notions of the field, that of 'relation-changing rule of grammar'.

Another of the central constructs examined in the volume is that of the notion 'grammatical relation' itself. Various authors are concerned with the claims that have been made concerning the nuclear terms of a clause, the subject and object. Schachter argues that, at least for Philippine languages, the concept of 'subject' is quite artificial. Instead he proposes that ideas such as 'topic' and 'agent', which converge as subject in many languages, are kept quite distinct in the languages of the Philippines. Lawler has also uncovered a language, Achenese, in which the identification of the subject is not a trivial matter. He suggests that membership in a relational category is a matter of degree, and that, indeed, the properties that are ordinarily thought of as defining grammatical relations are themselves not discrete.

The recognition of the direct object is also not straightforward, as several of the chapters show. Kisseberth and Abasheikh's contribution discusses the implications of the fact that the typical properties of direct objects are split between two distinct noun phrases in Chi-Mwi:ni. Gary and Keenan argue that Kinyarwanda allows two direct objects in certain sentences. In contrast, for German double-accusative constructions, Harbert argues that only one noun phrase should be considered a direct object, while the other, despite its accusative case marking, is in fact an indirect object.

A rather different problem with respect to the identification of subjects and objects is presented by ergative languages. Woodbury describes West Greenlandic Eskimo, one of the most thoroughly ergative languages known, with the problem of identifying the nuclear terms in mind. He concludes that whether a rule or even an aspect of a rule will follow the accusative or ergative arrangement depends to a large extent on the nature of the process involved.

One of the significant advances to come out of the relational model is the discovery that the various grammatical relations may be arranged in a hierarchy that can be used to explain numerous universal syntactic facts. The refinement and extention of this hierarchy is the concern of three of the contributions in this volume. Keenan and Gary's work on Kinyarwanda shows that not all positions on the hierarchy are necessarily represented in every language and that, indeed, the same position may in some cases be occupied by two constituents in individual sentences. Cole et al. demonstrate that an extension of the hierarchy can be put to use in explaining island constraints. The utility of this unexpected benefit of the relational approach is illustrated with respect to several languages. As Pullum shows, the relational hierarchy can serve in yet another sphere for which it was not originally postulated, namely word order universals. Pullum argues that there is a very simple relation between the hierarchy and the order of basic clause constituents in all human languages.

It is a central hypothesis of Relational Grammar that the linear order of constituents plays almost no role in the working of major syntactic processes. Anderson and Chung support this hypothesis by showing that Berman's arguments against McCawley's treatment of English as a VSO language hold equally well for languages that ARE VSO. They conclude that these arguments demonstrate that rules affecting grammatical relations are completely independent of the linear order of constituents.

Other chapters concern themselves with the nature of relational rules and the laws governing them. Harbert seeks to understand better the process called Clause Union, and Woodbury, as previously mentioned, is interested in the nature of ergative versus accusative rules. Comrie argues that, contrary to the popular view, languages display rules that are best stated as demotions of a term to nontermhood.

There is, finally, one very important chapter that does not fit neatly into any of the classes above. This is Fillmore's exegesis of his own theory of Case Grammar, a theory that in some ways is a precursor of today's Relational Grammar. Fillmore explains what he felt Case Grammar was all about, answers several criticisms of the theory, and relates the notion of deep case to that of grammatical relation.

The volume thus presents a spectrum of work in Relational Grammar, from the basics of the theory to the detailed examination of its utility in describing individual languages. The chapters will therefore give the reader an overview of the relational model and an appreciation for the problems which concern those working in the new paradigm.

# CONTENTS OF PREVIOUS VOLUMES

## Volume 2

## Volume 3

## Volume 4

## Volume 5

# ON GRAMMATICAL RELATIONS AND
# CLAUSE STRUCTURE IN VERB-INITIAL LANGUAGES

*STEPHEN R. ANDERSON*
*University of California, Los Angeles*

*SANDRA CHUNG*
*University of California, San Diego*

## INTRODUCTION

In one of the fundamental papers of the Generative Semantics literature, McCawley (1970) argued that the underlying word order in English clauses is not verb medial (SVO), as might be expected on the basis of surface structure, but rather verb initial (VSO). This somewhat surprising conclusion follows, according to McCawley, from considerations internal to the syntax of English: A number of syntactic processes are argued to be stated more directly or more perspicuously, or with less theoretical apparatus, on the basis of such structures. The required rule to produce the verb-medial order of surface structures is also claimed to be independently necessary. It is to be simply the inverse of the rule that would otherwise be necessary to produce verb-initial order in inverted structures such as questions.

McCawley's position is criticized at length and in detail by Berman (1974). Her arguments are essentially of two sorts. First, she attempts to demonstrate that there is in fact no reason to posit underlying VSO structures for English at all, since the rule simplifications claimed by McCawley are either illusory or incorrect. Berman's aim in this case is to establish that English has underlying verb-medial order; insofar as her essentially negative arguments against McCawley are accepted, they would probably be taken by most linguists to establish a case ex silentio for underlying structures that look, in this respect

1

at least, like surface structures. We will not be further concerned here with these issues, internal to the study of English.

Berman goes on to give a second class of arguments, however, which are of more general interest. By showing that there are some syntactic processes in English (and perhaps in other languages for which the same issue could arise) for which such an order is actually necessary, these points are intended to establish a positive case for verb-medial structures. The arguments of this second type which Berman provides have the following form, in outline: In a verb-initial structure, both subject and object NP are directly dominated by the node S. There is, therefore, no structural difference between these NPs apart from their relative order. As a consequence, a rule which removed one or the other of them would produce a structure which would be formally indistinguishable from that of a basic intransitive clause. That is, there would be no way to identify whether the remaining NP in such a reduced transitive clause was originally subject or object. Thus on this hypothesis the single remaining NP in such a clause ought to behave, for the purpose of further syntactic operations, exactly the same as does the subject of an intransitive clause. Berman's arguments then take the form of showing that this conclusion is false. Certain rules apply to a clause which consists of just a verb and a single NP differentially, depending on whether that NP represents an original subject or the object of a reduced clause. If this is correct, and if, furthermore, transformations are to be stated in terms of the structural properties of phrase markers, then it must follow that subject and object are structurally distinct in some way that persists even after the subject has been removed from a transitive structure. On the hypothesis of VSO order, there is no obvious structural property which can perform this function, as was just noted. There is one obvious property, however; if SVO structures are basic: Subjects are preverbal, while objects are postverbal, regardless of whether the subject is still present. Reduced transitive clauses are distinguished from basic intransitives as VO versus SV, a property to which syntactic rules can have access.

It should be clear that Berman's arguments, even if correct in every detail, do not really establish a case for SVO order. That is, the argument outlined in the preceding paragraph makes no reference whatsoever to the actual order of elements in the clause, except inferentially: While it would certainly be possible to distinguish subject from object in terms of position relative to the verb, this is by no means the only possibility. For instance, if the verb and its object(s) form a subconstituent of the clause (namely, a VP), of which the subject is not a member, then the required differentiation between subject and object could be carried out on the basis of constituent structure alone, without reference to order. This is essentially the approach to grammatical relations taken by Chomsky (1965); it represents a position which enjoys wide acceptance among contemporary syntacticians. On this approach, underlying SOV order would be just as satisfactory as would SVO from the point of view of the argument developed by Berman. Yet another possibility would be simply to treat 'subject' and '(direct) object' as primitives of clause structure, not defined in terms of any other properties, but rather the basic relations that determine the makeup of clauses. This is, of course, the position of Relational Grammar.[1] On this line, any order whatsoever of the basic constituents of the clause (or indeed a totally unordered structure) would be equally satisfactory, since the problems raised by Berman would be resolved directly by a sort of deus ex machina which is independent of clause-internal ordering.

Insofar as Berman's argument is valid, then, it demonstrates the need for some mechanism in terms of which the grammatical relations borne by NPs within a clause can be distinguished, without determining the form of such a mechanism. Berman notes in her paper that an important source of further information on this score would be provided by the investigation of languages for which there is no reason to doubt the correctness of underlying VSO order. In such a language, where VSO structures are not to be derived from some other order at more abstract levels of representation, it would apparently be impossible for the internal structure of clauses to involve a subconstituent of the type VP, since the verb and its object(s) are separated by the subject, and hence are noncontiguous. If, in such a language, facts of the same sort as those underlying Berman's arguments from SVO languages could be shown to obtain, this would show that internal constituent structure of the usual type could not form the basis for the required differentiation. In the absence of evidence to the contrary, we assume that in VSO languages there is no basis for positing a sort of pseudo-VP consisting of the verb and the subject, excluding the object(s), which could serve the same function. Constituent structure would apparently not be adequate to resolve our problem, then. Clearly, order relative to the verb (or anything else?) would be no more satisfactory; this was the basis of Berman's argument against a VSO analysis for English. Arguments of this type from VSO languages, then, would seem to be intimately related to the claims of Relational Grammar that grammatical relations are primitives of clause structure which are not to be defined derivatively in terms of other aspects of phrase-marker structure. If such arguments can be found, they would support the need for such a notion. On the other hand, if such arguments are lacking precisely for the class of VSO languages, this would indicate that another device—such as order relative to the verb (available only for SVO languages) or clause-internal constituent structure (available for SVO, SOV, and VOS but not for VSO languages)—is a more appropriate way to define grammatical relations. A negative demonstration of this sort, to the effect that no arguments of a given type can be found within a certain domain, is, of course, next to impossible to construct; fortunately, we do not have to do this.

---

[1] As represented in several chapters in this volume, and most notably in the work of Perlmutter and Postal (forthcoming).

It is the aim of this paper to present some arguments of the type originally provided by Berman,[2] taken from languages whose VSO typology is not seriously in question. The languages at issue are Tongan and Samoan, from the Polynesian family, and Breton, a Celtic language. Despite some processes of topicalization in all three languages which can lead to some surface structures which are NOT VSO, it is quite clear that the basic typology of these languages IS VSO, and that it is such a structure that forms the input to essentially all of the rules of their syntax. For general discussion of the syntactic properties of verb-initial languages, see Keenan (forthcoming); for a discussion of the syntax of Polynesian languages, see Chung (1976); and for a sketch of the relevant aspects of the syntax of Breton see Anderson (forthcoming). From the evidence of these languages, to be presented below, it would appear to follow (as outlined above) that a strong argument can be constructed for an approach to syntax in which grammatical relations are primitives. Nonetheless, at the end of this chapter we will discuss some data from Breton which suggest that a notion of constituent structure at variance with the traditional one may possibly play a role in the description of VSO languages; these data suggest that the argument for the elementary character of grammatical relations in clause structure is weaker than it first appears.

## EXAMPLES FROM POLYNESIAN LANGUAGES

We consider first an argument from the interaction of an Equi-NP Deletion rule and Subject-to-Object Raising in Samoan. The Equi rule in Samoan optionally deletes an embedded subject under identity with a controller NP in the next higher clause. The problems of selecting a controller are much the same as the familiar ones which arise in English and other languages; the NP deleted in the lower clause, however, is always a subject. The rule need not apply, as in the sentences of (1S):[3]

(1S)      a. '*Ua mānana'o tagata e   mālō lātou i  le  pālota.*
           perf want-pl   people fut win   they in the election
           'People wanted to win in the election.'

      b. '*Ua māfaufau Tupu e  fa'alogo 'oia i  le  lāuga.*
           perf decide    Tupu fut listen   she to the sermon
           'Tupu decided that she would listen to the sermon.'

---

[2] The arguments below are presented in the framework of "classical" generative syntactic description. In particular, we ignore the possible implications for our analyses of recent proposals for a "trace theory of movement rules." Such a theory, since it allows a degree of 'global' reference to earlier stages of a derivation (cf. Chomsky 1975 for some discussion), would have extensive implications for the sort of rules discussed here.

[3] The languages from which the examples are taken are indicated by letters: e.g. (1S) is from Samoan, (7T) from Tongan, (18B) from Breton, and (44E) from English.

If Equi applies to these sentences, it results in the sentences of (2S):

(2S)          a. *'Ua mānana'o tagata e    mālō i le   pālota.*
                     perf want-pl   people fut win  in the election
                     'People wanted to win in the election.'

         b. *'Ua māfaufau Tupu e   fa'alogo i  le   lāuga.*
                     perf decide    Tupu fut listen    to the sermon
                     'Tupu decided to listen to the sermon.'

The Samoan rule of Subject-to-Object Raising is also analogous to the English rule. This rule optionally raises the subject of an embedded clause, which becomes the direct object of the higher clause. In (3S), the rule has not applied:

(3S)          a. *Sā   mana'o Tupu e  'emo le  uila.*
                     past want    Tupu fut flash the lightning
                     'Tupu wanted the lightning to flash.'

         b. *E mānana'o tagata 'ia    manuia le  pālota.*
                     fut want-pl   people irreal be-well the election
                     'People want the election to turn out well.'

When Subject-to-Object Raising applies, the sentences of (4S) result:

(4S)          a. *Sā   mana'o Tupu i  le  uila     e  'emo.*
                     past want    Tupu at the lightning fut flash
                     'Tupu wanted the lightning to flash.'

         b. *E mānana'o tagata i  le  pālota 'ia    manuia.*
                     fut want pl    people at the election irreal be-well
                     'People want the election to turn out well.'

Both Equi and Raising are subject to some further conditions and qualifications (cf. Chung 1976 for details), but the two rules are clearly part of the grammar of Samoan, and distinct from one another.

Significantly, there are a few verbs in Samoan which govern both Subject-to-Object Raising and Equi. *Mana'o* (plural *mānana'o*) 'want', for instance, allows either rule to affect its complement [cf. (2Sa) versus (4Sb), for example]. Now both of these rules affect subjects; since Samoan has an underlying VSO word order, both would be stated so as to affect the first NP following the verb (in the absence of any further internal structure). In that case, however, the application of one of these rules to a transitive complement ought to produce a reduced clause superficially like a basic intransitive. If this is indeed true, it ought to be possible now to apply the other of the two rules. From a sentence to which Equi has applied, like (5Sa), it should be possible to derive (5Sb) by Raising:

(5S)         a.  *Sā  mānana'o tagata e   pu'e  le  gaoi.*
                 past want-pl   people fut catch the burglar
                 'People wanted to catch the burglar.'

             b.  *\*Sā  mānana'o tagata i  le   gaoi   e  pu'e.*
                 past want-pl   people at the burglar fut catch
                 'People wanted the burglar to catch.'


Sentence (5Sb), however, is not possible: Subject-to-Object Raising cannot apply to objects, regardless of whether the subject is still present.

The converse of the facts in (5S) is also true of Samoan. Where Raising has applied to remove the subject NP from a complement, as in (6Sa), we might expect to be able to apply Equi to delete the NP that is left in the reduced clause:


(6S)         a.  *E  le'i     mana'o Tupu i  leoleo e  pu'e  'oia.*
                 fut not-yet want    Tupu at police fut catch her
                 'Tupu didn't want the police to catch her.'

             b.  *\*E  le'i     mana'o Tupu i  leoleo e  pu'e.*
                 fut not-yet want    Tupu at police fut catch
                 'Tupu didn't want the police to catch.'


The ungrammaticality of (6Sb) shows, however, that this is not the case: Objects cannot be deleted by Equi even when the subject is no longer present in the clause.

The impossibility of constructions like (5Sb) and (6Sb) cannot be accounted for if linear order relative to one another is the only parameter which distinguishes subject from object structurally in a VSO language like Samoan. On this view, there would be no natural way of preventing Equi and Subject-to-Object Raising from applying to one another's outputs on a purely structural basis. The fact that the two rules do not interact in such a way would follow immediately, however, from a proposal which distinguished subject and object in some other terms. In such a framework, the rules would not be stated to affect the NP following the verb, but rather the NP which has the structural properties of a subject. If one rule removes the subject, there is no reason to expect that another NP in the clause (the object) would "inherit" the subject properties. Thus, neither rule could apply to the output of the other.

One serious objection to this argument is the probability that semantic conditions are involved in the operation of Equi and of Raising, with the possible consequence that such conditions might be invoked to prevent the generation of (5Sb) and (6Sb). Equi, in particular, seems to be constrained so as to apply only where the controller in the higher clause has some possibility of effecting the action of the lower clause. This might account for the absence of (6Sb); (5Sb) could then be prevented by ordering Raising before Equi. It is difficult to escape the feeling that semantic conditions are involved in these constructions, and that the ungrammaticality of (5Sb) and (6Sb) is due to something other than the faulty application of syntactic processes. The reason for including such an argument here is that Berman provides an exactly parallel argument for English, against which exactly parallel objections could be raised. The point of this discussion is that the argument is exactly as good (or bad) for Samoan as it is for English.

It seems much less likely that semantic conditions are involved in the next rule to be discussed. We are concerned here with a rule of Clitic Placement, which exists in similar forms in many Polynesian languages. Generally, the rule can be argued to perform the following operations: First, a clitic pronoun copy of a pronominal subject is created, and positioned before the verb. Then, if the pronoun subject is unemphatic, it is deleted, leaving the clitic copy as the only residue of the original subject. The important property of this rule for our purposes is the fact that it applies only to produce clitic copies of pronoun SUBJECTS: It cannot ever apply to copy a pronoun object, regardless of whether the subject is still present in its clause.

We discuss below the interaction of this rule in Tongan with another rule which can remove the subject NP from a clause. Tongan contains a rule of Subject-to-Subject Raising which applies in the subject complements of a highly restricted class of verbs (typically *lava* 'be able'). These subject complements can occur unaltered, as in (7T):

(7T)       a. *Na'e lava pē   ke 'alu 'a  e  tangata.*
           past able emph irr walk abs art man
           'It was possible for the man to walk.'

       b. *'Oku lava ke hua'i 'e Siale  'a  e  hu'akau.*
           pres able irr throw erg Charlie abs art milk
           'It is possible for Charlie to throw out the milk.'

Or else the subjects of the complements can be raised:

(8T)       a. *Na'e lava pē    'a  e  tangata 'o   'alu.*
           past able emph abs art man    comp walk
           'The man could walk.'

       b. *'Oku lava 'e Siale   'o   hua'i 'a e  hu'akau.*
           pres able erg Charlie comp throw abs art milk
           'Charlie can throw out the milk.'

The fact that Raising, rather than an Equi-NP type Deletion, has taken place in the sentences in (8T) follows from the case marking. Thus, in (8Ta), where the lower clause is intransitive, the (raised) subject is appropriately marked with the absolute particle *'a*. In (8Tb), however, the lower clause is transitive, and the raised subject is marked with the ergative particle *'e* to reflect this fact.

Tongan also has a rule of Clitic Placement, of the sort discussed above. The rule copies pronominal subjects into the position between the tense marker and the verb in the clause. This copying is obligatory for pronouns other than third-person singular; it is generally followed by deletion of the original pronoun:

(9T)　　　a.　(i)　*'Oku 'ahuina　　au.*
　　　　　　　　　　pres　smoke-suff I
　　　　　　　　　　'I'm covered with smoke.'

　　　　　　　(ii)　*'Oku ou 'ahuina.*
　　　　　　　　　　pres　I　smoke-suff
　　　　　　　　　　'I'm covered with smoke.'

　　　　　　b.　(i)　*\*Na'e 'ilo 'e　kinautolu 'a　e　tangata 'i he 'ana.*
　　　　　　　　　　past find erg they　　　abs art man　　in art cave
　　　　　　　　　　'They found a man in the cave.'

　　　　　　　(ii)　*Na'a nau 'ilo 'a　e　tangata 'i he 'ana.*
　　　　　　　　　　past they find abs art man　　in art cave
　　　　　　　　　　'They found a man in the cave.'

The rule is optional for third-person-singular pronoun subjects;

(10T)　　　　　　a.　(i)　*Na'e puke ia.*
　　　　　　　　　　　　past sick she
　　　　　　　　　　　　'She was sick.'

　　　　　　　　　(ii)　*Na'a ne　puke.*
　　　　　　　　　　　　past she sick
　　　　　　　　　　　　'She was sick.'

　　　　　　　　b.　(i)　*Na'e taa'i pē　ia　'e ia.*
　　　　　　　　　　　　past hit　emph him erg he
　　　　　　　　　　　　'He hit himself.'

　　　　　　　　　(ii)　*Na'a ne taa'i pē　ia.*
　　　　　　　　　　　　past he hit　emph him
　　　　　　　　　　　　'He hit himself.'

As these examples show, the pronoun copies which the rule produces have distinct forms from the independent pronouns. They form a single phonological unit with the tense marker, contrary to the apparent word division in the orthographic representations.

It is strictly irrelevant to the point we wish to make below whether the rule is a copying process, as we have suggested, or a movement rule, as might appear from the examples given thus far. Our analysis is supported, however, by the fact that the original pronoun, if emphatic, may remain in the clause even though Clitic Placement has occurred:

(11T)       a. *Na'a ma 'ave 'e  kimaua ho'o telefone.*
               past we take erg we      your telephone
               'We took away your telephone.'

            b. *Na'a ne taa'i 'e  ia pē    ia.*
               past he hit  erg he emph him
               'He hit himself.'

This behavior is exactly parallel to that of a great many languages in which, when the person and number of the subject are marked in the verb (generally by an agreement rule), all but emphatic pronoun subjects are then deleted.

It is important to note that only subject pronouns can undergo Clitic Placement:

(12T)       a. *\*Na'a ne ui 'e  he tangata.*
               past she call erg art man
               'The man called her.'

            b. *\*Te u 'omi 'e  Sione 'a  e   siaine.*
               fut I bring erg John  abs art banana
               'John will bring me some bananas.'

We turn now to the interaction of Clitic Placement with Raising. Let us note first that Clitic Placement can occur in embedded subject clauses that have not undergone Raising:

(13T)   *'E lava ke ke  lau ('e  koe) 'eku mata'itohi?*
        fut able irr you read (erg you) my   handwriting
        'Is it possible that you (/**you**) can read my handwriting?'

Clitic Placement can also apply in the matrix clause if Subject-to-Subject Raising has applied:

(14T)   *Te ke  lava ('e  koe) 'o    lau 'eku mata'itohi?*
        fut you able (erg you) comp read my  handwriting
        'Can you (/**you**) read my handwriting?'

However, Clitic Placement CANNOT apply in the lower clause if Subject-to-Subject Raising has applied:

(15T)   *\*Te ke  lava ('e  koe) 'o    ke  lau ('e  koe) 'eku mata'itohi?*
        fut you able (erg you) comp you read (erg you) my   handwriting
        'Can you (/**you**) read my handwriting?'

Clearly, Clitic Placement must be able to follow Raising in order to derive sentences like (14T). If Clitic Placement were a cyclic rule, we would expect it to be possible to apply it on the lower clause cycle, and then to apply Raising on the matrix cycle. In that case, however, we would derive the ungrammatical (15T). The most plausible account of these facts would be as follows: Let Clitic Placement be a postcyclic rule, applicable both to embedded and to matrix clauses [cf. (13T) and (14T)]. Whether or not Raising is cyclic, it must precede Clitic Placement. In that case, the ungrammaticality of (15T) will follow from the fact that, if Raising applies, there is no longer any subject NP present in the lower clause for Clitic Placement to apply to.

The import of this argument is to establish that Clitic Placement does not apply to embeddings until after Raising has (perhaps) removed the subject from such a clause. Now recall that Clitic Placement must be restricted to apply to subjects only, as was shown in (12T). If transitive clauses have no internal structure beyond a verb followed by two structurally equivalent NPs, this must be stated as CLITIC PLACEMENT APPLIES TO THE NP IMMEDIATELY FOLLOWING THE VERB. But in that case, when Raising removes the subject of an embedding, the result will be that the original object will become the NP immediately following the verb. If our statement is correct, then, we would expect that where Raising applies the original object can undergo Clitic Placement. However, this is not correct:

(16T)     a.   *'Oku lava ke taa'i 'e   he  tangata au.* ⇒ **raising**
               pres able irr hit   erg art man    me
               'It is possible for the man to hit me.'

          b.   *'Oku lava 'e   he  tangata 'o       taa'i au.* ⇒ **cliticization**
               pres able erg art man     comp hit   me
               'The man can hit me.'

          c.   **'Oku lava 'e   he  tangata 'o       u taa'i (au).*
               pres able erg art man     comp I hit   (me)
               'The man can hit me (**me**).'

In the first sentence in (16T), nothing has happened, and Clitic Placement is of course inapplicable. In the second sentence, Raising but not Clitic Placement has applied; in the third, both Raising and Clitic Placement have applied, yielding an ungrammatical sentence. If Clitic Placement were in fact applicable to the first NP after the verb, we would expect (16Tb) to be ungrammatical (recall that Clitic Placement, where applicable, is obligatory for pronouns other than third-person singular) and (16Tc) to be grammatical. We conclude, therefore, that this is not the correct statement of the Clitic Placement rule. Rather, the rule should be stated as it was originally: Clitic Placement applies only to pronoun SUBJECTS. From that, however, we can conclude that there must be some structural difference between subjects and objects which persists even after the subject of a clause has been removed (here, by Raising).

We should note, incidentally, that the ungrammaticality of (16Tc), and also of (15T), cannot be explained by saying that Clitic Placement does not occur in clauses introduced by the complementizer *'o*. This is not the case:

(17T)    *Mou   tutu ho'omou tūhulu, 'o    mou ō       mai!*
         you-pl light your-pl  torches comp you come-pl toward
         'Light your torches and come!'

It is precisely clauses in *'o* from which the subject has been removed in which Clitic Placement is blocked. Our conclusion that Clitic Placement refers to a property of subjects other than simply postverbal position is reinforced.

Other, similar arguments could be adduced, but the above should be sufficient to establish our conclusion. In the languages of Polynesia, rules referring to subjects must have access to some structural difference between subjects and nonsubjects, and linear order with respect to other NPs or to the verb is not sufficient. In the absence of any evidence to the contrary, we assume that the basic order in languages like Samoan and Tongan is VSO, as in surface structure. Subject cannot be distinguished from object, then, by order relative to the verb. Since the argument is directly parallel to that of Berman for English, we must conclude that, in general, arguments of this sort establish the need for a structural difference between subject and object, and are irrelevant to the question of whether English has basic SVO order.

## EXAMPLES FROM BRETON

Arguments of the sort we have just discussed are by no means confined to the languages of Polynesia. We turn now to a similar argument from Breton.[4] While this language is undoubtedly to be analyzed as having basic VSO order, this fact is not as clear from surface structures as it was in the case of Polynesian languages. A frequent word order, in fact, involves the subject in initial position:

(18B)    *Yannig a   zebro       krampouezh e  Kemper  hiziv.*
         Johnny prt eat-fut-3sg crepes        in Quimper today
         '**Johnny** will eat crepes in Quimper today.'

---

[4] The Breton described here is primarily the semistandardized modern literary language, based essentially on forms from the Leon dialect. Trépos (n.d.) covers more of the syntax of the language than do other reference grammars. As far as the syntactic points discussed here are concerned, there does not appear to be much dialectal difference. We will not go into the rather complex morphology of the language here; the system of mutations, in particular, can often have the effect of obscuring the relationship between forms of the same word. The orthography is to be interpreted as follows: vowels have the obvious values, except that *ou* = [u], *u* = [ü], and *eu* = [ö]; of the consonants, *ch* = [š], *c'h* = [x], *j* = [ž], and *h* = ∅. The combination *zh* represents a segment which is phonetically [z] in the dialects of relevance here, corresponding to [h] in the dialect of Vannes. The symbol *ñ* does not represent a nasal consonant, but simply marks nasality of a preceding vowel. In many modern dialects, this nasality is increasingly lost, especially in infinitive endings and other common morphemes.

This word order, however, is to be analyzed as due to the operation of a rule of Topicalization. Sentence (18B) is exactly on a par[5] with the following variants, in each of which some other element appears in sentence-initial position:

(19B)    a. *Krampouezh a    zebro        Yannig e Kemper  hiziv.*
            crepes        prt eat-fut-3sg Johnny in Quimper today
            'Johnny will eat **crepes** in Quimper today.'

         b. *E Kemper  e    tebro        Yannig krampouezh hiziv.*
            in Quimper prt eat-fut-3sg Johnny crepes        today
            'Johnny will eat crepes **in Quimper** today.'

         c. *Hiziv e    tebro        Yannig krampouezh e  Kemper.*
            today prt eat-fut-3sg Johnny crepes        in Quimper
            'Johnny will eat crepes in Quimper **today**.'

The differences among these sentences reside in the areas of emphasis, topic-comment structure, and so forth. Though we have glossed them as if the sentence-initial element were actually emphasized, this is an exaggeration: This element is merely the topic of the sentence, and need not be emphatically or contrastively stressed. Since virtually every sentence has SOME topic, this topicalization process simply makes explicit an aspect of the sentence's information structure which is revealed in subtler ways in other languages (cf. Kuno 1972 for some general discussion). For our purposes, the point is simply to note that none of the above orders enjoys any privileged status: Under appropriate discourse conditions, any of them is equally possible.

Under other circumstances, however, word order is fixed more rigidly. Thus, in object complements, the order with no constituent preceding the verb is preferred:

(20B)    a. *Ma mamm a    c'houlenn e    chomfen        er      gêr.*
            my mother prt ask-3sg   prt stay-condit-1sg in-the house
            'My mother asks that I stay in the house.'

         b. *C'hwi a    ouie      e    oa  bet   korseriou e Sant Malo*
            you(pl) prt knew-3sg prt was been pirates    at Saint-Malo
            *gwechall?*
            formerly
            'Did you know that there used to be pirates in Saint-Malo?'

In these sentences, the complement clause is introduced by the verbal particle *e*, followed directly by the verb. The same order is obligatory after certain

[5] In fact, grammars often warn language learners (essentially Frenchmen, who have a background of SVO structures) against overuse of subject-fronted structures like (18B) in circumstances where no special emphasis is intended.

conjunctions, such as *ma* 'if', *pa*, 'when', and others:

(21B)   a. *pa   welo     da   vamm-gozh   da   gaier-notennou*
           when see-fut-3sg your grandmother your notebook
           'when your grandmother sees your notebook'

         b. *Plijet  e  vo      tad   ma   labour mat e  vab?*
           pleased prt be-fut-3sg father if     works hard his son
           'Will father be pleased if his son works hard?'

Similarly, in negative main clauses no other element precedes the verb:

(22B)   a. *Ne vije      ket bet  lazet  ar  paour-kez den.*
           ncg would-be neg been killed the poor     man
           'The poor man wouldn't have been killed.'

         b. *Ne blij   ket din   mont e kêr pa   ne  vez ket ret.*
           neg please neg to-me to-go to town when neg is   neg necessary
           'I don't like to go to town when it isn't necessary.'

Thus, in these circumstances the word order VSO is fixed, while elsewhere any element of the sentence which is the topic can be placed before the verb.[6] The natural account of these facts is to take VSO order as basic, and to posit a rule of Topicalization which is blocked in environments such as those of (20B)–(22B).

For our purposes, the most interesting property of the Topicalization rule is the fact that, when nonsubjects are topicalized, a NP leaves an optional pronominal copy behind. When the topicalized NP is a possessor, it obligatorily leaves behind a possessive pronoun:

(23B)                a. *Per  a  zo klañ e  vab.*
                   Peter prt is sick   his son
                   '**Peter's** son is sick.'

                b. *An den  a    varvas e   vuoc'h.*
                   the man prt died   his cow
                   '**The man's** cow died.'

When the NP which is topicalized is the object of a preposition, the pronoun

---

[6] It should be noted that it is also possible to have nothing fronted in main clauses: thus, *e tebro Yannig krampouezh e Kemper hiziv* is a grammatical, though stylistically odd, variant of the sentences in (19B), Where nothing else is topicalized, another construction involving fronting of the verb (to be discussed below) is the most usual form for informationally neutral main clauses.

copy which is left behind merges with the preposition to form an 'inflected
preposition':

(24B)        a. *An dud-se      a     torner    dezho   hiziv.*
                the people-dem prt one-fights for-them today
                'One fights for **those people** today.'

             b. *Ar boteier a    sell    an den outo    er      stal.*
                the shoes   prt looks the man at-them in-the store
                'The man is looking at **the shoes** in the store.'

In (24Ba), we find a form of the proposition *da* 'for', because the topicalized
NP is a benefactive; in (24Bb) we find a form of *ouzh* 'at', with which objects
of *sellout* 'to look' are idiosyncratically marked. When a nonsubject which is
not part of any prepositional phrase is topicalized (e.g. a direct object of a verb
which takes no preposition), the pronominal copy which is left behind is a
form of the preposition *a* 'from', used also for noncopy pronouns, as in (25Ba):

(25B)        a. *Da    voereb he deus pedet   ac'hanomp.*
                your aunt    has     invited *a* + 1pl
                '**Your aunt** has invited us.'

             b. *Ar vuoc'h a    breno    ma zad    anezhi    warc'hoaz.*
                the cow    prt will-buy my father *a* + 3sgf tomorrow
                'My father will buy **the cow** tomorrow.'

Note that when a subject is topicalized no copy can be left behind, in the form
of either an independent pronoun or a form of *a*:

(26B)        a. *\*Yannig  a    louzo*  $\begin{Bmatrix} e\tilde{n} \\ anezha\tilde{n} \end{Bmatrix}$ *e    zilhad.*

                Johnny prt dirtied $\begin{Bmatrix} \text{he} \\ \text{him} \end{Bmatrix}$    his clothes

                '**Johnny** got his clothes dirty.'

             b. *Yannig  a    louzo  e    zilhad.*
                Johnny prt dirtied his clothes
                '**Johnny** got his clothes dirty.'

This fact can sometimes be used to disambiguate a sentence which would otherwise have two potential sources:

(27B)                 a. *Ar bleiz a    lazas  ma c'hi.*
                         the wolf prt killed my dog
                         $\begin{Bmatrix} \text{'**The wolf** killed my dog.'} \\ \text{'My dog killed **the wolf**.'} \end{Bmatrix}$

    b. *Ar bleiz a    lazas  ma c'hi anezhañ.*
       the wolf prt killed my dog *a* + 3sgm
       'My dog killed **the wolf**.'

Sentence (27Ba) is ambiguous, since there is no way to determine whether *ar bleiz* 'the wolf' has been topicalized from subject or from object position. In (27Bb), on the other hand, it is clear that *ar bleiz* must represent the original object; otherwise it could not have left a pronominal copy behind when it was topicalized.

We have thus far argued that Breton has a rule of Topicalization which applies to VSO structures to front any constituent of the clause. We will discuss below the meaning of 'any constituent' in this statement, but our concern at this point is with another aspect of the rule. Topicalization can leave behind a pronominal copy when it applies to other than a subject NP, where such a copy will be reinforced with the preposition *a* if it is not otherwise part of a prepositional phrase. There are two possible approaches to this aspect of the rule: Either we could state explicitly that copies are produced of all and only nonsubject NPs as an optional correlate of Topicalization, or we could allow Topicalization to produce copies of any fronted NP, and then delete copies that represent original subjects. Presumably the appropriate way to do this would be to copy any NP as an optional by-product of Topicalization, mark object pronouns that are not part of prepositional phrases with the preposition *a* [necessary in any case to derive sentences like (25Ba), where the object pronoun is independent of Topicalization], and then delete any unsupported postverbal pronouns (i.e. subject pronouns).

The evidence is fairly strong that this latter approach is correct. As we have noted, the rule which marks unsupported object pronouns with *a* is needed in any event. Further, the rule to delete postverbal (i.e. nontopicalized) subject pronouns is also needed in any event, since these pronouns never appear in surface structure except where they have been fronted by Topicalization:

(28B)      a. *Al levr   brezhoneg a   lennan (anezhañ).*
          the book Breton     prt I-read (*a* + it)
          'I read **the Breton book**.'

      b. *Me a  lenn al  levr   brezhoneg.*
          I    prt read the book Breton
          'I read the Breton book.'

      c. *\*Al levr   brezhoneg a    lenn(an)   me (anezhañ).*
          the book Breton     prt read(1sg) I   (*a* + it)
          'I read **the Breton book**.'

      d. *\*Me a   lenn(an)  me al  levr   brezhoneg.*
          I    prt read(1sg) I   the book Breton
          'I read the Breton book.'

Sentences (28Bc–d) are ungrammatical because an unsupported subject pronoun has not been deleted in postverbal position.

Since both *a*-marking and postverbal subject pronoun deletion are independently needed in Breton, it is clear that the facts concerning copies left behind by Topicalization can be accounted for simply by allowing the rule to leave a pronoun in the original position of a NP which has been topicalized, without regard to its function. It will then be marked with *a*, if an object; cliticized to a preceding preposition; or deleted if left unsupported. What is of interest for our purposes is that an object NP cannot be marked with *a* until after Topicalization has applied: this is because nontopicalized objects when full NPs must not be marked with *a*:

(29B)        a.  *Me 'm eus    tapet    daou louarn.*
                 I    have-1sg caught two  foxes
                 'I have caught two foxes.'

             b.  **Me 'm eus    tapet    a      zaou louarn.*
                 I    have-1sg caught from two  foxes
                 'I have caught two foxes.'

             c.  *Al  louarn am eus    tapet    anezhañ.*
                 the fox      have-1sg caught *a* + it
                 'I have caught **the fox**.'

We must therefore prevent *a*-marking from applying to full NPs, as in (29Bb), and restrict it to pronouns. Until Topicalization has applied, however, the NP which will be topicalized is in general not pronominal, as in (29Ba). We cannot avoid this consequence by marking all objects with *a* and then deleting *a* before full NPs after Topicalization has applied, since that would incorrectly predict the deletion of a host of *a*'s that have nothing to do with object marking:

(30B)        a.  *Sell  pegement   a  granked!*
                 look  how-many of crabs
                 'Look at how many crabs there are!'

             b.  **Sell  pegement   kranked!*
                 look  how-many crabs
                 'Look at how many crabs there are!'

We conclude that *a*-marking applies only to object pronouns; since these pronouns are created by Topicalization, it follows that *a*-marking cannot apply to them until after Topicalization.

This observation leads immediately to an argument of the sort we are looking for. Topicalization may remove any element from the clause without residue, since resumptive copies are completely optional. Object Marking, as we have seen, applies after Topicalization; thus, when it comes to apply, there may be only one NP left in the clause, and the rule must be able to determine whether that NP is a subject or an object. If it is a (pronominal) object, *a*-marking can apply; otherwise *a*-marking must be blocked. Consider the following partial paradigm:

(31B)          a.   *Me 'm eus     gwelet anezhañ.*
                    I     have-1sg seen     *a* + him

               b.   *Hennezh am eus     gwelet.*
                    him          have-1sg seen

               c.   **Me 'm eus     gwelet.*
                    I     have-1sg seen

               d.   **Hennezh am eus     gwelet ac'hanon.*
                    him          have-1sg seen     *a* + I
                    'I have seen him.'

Object pronouns are *a*-marked [cf. (a)] and are not deleted [cf. (c)]. Subject pronouns are deleted postverbally [cf. (b)] and are not *a*-marked [cf. (d)].

Object Marking needs to be able to distinguish subjects from objects. If Breton underlying structures are indeed VSO, as we have argued, and if the two NPs in a transitive clause are structurally equivalent except for order, there is no way to distinguish the results of topicalizing the subject from the results of topicalizing the object: In both cases, if no pronoun copy is left behind, the output is a structure [$_S$NP V NP]. Thus, some additional structure must be posited from which the subject-object distinction can be recovered.

It might be suggested that even after a subject is topicalized a subject pronoun copy will remain behind as a place holder from which the required distinction could be made. This cannot be true, however. Object pronouns cannot in general be deleted [cf. (31Bc)]; only pronoun copies have this property. It seems plausible to account for this by saying that copying is optional, a part of the Topicalization rule itself. But *a*-marking for objects is not optional, as would have to be the case if topicalized subjects sometimes left a copy and sometimes did not, and if this subject place holder were essential to the structural description of *a*-marking. The only alternative would be to say that copying is obligatory when Topicalization applies to subjects. This is clearly unmotivated, however, since it is precisely when Topicalization applies to subjects that a pronoun copy can never appear in surface structure [cf. (28Bd) above]. We conclude, therefore, that a single NP must be identifiable as either subject or object of a clause in which it appears—independent of the issue of whether another NP also appears in that clause.

Another argument in the same direction can be constructed from the inter-

action of Topicalization and subsequent *a*-marking of object pronoun copies
with a rule which deletes subjects. Breton has rules of Complement Subject
Deletion rather similar to English Equi-NP Deletion (and Super-Equi, if such
a rule exists). Here we will not justify the positing of such rules, but will simply
note their effects. We have already seen the form of embedded clauses: These
appear in the same form as main clauses, except that Topicalization is generally
not applicable in them. In the following cases, the complement clauses are
introduced directly by the verbal particle *e* (which also has phonological
variants *ez*, *ec'h*), and the remainder of the complement is exactly like a main
clause:

(32B)   a. *Gouzout a   ran   e   teuio          d'ar   gêr   abarz- pell.*
            know    prt I-do prt he-will-return to-the house before-long
            'I **know** he will return to the house before long.'

        b. *Mamm a   lavaras din   ec'h ev     he zad.*
            mother prt she-said to-me prt  drinks her father
            '**Mother** told me that her father drinks.'

When the subject of the lower clause is identical with an appropriate controller NP in the matrix clause, the lower subject is deleted, the verbal particle
disappears, and the verb is replaced by an infinitive form:

(33B)       a. *ma ouifes              bleniañ  eur c'harr*
               if  know-condit-2sg to-drive a   car
               'if you knew how to drive a car'

            b. *Mamm a   lavaras din    nompas ober   trouz.*
               mother prt she-said to-me neg       to-do noise
               '**Mother** told me not to make noise.'

In general, these reduced clauses consist of only the infinitive and its complements. Some verbs, however, take a complement preceded by a preposition;
similarly, complements in other than direct-object position usually have this
form:

(34B)       a. *Me 'm eus    c'hoant da gousket.*
               I    have-1sg desire   for to-sleep
               '**I** want to sleep'

            b. *Mont a   raio    ar merc'hed da welout ar staliou.*
               to-go prt will-do the women    for to-see the shops
               'The women will **go** (to town) to see the shops.'

There is also a participial form, consisting of the infinitive preceded by the
particle/preposition *o*, forming a sort of reduced relative. This form is also used
as the complement of certain auxiliaries (typically *bezañ* 'to be', used to form a

progressive tense), and is presumably to be derived by Complement Subject Deletion:

(35B)  a. *Setu an noz o tont.*
      voila the night prt to-come
      'Look at the night coming.'

    b. *Pelec'h e vezit bemdez o tebriñ koan?*
      where prt be-habit-2sg every-day prt eat supper
      'Where do you eat supper every day?'

The importance of Subject Deletion from our point of view comes from its interaction with Topicalization. Topicalization, basically, is upward-bounded: a topicalized NP cannot escape from its clause if it remains a full clause:

(36B)  a. *Lavaret en deus an aotrou Kere e oa ret*
      said have-3sg the Mr. Quere prt was necessary
      *dit deskiñ mat da genteliou.*
      to-you to-learn well your lessons

    b. ??*Lavaret en deus an aotrou Kere da genteliou a*
      said have-3sg the Mr. Quere your lessons prt
      *oa ret dit deskiñ mat.*
      was nec. to-you to-learn well

    c. *\*Da genteliou en deus lavaret an aotrou Kere e*
      your lessons have-3sg said the Mr. Quere prt
      *oa ret dit deskiñ mat.*
      was nec. to-you to-learn well
      'Mr. Quéré said it was necessary for you to learn your lessons well.'

In (36Bb), Topicalization has applied in the complement. Though this is sometimes at least marginal, it is usually impossible. In (36Bc), however, Topicalization has applied not within the lower clause, but to raise an element of that clause into topic position in the upper clause. This is completely impossible, as the ungrammaticality of (36Bc) makes clear.

When the subject of the complement is removed, however, by the process(es) illustrated above in (33B)–(35B), Topicalization is possible:

(37B)  a. *E vreur emañ Perig o klask er c'hoad.*
      his brother is Peter prt look-for in-the woods
      'Peter is looking for **his brother** in the woods.'

    b. *Ar boteier a oa an den er stal o sellout outo.*
      the shoes prt was the man in-the shop prt to-look at-them
      'The man was in the shop looking at **the shoes**.'

    c. *Ar staliou a    yelo     ar  merc'hed da  welout warc'hoazh.*
       the shops prt will-go the women   for to-see  tomorrow
       'The women will go (to town) to see **the shops** tomorrow.'

Thus, Equi-NP Deletion has the effect of reducing a clause to a form from which Topicalization can remove an element into the matrix sentence. It follows, therefore, that in these cases Topicalization follows Equi-NP Deletion.

But Topicalization from such a reduced clause can remove the object, and when it does it may leave a pronoun copy behind. Like other object pronoun copies, these are marked with *a*:

(38B)    a. *Ho ti    a   oamp   o   klask da brenañ anezhañ.*
          your house prt were-lpl prt seek   for buy     *a* + it
          'We were looking to buy **your house**.'

    b. *E  vreur   emañ Perig o   klask anezhañ er      c'hoad.*
          his brother is     Peter prt seek   *a* + him in-the woods
          'Peter is looking for **his brother** in the woods.'

The pronouns in (38B) are produced as a result of Topicalization. They undergo *a*-marking as objects; this application of *a*-marking must follow their creation, and hence must follow Topicalization. But Topicalization, in turn, must follow Equi-NP Deletion, as we saw above. Thus, when *a*-marking comes to apply, the object pronoun is the only remaining NP in its (reduced) clause. It cannot be the case, then, that the presence of the subject in the clause is crucial to the structural description of the Object *a*-marking rule. There must be some other structural feature of the clause from which the status of the pronoun as an object can be determined. We have thus arrived at our conclusion once again: The status of a NP as object rather than subject must be related to some aspect of clause structure other than simple relative order of NPs within a homogeneous $[_s V\ NP\ NP]$ structure in a VSO language.

## CONCLUSION: ON CLAUSE STRUCTURE IN VSO LANGUAGES

We have demonstrated above that Berman's conclusion concerning the need for a structural difference between subject and object can be shown to follow in languages such as Samoan, Tongan, and Breton, where the basic order is VSO. It thus cannot be the case that her argument demonstrates the need for underlying SVO order in English, though of course there may well be (indeed, we feel there are) independent arguments establishing this conclusion. If subject and object are to be structurally distinguished in a VSO structure, though, it clearly cannot be by order relative to the verb (i.e. with subject specified as $NP/\_V$, and object as $NP/V\_$). It would appear to be the case that a constituent VP, including the verb and its object(s), is impossible, since the subject intervenes between these elements. Thus, there does not seem to be a natural constituent structure division of the clause that will accomplish the desired effect. We would appear to have arrived at a strong argument in favor of the basic position of Relational Grammar, to wit, that grammatical relations must be taken as primitives of clause structure, neither ignored nor defined solely in terms of other structural properties of clauses such as linear order or internal constituency and domination.

As the alert reader will no doubt have perceived from our choice of words in the preceding paragraph, however, the evidence does not seem unambiguous in support of this conclusion. In particular, there is some evidence from Breton that a constituent VP, consisting of just the verb and its object(s), may need to be posited despite the fact that this unit could not form a continuous constituent of the usual sort.

As we have discussed at some length above, Breton has a rule of Topicalization which can apply in main clauses to front any single constituent. But Topicalization cannot apply to more than one constituent in a single clause:

(39B)       *Hiziv e  Kemper  e   tebro   Yannig krampouezh.
            today in Quimper prt will-eat Johnny crepes
            'Johnny will eat crepes **in Quimper today**.'

As can be seen from the grammaticality of (19Bb–c), either *hiziv* 'today' or *e Kemper* 'in Quimper' can be topicalized by itself, but together the two do not form a larger constituent, and so both cannot be fronted at the same time. On the other hand, where two elements do form a single constituent, they can be topicalized together. Thus, we saw above that a possessor of a NP could be topicalized by itself, as in (23B). We can also topicalize the head along with the possessor:

(40B)                    a. *Mab Per   a   zo klanv.*
                            son Peter prt is  sick
                            '**Peter's son** is sick.'

                         b. *Buoc'h an den  a   varvas.*
                            cow     the man prt died-3sg
                            '**The man's cow** died.'

We conclude that the Topicalization rule applies to exactly one constituent of a clause.

Thus far, most of our examples of Topicalization have involved the fronting of either an NP or an adverb. There is another kind of Topicalization, however, which is statistically of high frequency in the language: It is also possible to topicalize the main verb of a clause. When this happens, the topicalized verb shows up in the form of an infinitive, and in the place of the original finite verb is found an inflected form of the verb *ober* 'to do', marked for person, number and tense. This option is not limited to activity verbs: It is applicable to any

verb in the language with the exception of *bezañ* 'to be' and the periphrastic
verb *endevout* 'to have'.[7] The 'do' in this case is thus closer to the *do* produced
in English by Verb-Phrase Deletion (*he ought to know that, but he doesn't*) than
to the verb of *do so* and related constructions:[8]

(41B)          a. *C'hoarzhiñ a   ra    ar baotred.*
                  to-laugh    prt does the boys
                  'The boys laugh.'

               b. *Mont a rin           ganit     d'ar    pardon.*
                  to-go prt do-fut-1sg with-you to-the pardon
                  'I will go with you to the pardon.'

Since the topicalization of the main verb has the effect of focusing on the action
rather than on one of the participants in it, it is appropriate for 'neutral' discourse, and accordingly the construction in (41B) is much used.

The interesting point about this construction for our purposes, though, is the
following: As we have noted, constituents are subject to Topicalization. Clearly
the verb itself is a constituent, and so we would expect to be able to topicalize
it. There is also another possibility, however: When the main verb is itself transitive, it is possible to topicalize just the verb, as in (42Ba) below, or alternatively
to topicalize the verb with its object(s):

(42B)          a. *Deskiñ   a    reomp Brezhoneg.*
                  to-learn prt do-1pl  Breton
                  'We are learning Breton.'

               b. *Deskiñ Brezhoneg a     reomp.*
                  to-learn Breton      prt do-1pl
                  'We are learning Breton.'

               c. *Lenn'   eul levr   brezhoneg a   ran      bemdez.*
                  to-read a  book Breton      prt do-1sg every-day
                  'I read a Breton book every day.'

How are we to account for this possibility? It seems clear that the construction
in (42Bb–c), which is in no way marginal but rather is perfectly productive in
the language, must be taken to imply that the verb together with its object(s)
form a constituent of some sort. While we will not describe all of these possibilities here, the material that can be treated as a 'verb phrase' for the purposes
of Topicalization in Breton is essentially the same as that which is usually taken
to make up the verb phrase in English: The verb together with direct and

---

[7] For some speakers; for others, this topicalization may be most acceptable for activity verbs
and less so for statives. The facts are rather unclear here.

[8] For some discussion of this distinction, cf. Anderson (1968).

indirect objects, reduced complement clauses, and directional adverbs, but not with adverbs of time, place, manner, and others generally thought of as 'sentence adverbials' rather than 'verb phrase adverbials'.

Two alternatives present themselves here. We might take the apparent VSO order of Breton to be derived: That is, at some more abstract level the language might be assigned SVO or SOV basic order, with a rule of Verb Fronting applying to yield the observed VSO structures. The most natural structure for Topicalization to apply to, though, is VSO, since we wish this order to result when Topicalization does not apply, and other orders to count as equivalent deviations from it. If VSO arises before Topicalization applies, however, the point of positing an order other than VSO disappears; recall that the motivation for an order other than VSO was exactly to account for the unity of verb phrases under Topicalization. Since there does not seem to be any positive evidence in the language which favors a basic order distinct from VSO, we reject this alternative.

The other possibility is to say that the material usually called a VP does indeed form a constituent of some sort, despite the fact that the verb itself is not contiguous with the rest of this "VP". Note that it is NOT possible to topicalize the verb and its subject, which are contiguous:

(43B)     a.   *_Deskiñ ni a ra Brezhoneg_
              to-learn we prt do Breton
              '**We** are **learning** Breton.'

         b.   *_Lenn Yannig a ra eul levr brezhoneg bemdez._
              to-read Johnny prt does a book Breton every-day
              '**Johnny reads** a Breton book every day.'

There are several ways we could envision the creation of a constituent with the appropriate properties. We might, for example, analyze all sentences in which Verb Topicalization is possible as having their apparent main verbs embedded as complements of a matrix verb _ober_ 'to do', with this structure undergoing Equi followed by a sort of incorporation rule which, if Topicalization has not taken place, would replace the inflected form of _ober_ with a form of the embedded verb. Mechanically, this is probably the most satisfactory alternative, but in the absence of any further evidence for the analysis of virtually all clauses in Breton as involving such embedding, we are somewhat uneasy about it.

Another solution to the problem would have to involve extending our notion of constituent structure in some way. We might simply allow discontinuous constituents, an option which has occasionally been suggested in the structuralist literature, but seldom taken seriously within the framework of generative grammer. Or, on the other hand, we might allow transformational rules to make reference to 'constituents' that are unitary only in some sort of semantic structure. Occasionally such a suggestion has been made to explain, for example, the possibility of passivizing the objects of certain prepositional phrases:

(44E)           a. *This bed was slept in by Herbert Hoover.*
                b. *Harry's proposal will be argued about for years.*

In these cases, *sleep in* and *argue about*, while not syntactic constituents, are in some sense semantically unitary elements similar in nature to simplex verbs; it is this fact which is responsible for the possibility of passivizing their objects but not those in (45E):

(45E)              a. *\*Cleveland was run amok in by John.*
                   b. *\*Saturday was slept on.*

Similarly, it has been proposed that *make the claim* (*that s*), *make the suggestion* (*that s*), *have the idea* (*that s*), etc., are in a way semantically equivalent to simplex verbs like *claim*, *suggest*, and *think*. This could then account for the fact that it is easier to extract elements from the complements of such expressions than from the structurally similar ones in (46Ed–f).

(46E)   a. *?This is the sort of sentence that no one would ever make the claim could be properly parsed.*

        b. *?Your dog, which I made the suggestion be chained, is none-theless a fine one.*

        c. *A play which I had the idea you might enjoy opened last week in London.*

        d. *\*This is the sort of sentence which no one would ever believe the claim could be properly parsed by machine.*

        e. *\*My dog, which I will not entertain a suggestion be chained, is not a biter.*

        f. *\*The play which I don't like the idea that you will appear in involves full frontal nudity.*

Thus, there is some precedent for such a notion of semantic constituents which are not syntactic constituents. The idea must be explored much more fully than it has been, however, before it could be taken seriously.

There is really no completely satisfactory solution to our problem, then. On the one hand, we must be able to treat the verb and its complements as a con-stituent of some sort for the purposes of Topicalization; on the other hand, no satisfying and well-motivated way to do this has been proposed thus far. Nonetheless, we can conclude that the verb and its complements do form a unit at some levels of structure in Breton, a unit which does not include the subject; and from this it follows that there may well be a way to distinguish subjects and objects in terms of constituent structure, at least of this (possibly extended) sort. In that case, it might no longer be necessary to take the relational terms as primitive. It would be interesting to see whether whatever device is appropriate here can be extended naturally to other languages in which a configurational definition of the fundamental relations in clause structure is apparently not available.

It seems to us that if such a move is feasible it would in fact be more interesting than a theory in which subject and object are taken as unanalyzable basic terms. The interest of a theoretical structure comes largely from the extent to which it reveals systematicities and relations among its basic terms. Work in Relational Grammar has uncovered an impressive array of properties associated with the fundamental grammatical relations; it would appear that the interest of such a theory could only be enhanced by showing that these notions themselves could be reduced to other independently motivated properties such as the internal constituent structure of clauses.

Regardless of the resolution of this issue, however, the thrust of our arguments above is the following: In VSO languages, as well as in other types of languages, rules exist which are sensitive to a structural difference between subjects and objects. The difference in question is independent of the linear position in the clause of the NP affected, and persists after the deletion of one or the other of the NPs involved in a transitive construction. From this it must follow that subject and object are structurally distinct; and in the nature of things, this distinction cannot be taken to refer to position relative to the verb in a VSO language. This, in turn, suggests that the distinction is probably not (solely) in terms of position relative to the verb in a language like English, either. Whether the required relational distinctions can be coded in terms of some notion of hierarchical constituent structure, or should be taken to be unanalyzable primitives, must remain at present an open question.

## REFERENCES

Anderson, S. R. (1968) "Pro-sentential Forms and Their Implications for English Sentence Structure," in Report NSF-20, Harvard University Computation Laboratory; to appear in J. D. McCawley, ed., *Notes from the Linguistic Underground*, Academic Press, New York.
Anderson, S. R. (forthcoming) "Breton," in E. L. Keenan, ed., *The Syntax of Verb-first Languages*.
Berman, A. (1974) "On the VSO Hypothesis," *Linguistic Inquiry* 5, 1–38.
Chomsky, N. (1965) *Aspects of the Theory of Syntax*, M.I.T. Press, Cambridge, Massachusetts.
Chomsky, N. (1975) *Reflections on Language*, Pantheon Books, New York.
Chung, S. (1976). *Case Marking and Syntactic Relations in the Polynesian Languages*, unpublished Doctoral dissertation, Harvard University, Cambridge, Massachusetts.
Keenan, E. L. (forthcoming) "Typological Properties of Verb-first Languages," in E. L. Keenan, ed., *The Syntax of Verb-first Languages*.
Kuno, S. (1972) "Functional Sentence Perspective," *Linguistic Inquiry* 3, 269–320.
McCawley, J. D. (1970) "English as a VSO Language," *Language* 46, 286–299.
Perlmutter, D. and P.M. Postal (forthcoming) *Relational Grammar*.
Trépos, Pierre (n.d.) *Grammaire bretonne*, Simon, Rennes.

# NOUN PHRASE ACCESSIBILITY AND
# ISLAND CONSTRAINTS

---

PETER COLE, WAYNE HARBERT, SHIKARIPUR SRIDHAR,
SACHIKO HASHIMOTO, CECIL NELSON, AND DIANE SMIETANA
University of Illinois

In this paper we define two approaches to island phenomena: the TRANS-
FORMATIONAL APPROACH and the ACCESSIBILITY APPROACH. Previously un-
reported cross-linguistic evidence—falsifying the former but consistent with
the latter—is presented. In the first part of the paper we shall outline the two
approaches, in the second part we shall present cross-linguistic evidence against
the Transformational Approach, and in the third part we shall present evidence
for the Accessibility Approach.

## THE TRANSFORMATIONAL AND ACCESSIBILITY APPROACHES

The existence has long been recognized of syntactic islands—configurations
such as coordinate structures and complex NPs—which block the application
of some syntactic processes. Since they were discovered, the exact nature of
the constraints has been a matter of great interest. Until recently, investigators
have attempted to explain island phenomena as constraints on particular types
of transformational operations, such as movement or deletion. For example,
Ross (1967) attempted to show that island constraints are universal restrictions
which prevent transformations from carrying out the operations of movement
or deletion over a variable. (We shall ignore putative feature-changing rules.)
Perlmutter (1972) argued that Ross's apparent cases of constraints on movement
should be reanalyzed as constraints on relative deletion, thereby reducing

27

island constraints to constraints on a single transformational operation: deletion. We would like to emphasize the affinity between Ross's and Perlmutter's
approaches. What is common to both is the attempt to define island constraints
as constraints on some class of transformational operation, such as movement
or deletion. We are not concerned with the very real differences between Ross's
and Perlmutter's positions; we refer to their joint approach as the Transformational Approach to island phenomena.

Despite the impressive results obtained by the Transformational Approach,
recent studies contain data suggesting that this approach is fundamentally
inadequate. James (1972) and Morgan (1975) have noted phenomena in English
that are sensitive to island constraints, but which seem, at least, not to be
explainable in terms of constraints on particular classes of transformational
operations. James notes that the referent of the exclamation *ah* cannot be in
an island. Thus in (1):

(1)      *Ah, it is reported by Newsweek that Kissinger is a vegetarian!*

which contains an extraposed sentential subject, *ah* can be an expression of
surprise that Newsweek made a certain report, or it can be an expression of
surprise with regard to the proposition reported. In (2):

(2)      *Ah, that Kissinger is a vegetarian is reported by Newsweek!*

however, where the sentential subject has NOT been extraposed and hence is
an island, *ah* can be interpreted only as an expression of surprise that Newsweek
made the report. It cannot be interpreted as surprise respecting the CONTENT
of the report. James provides similar examples which show that *ah* cannot
refer to material inside complex NPs or coordinate structures.

Morgan shows that nondirect replies are sensitive to islands. In reply to (3),
(4) is felicitous, but (5) is not:

(3)      *Why was Angela arrested?*

(4)      *The man who lives next door thinks she bought some guns.*

(5)      *The man who thinks she bought some guns lives next door.*

The infelicity of (5) as a nondirect reply to (3) seems to be due to the fact that
the relevant information (*she bought some guns*) is inside an island—a complex
NP—in (5). This is not the case with respect to (4). Thus (4) is felicitous.

Data like those reported by James and Morgan cannot be easily explained
in terms of constraints on movement or on deletion. In fact, they would seem
incompatible with any transformational approach.

There is an approach to island phenomena which appears to offer an explanation for the difficult problem noted by James and by Morgan. It is the Accessibility Approach, the approach for which we shall argue here. Following a proposal by Keenan (1972), we shall contend that island constraints apply only to processes having the effect, roughly, of making a noun phrase the most prominent element in its clause. (Relativization, Wh-question Formation, and Topicalization are instances of processes which usually have such a function, regardless of the transformational operations employed in these processes in particular languages.) The question of which structures constitute islands is determined in terms of a UNIVERSAL HIERARCHY OF NP ACCESSIBILITY, an extended version of the Keenan-Comrie hierarchy. (See Keenan and Comrie, to appear.) Keenan and Comrie's hierarchy is reproduced in (6):

(6)   The Universal NP Accessibility Hierarchy:

   a. *Subject* ≥ *Direct Object* ≥ *Indirect Object* ≥ *Object of Preposition*
      ≥ *Possessor NP* ≥ *Object of Comparative Particle*

   b. *if X* ≥ *Y and Y dominates Z, then X* > *Z*

      (≥ means 'greater than or equal to in accessibility'.)

Particular languages differ with regard to how far down on the hierarchy processes like Relativization and Question Formation may go. According to the Accessibility Approach, islands are islands simply because they are very low on the Accessibility Hierarchy [presumably, lower than the positions in (6)]. NP accessibility is also affected by the degree to which the strategies of relativization, etc., preserve superficial sentential structure. Thus, if a language has two relativization strategies, a deletion strategy and a pronoun retention strategy, the latter would allow the relativization of less accessible NPs than would the former. For example, in Modern Hebrew both deletion and pronoun retention are possible. The Accessibility Approach would predict that pronoun retention would allow the relativization of less accessible environments than would deletion. This prediction is correct. Sentence (7) is ungrammatical when a relativized NP in a conjoined structure is deleted. When a pronoun is retained, however, as in (8), the sentence is fully grammatical:

(7)        *Ze      haiš še ∅  veMiriam    xaverim tovim.
           this the man that and Miriam friends  good
           'This is the man that and Miriam are good friends.'

(8)        Ze      haiš še   hu veMiriam    xaverim tovim.
           this the man that he and Miriam friends  good
           'This is the man that he and Miriam are good friends.'

## CROSS-LINGUISTIC EVIDENCE

We shall now turn to cross-linguistic evidence which is consistent with the Accessibility Approach to islands but which is inconsistent with the Transformational Approach of Ross and Perlmutter. The Ross–Perlmutter approach makes two falsifiable claims, which are given as (9) and (10):

(9)   *Relativization, wh-question formation, etc., will not be constrained by island constraints **unless** the syntactic rule employed involves deletion or movement.*

(10)  *When a rule of relativization, etc., involves deletion or movement, island constraints always apply.*

Note that (9) predicts that relativization strategies, in which the relativized NP appears as a pronoun or as a full lexical noun phrase, would NOT be affected by island constraints. Nor would questioned NPs when the question strategy does not involve movement or deletion. The evidence to be presented will show that both (9) and (10) are false.

The evidence against (9) is based on data from Hindi, Kannada, and Mandarin. We shall consider the data from Hindi and Kannada first. The Hindi data are drawn in part from the work of Kachru (to appear) and Bhatia (1974); the Kannada data are derived in part from Nadkarni (1970).

In Hindi and Kannada, there are two strategies of relativization, one involving the deletion, the other the retention of the relativized noun phrase (a full lexical noun phrase, not a pronoun). Following Nadkarni (1970), we shall refer to the two strategies as the PARTICIPIAL and the NONPARTICIPIAL strategies. In the Participial Strategy, the main verb of the relative clause is changed to a participle, and the coreferential NP is deleted. This is illustrated in examples (11a) (Hindi) and (11b) (Kannada):

(11)          a. *Us    lərkī kī likhī huī kəvita ∅ əcchī hɛ.*
                 that girl of   written poem    good is

              b. *Ā huḍugi ∅ bareda  kavite cennāgide.*
                 that girl   written poem  good is
                 'The poem which that girl wrote is good.'

In the Nonparticipial Strategy, Hindi allows three surface realizations of the relative clause. In the realization with which we shall be concerned [example (12a)], the relative clause precedes the head and the relativized NP is retained in surface structure. In Kannada, relative clauses always appear to the left of their heads. The relativized NP is retained on the surface. This is shown in example (12b):

(12)    Nonparticipial Relative Clause:

    a. *Jo kəvita us    ləṛkī ne likhī   vəh ∅ əcchī hɛ.*
       rel poem that girl     wrote correl good is

    b. *Yāva kaviteyannu ā   huḍugi baredaḷō     adu cennāgide.*
       rel   poem acc   that girl    wrote enclitic that good is
       'The poem which that girl wrote is good.'

In both Hindi and Kannada, when the deletion strategy is employed, all the island constraints hold.

Notice that in neither language does the Nonparticipial (or retention) Strategy involve movement or deletion. Yet the island constraints hold—most of them in the case of Hindi, and some of them in Kannada—as the following data illustrate. First, consider the following examples from Hindi:

(13)    Complex NP (Relative Clause):

    $*_{s_1}$[*jis admi$_i$ ne    vəh    sūp$_j$ bənaya* $_{s_2}$[*jo* ∅$_j$ *əccha hɛ*]$_{s_2}$]$_{s_1}$ *vəh* ∅$_i$
       rel man  agent correl soup made     rel  good is     correl
    *bhaśa-vijnani hɛ.*
    linguist     is
    'The man who the soup which is good made is a linguist.'

(14)    Complex NP (Sentential Complement of a Noun):

    $*_{s_1}$[*jis kar$_i$ ko* $_{s_\perp}$[*vəh bat   səc hɛ ki   gopal ne* ∅$_i$ *xərīdī*]$_{s_2}$]$_{s_1}$
       rel car  postp this news true is that Gopal    bought
    *vəh   sundər hɛ.*[1]
    correl pretty is
    'The car which the news that Gopal bought is true is pretty.'

(15)    Coordinate NP:

    $*_s$[*jis sofa$_i$ ɔr   kursi ke   bīc     me unhõne mez rəkha hɛ*]$_s$
       rel sofa and chair poss between in they    table placed have
    *vəh* ∅$_i$ *purana hɛ.*
    correl old    is
    'The sofa which they have placed a table between and a chair
    is old.'

---

[1] The relativized noun phrase is fronted by an optional fronting rule from the preverbal position in $S_2$. The unfronted version is ambiguous between (14) and a grammatical sentence, for which the gloss is 'The news that the car which Gopal bought is beautiful is true.' We have given the fronted version in order to eliminate the irrelevant, grammatical reading. For the conditions on fronting, see Kachru (to appear).

(16)    Coordinate VP:

*$_S$[jo  kahãniyã$_i$  Sīta likhtī  hɛ]$_S$ ɔr $_S$[kavita pəṛhtī hɛ]$_S$]$_{S_1}$ ve $\emptyset_i$
rel stories     Sita writes aux and poems reads aux     correl
əcchī hotī hɛ̃.
good are
'The stories which Sita writes and reads poems are good.'

(17)    Coordinate S:

*$_S$[jo  kəhãniya$_i$  Sīta likhtī  hɛ]$_S$ ɔr $_S$[vəh patrikaõ    ko kəvita
rel stories     Sita writes aux and she magazines to  poems
bhejtī hɛ]$_S$ ve $\emptyset_i$  əcchī hotī hɛ̃.
sends aux correl good are
'The stories which Sita writes and she sends poems to magazines are
good.'

While in the case of the islands illustrated above the constraints hold, Hindi
does allow relativization into sentential subjects, using the retention strategy:

(18)      Sentential Subject:

$_{S_1}$[$_{S_2}$[mera jo  topi$_i$ lana]$_{S_2}$  əjib      tha]$_{S_1}$ vəh $\emptyset$  fransīsi hɛ.
my  rel hat  bringing strange was  correl French is
'The hat which that I brought was strange is French.'

Hindi also permits relativization into complex NPs (relative clauses), provided
that the NP being relativized is contained within a participial relative clause
and that the Nonparticipial Strategy is employed to relativize the NP in question:

(19)    Complex NP (Relative Clause):

$_{S_1}$[$_{S_2}$[jis admi$_i$ ka  $\emptyset_j$ bənaya]$_{S_2}$ sup$_j$  əccha hɛ]$_{S_1}$ vəh $\emptyset_i$ bhasa vijnani hɛ.
rel man poss made     soup good is     correl linguist     is
'The man who the soup which is good made is a linguist.'

A similar pattern is found in Kannada which also blocks relativization into
nonparticipial relative clauses, coordinate VPs, and coordinate sentences [cf.
(20)–(22)]. The difference between Hindi and Kanada is that Kannada permits
relativization into certain additional islands which are inaccessible in Hindi.
Thus, in Kannada one can relativize not only into sentential subjects [cf. (23)]
and relative clauses of the type illustrated in (19) [cf. (24)], but into sentential

complements of nouns [cf. (25)] and of coordinate NPs [cf. (26)]:

(20) Complex NP (Relative Clause):

*[ *yāva manushyanu$_i$* [*yāva sūpannu avanu māḍidanō*] *adu*
rel man nom rel soup acc he made enclitic that
*cennāgide ā manushya$_i$ bhāshā vijnani.*
good is that man linguist (is)
'The man who the soup which is good made is a linguist.'

(21) Coordinate VP:

*[ *yāva kategaḷannu$_i$ sīte bareyuttāḷō*] *mattu* [*kaviteyannu ōduttāḷe*]
rel stories acc Sita writes + enclitic and poetry acc reads
*avu$_i$ cennāgiruttave.*
they good are
'The man who the soup which is good made is a linguist.'

(22) Coordinate S:

*$_{S_1}$[*yāva kategaḷannu$_i$ sīte bareyuttāḷo*]$_{S_1}$ *mattu* $_{S_2}$[*avaḷa gaṇḍa avaḷa*
rel stories acc Sita writes enclitic and her husband her
*kavanagaḷannu patrikegaḷige kaḷisuttāre*]$_{S_2}$ *avu$_i$ cennāgiruttave.*
poems acc to magazines sends they good are
'The stores which Sita writes and her husband sends her poems to
magazines are good.'

(23) Sentential Subject:

[*yāva karannu gōpalānu kondanembudu nijavō*]$_S$
rel car acc Gopal bought that true (is) enclitic
*adu sundaravāgide*
that pretty is
'The car which that Gopal bought is true is pretty.'

(24) Complex NP (Relative Clause):

[*yāva manushyanu$_i$ ∅$_j$ māḍida sūpu$_j$ cennāgideyō*] *avanu$_i$*
rel man made soup good is enclitic he
*bhāsha vijnāni.*
linguist (is)
'The man who the soup which is good made is a linguist.'

(25)　Sentential Complement of a Noun:

[*yāva kārannu$_i$ gōpālanu koṇḍanemba sangati nijavō*]$_S$
rel　car acc　Gopal　bought that news　true (is) enclitic
　　*adu$_i$ cennāgide.*
　　that good (is)
'The car which the news that Gopal bought is true is good.'

(26)　Coordinate NP:

[*yāva sōfa$_i$ mattu kurciya　naḍuve　avaru mējannu*
rel　sofa and　chair poss between they　table acc
　*iṭṭiddārō*]　　　　*adu$_i$　haḷeyadu.*
　placed have enclitic that (is) old
'The sofa which they have placed a table between and
　a chair is old.'

Similar differences between Hindi and Kannada are found in wh-questions. In both languages Wh-question Formation does not involve movement or deletion, but only the substitution of a question word for the questioned constituent. But the island constraints hold in Hindi except in the case of participial relative clauses and sentential subjects [see the (a) examples of (27)–(32) below]. Kannada, on the other hand, allows the questioning of elements within coordinate and complex NPs other than nonparticipial relative clauses, as illustrated in the (b) examples of (27)–(32):

(27)　Participial Relative Clause Question:

a.　*Kiski likhī huī kəhāniyā tumhe pəsənd hɛ̃?*
　　whose written　stories　　to you liking　are

b.　*Yāru bareda kategaḷu ninage ishṭa?*
　　who　written stories　to you favourite
　　'The stories written by who do you like?'

(28)　Complex NP (Sentential Complement of a Noun) Question:

a.　*\*yəh bat　səc hɛ ki　gopal ne　kya xəridi?*
　　it　news true is that Gopal agent wh- bought

b.　*Gopālanu ēnu koṇḍa　emba sangati nija?*
　　Gopal　wh- bought that　news　true
　　'What, the news that Gopal bought is true?'

(29)　Sentential Subject Question:

a.　[*gopal ka　kya lana*]　*əjib　tha?*
　　Gopal poss wh- bringing strange was

    b. [*gopālanu ēnu tandanembudu*] *vicitravāgittu?*
       Gopal   wh- brought that   strange was
       'What that Gopal brought was strange?'

(30)   Coordinate NP:

    a. \**Sōfa or   kiske bīc mẽ   unhõne mēz rəkha hɛ?*
       sofa and what between they   table placed have

    b. *Sofa mattu yētara   naḍuve avaru mējannu iṭṭiddāre?*
       sofa and   of what middle they   table acc placed have
       'What have they placed the table between the sofa and?'

(31)   Coordinate VP:

    a. \**Sīta kya likhīT hɛ ɔr   kəhãniyã pəṛhti hɛ?*
       Sita wh- writes   and stories   reads

    b. \**Sita yēnannu   bareyuttāḷe mattu kategaḷannu ōduttāḷe?*
       Sita what acc writes   and   stories acc   reads
       'What does Sita write and reads poems?'

(32)   Coordinate S:

    a. \**Sīta kya   likhti hɛ ɔr   vəh unko pətrikaɔ̀   ko bhejti hɛ?*
       Sita what writes   and she them magazines to sends

    b. \**Sita yēnannu   bareyuttāḷe mattu avaḷu avannu   patrikegaḷige*
       Sita what-acc writes   and   she   them acc magazines to
       *kaḷisuttaḷe?*
       sends
       'What does Sita write and she sends them to the magazines?'

The Hindi–Kannada data constitute evidence for the falsity of (9) because in these languages (some of) the constraints hold even though the processes of Relativization and Question Formation do not involve deletion or movement. It should be noted that the languages differ with regard to which NPs can be relativized even though almost identical relativization strategies are employed.

We shall now turn to Mandarin. The analysis of Mandarin relativization presented here is drawn from Chen (1974). Mandarin employs two relativization strategies, one where the relativized noun phrase is deleted, and the other where a pronominal token of the relativized noun phrase is retained in surface structure. Deletion is usually obligatory when the relativized noun phrase is the subject of the relative clause, and optional (with deletion preferred) when it is the direct object. Example (33) illustrates the relativization of a direct object:

(33)      *Zhe jiushi* [*wo zuotain     kanjian* $\left\{\begin{matrix} \emptyset \\ \surd\,?ta \end{matrix}\right\}$ *de*] *neige ren.*

       this is     I     yesterday see     $\left\{\begin{matrix} \emptyset \\ he \end{matrix}\right\}$     rel that  person

       'This is the man that I saw yesterday.'

       (The symbol $\surd$? means that the sentence is awkward,
          slightly less than fully grammatical.)

When the relativized noun phrase is within a complement clause, pronoun re-tention is preferred. This is true even when the relativized noun phrase is the subject of the complement clause, as in (34):

(34)   *Zhe jiushi* [*Lao Wang shuo* $\left\{\begin{matrix} ?\emptyset \\ ta \end{matrix}\right\}$ *hen   xihuan tiaowu de*] *neige ren.*

    this is     Lao Wang say     $\left\{\begin{matrix} \emptyset \\ he \end{matrix}\right\}$ very like     dance rel that  person

    'This is the man who Lao Wang said that he loved dancing very
       much.'

   Having established that pronoun retention is a permissible relativization strategy in Mandarin, we shall now consider the effect of pronoun retention on the grammaticality of relativization into islands. Sentences (35)–(38) are cases in point. Although all are ungrammatical, pronoun retention improves their comprehensibility, while deletion leaves them mere gibberish:

(35)   Complement of Noun Head:

    \**Zhe jiushi* [*Lao Wang chengren*     [*women dou kanjian* $\left\{\begin{matrix} \emptyset \\ ta \end{matrix}\right\}$ *de*]

    this is     Lao Wang acknowledge we     all   see     $\left\{\begin{matrix} \emptyset \\ he \end{matrix}\right\}$ rel

      *zheige shishi de*] *neige ren.*
      this    fact   rel that  person
    'This is the man Lao Wang acknowledged the fact that we all
      saw him.'

(36)   Relative Clause:

    \**Zhe jiushi* [[*women dou hen   zunjing* $\left\{\begin{matrix} \emptyset_i \\ ta_i \end{matrix}\right\}$ *xihuan* $\left\{\begin{matrix} \emptyset_j \\ ta_j \end{matrix}\right\}$ *de*] *neige*

    this is     we     all  very respect $\left\{\begin{matrix} \emptyset \\ he \end{matrix}\right\}$ like     $\left\{\begin{matrix} \emptyset \\ she \end{matrix}\right\}$ rel that

      *ren_i    de*] *neiwei nulaoshi_j.*
      person rel that   woman teacher
    'This is the woman teacher that we all respect the man who
      likes her.'

(37)   Coordinate NP:

*Zhe jiushi [wo zuotian   kanjian $\begin{Bmatrix} \emptyset \\ ta \end{Bmatrix}$ gen Lao  Wang de] neige ren.

this is     I    yesterday see    $\begin{Bmatrix} \emptyset \\ he \end{Bmatrix}$ and Lao Wang rel that  person

'This is the man that I saw and John yesterday.'

(38)   Sentential Subject:

*Ta  renshi ((Lao Li zuotian    ma    le    $\begin{Bmatrix} \emptyset \\ ta \end{Bmatrix}$     shi    wo hen

she know    Lao Li yesterday scold aspect $\begin{Bmatrix} \emptyset \\ him \end{Bmatrix}$ make I    very

bu  gaoxing de) neige ren.)
not happy   rel that  person
'She knew the person whom that Lao Li scolded him made me
very unhappy.'

We have presented evidence showing the falsity of (9). In Hindi, Kannada,
and Mandarin, island constraints are not restricted to syntactic rules of deletion
and movement. These facts are compatible with the Accessibility Approach but
incompatible with the Transformational Approach.

The second claim of the Transformational Approach [(10)] is that, if relativization and similar processes involve deletion or movement, island constraints
should always apply. An examination of relativization in Japanese, however,
shows that this position cannot be maintained.

Japanese relativization is effected normally by the deletion of the relativized
NP with its case marker, as illustrated in example (39):

(39)        a. Watashi wa    kinoo     sono uchi  o    mita.
               I          topic yesterday the   house acc saw
               'I saw a house yesterday.'

            b. (Watashi ga      kinoo $\emptyset$   mita) uchi   wa    asoko da.
               I          subject yesterday saw   house topic there  is
               'The house which I saw yesterday is there.'

In some instances of relativization of a possessor NP, a pronominal reflex of
the relativized NP must be retained:

(40)    (Tom ga       $\begin{Bmatrix} *\emptyset \\ sono \end{Bmatrix}$  tomodachi ni   atta) Mary wa     asoko da.
            subject pro   friend     dat met        topic there  is
        'Mary whose friend Tom met is there.'

Pronoun retention is fully grammatical ONLY with possessor NPs. Consequently, the primary strategy of Relative Clause Formation in Japanese is
deletion.

An approach treating island phenomena as constraining Relative Deletion would predict, therefore, that Japanese relativization would be sensitive to island constraints. In fact, this is true in some cases. Japanese relativization is blocked from applying into one member of coordinate NPs joined by some conjunctions—as in sentence (41a)—although not in others—as in sentence (41b)![2]

(41)   Coordinate NP:

a. *Kore wa   (watashi ga ∅   ringo mo tabenakatta) banana da.
   this topic I      subject apple or  eat neg past banana is
   'This is the banana that I didn't eat or an apple.'

b. (Watashi ga ∅   ringo to              tabeta) banana wa
   I         subject apple commitative ate     banana topic
   oishikatta.
   delicious was
   'The banana which I ate and an apple was delicious.'

Under no circumstances is relativization possible into one member of a co-ordinate VP. Example (42) illustrates this constraint:

(42)     Coordinate VP:

*(Watashi ga ∅   yonda soshito terebi o   mita) hon   wa
 I          subject read  and    T.V.  acc saw  book topic
 omoshirokatta.
 interesting was
 'The book which I read and watched T.V. was interesting.'

The fact that relativization is not possible into coordinate structures in Japanese would, assuming for the moment the correctness of Perlmutter's approach,[3] require that an island-sensitive rule of deletion be assumed to exist in the grammar of Japanese. There are some islands, though, into which Japanese relativization can operate rather freely. Among such islands are complex NPs. Relativization can operate into sentential complements of nouns, as in example (43) (adapted from McCawley 1972), into relative clauses, as in

---

[2] Susumu Kuno (personal communication) has suggested that *to* in (41b) is a postposition, more or less equivalent to 'with', rather than a conjunction, equivalent to 'and'. If this is correct, the disparity between (41a) and (41b) is explained, and we can conclude that in Japanese relativization out of coordinate NPs is blocked. We shall tentatively adopt Kuno's suggestion.

[3] Perlmutter (1972) claimed that island constraints do not apply in Japanese, and argued that for various reasons this fact favored the shadow pronoun hypothesis. We reject Perlmutter's factual claim on the basis of the data presented in the body of this paper. Thus, we shall not discuss the conclusions which he drew from the putative facts.

example (44) (adapted from Kuno 1973), and into sentential subjects, as in example (45):

(43)   Complex NP (Sentential Complement of a Noun)

(∅ *shikakui to yuu uwasa o   shinzite ita*)        *chikyuu wa     marukatta.*
square   comp rumor acc believe  post prog earth     topic round was
'The earth which they believed the rumor that was square was round.'

(44)   Complex NP (Relative Clause):

((∅ ∅ *kawaigatte ita*)        *inu ga       shinda*) *kodomo wa*
      pet           past prog dog subject died    child     topic
*kanashi sooda.*
sad       looks
'The boy that the dog that was petting died looks sad.'

(45)   Sentential Subject:

((*Anata ga ∅     au     koto*)) *ga       mazui        hito    wa    kokoni*
you    subject meet nom     subject unfavorable person topic here
*wa    inai.*
topic is neg
'The person whom that you see is unfavorable is not here.'

If island constraints are constraints on specific transformational operations, then they should be expected to apply consistently to block such operations into ALL island configurations. In Japanese, however, in which relativization involves deletion in virtually all cases, it is possible to relativize into some syntactic islands, but not into others. The Transformational Approach, therefore, fails to account for the facts of Japanese relativization.

The Accessibility Approach, however, argues that island constraints are restrictions on making elements prominent from structures ranking low on the universal Accessibility Hierarchy. It predicts that there are degrees of islandhood, and that each language differs with regard to how far down the hierarchy it can go. This view is consistent with the evidence from Japanese relativization.

We have seen that Japanese constitutes a counterexample to (10). Modern Hebrew also contains counterevidence to (10). In Modern Hebrew, elements in sentential subjects may be relativized by the use of deletion or pronoun retention. But elements in complex NPs and coordinate NPs cannot be relativized unless a pronoun is retained. The possibility of relative deletion within sentential subjects is a counterexample to (10). Examples from Modern Hebrew are given in (46)–(48):

(46)   Sentential Subject:

a. *Zot iša      še    leehov ∅ lo   kidai.*
this woman    that to love  not worthwhile
'This is a woman that to love isn't worth it.'

b. *Zot iša     še   leehov ota lo   kidai.*
this woman that to love her not worthwhile
'This is a woman that to love her isn't worth it.'

(47)   Complex NP:

   a. **Hine   hakadur še   hikiti et   hayeled še    zarak ∅ elai.*
here is the ball that I hit  acc the boy that threw   at me
'Here is the ball that I hit the boy that threw at me.'

   b. *Hine   hakadur še   hikiti et   hayeled še    zarak oto elai.*
here is the ball that I hit  acc the boy that threw it   at me
'Here is the ball that I hit the boy that threw it at me.'

(48)   Coordinate NP:

   a.**Ze haiš     še   Miriam ohevet ∅ veet     axiv.*
this the man that Miriam loves    and acc his brother
'This is the man that Miriam loves and his brother.'

   b. *Ze  haiš     še   Miriam ohevet oto  veet     axiv.*
this the man that Miriam loves  him and acc his brother
'This is the man that Miriam loves him and his brother.'

We have presented data from Japanese and Modern Hebrew which show that relativization strategies involving deletion are not always constrained by island constraints. This contradicts claim (10) of the Transformational Approach.

## EVIDENCE FOR THE ACCESSIBILITY APPROACH

The bulk of this paper so far has been devoted to presenting cross-linguistic evidence against the Transformational Approach. We believe that the evidence we have presented is quite conclusive and that the Transformational Approach should be rejected. We have not, however, presented direct evidence in favor of the Accessibility Approach. Admittedly, the evidence in favor of the Accessibility Approach is less conclusive than that against the Transformational Approach, but we feel that the case for the Accessibility Approach is persuasive.

The Accessibility Approach makes two empirical claims. There are summarized as (49) and (50):

(49)   *Islandhood is a reflection of the relative inaccessibility of certain structures on an Extended Accessibility Hierarchy.*

(50)   *The preservation of superficial sentential form allows a rule access to structures which would otherwise be less accessible.*

A wide variety of data supporting (50) has been adduced by Keenan (1972). The evidence from Mandarin cited earlier [(35)–(38)] constitutes further support for (50). Pronoun retention is seen to increase the acceptability of relativization in islands, but not to the extent that the resulting sentences could be considered grammatical. On the basis of (50), this is not surprising, but such facts are incompatible with (9). We shall assume that (50) has been established, and turn our attention to (49).

Two claims are implicit in (49). The first is that island structures vary in strength in a hierarchical fashion. The second is that this hierarchy is a sub-hierarchy of an EXTENDED ACCESSIBILITY HIERARCHY. There is considerable reason to believe that islands vary in strength hierarchically. Consider the relevant data from languages discussed earlier: Modern Hebrew, Japanese, Mandarin, Hindi, and Kannada. We saw that, in some languages, relativization out of certain islands was possible by means of a deletion strategy. In other cases, relativization was possible if an NP retention strategy was employed, while in further cases relativization was impossible regardless of the relativization strategy. The pattern of relativization possibilities is summarized in (51):

(51)    Relativization Possibilities

|            | Sentential Subject | Complex NP | Coordinate NP | Coordinate VP and S |
|------------|--------------------|------------|---------------|---------------------|
| Deletion:  | Hebrew Japanese    | Japanese   | _____        | _____              |
| Retention: | Hebrew Hindi Kanada | Hebrew Hindi* Kannada* | Hebrew Kannada | Hebrew |

*All complex NPs except nonparticipial relative clauses.

From (51) the gross outlines of an ISLAND HIERARCHY can be seen:

(52)    The Island Hierarchy

Sentential Subject ≥ Complex NP ≥ Coordinate NP ≥ Coordinate VP and S

Note that there is no language in which, for example, relativization out of sentential subjects is blocked regardless of the strategy employed, but in which coordinate NPs are relativizable by deletion. The only anomaly in the hierarchy which we have found so far is the fact that coordinate NPs are more accessible in Kanada than are nonparticipial relative clauses. But this may not be a true counterexample to our claims. Avery Andrews (personal communication) has suggested that nonparticipial relative clauses are not syntactically subordinate to their heads, and, as a result, may not be genuine complex noun phrases. Thus, on the basis of (51), we feel justified in advancing the tentative claim that island strength varies hierarchically along the lines of (52). This claim is strengthened by the existence of English-specific evidence for an islandhood hierarchy reported by Lakoff (1973) and Neeld (1973).[4]

Finally, we would like to examine whether (52) is, as we have claimed, a relatively inaccessible subhierarchy of an Extended Accessibility Hierarchy, and not a separate hierarchy. The question can be approached only in a negative fashion: that is, is there any evidence inconsistent with the hypothesis that (52) is a subhierarchy of an Extended Accessibility Hierarchy? For example, is there any language in which a relatively accessible position on the Accessibility Hierarchy (such as indirect object) requires a retention strategy, but in which some island structure (much lower on the combined hierarchy than indirect objects) permits relativization by deletion? The existence of such facts would suggest that the Island Hierarchy and the Accessibility Hierarchy are distinct.

We are, in fact, aware of a case of this sort. But it will be seen that it results from language-specific factors and thus is not a true counterexample to the hypothesis. In Modern Hebrew, subjects and direct objects may be relativized by deletion or pronoun retention. All other relativizable environments, for example, indirect objects, allow relativization only if a pronoun is retained:

(53)      Subject:

    *Ze      haiš      še (hu) maca et hakelev      šeli.*
    that (is) the man that     found acc the dog of mine
    'That's the man that found my dog.'

(54)      Direct Object:

    *Ze      haiš      še hakelev šeli      maca (oto)      al*
    that (is) the man that the dog of mine found acc + him upon
    *hahar.*
    the mountain.
    'That's the man that my dog found on the mountain.'

(55)      Indirect Object:

    a. *Ze      haiš      še      natati lo      et hasefer.*
       that (is) the man that (I) gave dat + him acc the book
       'That's the man to whom I gave the book.'

---

[4] It should be noted, however, that the hierarchy proposed by Neeld differs from that argued for in this paper. On the basis of data limited to English, Neeld contends that elements within coordinate VPs and S's are more accessible to relativization, etc., than are coordinate NPs. The data presented in the present study contradict Neeld's claims. While we shall not discuss the discrepancies between Neeld's results and our own at length, it is important to realize that the set of rules considered as possible candidates for island constraints differs in the two papers. Neeld defines the rules under consideration in terms of such formal operations as movement and deletion over a variable, while we consider rules having the effect of making an element prominent over a variable. These differences make the two studies less than fully comparable.

    b. *Ze    haiš    še    natati ∅ et  hasefer.
      that (is) the man that (I) gave  acc the book

(56)    Oblique Case NPs:

    a.     RNP with *be* 'in':

        i.   *Ze     haet    še  ani kotev bo.*
           that (is) the pen that I   write in it
           'That's the pen I write with.'

        ii. *\*Ze    haet    še  ani kotev ∅.*
           that (is) the pen that I   write

    b.     RNP with *al* 'upon':

        i.   *Zot    hatmuna   še  ani ohev lehistakel aleha.*
           that (is) the picture that I   love to look   upon it
           'That's the picture I love to look at.'

        ii. *\*Zot    hatmuna   še  ani ohev lehistakel ∅.*
           that (is) the picture that I   love to look

It will be remembered, however, that NPs within sentential subjects may be relativized by deletion. The relevant example is repeated here as (57):

(57)        *Zot iša    še  leehov ∅ lo  kidai.*
           this woman that to love  not worthwhile
           'This is a woman that to love isn't worth it.'

On the basis of (53)–(57), it would appear—at least in Modern Hebrew—that elements in sentential subjects are more accessible than are indirect objects. This would conflict with the claim that sentential subjects, like other islands, are relatively inaccessible points on the Extended Accessibility Hierarchy.

However, the pattern illustrated in (53)–(57) can be shown to be a false counterexample to the unity of the Accessibility Hierarchy and the Island Hierarchy. In fact, the ungrammaticality of (55b), (56aii), and (56bii) is not due to the inaccessibility of indirect objects, but rather to a language-specific constraint against preposition stranding in Modern Hebrew. (This is argued for at length in Cole, to appear. We shall restrict ourselves to a short summary here.) The effect of the deletion of NPs other than subjects and direct objects is, in general, preposition stranding. This is because, except for nominative and accusative relativized NPs, the language usually provides no device which allows for the nonappearance of a preposition as case marker.

Preposition stranding explains the ungrammaticality of (55b), (56aii), and (56bii).[5] For at least some speakers, however, deletion of indirect object and

---

[5] That is, there are no derivations for these sentences. The normal application of the rules of the language would result in derived structures with stranded prepositions. This would violate an independently motivated constraint against preposition stranding. See Cole (to appear) for details.

oblique case relativized NPs is possible. As G. Ben-Horin (personal communication) and Givón (manuscript) have noted, for these speakers the relativized NP may be deleted under identity, with the preposition preceding the head:

(58)  a.  *Natati  sefer  le  oto    yeled še    Miriam natna ∅ sefer.*
          (I) gave book dat same boy  that Mary   gave    book
          'I gave a book to the boy to whom Mary gave a book.'

      b.  *Natati  sefer  le  oto    yeled še    Miriam natna lo        sefer.*
          (I) gave book dat same boy  that Mary   gave  dat him book
          'I gave a book to the boy to whom Mary gave a book.'

      c.  *\*Raiti  et  oto    hayeled še    Miriam natna ∅ sefer.*
          (I) saw acc same the boy that Mary    gave    book

      d.  *Raiti  et  oto    hayeled še    Miriam natna lo        sefer.*
          (I) saw acc same the boy that Mary    gave  dat him book
          'I saw the very boy to whom Mary gave the book.'

(59)  a.  *Yašavta  al    kise  še    Ben-Gurion  yašav ∅.*
          (you) sat upon chair that Ben-Gurion sat
          'You sat on a chair on which Ben-Gurion sat.'

      b.  *Yašavta  al    kise  še    Ben-Gurion  yašav alav.*
          (you) sat upon chair that Ben-Gurion sat    on it
          'You sat on a chair on which Ben-Gurion sat.'

      c.  *\*Raita     kise  še    Ben-Gurion  yašav ∅.*
          (you) saw chair that Ben-Gurion sat

      d.  *Raita     kise  še    Ben-Gurion  yašav alav.*
          (you) saw chair that Ben-Gurion sat    on it
          'You saw a chair on which Ben-Gurion sat.'

(60)  a.  *Histakalti bamilon          še    ata histakalta ∅.*
          (I) looked at (the) dictionary that you looked
          'I looked at the dictionary that you looked at.'

      b.  *Histakalti bamilon          še    ata histakalta bo.*
          (I) looked at (the) dictionary that you looked    in it
          'I looked at the dictionary at which you looked.'

      c.  *\*Raiti  et  hamilon          še    ata histakalta ∅.*
          (I) saw acc the dictionary that you looked

      d.  *Raiti  et  hamilon          še    ata histakalta bo.*
          (I) saw acc the dictionary that you looked    in it
          'I saw the dictionary which you looked at.'

Examples (58)–(60) show that the ill-formedness resulting from the deletion of such relativized NPs as those of (55b), (56aii), and (56bii) is not due to the inaccessibility of those NPs, but rather to language-particular constraints on the output of the deletion. Thus, the ungrammaticality of (55b), (56aii), and (56bii), in contrast to the grammaticality of (57), does not indicate that the Accessibility Hierarchy and the Island Hiererachy are distinct entities.

Furthermore, the data just presented from Modern Hebrew suggest that apparent counterexamples to the claim that the Island Hierarchy is a sub-hierarchy of the Accessibility Hierarchy should be scrutinized carefully. Language-specific factors, as in Modern Hebrew, may lead to the appearance of incompatibility between the Island Hierarchy and the Accessibility Hierarchy when, in fact, no such incompatiblity exists.

## CONCLUSION

We have shown that the Transformational Approach is seriously flawed and should, we think, be abandoned. We have examined some of the predictions of the Accessibility Approach and have found them to be almost entirely correct. Further research is called for to expand the data presented in (51) with information on other languages. We hope to be able to present the results of that research in the not-too-distant future.

## ACKNOWLEDGMENTS

This paper reports on research growing out of three sources. The discussion of island phenomena and other syntactic data from Modern Hebrew is based on research on Modern Hebrew syntax conducted from 1973 to 1976 by the senior author (Cole), with the assistance of the Research Board of the University of Illinois. The data on Hindi, Kannada, and Japanese were gathered during a graduate seminar on syntax during the spring of 1975. The analysis of that data was carried out within the framework of the seminar and also within the framework of the Illinois Project on Universals of Grammatical Organization, National Science Foundation grant SOC75–00244. We are grateful to the Research Board and to the National Science Foundation for their support.

We would like to thank those individuals who served as informants and also those who provided helpful criticism of earlier versions of this paper. Special thanks are due to Yamuna Kachru for assisting us in our analysis of Hindi, to Gad Ben Horin and Yael Ziv for their invaluable assistance throughout the Modern Hebrew syntax project, and to Ching-Hsiang Chen for her generous help on Mandarin.

An earlier version of this paper was presented at the Eleventh Regional Meeting of the Chicago Linguistic Society.

## REFERENCES

Bhatia, T. K. (1974) "Testing Four Hypotheses about Relative Clause Formation and the Applicability of Ross's Constraints in Hindi," unpublished paper, University of Illinois, Urbana, Illinois.

Chen, C. (1974) *Aspects of Noun Phrase Structure and Constraints on Question Formation in Mandarin Chinese*, unpublished Doctoral dissertation, University of Illinois, Urbana, Illinois.

Cole, P. (to appear) "The Interface of Theory and Description: Notes on Modern Hebrew Relativization," *Language*.

Givón, T. (ms) "Some Trends in Spoken Hebrew Relativization."

James, D. (1972) "Some Aspects of the Syntax and Semantics of Interjections," in P. M. Peranteau, J. N. Levy, and G. C. Phares, eds., *Papers from the Eighth Regional Meeting of the Chicago Linguistic Society*, University of Chicago, Chicago, Illinois.

Kachru, Y. (to appear) "Pronominalization vs. Deletion: Evidence from Relative Clause Formation in Hindi-Urdu."

Keenan, E. L. (1972) "On Semantically Based Grammar," *Linguistic Inquiry* 3, 413–462.

Keenan, E. L. and B. Comrie (to appear) "Noun Phrase Accessibility and Universal Grammar," *Linguistic Inquiry*.

Kuno, S. (1973) *The Structure of the Japanese Language*, M.I.T. Press, Cambridge, Massachusetts.

Lakoff, G. (1973) "Fuzzy Grammar and the Performance/Competence Terminology Game," in C. Corum, T. C. Smith-Stark, and A. Weiser, eds., *Papers from the Ninth Regional Meeting of the Chicago Linguistic Society*, University of Chicago, Chicago, Illinois.

McCawley, J. D. (1972) "Japanese Relative Clauses," in P. M. Peranteau, J. N. Levi, and G. C. Phares, eds., *The Chicago Which Hunt: Papers from the Relative Clause Festival*, Chicago Linguistic Society, University of Chicago, Chicago, Illinois.

Morgan, J. L. (1975) "Some Interactions of Syntax and Pragmatics," in P. Cole and J. L. Morgan, eds., *Syntax and Semantics: Speech Acts*, vol. 3, Academic Press, New York.

Nadkarni, M. V. (1970) *NP Embedded Structures in Kannada and Konkani*, unpublished Doctoral dissertation, University of California, Los Angeles, California.

Neeld, R. (1973) "On the Variable Strength of Island Constraints," in C. Corum, T. C. Smith-Stark, and A. Weiser, eds., *Papers from the Ninth Regional Meeting of the Chicago Linguistic Society*, University of Chicago, Chicago, Illinois.

Perlmutter, D. M. (1972) "Evidence for Shadow Pronouns in French Relativization," in P. M. Peranteau, J. N. Levy, and G. C. Phares, eds., *The Chicago Which Hunt: Papers from the Relative Clause Festival*, Chicago Linguistic Society, Chicago.

Ross, J. R. (1967) *Constraints on Variables in Syntax*, unpublished Doctoral dissertation, M.I.T., Cambridge, Massachusetts.

# IN DEFENSE OF SPONTANEOUS DEMOTION: THE IMPERSONAL PASSIVE

*BERNARD COMRIE*
*University of Cambridge*

Within the theory of Relational Grammar, the derivation of a passive sentence like *John was kissed by Mary* involves two changes of syntactic relation to the underlying structure, similar to the corresponding active *Mary kissed John*. On the one hand, an object (in this case, the direct object) is changed into a subject; on the other, the subject is changed into a syntactic relation which is neither subject, direct object, nor indirect object.[1] If the theory of Relational Grammar is supplemented by a hierarchy of syntactic relations, *Subject—Direct Object—Indirect Object—Oblique Object* (= *X-rated NP*) (Keenan and Comrie, to appear; and similarly in work by Paul Postal and David Perlmutter on Relational Grammar)—with subject at the top of the hierarchy then we can say that the passive in English involves promotion up the hierarchy of an object and demotion down the hierarchy of the subject. Another possibility is for the subject to be deleted, rather than demoted, as in *John was kissed*. For the time being, I shall assume that deletion and demotion should be treated separately, although I shall return to the relation between them at the end of the paper.

Since the English passive involves two processes—OBJECT PROMOTION and SUBJECT DEMOTION or SUBJECT DELETION—a reasonable question to ask is whether, in other languages, these two exist independently, i.e. whether there

---

[1] In work on relational grammar it is usually said that the subject is X-RATED; in Keenan and Comrie (to appear) the term OBLIQUE OBJECT is used to correspond approximately to instances of X-rating. The differences between the Keenan-Comrie and Postal-Perlmutter terminologies are not relevant to the present discussion.

are languages with passives involving only Subject Demotion, or involving only Object Promotion. The latter possibility would give rise to a derived structure with two subjects, and while I am not convinced that such a structure must be excluded from linguistic theory (for some discussion, see Comrie, forthcoming: Section 3.3), I know of no languages where the passive illustrates this possibility, and it may be discounted for present purposes. However, there are several languages with passives having subject deletion or subject demotion, but lacking object promotion, such as Spanish, Latin, German, Dutch, Polish, Welsh, and Finnish.[2] It is with such constructions in these languages that this paper will be primarily concerned.

The existence of such constructions is of crucial importance to the general theory of Relational Grammar. One of the constraints which some of those working on Relational Grammar have tried to impose on the theory is that there can be no rules of spontaneous demotion. In the derivation of the English passive, for instance, although the subject is indeed demoted, its demotion is a direct result of the promotion of the object: If an object is promoted to subject position, then, given that a sentence cannot have two subjects, the old subject must be removed, i.e. deleted or, if not deleted, demoted. Such demotion is thus not spontaneous. In the impersonal passive, however, where the underlying subject turns up as an oblique object (X-rated), there does appear to be spontaneous demotion of a subject, not caused by promotion of some other noun phrase to subject. The admissibility of rules of spontaneous demotion is controversial within the theory of relational grammar: Thus Johnson (1974:118–119), in discussing impersonal passives similar to some of those treated below, suggests that one possibility is a rule of spontaneous demotion (abdication), although it is not clear from the discussion whether this is his definitive final conclusion. In this study I attempt to demonstrate that the existence of spontaneous demotion rules should be accepted.

From the above discussion, it follows that an impersonal passive will have no derived subject, and that if there are objects (direct or not) in the underlying structure, then these will be retained in the derived structure and will not be promoted to subject. The underlying subject will either be completely absent or will be present as an oblique object. In a number of languages with imper-

---

[2] Examples from these languages, and noncontroversial interpretations of the data, are taken or adapted without detailed reference from Harmer and Norton (1957: Chapter 21) (Spanish); Hartung (1966) (German); Kirsner (1974) (Dutch); Wiese (1969) (Polish); Morris Jones (1913) and Awbery (1973) (Welsh). The Latin examples were provided by Dilys Cousins; to avoid irrelevant detail, made-up Latin examples are used below, although attested examples illustrating the various constructions are given in Cousins (1975). Welsh and Finnish examples arose in the course of informant work with Gwenllian Awbery and Varpu Porter, respectively.

The question of whether such subjectless (impersonal) passives should, in fact, be treated as passives is controversial in the traditional grammars of many of these languages, and for most of the present discussion 'personal passive' and 'impersonal passive' may be treated as convenient labels; toward the end of this chapter I try to justify the treatment of both as passives. For discussion on many aspects of relational grammar, I am grateful to David Johnson and Geoffrey Pullum.

sonal passives, it is in fact impossible to give overt expression to the underlying subject, i.e. this subject must be deleted rather than demoted. Compare the following examples [(1)–(3) are from Spanish, (4)–(7) from Polish]:

(1)       *En Europa no se nos conoce* (*\*por los periodistas*).
          in Europe not  us  is-known by  the journalists
          'In Europe we are not known (by the journalists).'

The verb *se conoce* is impersonal (morphologically third-person singular), and does not agree with *nos* 'us'.

(2)       *No se habla   de música* (*\*por los estudiantes*).
          not is-spoken of music     by  the students
          'Music isn't spoken of (by the students).'

(3)       *¿Por dónde se sale    (\*por los viajeros)?*
          for  where is-departed by  the travelers
          'Where are people (the travelers) departing for?'

(4)       *Dokonuje się prace* (*\*przez uczonych*).
          is-completed works  by    scientists
          'The works are being completed (by the scientists).'

(5)       *Dokonano       prace* (*ᵐprzez uczonych*).
          was-completed works  by     scientists
          'The works have been completed by the scientists.'

The impersonal form *dokonuje się* is morphologically third-person singular, but in the past tense Polish has a special impersonal form, *-o*, which is distinct from all forms with a subject [including the third-person singular neuter *jest dokonane* '(it) has been completed']:

(6)       *Zapukano      do drzwi* (*\*przez sąsiada*).
          was-knocked at door  by    neighbor
          'There was a knock at the door.'

(7)       *Idzie się   szybko* (*\*przez uczniów*).
          is-walked quickly by    schoolboys
          'One walks quickly.'

(8)       *Hänet jätettiin kotiin* (*\*äidi-   llä-nsä*).
          him    was-left home    mother by his
          'He was left at home (by his mother).'

In the Finnish example, above [(8)], *hänet* is accusative (compare nominative *hän*); the case marking of direct objects of Finnish impersonal passives is complex, although there is good evidence (Comrie 1975) that the construction is always impersonal, and never involves promotion of an object to subject:

(9)                       *Suomesta pidetään* (*\*Peka- lla*).
                          Finland   is-liked      Pekka by
                          'Finland is liked (by Pekka).'

The Finnish verb *pitää* 'to like' does not take a direct object, but a noun phrase in the elative case (suffix *-sta/-stä*, basic meaning 'from'):

(10)                      *Täällä eletään hauskasti* (*\*tytöi-llä*).
                          here    is-lived pleasantly   girls by
                          'Life is pleasant here.'

The above examples contain instances of verbs with direct objects, verbs with nondirect objects, and verbs with no object at all.

If it were always the case that impersonal passives were agentless (i.e. no overt expression of the underlying subject), and even more so if it were also the case that personal passives always allowed overt expression of the underlying subject, then this would be good evidence in favor of the assertion that spontaneous demotion is impossible, and moreover of the strict separation of demotion from deletion. I shall try to show that, in some other languages, there are in fact impersonal passives which allow overt expression of the underlying subject. There may be some weaker correlation between impersonal versus personal passive and impossibility versus possibility of overt expression of the underlying subject, although much more data would have to be collected to verify such a correlation. It cannot be more than a correlation, given the presence of impersonal passives with expressed agents, as discussed below, and also of languages like Latvian which have a personal passive but still do not allow expression of the agent (Budiņa Lazdiņa 1966:165):

(11)                      *Es tieku mācīts* (*\*no mātes*).
                          I   am    taught    by mother

Although the following Arabic and Persian personal passives with expressed agent are possible in modern written Arabic (12) and Persian (13), they are not found in more traditional styles, and probably arose only under the influence of European languages:

(12)                      *Kutiba       t-  tamrīnu min  ṭarafi ṭ-  ṭālibi.*
                          was-written the exercise from side   the student-of
                          'The exercise was written by the student.'

(13)　　　　　　　*Juje　　tavassote mard košte šod.*
　　　　　　　　　chicken by　　　man killed was
　　　　　　　　　'The chicken was killed by the man.'

More traditional styles would allow these passives without overt expression of the underlying subject: *kutiba t-tamrīnu* 'the exercise was written' and *juje košte šod* 'the chicken was killed'.

In German, transitive verbs—i.e. those taking a direct object—do not form impersonal passives, but only personal passives, as in English:

(14)　　　　　　　*Hans wurde von Marie geküsst.*
　　　　　　　　　Hans was　by　Marie kissed
　　　　　　　　　'Hans was kissed by Marie.'

Intransitive verbs, i.e. those taking an object other than a direct object—and those that take no object at all—have only impersonal passives. In German, impersonal forms are morphologically the same as third-person singulars, and sometimes occur with the third-person singular neuter pronoun *es* 'it' (this applies to all impersonal forms, not only impersonal passives):

(15)　　　　　　　*Der Lehrer half　dem Schüler.*
　　　　　　　　　the teacher helped the pupil

(16)　　　　　　　*Es wurde dem Schüler geholfen.*
　　　　　　　　　it was　the pupil　helped
　　　　　　　　　'The pupil was helped.'

The German verb *helfen* 'to help' does not take a direct object, but rather an indirect object in the dative case (*dem Schüler*). If some other element is placed before the verb, *es* does not occur:

(17)　　　　　　　*Dem Schüler wurde geholfen.*

(18)　　　　　　　*Wir tanzten gestern.*
　　　　　　　　　we danced yesterday

(19)　　　　　　　*Es wurde gestern　getanzt.*
　　　　　　　　　it was　yesterday danced
　　　　　　　　　'There was dancing yesterday.'

(20)　　　　　　　*Gestern wurde getanzt.*

The crucial point about such German constructions is that they may include the underlying subject, expressed by the preposition *von*, just as in the personal passive:

(21)              *Es wurde dem Schüler vom Lehrer geholfen.*

(22)              *Dem Schüler wurde vom Lehrer geholfen.*

(23)              *Es wurde gestern von uns getanzt.*

(24)              *Gestern wurde von uns getanzt.*

Apparently, then, such passive sentences have spontaneous subject demotion. Before accepting this analysis, however, a number of other possibilities must first be discussed.

In the case of a sentence like (21), *es wurde dem Schüler vom Lehrer geholfen,* one might argue that, despite the dative case of *dem Schüler*, this noun phrase is really the direct object in underlying structure, and that the peculiarity of (21) is due to some idiosyncrasy in the assignment of morphological case to syntactic relations in German, rather than to rules that change syntactic relations. Such a solution becomes less attractive with (23), *es wurde gestern von uns getanzt*, since here there is no object at all. One can, of course, always argue that in underlying structure there is a direct object which is deleted in the course of the derivation, but in the absence of any independent evidence for such a direct object this analysis serves no purpose other than to save the claim that there are no spontaneous demotion rules from any possible counterexample.[3] A second possibility would be to argue that the demotion of the subject in such sentences is a direct result of the introduction of the subject *es*. That is to say, in the derivation of an impersonal passive, in addition to the change of the verb to the passive form, there is a special rule which inserts *es* as subject, whence the underlying subject must be demoted by the general principle that a sentence cannot have more than one subject.[4] There is perhaps no empirical evidence against such an analysis for German, though I shall try to show below that there are languages, in particular Welsh, for which such an analysis would not work. At best, the only motivation for this analysis would be the desire to exclude spontaneous demotion, since elsewhere *es*-insertion in German is usually considered to be conditional on the absence of an overt subject at the

---

[3] I am assuming throughout that the claim that there is no spontaneous demotion is a claim about language, and not an arbitrary decision by a linguist or linguists to analyze all data of a certain kind in a certain way. For German, one might conceivably claim that the normally deleted direct object of intransitive verbs turns up as the subject *es* in (21) and (23) [though there would still be problems with the lack of *es* in (22) and (24)], but in the discussion of Latin and especially Welsh below we shall see that for these languages even this possibility is excluded.

[4] This analysis was suggested to me as a logical possibility by Geoffrey Pullum.

appropriate level of derivation, rather than itself conditioning the absence or demotion of the subject. For the time being, we may leave this latter suggestion as a logical possibility, to which we shall return in the discussion of Welsh.

Impersonal passives in Dutch follow essentially the same pattern as in German:

(25)          *De soldaten verwoestten de huizen.*
              the soldiers destroyed   the houses

(26)          *De huizen werden (door de   soldaten) verwoest*
              the houses were    by    the soliders  destroyed
              'The houses were destroyed (by the soldiers).'

(27)          *De jongens floten.*
              the boys    whistled

(28)          *Er werd (door de  jongens) gefloten.*
              it  was   by  the boys     whistled
              'There was whistling (by the boys).'

In Latin, as in German and Dutch, transitive verbs (with direct objects) have only the personal passive, whereas other verbs have only the impersonal passive:

(29)          *Alexander          Dareum        vicit.*
              Alexander (nom) Darius (acc) conquered
              'Alexander conquered Darius.'

(30)          *Dareus         ab Alexandro victus       est.*
              Darius (nom) by Alexander conquered is
              'Darius was conquered by Alexander.'

(31)          *Boni cives     legibus parent.*
              good citizens laws-to obey
              'Good citizens obey the laws.'

Latin *parere* 'to obey' takes an indirect object in the dative:

(32)          *Legibus (a   bonis civibus) paretur.*
              laws-to   by good citizens  is-obeyed
              'The laws are obeyed (by good citizens).'

(33)                    *Milites  acriter  pugnaverunt.*
                       soldiers fiercely fought
                       'The soldiers fought fiercely.'


(34)                    *Acriter* (*a   militibus*) *pugnatum est.*
                       fiercely  by soliders  fought     is
                       'There was fierce fighting (by the soldiers).'


The Latin data lead to essentially the same conclusions as the German, except
that in Latin we do not normally find any dummy pronoun corresponding to
German *es* 'it' (this is also true of other impersonal sentences), so that in Latin
there is even less motivation than in German for analyses that would save the
constraint against spontaneous demotion by making the demotion dependent
on the introduction of the subject 'it'. The only other motivation for such an
analysis in Latin would be to account for the third-person-singular morphology
of the Latin impersonal verb. Traditionally this morphology is considered
rather to reflect the unmarkedness of the third-person singular, i.e. in the
absence of any subject to trigger verb agreement, the verb goes into the least
marked form. This more traditional analysis also serves to explain why, in
languages that lack specifically impersonal forms, impersonal forms are always
morphologically the same as the third-person singular, on the basis of the
general claim that this is the least marked form in all languages; if the Latin
third-person-singular morphology were to be accounted for by positing the
insertion of a third-person-singular subject, then we should expect to find other
languages where the inserted subject was of some other person or number.
    As the last example of a language with impersonal passives, we shall consider
Welsh. Since the Welsh data are in many ways crucial to the present argument,
they will be treated in some detail in what follows. In Welsh, the same impersonal passive forms are used with all verbs, whether transitive or intransitive,
and expression of the underlying subject is possible:


(35)                    *Lladdodd draig    ddyn.*
                       killed      dragon man
                       'A dragon killed a man.'


(36)                    *Lladdwyd  dyn* (*gan ddraig*).
                       was-killed man  by  dragon
                       'A man was killed (by a dragon).'


(37)                    *Aeth llawer yno   yn yr   haf.*
                       went many  there in the summer
                       'Many people went there in summer.'

(38)           *Eir        yno  (gan lawer) yn yr  haf.*[5]
               was-gone there by  many  in the summer

With intransitive verbs, the impersonal nature of the construction is apparent;
it seems to be noncontroversial. The morphology of the impersonal passive verb
is quite different from all other forms of the verb, and in particular there is no
reason to call this verb third- person singular, rather than simply impersonal.[6]
With transitive verbs, the claim is more controversial, although I shall try to
show that the passive of transitive verbs is also an impersonal construction.

The clearest evidence for the derived direct object status of the noun phrase
associated with the passive form of a transitive verb can be found when the
noun phrase in question is a pronoun. Here, Welsh has a special construction,
not possible with nonpronominal noun phrases, where the sentence is introduced by a particle *fe* followed by a clitic form of the pronoun:

(39)           *Fe'i      lladdwyd   (gan ddraig).*
               him was-killed  by  dragon
               'He was killed by a dragon.'

This clitic form *'i*, in the construction *fe'i*, does occur in active sentences in
Welsh, but only where the pronoun is direct object:

(40)           *Fe'i      lladdodd draig.*
               him killed     dragon
               'A dragon killed him.'

To say 'he killed a dragon' one could not use this form, but would have to say:

(41)           *Lladdodd ef ddraig.*
               killed     he dragon

Thus there is evidence from elsewhere in Welsh that the form *'i* is a direct object,
in fact that this is its only use in Welsh. (39) is thus a clear instance of an impersonal passive with the underlying direct object not promoted, but with the
underlying subject demoted, i.e. a clear instance of spontaneous demotion.
Where we have the passive of a transitive verb with a nonpronominal underlying direct object, the position is rather more complex, and has given rise to
much controversy traditionally as to whether the noun phrase in question is

---

[5] Example (38), with the inclusion of *gan lawer*, was considered very literary by my informant,
but not absolutely excluded. The example is taken from Bowen and Rhys Jones (1960:139).

[6] This is true synchronically; diachronically, it is unclear whether such forms in Celtic and other
branches of Indo-European were originally impersonal, or originally third-person singular (or
both).

derived subject or direct object; with pronouns, in addition to the construction discussed above, the construction paralleling that of nonpronominal noun phrases is also possible. In Welsh, direct objects are marked in active sentences by lenition (soft mutation), i.e. a change in the initial consonant of the direct object noun phrase, in particular of *d* to *dd* (the orthographic symbol for a voiced dental fricative):[7]

(42)                     *Lladdodd draig    ddyn.*
                         killed      dragon man
                         'A dragon killed a man.'

(43)                     *Lladdodd dyn    ddraig.*
                         killed      man dragon
                         'A man killed a dragon.'

In the passive, the underlying direct object turns up without lenition, which seems prima facie evidence that in derived structure it is subject, i.e. that it has been promoted:

(44)                       *Lladdwyd  dyn.*
                           was-killed man
                           'A man was killed.'

In Comrie (1975) it is claimed that Welsh (like Finnish) is an antiergative language, i.e. that there is a special case (marked by lenition) for the direct object if and only if there is also a subject in the same simplex sentence. Thus in (44), *lladdwyd dyn*, *dyn* would be direct object, but would not be marked by lenition because the sentence contains no subject. Essentially the same argument as was used for similar constructions in Finnish in Comrie (1975) can be used with respect to the Welsh data. We have already noted that with pronouns, in addition to the regular construction [as in (45)], there is also the special construction with *fe* and a clitic pronoun; the latter is clearly impersonal [as in (46)]:

(45)                     *Lladdwyd ef (gan ddraig).*
                         was-killed he  by  dragon
                         'He was killed (by a dragon).'

(46)                     *Fe'i     lladdwyd (ef) (gan ddraig).*
                         him was-killed him by    dragon
                         'He was killed (by a dragon).'

---

[7] The preposition *gan* 'by' also requires lenition, whence *gan ddraig* 'by a dragon' [see example (36)].

In (46) the repetition of the pronoun by *ef* is possible, but not required.[8] It is possible to take construction (46) and coordinate the pronoun *ef* with a non-pronominal noun phrase, for instance:

(47)      *Fe'i    lladdwyd ef  a   'i  gi  (gan ddraig).*
          him was-killed him and  his dog  by  dragon
          'He and his dog were killed (by a dragon).'

The possibility of this coordination follows from the fact that both the pronominal and the nonpronominal noun phrases stand in the same derived syntactic relation, namely, both are direct objects. Coordination of a subject and a direct object would not be possible.[9]

Welsh thus provides a clear example of a language where Subject Demotion may take place spontaneously, without any Object Promotion. The attempts to save the claim that spontaneous demotion does not occur in German, Dutch, and Latin cannot be applied to the Welsh data. The passive forms do not have any overt subject like German *es* or Dutch *er* to trigger demotion of the underlying subject; the morphology of the passive form is not third-person singular, so even the argument from a putative subject controlling verb agreement is not open to us, as it may be in Latin. Moreover, positing underlying direct objects with intransitive verbs, which are promoted and then deleted after having demoted the underlying subject, as has been suggested for German and Latin, does not work in Welsh, because even transitive verbs form an impersonal passive, i.e. in the only clear cases of underlying direct objects they are not in fact promoted.

---

[8] Note that the form *ef* can be either subject or direct object; compare also *lladdodd ef ddraig* 'he killed a dragon'. In the first-person singular there are distinct forms, *i* and *fi*, as in *Carwn i* 'I used to love', but *cerwch fi!* 'love me!'. Morris Jones (1913:316–317) notes that with the passive we have *cerid fi* 'I used to be loved', with the same form as marks the direct object of *cerwch fi!*, rather than *\*cerid i* with the subject form, as in *carwn i*. However, this is not a telling criterion either way, since the distribution of *i* and *fi* does not parallel the subject-direct object distinction. *I* is used if and only if there is some other marker of the person and number of the pronoun, e.g. by the verb ending (*carwn i*) if the pronoun is subject; or by a clitic pronoun (*fe'm carai i* 'he/she used to love me', compared with *carai* 'he/she used to love'; unstressed subject pronouns may be omitted in Welsh) as direct object; or even by a possessive pronoun (*fy nhy i* 'my house', literally 'my house I/me'). *Cerid fi* thus has *fi* because there is no other marker of first-person singular. In the passive construction with a clitic pronoun, we have *fe'm cerid i*, with *i* because *'m* already marks first-person singular.

[9] For completeness, some further details of Welsh morphology should be noted. The word for 'his' in (47), *'i* (in isolation written *ei*), is in itself identical with the direct object pronoun *'i* of *fe'i* 'him', but differs from the latter in that it requires lenition of the following word; the citation form of the word for 'dog' is *ci*. The Welsh for 'he and a dragon were killed' would be *fe'i lladdwyd ef a draig*; the lack of lenition in *draig* here, however, tells us absolutely nothing about syntactic relations, since in Welsh lenition affects only the initial consonant of the whole direct object, and in the coordinate direct object *ef a draig* there is no initial consonant to be lenited. Compare *lladdodd draig gi a dyn* 'a dragon killed a dog and a man', where *ci* is lenited to *gi* since *c* is the initial consonant of the direct object, but *dyn* is not lenited.

At the beginning of this chapter we noted that the passive in English has two results: on the one hand, promotion of an object; on the other, demotion or deletion of the subject. There has been a tendency in work on Relational Grammar (and elsewhere) to concentrate on the promotional properties of the passive, and to relegate its demotional properties to secondary status. The concomitant result has been that subject demotion and subject deletion are treated as radically different, it being accidental that the passive in English (and many other languages) serves equally as a means to demote and to delete subjects. If we subsume demotion and deletion under the general term REMOVAL, and give the functions of the English passive—and of the personal passive in other languages—as both SUBJECT REMOVAL and OBJECT PROMOTION, then we have a more unified account of the nature of the personal passive. This kind of passive now has two functions, rather than three, and one of these functions— removal of the subject—is true equally of the impersonal passive. It is precisely subject removal that links personal and impersonal passives, and only if we accept removal as a possibility independent of promotion (i.e. spontaneous removal, including demotion without deletion) do we have an explanation for the similarities, down to morphological identity in many cases, between personal and impersonal passives in various languages.

## REFERENCES

Awbery, G. M. (1973) *The Passive in Welsh*, unpublished Doctoral dissertation, University of Cambridge, Cambridge.
Bowen, J. and T. J. Rhys Jones (1960) *Teach yourself Welsh*, English Universities Press, London.
Budiṇa Lazdiṇa, T. (1966) *Teach yourself Latvian*, English Universities Press, London.
Comrie, B. (1975) "The Antiergative: Finland's Answer to Basque," in R. E. Grossman, L. J. Sam, and T. J. Vance, eds., *Papers from the Eleventh Regional Meeting of the Chicago Linguistic Society*, University of Chicago, Chicago, Illinois.
Comrie, B. (forthcoming) "Causatives and universal grammar," *Transactions of the Philological Society* (1974).
Cousins, D. A. (1975) *The impersonal passive in Latin*, unpublished diploma in linguistics dissertation, University of Cambridge, Cambridge.
Harmer, L. C. and F. J. Norton (1957) *A Manual of Modern Spanish*, 2 ed., University Tutorial Press, London.
Hartung, W. (1966) "Die Passivtransformationen im Deutschen," *Studia Grammatica* 1, 90–114.
Johnson, D. E. (1974) *Toward a Theory of Relationally-based Grammar*, unpublished Doctoral dissertation, University of Illinois, Urbana, Illinois.
Keenan, E. L. and B. Comrie (to appear) "Noun Phrase Accessibility and Universal Grammar," *Linguistic Inquiry*.
Kirsner, R. S. (1974) "On Pragmatic Inference and Communicative Strategies: The Problem of the Dutch 'Pseudo-passive'," presented at the Annual Meeting, Linguistic Society of America.
Morris Jones, J. (1913) *A Welsh Grammar, Historical and Comparative: Phonology and Accidence*, Clarendon Press, Oxford.
Wiese, E. (1969) "Die Struktur Unbestimmt-persönlicher Sätze im Modernen Polnischen," *Zeitschrift für Slawistik* 14, 51–68.

# THE CASE FOR CASE REOPENED

*CHARLES J. FILLMORE*
*University of California at Berkeley*

## 1

Several years ago I wrote a fairly long article (Fillmore 1968) with the punning title, "The Case for Case." In it I presented a notion I referred to as DEEP STRUCTURE CASES, together with a number of proposals on how the notion could be incorporated into a generative grammar. Since that time, I have become aware—through the many published and unpublished reactions to the piece that have reached my desk—not only of some of my own mistakes, but also of a number of ways in which readers have misunderstood my intentions or have acquired expectations for the theory which went beyond anything I had in mind.

Here is what I am going to try to do in this chapter: I will locate the concept of deep cases within traditions of semantic and grammatical inquiry; I will review a few of the basic assumptions of case theory and will point out what I originally thought of as its advantages; I will discuss some of the most important challenges to the theory, including the serious one of how one can know what the cases are and how many of them there are; and I will fail to offer a satisfying solution to this problem. I will instead propose a new interpretation of the role of cases in a theory of grammar and a new method of investigating the question of their number and identity. I consider this new interpretation as a position in the theory of grammatical relations and as a position in semantic theory with which one could associate this slogan: MEANINGS ARE RELATIVIZED TO SCENES.

To illustrate my points, I will mainly use the same examples that I have used in earlier writings, including, of course, many that I borrowed from other authors. This is not because I can't think of any new ones, but because I wish to show with examples that might be familiar some of the ways in which the new interpretation is different.

## 2

Within semantics in general, the notion of deep cases is a part of what might be called INTERNAL, as opposed to EXTERNAL, semantics; that is, it concerns, not the semantics of truth or entailment or illocutionary force, but rather the semantic nature of the inner structure of a clause. Within internal semantics, the concern is SYNTAGMATIC rather than PARADIGMATIC; that is, deep cases are among the types of semantic relations that elements of sentence structures have with each other in context, rather than with the system of contrasts and oppositions that differentiate constituents paradigmatically. The concern is with the inner structure of clauses rather than with the semantics of interclausal connections through the devices of coordination and subordination.

Within grammatical theory the concept of deep cases can be thought of as a contribution to the theory of grammatical levels, to the theory of grammatical relations, to the description of valences and collocations, and to the general theory of the functions of sentence constituents. The proposal is that there is a level of structural organization for a sentence which is distinct from what is usually thought of as a semantic representation and which is distinct likewise from the familiar notions of deep and surface structure syntactic representations. The theory is concerned with the determination of the nuclear grammatical relations in a sentence—subject, object, and indirect object—in that it addresses itself to the question of how particular aspects of the meaning of an utterance determine which constituent will appear as the (deep structure) subject, which as the object. The theory of cases can also be seen as offering at least part of the SEMANTIC VALENCE descriptions of verbs and adjectives, comparable to the syntactic valence descriptions given by certain European linguists (Tesnière 1959, Helbig 1971, Helbig and Schenkel 1969, Emons 1974). And, lastly, it may add something to the theory of the functions of sentence constituents. Katz (1972:113) has distinguished three kinds of sentence-constituent functions: the GRAMMATICAL, illustrated by the notions of 'subject' and 'object'; the RHETORICAL, illustrated by such oppositions as 'given' versus 'new', 'topic' versus 'Comment', etc.; and the SEMANTIC, illustrated by such notions as 'agent', recipient', 'means', 'result', etc. In his discussion of these functions, Katz claims that Chomsky's failure in the Extended Standard Theory (Chomsky 1970) is one of confusing the grammatical and the rhetorical functions, and that my failure in "The Case for Case" is that of confusing the grammatical and the semantic functions. There is, I believe, a fourth way of looking at the functional structure of the parts of sentences, something for which such words as ORIENTATION and PERSPECTIVE suggest what I have in mind. The parts of a message can be divided into those that are "in perspective" and those that are "out of perspective". My current position is that it is the orientational or perspectival structuring of a message which provides the subject matter for the theory of cases, and that the case notion figures very differently in grammatical description from what I originally had in mind.

One essential feature of the theory of deep cases is the CASE FRAME (Fillmore 1968:27), the function of which is to provide a bridge between descriptions of situations and underlying syntactic representations. It accomplishes this by assigning semantico-syntactic roles to particular participants in the (real or imagined) situation represented by the sentence. This assignment determines or constrains the assignment of a PERSPECTIVE on the situation by means of what I have called SUBJECT SELECTION PRINCIPLES and the CASE HIERARCHY.

Some of the Subject Selection principles seem to be language-universal. Thus, given certain qualifications for the interpretation of ergative systems, one candidate for a universal Subject Selection Principle is this: If there is an agent which is brought into perspective, the nominal which represents it must be the (deep) subject.

Other Subject Selection principles appear to be language-specific. Japanese, according to Kuno (1973:31), and German, according to Rohdenburg (1970), do not allow certain kinds of enabling or occasioning causes to be chosen as subjects of their sentences, whereas English does tolerate such choices, as in sentences like those in (1):

(1)    a. *Fifty dollars will buy you a second-hand car.*
      b. *The smell sickened me.*
      c. *The accident killed the woman.*

Still other Subject Selection principles appear to be word-specific. This appears to be true, for example, of (at least) one member of the pair *regard* and *strike*, as in Chomsky's examples (1965:162) given here in (2):

(2)       a. *I regard John as pompous.*
        b. *John strikes me as pompous.*

Lastly, but not surprisingly, Subject Selection principles are capable of changing in time. Jespersen (1924:160) speaks of the changes in the history of English from expressions of the type seen in (3a) and (3b) to expressions of the type seen in (3c) and (3d) as involving changes in the MEANINGS of these verbs:

(3)       a. *Me dreamed a strange dream.*
        b. *Me like oysters.*
        c. *I dreamed a strange dream.*
        d. *I like oysters.*

There is, of course, a way of construing the word *meaning* so that Jespersen's description can seem sensible; but one could more revealingly say that what changed were the workings of the Subject Selection principles operating in the language, these changes having to do with the interaction of ordering principles and case-marking principles in a period after which most surface case distinctions on nouns and pronouns were lost.

The advantages that I saw in the notion of deep-structure case were that case-structure descriptions of words and sentences offered a level of linguistic organization at which universal properties of lexical structure and clause organization were to be found, and, moreover, that such descriptions were in some sense intuitively relatable to the ways people thought about the experiences and events that they were able to express in the sentences of their language.

## 3

It was misleading for me to use the phrase CASE GRAMMAR to describe the proposals I made in "The Case for Case." My proposals did not cohere into a model of grammar. Instead, they were suggestions about a level of organization of a clause that was relevant to both its meaning and its grammatical structure; that provided a way of describing certain aspects of lexical structure; and that offered convenient classifications of clause types. From the fact that I have frequently received mail asking me questions like, "How does case grammar handle intonation?", I have become aware that my writings somehow gave the impression that case grammar so-called was being presented as a general model of linguistic structure. Nowadays I try to be more careful about the phrase 'case grammar'.

Criticism of the deep case proposals have come from many places and represent many points of view. Some of them are based on misunderstandings (possibly invited misunderstandings); some of them are valid but require "patching" rather than deep changes in my position; and a number of them are very much worth worrying about.

When I wrote "The Case for Case" the Generative Semantics position had not yet been formulated, or, rather, had not yet been formulated in my hearing except in its preliminary version as Abstract Syntax. In the section of my article which touched on surface case morphology, I described the traditional way of treating cases, which consisted in identifying the cases through their forms and then, one by one, describing their functions within larger constructions. What I suggested was that things should be turned around, so that the organization of the sentence as a whole should be taken as the framework within which the functions of the individual grammatical morphemes could be stated. As a catchword for this position I spoke of the CENTRALITY OF SYNTAX.

Walter Cook, in his article "A Set of Postulates for Case Grammar" (1972), claims to be taking a position in opposition to mine in a postulate which assigns centrality to semantics, not syntax. I suspect that if I knew precisely what it meant, Cook's is a position I might take, too. But, in any event, it was not an opposition between semantics-at-the-bottom and syntax-at-the-bottom that I had in mind, but rather between analysis that begins with the morpheme and analysis that begins with the sentence.

I have used various forms of arguments in trying to justify specific claims about deep case distinctions. One of these argument forms has two steps. In the first step we recognize an ambiguous sentence whose ambiguity can be accounted for only by assuming that one of its nominals is interpretable as bearing either of two semantic roles in the sentence. As an illustration of this point, we can consider the ambiguous sentence (4a). To see that this sentence is ambiguous, imagine a situation in which you see that I have a letter on my desk, that you see me make a copy of it, and that then you hear me say sentence (4b). If you speak the same version of English that I do, you can't know for sure, from my instructions, which of the two letters I have in mind.

(4)     a. *I copied the letter.*
        b. *Point to the letter which I copied.*
        c. *I copied this from that.*

The second step in this argument form consists in exhibiting the same verb in a sentence where it takes two different nominals, each with just one of the two semantic roles sensed in the earlier ambiguous sentence. This property is found in our verb *copy*, as can be seen in sentence (4c), in which exactly the two previously sensed roles noticed in (4a) are parcelled out among two separate nominals. Having both types of evidence—as provided in the two steps of this argument—makes it believable that we are dealing with two different case roles rather than with simply a matter of vagueness.

In a second kind of argument, also with two steps, I have suggested that we may be dealing with different case relationships whenever we find a single verb collocating with two seemingly disparate classes of nominals in a given grammatical relation, with the nominals from the two classes seeming to exemplify different semantic roles in their sentences. Examples for this point are the possibilities for the subject-nominal in sentences (5a) and (5b). And, again, the argument can be taken as completed if, as step two, we can find a single sentence with the same two roles parcelled out between two separate nominals, as in (5c):

(5)     a. *My foot hurts.*
        b. *This shoe hurts.*
        c. *This shoe hurts my foot.*

These kinds of arguments have seemed particularly weak to a number of European critics, who have suggested that the method of analysis is based on accidental properties of English words. Other languages, this particular counter-argument goes, might use different words for the different senses of *hurt* and *copy*, and so, for purely nonsystematic reasons, the method would yield different results for these other languages.

This objection, too, I take as a misunderstanding. These arguments are not offered as definitions of cases, but rather as steps for pointing out case distinctions in sentence sets where sense differences are only, or are primarily, matched by case role differences. I have been just as interested in similarities in underlying case structure in sentences with different verbs and different relational organization. In a third kind of argument that I have used, different surface verbs are taken from single vocabulary fields—pairs like *rob* and *steal* or *buy* and *sell*—verbs which have matching (or partly matching) case structures but different assignments of grammatical relations. I feel sure, in other words, that an analyst looking at, say, Swedish, would be able to discover, in expressions of physical pain, roles involving such things as the source of the pain, the location of the pain, the experiencer of the pain, and so on; and this could be done independently of whether the same verb or different verbs were used, independently of whether the same or different choices were made in the selection and orientation of the cases.

A criticism that has come from some European workers in Valence Theory (Emons 1974 and Panevová 1974) has been that I have obscured the various senses in which it is possible to speak of optional constituents in a sentence. Sometimes some aspect of an event or situation is a part of the speaker's and the hearer's understanding of the meaning of a sentence, yet there is nothing in the sentence which expresses it; and sometimes the absence of a constituent in the surface sentence reflects the absence of the associated notion from the conceptualization that is being communicated. It is true that there have been some places where I was wrong in detail in the description of given sentences in just this regard; but my intention was that all of the various senses of optionality could be accounted for by the fact that the system I proposed had CASE FRAMES, indicating the case notions conceptually present in a sentence; CASE FRAME FEATURES, indicating the case notions that could be combined in construction with a given lexical item; and DELETION TRANSFORMATIONS, by which, under various conditions, a given constituent could be, or maybe had to be, absent from the surface structure. I think that in principle my proposals take care of optionality sufficiently well.

Several specific suggestions that I made in "The Case for Case" seem to have been bad ones, and I have been quick to abandon them. I proposed, for example, that all nominals in English sentences are initially provided with prepositions; this position required that the processes of forming subjects and direct objects had to involve preposition deletion. My motivation was partly that of wanting to make English and Japanese seem more comparable than they might have otherwise. Japanese has POSTPOSITIONS marking all nominal functions in a sentence, INCLUDING THE NUCLEAR GRAMMATICAL RELATIONS (subject and object). I thought that the basic typological differences between the two languages could be captured as follows: In deep structure, English has the verb at the beginning, Japanese, the verb at the end, of each sentence; the language with the verb at the beginning has prepositions on all the nouns; the language with the verb at the end has postpositions on all the nouns. Apart from these differences—which a mirror would show are really similarities—the two languages differ in that the verb-initial language—English—has a Subject-fronting rule, by which the verb ends up in second position, and it has preposition-deletion processes for the subject and direct object. These two language types, then, can be compared with a third type, exemplified by Tagalog, which lacks Subject Fronting and which keeps prepositions in front of all its associated nominals.

As part of an informal general typological sketch, this way of looking at things is not bad, I think; but the specific proposals I had for the assignment of the individual lexical preposition made the system look fairly inefficient. In particular, as I tried to construct a grammar using these proposals, my initial association of the preposition *by* with the agent case had to yield in favor of a more complicated principle associating *by* with the highest-ranking case in the sentence, whatever that case might have been. This decision made it possible to account correctly for the *by* in *eaten by George*, *destroyed by fire*, and *assumed by everybody* (as long as it was constrained to allow *known to me*, etc.). In the end, however, such provisions did not look any better than an account according to which the preposition *by* gets introduced by means of a Passive transformation.

In "The Case for Case" I described the agent and the dative cases as necessarily animate. This, by a curious kind of bad logic, led some people, for example me, to assume that obligatory animacy in a verbal complement implied that the associated nominal had to be in one of these two cases. By that kind of reasoning, the subjects of *die* and *melt* (to use examples from Huddleston's 1970 critique) were dative and patient (object), respectively, and the two sentences in (6) would have to be given different case structure analyses:

(6)       a. *The man died.*
        b. *The snow melted.*

I am now more careful about keeping relational notions and categorial notions distinct.

Some workers, for example Nilsen (1972), have provided binary opposition analyses of the basic cases, analyzing agent and instrument as animate and inanimate causes, respectively; and experiencer (dative) and patient (object) as animate and inanimate effects, respectively. The initial appeal of this analysis fades when one realizes that it is a confusion of categorial and relational notions, but begins to reappear when one tries to see it as an account of the basic properties of the prototype scenes in terms of which actions and experiences can be structured.

In an attack on case grammar recently published in Germany, Peter Finke (1974) concentrated on what he took to be the categorial implications of cases, and interpreted case theory as a version of many-sorted logic. To say that a verb takes an agent and a patient is to say, Finke would claim, that the two arguments of the verb have to meet different SORTAL SPECIFICATIONS, and that in general cases are to be defined in terms of sortal specifications. Agents are things having one set of properties, instruments are things having some other set of properties, and so on.

Finke's main point, if I understand him correctly, is that a case grammar makes an ontological commitment about the number of sorts of objects that can exist in a universe, that number equal to the number of cases. If such a strong claim is implied by the theory, according to Finke, then the fact that case grammarians have not been able to come up with a common and stable collection of cases shows that the theory is not to be taken seriously. The reply is, of course, that even if some universe contained only one sort of object— say, human beings—the role-identifying function of the cases could still be maintained. One person could pick up another person, use that person's body for knocking down a third person, that third person could feel embarrassment, and so on. In a universe with only one sort of object, in short, the case relations of agent, instrument, patient, and experiencer could all be easily imagined. Perhaps it was my misleading statements about animacy that created the impression that case notions were to be understood as categories rather than as types of relations.

A challenge to case grammar that I have recently heard comes from a writer (Raible 1975) who was concerned with how case theory could account for the very complicated set of case functions in a language like Finnish. The author of this challenge had taken my suggestion that when looking at a system of cases we should distinguish case FORMS from case USES, and that we should build a theory of deep cases whose repertory of case concepts was more or less equivalent to the repertory of case uses. Finnish presents special problems, and in two ways. First, because of the system of locative and directional cases which combine, in one and the same surface case category, both locational notions and assumptions about the topology of the reference object (the entity in terms of which something is being located or with respect to which something is being oriented); and, second, because there is a semantic difference, in what is thought of as the direct object, between choosing the nominative, the accusative, or the partitive case. The difference between choosing the accusative rather than the partitive, for example, appears to involve such notions as definiteness, completion, and totality. My answer has to be, of course, that the morphemes in surface case systems encode more than nominal functions, and that therefore an account of the uses of surface-structure cases requires more than a theory of deep cases.

## 4

There are four more kinds of criticisms of case theory that I wish to mention, two that I do not know how or whether to worry about, and two that seem clearly very serious indeed. The first of the puzzling ones is the collection of criticisms that take the form, "I can do anything you can do"—the argument of MERE NOTATIONAL VARIANCE. One version of the argument goes like this: I have claimed that in the structure underlying expressions containing a verb like English *seem* there is what I call an EXPERIENCER, the person for whom something seems; and I have claimed that this sometimes is manifested on the surface as a *to*-phrase, as in (7):

(7)      a. *To me, Harry seems intelligent.*
         b. *It seems to me that Harry is intelligent.*

This, the argument goes, is pointless. There is no particular advantage to giving theoretical prominence to terms like experiencer, agent, instrument, and the rest. We could just as well state that *seem* is a MENTAL STATE VERB, meaning that it has a semantic marker 'mental'; and we can then say that selection restrictions for verbs containing this marker require one of their coconstituents to be 'animate' nominal; we can say of the verb *seem* that it has a selectional restriction requiring its associated animate argument to be part of a preposition phrase marked by *to*; and we could even provide a principle which declared that, for any argument of a mental verb which is obligatorily animate, a semantic marker 'experiencer' can be added to the representation of that nominal in the finished semantic reading of the sentence.

This argument (found in Chomsky 1970, Katz 1972, and Mellema 1974) has something to say for it, of course. It is a version of the view that a change in a scientific paradigm should be tolerated only when the possibilities of the existing paradigm have been exhausted AND when a more satisfactory paradigm can be shown to exist. I sympathize with this view in general; my position, however, is that alternative paradigms—or even alternative notations—should be valued for the kinds of questions they force an analyst to ask. A strong assumption about deep structure cases forces the analyst to ask certain questions about the number and variety of the semantic functions of the parts of sentences. Whether the answers to these questions can be WRITTEN DOWN within the terms of some other paradigm does not always seem important to somebody primarily concerned with whether the questions are important ones and whether they can be answered at all.

Next there are the trivializing objections to case grammar leveled by Ray C. Dougherty (1974). Dougherty's main point is that case grammar so-called offers at best a possibly interesting but theoretically unimportant classification of verbs. Verbs, in this system, are classified on the basis of intuitive judgments about their complements. This—Dougherty goes on—might seem harmless enough, possibly comparable to classifying words by the number of letters, as in the New York Times Crossword Puzzle Dictionary; but it is not harmless, because Fillmore has deceitfully superimposed on this mere taxonomy the trappings of a generative grammar.

If the mere taxonomy charge is valid, then I should probably repeat that the deep case proposal was not intended as a complete model of grammar, but only as a set of arguments in favor of the recognition of a level of case structure organization of sentences. If the mere notational variant evidence is valid, this should not be taken as a reason for dismissing case theory, but rather as a challenge for considering such questions as which of the many possible notational variants of the final correct theory offers the greatest convenience for making generalizations about language typology, about lexical classification, about child language acquisition, and so on. In short, I see the notational and taxonomic possibilities of case theory as standing or falling together. A taxonomy is to be valued if it provides a convenient and revealing conceptual organization of the entities in its realm, in our case something in terms of which grammatical and semantic generalizations can be easily formulated; a notation is to be valued if it allows the formation of such a taxonomy in a simple and straightforward way.

The two sorts of objections I have just been discussing have been that case theory is AT BEST a mere notational variant of some preferred theory, or is AT BEST a mere taxonomy. The critics who have raised these issues have other objections, too, several of them relating to points discussed elsewhere in this paper.

But now let me turn to objections that require action. Stephen Anderson, in a paper called "On the Role of Deep Structure in Semantic Interpretation" (1971), challenged my claim that it would be possible to do without a level of deep structure in the sense of the Standard Theory. The position I had taken was that grammatical theory needs a level of case structure, which I thought of as being, or as being close to, a level of semantic representation; this position recognizes, by means of the grammar's transformational rules, the levels of surface structure. But, for reasons like those given by Halliday (1967:39), there was thought to be no need for a separate level of deep structure.

I would say, for example, that in the case of the English verb *break* used transitively, its two arguments could have the case functions agent and patient, the agent being the entity responsible for the breaking, the patient being the entity which broke. In the surface structure, one of these arguments has to become the subject of the sentence. One possibility is for the agent to become the subject, as in (8a); another, which has side effects on the form of the verb, is for the patient to become the subject, as in (8b):

(8)                a. *John broke the vase.*
                   b. *The vase was broken by John.*

I presented these as optional choices provided by a Subject Selection rule. The important point to notice is that, in the history of the formation of a passive sentence, no level of representation was posited according to which the sentence had a subject that was different from the surface subject. It had a case structure and a surface structure, but no intermediate structure within which the notions of subject and object could be defined.

Anderson, defending the Standard Theory, argued on grounds of the simplicity of the semantic component for the existence of deep-structure subjects and objects. His argument took the form of a claim that there are certain semantic generalizations which can be formulated simply only at the standard deep-structure level. There are two situations covered by Anderson's arguments. The first is that in which certain transformations, like Passive and Dative Movement, are viewable as changing an original assignment of deep-structure subject or object; the second is that in which a given predicate allows more than one way for its arguments to be parcelled out as terms of grammatical relations. In either case, Anderson's argument is that frequently there is a difference between a HOLISTIC and a PARTITIVE interpretation given to a noun phrase, depending on whether or not it has one of the primary grammatical relations (subject or object) at the deep-structure level. To illustrate Anderson's point from familiar examples, we can say that the difference between (9a) and (9b) is that the sentence with *the garden* in subject position conveys the idea of the whole garden containing bees, whereas in the other no such assumption is necessary; and that the difference between (9c) and (9d) is that the sentence with *the truck* in direct-object position conveys the idea of the truck being entirely filled with hay, an assumption not necessary with the other sentence:

(9)                a. *Bees were swarming in the garden.*
                   b. *The garden was swarming with bees.*
                   c. *I loaded hay onto the truck.*
                   d. *I loaded the truck with hay.*

New examples suggested by Mellema (1974) are the sentences in (10):

(10)                                a. *He read from his speech.*
                                    b. *He read his speech.*

Having in mind the reading-aloud sense of *read*, the sentence with *his speech* in direct-object position gives the impression that the entire speech was read, while the other sentence definitely does not.

Without feeling required to concede that these arguments support the version of deep structure that Anderson had in mind, I believe I must concede that a level of representation including the grammatical relations subject and object—or something else which recognizes the kind of close participation in the nuclear part of a clause that we find with subjects and objects—is probably necessary for grammatical theory. This does not mean, however, that a level of representation which recognizes case functions is spurious. We still have, after all, the problem of determining, from an understanding of what is being said, which of the arguments of a multiplace predicate are to appear as its subject, and which, if any, as its object.

The next truly worrisome criticism of case theory is the observation that nobody working within the various versions of grammars with 'cases' has come up with a principled way of defining the cases, or principled procedures for determining how many cases there are, or for determining when you are faced with two cases that happen to have something in common as opposed to one case that has two variants. In his careful paper "Some Thoughts on Agentivity" (1973), D. A. Cruse examined a number of linguists' statements about agentivity, found not only that different linguists disagree on the definition of agentivity, but also that the notions that enter into these definitions do not appear to be comparable enough to lend themselves to a uniform definition of a coherent concept.

I have thought of the problem of determining the cases as being somewhat analogous to that of determining the phonological units of language. Since *pie* and *buy* are different words in English, we have good reason to believe that we have a /p/ phoneme that is distinct from a /b/ phoneme. In *spy*, however, we have a problem. Should we analyze its stopped segment as /p/ or as /b/, or as something distinct from either of these? If it is not a /p/ or a /b/, should it be seen as something which in some sense includes both the /p/ and the /b/ phonemes, something which is exactly neutral between the /p/ and the /b/, or something conceptually distinct from those two phonemes altogether—something taking part in a different phonological system? The data do not dictate the correct answers to these questions. American phonemicists tend to regard the segment as /p/, but Danish phonologists, facing a similar problem in their language, choose /b/. Firthian linguists would tend to regard it as a systematically different item entirely; phonologists who allow certain kinds of abstractions might regard it as a category that includes both /p/ and /b/, and, if they make special assumptions about the feature composition of phonemes, they would recognize it as a segment containing features shared by both /p/ and /b/ but lacking any of the features which distinguish those two segments from each other.

An analogous array of positions could be taken on the problem of the identity of cases. Huddleston (1970) examines my arguments that in (11a) *John* functions as agent and that in (11b) *this key* functions as instrument. Here we are dealing with what might be called 'indirect cause' and 'direct cause', respectively. A reason for feeling sure that the two roles are distinct is that the same two nouns, preserving their case roles, can also occur together, with *open*, in a single sentence, as in (11c). The problem, Huddleston suggests, is what to decide about the causal element in (11d). Deciding on the case role of the subject in (11d) is like deciding on the "emic" status of the stopped consonant in *spy*.

(11)                        a. *John opened the door.*
                            b. *This key opened the door.*
                            c. *John opened the door with this key.*
                            d. *The wind opened the door.*

One possibility is that the wind, like John in the earlier sentence, is using its own energy rather than energy provided by something or someone else, and that therefore it is the agent. A second way of looking at it is that, since the wind is the direct cause of the door's opening, it should be seen as the instrument. A third view is that the wind in (11d) has a role that is distinct from both agent and instrument—call it force—since we have neither manipulator nor manipulated, but only a self-sufficient force. Another view, of course, is that there is a case feature cause that is ONE of the features of both agent and the instrument case; in the subject noun phrase for our sentence about the wind opening the door, the cause feature is present, but the features that distinguish an agent from an instrument are absent.

Since there are all of these possibilities to draw from—each sanctioned by one or another respectable linguistic tradition—there is little wonder that scholars who have tried to make the case theory work have not been able to agree. Furthermore, since linguists differ in the kinds of sentences they concentrate on and in the various positions that can be taken on the degree of closeness between case structure and semantic structure, and since not every linguist will think of the full range of possible alternatives, scholars working with caselike notions have all come up with different lists. The shortest list is John Anderson's (1971): 'nominative', 'ergative,' and 'locative'. The longest, I think, is that of William Martin (1972), who has separate case labels for the nouns found in the phrases *at the station, on the table, in the box, from the station, off the table, out of the box, to the station, onto the table,* and *into the box.* The principle seems to be that there are at least as many deep-structure cases as there are surface-structure cases or types of prepositional phrases.

Halliday (1967) recognizes a small number of different kinds of clauses, and assigns separate kinds of caselike structures to each of them. The method of L. Stephen Coles (1972), by contrast, is to divide verbs into a number of types (he finds sixteen), specifying a framework of caselike concepts for each type. With verbs of construction, for example, he distinguishes the resulting constructed object, such as the house that got built; the material out of which the thing got built; the people who performed the constructing act; the implements that were used; the time of the event; the location of the event; the time span from the beginning of the task to the end of the task; and so on. In Coles's case, if I understand his purposes, there is no concern with whether the resulting-object case with a verb of construction is or is not the same as some particular case in the conceptual framework posited for some other verb class.

## 5

I believe now that there might be a solution. It involves what I said earlier about meanings being relativized to scenes. One way for me to lead into this question is to point out that, as I have conceived them, the repertory of cases is NOT identical to the full set of notions that would be needed to make an analysis of any state or event. One of the cases in the system I proposed was the agent, identifying the role of an active participant in some event; yet EVENTS are not restricted in the number of active participants they can have. For example, in what I shall be calling the COMMERCIAL EVENT, two different individuals are agentively involved, and the actions of EACH of the two are part of our understanding of ANY of the lexical items that can be used for describing this kind of event or any of its aspects. The point I want to make here is that a case frame need not comprise a description of all of the relevant aspects of a situation, but only a particular piece or section of a situation.

One of the individuals in the commercial event—the buyer--hands over some money and takes the goods; the other—the seller—surrenders the goods and takes the money. A complete description of the commercial event would identify the buyer, the seller, the money, and the goods.[1] A prototypic commercial event involves all of these things, but any single clause that we construct in talking about such an event requires us to choose one particular perspective on the event. In the usage that I suggest, any verb identifying any particular aspect of the commercial event will constrain us to bring one or more of the entities in the event INTO PERSPECTIVE, the manifestation of this choice for English being the selection of grammatical functions corresponding to the notions of underlying subject and direct object. For example, if I wish to take the perspec-

---

[1] A really careful analysis, in fact, would require that reference to the money be made from two points of view, the CASH and the VALUE. This would make it possible to distinguish:

   i.   *I bought it with a two-dollar bill.*
   ii.  *I bought it for two dollars.*

tive of the seller and the goods, I will use the verb *sell*. Should I wish to take the perspective of the buyer and the money, I will use the verb *spend*. If I wish to bring into perspective either the buyer and the money or the buyer and the seller, I will use the verb *pay*. Should I wish to take the perspective of the goods and the money, I will use the verb *cost*. And so on.

In each of these cases, the speaker is required to construct a sentence in which one of the two or three entities that have been put into perspective becomes the subject: and, maybe, one becomes the direct object. The new question for the theory of cases is this: What do we need to know about the various participant roles in a situation in order to know which of these roles or which combinations of them can be put into perspective, and then, for those which have been put into perspective, which is to become the subject and which is to become the direct object?

The connection with the notion of 'scenes' can be stated this way. The study of semantics is the study of the cognitive scenes that are created or activated by utterances. Whenever a speaker uses ANY of the verbs related to the commercial event, for example, the entire scene of the commercial event is brought into play—is "activated"—but the particular word chosen imposes on this scene a particular perspective. Thus, anyone who hears and understands either of the sentences in (12) has in mind a scene involving all of the necessary aspects of the commercial event, but in which only certain parts of the event have been identified and included in perspective. The buyer and the goods are mentioned in (12a), the buyer and the money in (12b). In each case, information about the other elements of the scene could have been included—via nonnuclear elements of the sentence, as in (12c) and (12d):

(12)       a. *I bought a dozen roses.*
           b. *I paid Harry five dollars.*
           c. *I bought a dozen roses from Harry for five dollars.*
           d. *I paid Harry five dollars for a dozen roses.*

One typical way of dealing with conceptually obligatory but superficially optional elements in a sentence is to claim that these elements are present in the deep structure but deleted or given zero representation on the surface structure. [Examples (12a) and (12b) represent different conditions for such deletion operations.] Within the view that meanings are relativized to scenes, however, it may not be necessary to believe that everything that is included in our understanding of a sentence is necessarily a part of the underlying grammatical structure of that sentence; it seems preferable to say that a word like *buy* or *pay* activates the scene of the commercial event; that everybody who understands the word knows what are the various components and aspects of such an event; and that a speaker's linguistic knowledge of the verb includes that knowledge of the grammatical ways in which the various parts of the event can be realized in the form of the utterance.

Any particular verb or other predicating word assumes, in each use, a given perspective. The grammatical functions of the nominals that represent the entities that are put into perspective are determined in part by something like a DEEP CASE HIERARCHY. Other parts of the associated scene can be introduced with prepositional phrases, with adverbials of various kinds, and with subordinate clauses. The "circumstantial" constituents of a sentence need not be aspects of scenes that are specifically required by a particular type of situation. Since any event takes place in time, any event sentence can contain a time adverbial; since many kinds of events take place in specific locations, sentences representing such events can contain locative adverbials; and so on.

Now when I say that meanings are relativized to scenes, what I mean is that we choose and understand expressions by having or activating in our minds scenes or images or memories of experiences within which the word or expression has a naming or describing or classifying function. For example, if we have occasion to say that a person has spent a certain amount of time *on land*, we know that this expression is chosen from a contrast set for which the opposing term is *at sea*, and that the terms from this set require a background scene involving in some way a sea voyage. Similarly, we know that if we describe somebody as being *spry* we have in mind a background scene of an age set for which the degree of activity and vigor we have in mind is relatively rare. The point is that, whenever we pick up a word or phrase, we automatically drag along with it the larger context or framework in terms of which the word or phrase we have chosen has an interpretation. It is as if descriptions of the meanings of elements must identify simultaneously 'figure' and 'ground'.

To say it again, whenever we understand a linguistic expression of whatever sort, we have simultaneously a background scene and a perspective on that scene. Thus, in our examples about buying and selling, the choice of any particular expression from the repertory of expressions that activate the commercial event scene brings to mind the whole scene—the whole commercial event situation—but presents in the foreground—in perspective—only a particular aspect or section of that scene.

## 6

Languages, and lexical items, differ in interesting ways in the options they present in taking particular perspectives on complex scenes. Consider, for illustrating this point, a scene of a person taking something and causing that thing to come into abrupt contact with something else.

The English verb *hit* allows either of two perspectives on such a scene. One is that of the actor and the manipulated object; the other is that of the actor and the affected object. Illustrating the first of these we have a sentence like

(13a); illustrating the second we have (13b):

(13)                              a. *I hit the stick against the fence.*
                                          b. *I hit the fence with the stick.*
                                          c. *I hit the stick.*
                                          d. *I hit the fence.*

The event referred to in (13a) and (13b) may be the same, but the perspectives are different.

I will refer to the elements that are brought into perspective—the elements that appear as subjects and direct objects—as NUCLEAR ELEMENTS in the sentence. The first thing to notice about nuclear elements, so defined, is that they are not identical with the obligatory elements of the sentence. In (13a), for example, the prepositional phrase is obligatory, yet it is not a part of the nucleus. Put differently, (13d) can be taken as an in-context abbreviation of (13b), but (13c) cannot be interpreted as an abbreviation of (13a).

A question that must be asked is under what conditions something can be brought into perspective. In the case of a hitting act in which the two objects that come into contact are both inanimate and neither is described as being interestingly affected by the event, it is difficult to imagine any particular salience difference between the two, and hence it is not easy to see the difference between the two perspectival choices. However, just in case one of the two entities brought together in an act of hitting is in some sense inherently more worthy of inclusion in perspective, inherently more salient, the force of the perspective choice begins to become noticeable. One possibility for enhancing the saliency of the affected entity is to make it be, not a fence, but a person. We will find, I believe, that it is in some sense more natural to say (14a) than (14b):

(14)                              a. *I hit Harry with the stick.*
                                          b. *I hit the stick against Harry.*

This must be because it is more natural to include human beings within perspective than to leave them out in favor of inanimate objects. It is not that there is not use for sentence (14b), but rather that in that sentence the decision to leave Harry out of perspective has the effect of treating him as a physical object rather than as a sentient being affected by the hitting act.

For scenes involving mechanical actions of the kind just considered, it is fairly easy to set up a conceptual framework which has parts that match caselike notions in a fairly straightforward way. Thus, the thing which gets manipulated is the patient, the thing on which the manipulated thing acts is the goal, and the manipulator is the agent. What we can say about the verb *hit* and a number of other verbs within the same semantic field is that certain perspectives are available: agent and patient, as in (14a), with agent as subject and patient as direct object; agent and goal, as in (14b), with agent as subject and goal as direct object; and, with the manipulator left out of perspective, patient and goal, with patient as subject and goal as direct object, as in (15):

(15)                    *The stick hit the fence.*

In sentence (15), the decision to leave the manipulator out of perspective has the effect of taking a smaller perspective on a larger event; one situation justifying this choice would be that in which the stick was thrown into space, so that its coming into contact with the fence could be seen as a separately individuated event.

The verb *beat*, by contrast, is associated only with a scene in which the agent is holding onto the manipulated object throughout the action. Thus we can say (16a–d), given the special interpretation required for (16c); but we cannot use sentence (16e) for the same scene:

(16)              a. *I beat the stick against the wall.*
                  b. *I beat the wall with the stick.*
                  c. *I beat the stick against Harry.*
                  d. *I beat Harry with the stick.*
                  e. *The stick beat Harry.*

Since *beat* necessarily involves an event in the history of the agent, there is no way of leaving the agent out of the perspective.

The verb *knock* offers a few special problems. Conceptually an act of knocking requires more than one participant, but only the agent need be put into perspective. Thus when we say (17) we have the agent's knocking action primarily in mind:

(17)                    *He knocked on the door with his fist.*

Thus we have seen how it is that the notion of perspective can be called on to explain (more honestly, to express) the subtle semantic differences, both in the grammatical organization of clauses having the same verb, and among sentences containing different verbs (*hit*, *beat*, and *knock*) within a single semantic domain.

One of the saliency conditions favoring inclusion in perspective, I have suggested, is humanness. Another is change of state or change of location. When an agent moves a patient against a goal, and as a result the goal participant moves or changes, the element in the goal case has acquired the saliency sufficient for it to be included in the perspective. We saw in (17) that with *knock on* the agent needs to be included in the perspective; but if in an act of knocking against a door, the door falls flat, we express this with the two-word verb *knock down* and include the door as direct object, as in (18):

(18)                        *He knocked the door down.*

Consider now the verb *push*, and suppose that I say (19a). Here we have a two-participant scene with a one-place perspective, meaning, if I am right, that it is the agent's action itself that is central. But now suppose that, as a result of my pushing against the table, the table moves. I can now say (19b), with the table in perspective, i.e. with *the table* in direct-object position.

(19)                        a. *I pushed against the table.*
                            b. *I pushed the table.*

The fact that some change occurred with the table is what made it natural to include it within the perspective.[2]

Suppose, now, that I manipulate one thing, bring it into contact with another thing, and, as a result, that second thing moves or undergoes a change. The thing which changes, as we have seen, gets included in the perspective, leaving the manipulated object as outside the nuclear system of grammatical relations. It has to be marked, if it is mentioned, with the preposition *with*. The notion that I referred to in my earlier writings as the instrument can thus be seen as a derived notion, involving the relationship between an entity in one event and the event which is caused by that first event. (This interpretation of one part of the notion instrument has been made particularly forcefully in Talmy 1972.) Thus, if I hit a hammer against a vase and the vase breaks, I express that as (20a); if, however, I strike a hammer against a vase and the HAMMER breaks, I express that as (20b):

(20)                        a. *I broke the vase with the hammer.*
                            b. *I broke the hammer on the vase.*

---

[2] One possible interpretation of these phenomena, brought to my attention by students of János Zsilka when I recently spoke in Budapest about direct object functions, is that instead of speaking here of "choosing" to put some nominal in direct object function by virtue of noticing an enhanced salience, we should speak of a lexicalization process of transitivization or some other sort of valence change. Hungarian has many instances of sentence relationships of the sort I have been considering, in which the lexical difference is in the presence or absence of a perfectivizing prefix *meg-* (Zsilka 1967). I think that the observations about perspective that I have been making in this paper are correctly seen as involving the functions of nuclear grammatical relations; but I agree that in a linguistic description these notions belong more appropriately to an account of aspect and lexicalization patterns than to a description of the reasons speakers have for assigning a grammatical organization to their sentence. I have taken this more "processual" view more as an easy way of talking about the phenomena than as a claim about their place in the operation of a grammar.

In each of the two-event scenes, the first part involves one thing moving toward another; the second part differs from one scene to another. The scene in which the hammer breaks requires *the hammer* to be realized as the direct object, *the vase* appearing in a construction with a goal preposition; the scene in which the vase breaks requires *the vase* to be the direct object *the hammer* appearing in a construction with the preposition *with*.

According to this interpretation, the relationship between a change-of-state verb and the entity which undergoes this change of state is reflected, not in the underlying case structure (at least not in the underlying case structure of the first part of the two-event scene), but in the grammatical relation DIRECT OBJECT. Having this in mind, we can now shed some light on the semantic difference between the sentences of (21):

(21)                              a. *I cut my foot on a rock.*
                                  b. *I cut my foot with a rock.*

In the sentence with *with* the foot has the goal relation to the action, and the rock is treated as the thing which acted against the foot; in the sentence with *on* the foot has the patient relation to the action, and the rock is seen as the thing against which the foot moved. The thing which underwent the change of state—in each case, the foot—is expressed uniformly as the direct object, independently of its case role in the underlying action scene.

My new way of treating these observations—using both caselike notions and grammatical relations—requires, for verbs of the kind we have been examining, no separate independent instrument case, but instead a process of setting aside by means of the preposition *with* (in some cases, *of*) any patient noun which, by virtue of there being another noun phrase with higher salience, does not become part of the sentence nucleus. A result of this change is that there is no need for embarrassment about the fact that the same preposition has both instrumental and noninstrumental uses. With the sentences of (21), and with sentences like (22):

(22)                              *I filled the glass with water.*

the generalization for the selection of *with* is uniform: The entity marked by *with* is the entity which moved with respect to something else but was left out of perspective by virtue of the higher salience of its competitor, the goal entity.

This last point enables us to add to our list of saliency criteria. I have been proposing that the perspective taken in a clause is determined by some sort of hierarchy of importance, which might be called the SALIENCY HIERARCHY. Humanness and change were the two conditions on this hierarchy that we have considered so far. I believe that definiteness and totality can be added to the list. With this decision we may be able to resolve some of the old problems with smearing mud and loading hay. In sentences (23a) and (23b) we have the idea that we are dealing with an event that more or less completely affects the truck or the wall—in particular, that the truck was filled or that the wall was covered as a result of the action. In the sentences that are typically paired with them, (23c) and (23d), no such assumption is necessary:

(23)                          a. *I loaded the truck with hay.*
                             b. *I smeared the wall with mud.*
                             c. *I loaded hay onto the truck.*
                             d. *I smeared mud on the wall.*

The condition seems to be that if, as a result of bringing something into contact with something else, that something else is affected in some complete way, that new status of the goal entity is sufficient for its inclusion in the clause's perspective.

Some verbs allow a choice of perspective—for example, most of those we have looked at so far. Others, as we are reminded in Mellema (1974), have fixed perspectives. *Cover*, for example, requires that the goal be taken as direct object; and *put*, by contrast, requires that the patient be taken as direct object. These facts are illustrated in the sentences of (24):

(24)                          a.  *I covered the table with a quilt.*
                             b. *\*I covered a quilt over the table.*
                             c.  *I put a quilt on the table.*
                             d. *\*I put the table with a quilt.*

Lexically specific requirements of this sort must be included in the technical description of the words; just as with *beat*, as noted above, the continued relation between the one who does the beating with the implement he uses for the beating must be specified.

7

What I have tried to do in the last part of this paper is to suggest that some of the problems of case analysis discussed in the earlier parts—in particular the vexing questions of the number and variety of cases—may be drawn a little closer to resolution if we separate from each other two things: one, the role analysis of the participants in a situation, of the kind for which proposals about deep cases have been made; and, two, the conditions under which a speaker can choose to draw certain situation participants into perspective. Since this perspectivizing corresponds, in English, to determining the structuring of a clause in terms of the nuclear grammatical relations, a consequence of this proposal is that it becomes necessary to recognize a level of grammatical structure which makes use of underlying grammatical relations, something I once thought it important to reject. I believe, however, that a level of case or role analysis is also needed, as a part of a general analysis of the scenes that get communicated with speech; and I believe that what unites these two sorts of structure is the notion of perspective that I have been trying to develop here. We recognize scenes or situations and the functions of various participants in these scenes and situations. We foreground or bring into perspective some possibly quite small portion of such a scene. Of the elements which are foregrounded, one of them gets assigned the subject role—in underlying or logical structure—and one of them—if we are foregrounding two things—gets assigned the direct object role in the clause. Something like a SALIENCY HIERARCHY determines what gets foregrounded, and something like a CASE HIERARCHY determines how the foregrounded nominals are assigned grammatical functions.

## REFERENCES

Anderson, J. (1971) *The Grammar of Case: Towards a Localistic Theory*, Cambridge University Press, Cambridge.

Anderson, S. R. (1971) "On the Role of Deep Structure in Semantic Interpretation," *Foundations of Language* 6, 197–219.

Chomsky, N. (1970) "Deep Structure, Surface Structure, and Semantic Interpretation," in R. Jakobs and S. Kawamoto, eds., *Studies in General and Oriental Linguistics*, TEC Corporation for Language Research, Tokyo.

Coles, L. S. (1972) "Techniques for Information Retrieval Using an Inferential Question-answering System with Natural-language Input," Technical Note No. 74, Project No. 8696, Stanford Research Institute, Stanford University, Stanford, California.

Cook, W. J. (1972) "A Set of Postulates for Case Grammar Analysis," *Languages and Linguistics Working Papers* No. 4, Georgetown University Press, Washington, D.C., 35–49.

Cruse, D. A. (1973) "Some Thoughts on Agentivity," *Journal of Linguistics* 9, 1–23.

Dougherty, R. C. (1974) "Generative Semantic Methods, a Bloomfieldian Counterrevolution," *International Journal of Dravidian Linguistics* 3, 255–286.

Emons, R. (1974) *Valenzen Englischer Prädikatsverben*, Niemeyer, Tiibingen.

Fillmore, C. J. (1968) "The Case for Case," in E. Bach and R. Harms, eds., *Universals in Linguistic Theory*, Holt, Rinehart and Winston, New York.

Finke, Peter (1974) *Theoretische Probleme der Kasusgrammatik*, Scriptor Verlag, Kronberg.

Halliday, M. A. K. (1967) "Notes on Transitivity and Theme in English, Part I," *Journal of Linguistics* 3, 137–181.

Helbig, G. (1971) *Beiträge zur Valenztheorie*, Mouton, The Hague.

Helbig, G. and W. Schenkel (1969) *Wörterbuch zur Valenz and Distribution Deutsche Verben*, VEB Zerlog Enzyklopädie, Leipzig.

Huddleston, R. (1970) "Some Remarks on Case Grammar," *Journal of Linguistics* 1, 501–510.

Jespersen, J. O. (1924) *Philosophy of Grammar*, Norton, New York.

Katz, J. J. (1972) *Semantic Theory*, Harper and Row, New York.

Kuno, S. (1973) *The Structure of the Japanese Language*, M.I.T. Press, Cambridge, Massachusetts.

Martin, W. (1972) *OWL*, Automatic Programming Group, M.I.T., Cambridge, Massachusetts.

Mellema, P. (1974), "A Brief against Case Grammar," *Foundations of Language* 11, 39–76.

Nilsen, D. L. F. (1972) *Toward a Semantic Specification of Deep Case*, Mouton, The Hague.

Panevová, Jarmila (1974), "On Verbal Frames in Functional Generative Description, Part I," *Prague Bulletin in Mathematical Linguistics*, No. 22, 3–3g.

Raible, W. (1975) "Partitiv, Akkusativ und Nominativ als Objekt," to appear in J. Petöfi, ed., Proceedings of Bielefeld Conference on Case Labels, April 1975.

Rohdenburg, G. (1970) "Zum Persönlichen Subjekt im Englischen," PAKS Arbeitsbericht No. 6, Lehrstuhl Anglistik, University of Stuttgart, Stuttgart, 133–164.

Talmy, L. (1972) *Semantic Structures in English and Atsugewi*, unpublished Doctoral dissertation, University of California.

Tesnière, L. (1959) *Éléments de Syntaxe Structurale*, Klincksieck, Paris.

Zsilka, J. (1967) *The System of Hungarian Sentence Patterns*, Indiana University Press, Bloomington, Indiana.

# ON COLLAPSING GRAMMATICAL RELATIONS IN UNIVERSAL GRAMMAR

*JUDITH OLMSTED GARY*

*EDWARD LOUIS KEENAN*
University of California, Los Angeles

The purpose of this study is to contribute to our understanding of the Relational Hierarchy (RH)—*Subject* (*Su*) > *Direct Object* (*DO*) > *Indirect Object* (*IO*) > *Oblique* (*Obl*)—in universal grammar. First, on pp. 83–84, we summarize some of the facts which justify including the RH in the statement of universal grammar. We present two contrasting views concerning the relation between the RH and the grammars of particular languages: a COMPARATIVE view versus a GENERATIVE view. We find that the generative view is the stronger of the two in that it provides some justification for the generalizations which the comparative view permits us to make. On pp. 87–114 we give a detailed analysis of Kinyarwanda (a Bantu language spoken in Rwanda and Burundi), which is shown to support the comparative view but not the generative view as stated. We then, on pp. 114–117, consider what revisions might be made in the generative view to make it compatible with the Kinyarwanda data and still permit the type of strong predictions it makes about the nature of human language. We conclude with a consideration of an alternate hypothesis (pp. 117–119).

## THE RELATIONAL HIERARCHY

### The Comparative View

The basic data which support the existence of the Relational Hierarchy in universal grammar come from the comparison of particular syntactic processes across languages. E.g. in Keenan and Comrie (1972 and to appear) it was argued that the distribution of relative clause types follows the Accessibility Hierarchy (AH)—*Su > DO > IO > Obl > Possessors > Object of Comparison*—in the following sense: First, Su is the easiest position to relativize, i.e. if a language can form relative clauses (RCs) at all it can form them on Su. Second, any particular RC-forming strategy which applies to Su may, in principle, apply continuously down the AH, cutting off at any point. Thus a human language may have (and some do have) RC-forming strategies that apply only to Su; others, RC-forming strategies which apply to Su and DO, but nothing else; still others, RC-forming strategies which apply to Su, DO, and IO, but nothing else, and so forth. And, more generally, any RC-forming strategy must apply to a continuous segment of the AH. Thus, for example, no possible language could relativize DOs and Obls in the same way unless it also relativized IOs in that way.

Another hierarchy generalization has been proposed in Johnson (1974a) and modified somewhat in Trithart (1975). There it is argued that, among other things, operations which promote NPs low on the RH to higher positions (as Passive promotes DOs to Su) distribute according to the RH. Thus if a language can promote locatives to Su (e.g. *the forest was seen-in a lion by John*) then it can necessarily promote IOs and DOs to SU (e.g. *Mary was shown the picture by John*).

Note that justifying the particular ordering of elements in the RH or the AH depends on comparative data from several languages. No one language, for example, has enough distinct ways of forming RCs to justify the particular ordering of the six elements in the AH. In Malagasy, for example, only subjects are relativizable (Keenan 1972), and on the basis of the Malagasy data alone there is no reason to think that DOs are in any sense more relativizable than are Obls.

Further, such comparative generalizations can be stated using only very weak assumptions concerning the relation between the RH and the grammar of an arbitrary language. We present two such assumptions, which will distinguish the comparative from the generative view of the RH.

*The Metalinguistic Assumption.* The RH—and more generally the AH— merely specify an ordered set of possible distinctions a language can make. But no one language need avail itself of all the distinctions. Within limits which will have to be determined empirically, languages are free to choose which distinctions they will use. Suppose, for example, that a language does not utilize a distinct category of IO, and that, further, objects of comparison are treated in all respects like objects of pre- or postpositions. Then the AH in that language will simply have this form: *Su > DO > Obl > Genitive.* But the hierarchy generalizations which are expressed in terms of the AH will remain unchanged in their application to that language. It will still be the case that any given RC-forming strategy must operate on a continuous segment of the (reduced) hierarchy, and that, if elements low on the hierarchy can be promoted to subject, then so can all intermediate elements. In fact, in Keenan and Comrie (to appear) it was stated, but not argued, that some languages do in fact collapse the Object of Comparison position with the Obl position, and that other languages collapse Obls with DO.[1] Further, it will be one of the major claims of this paper that Kinyarwanda does not realize the IO slot in the RH.

We should note here that, in our opinion, it is a defect of all work on both the AH and the RH that no explicit, universal definition of the positions in the hierarchies has been given. (For an attempt at a universal definition of Su see Keenan 1975b.) Thus the universality of the positions in the hierarchies and the generalizations stated in terms of these positions remain in doubt. Nonetheless, linguists will agree for many sentence types in many languages which NPs are to be called Su, which are to be called DO, etc. And, by beginning with the distinguishing properties of these categories in the relatively clear cases, we can at least construct noncircular arguments that the putatively universal hierarchy generalizations fail in some particular case, or that no class of NPs in some language exhibits the properties which normally distinguish IOs from DOs, for example.

*The Nonuniqueness Assumption.* The hierarchy generalizations allow in principle that a given position on the hierarchy be manifested by more than one NP in a given sentence. This is clearly the case for Obliques. Thus *The pudding was put in a bowl with a spoon by John* presents three oblique NPs. Further, the hierarchy generalizations will have to be made sensitive to subclasses within a given hierarchy position. E.g. Trithart (1975) has argued that in Chicewa (a Bantu language of Malawi) only certain subclasses of locatives can be promoted to DO, while others cannot. Similarly, in English certain subclasses of DOs cannot be passivized to Su. E.g. the DOs of highly stative verbs like *resemble, fit (The dress fits Mary, \*Mary is fitted by the dress), suit, have, cost (That cost me my job, \*I was cost my job by that), strike (John struck me as clever, \*I was struck as clever by John)*, etc., do not passivize. In addition, although many would claim there is a Dative rule which converts IOs to DOs in English (*John gave the toy to Mary → John gave Mary the toy*), only a small subclass of IOs undergo this rule—those of common verbs like *give, tell, show*, and *teach*. But in very many sentences containing IOs the IOs cannot be promoted to DOs: *add (John added a book to the pile, \*John added the pile a book), describe, contribute, praise, entrust, introduce, dedicate, talk/sing (Mary sang to the children, \*Mary sang the children), refer (John referred Bill to the special services department, \*John referred the special services department Bill)*, etc.

---

[1] We refer to languages which exhibit serial verb constructions, such as Akan and many other West African languages, as well as Tai, Vietnamese, and a number of other languages of South Asia. In such languages *John killed the chicken with a knife* might be rendered as *John use knife kill chicken*, and *John brought the book to Bill* as *John take book go Bill*: The apparently simplex sentence presents two verbs, both of which occur independently in that form as single verbs of main clauses. For some discussion of the analysis of such constructions within a "classical" transformational framework see Schachter (1974).

It seems clear, then, that more exact statements of hierarchy generalizations than we have given to date will require us to distinguish subtypes of NPs which occupy the same position on the hierarchy. But the generalizations do not place any restrictions on the number of NPs of any given hierarchy category or subcategory which may be present in a simplex sentence. (A sentence like *John was born in Wyoming in a log cabin* illustrates the cooccurrence of two NPs from the same locative subcategory.) Of course, if there are universally valid restrictions of this sort, then that is a further constraint on the form of possible human languages that we can give in terms of the hierarchy. Perhaps, for instance, no language can present basic sentences having more than one IO. Perhaps. But the question is an empirical one and cannot be decided a priori. For example, many languages in general treat IOs and Benefactives in the same way. In such languages then we might expect the translation of *John wrote a letter to the president for Mary* to present two IOs.

In this paper we argue explicitly that in Kinyarwanda (KR) the category DO allows more than one exponent in a given sentence, and thus is like the category Oblique in English.

## The Generative View

The generative view of the RH which we present here is based on lectures by David Perlmutter and Paul Postal at the 1974 Linguistics Institute, University of Massachusetts, Amherst [hereinafter Perlmutter and Postal, 1974]. The inferences we draw from their work, however, may not be in accordance with their views. The essential property of the generative view, in the respects which concern us, is that the categories in the RH are among the primitive categories in the generative grammar of each language. These categories are interpreted as relations which NPs bear to their verbs. The first three relations on the RH— Su, DO, and IO—are called GRAMMATICAL RELATIONS, and NPs which bear those relations to a verb are called the TERMS (of those relations). Relations like INSTRUMENT, GOAL-LOCATIVE, etc., which oblique NPs bear to their verbs are not GRAMMATICAL relations; such NPs are called NONTERMS.

The transformations which generate complex structures from simpler ones reference these relations explicitly. Thus Passive is defined, in essence, as an operation which promotes DOs to Su status; Dative promotes IOs to DO status; and still further operations (prominent in many Bantu languages) can promote Instrumentals, Locatives, etc., to DO or to Su.

In common with other work in generative grammar, a major motivation of this approach is to define 'possible grammar of a natural language' in such a way as to permit the statement of constraints on the form of possible human languages. Some such constraints (called "laws" by Perlmutter and Postal, 1974), with which we shall be concerned in what follows, are:

CYCLICITY LAW: *Operations which alter the termhood status of NPs are cyclic.*

RELATIONAL ANNIHILATION LAW: *NPs whose grammatical relations have been taken over by another (as in Passive, when an underlying DO takes over the SU relation of the active subject) cease to bear any grammatical relation to their verb. That is, they are* DEMOTED *to nonterm status.*

*Certain operations like controlling verb agreement, controlling reflexivization, controlling coreferential NP deletions, and being the NP slot to which other NPs can be raised are universally restricted to terms.*

In keeping with the spirit of these laws (i.e. to constrain the form of possible human languages) it is natural to assume, pending evidence to the contrary, (i) that no more than one NP in any given sentence in any language can bear a given grammatical relation to a given verb, and (ii) that the grammar of each language distinguishes all three grammatical relations: Su, DO, and IO. The alternate assumptions in each case would allow for a larger class of possible human languages. We argue in this paper that both of these assumptions are in fact violated in Kinyarwanda, and thus that the generative view (as we present it) is incorrect. We consider it important, however, to modify the generative view to handle the Kinyarwanda data, since this view provides a basis for explaining the hierarchy generalizations we want to make on the comparative view. That is, if categories like Su and DO figure in the operations which define the class of human languages, then it is natural that we can make cross-language generalizations in terms of them. But, if such notions do not figure in the grammar of any particular language, then it remains mysterious why cross-language generalizations should be statable in terms of them. To take one such example, why should the cross-language distribution of relative clause types or voicing rules be sensitive to categories which are irrelevant to the grammar of each language?

## THE RELATIONAL HIERARCHY IN KINYARWANDA

Below we present the properties characteristic of DOs in Kinyarwanda, indicating those properties which differentiate DOs from the clear cases of nonterms (pp. 88–91). We then consider the properties of NPs which express the semantic role of IOs and Benefactives in languages for which such categories are attested and show that, on the surface, they do not differ in syntactically significant ways from DOs (pp. 91–94). On pp. 106–114 we contrast our analysis of KR, which supports the metalinguistic assumption and the non-uniqueness assumption, with the generative view inherent in Perlmutter and Postal (1974). We argue that our proposal is both simpler and capable of capturing more generalizations than is that of Perlmutter and Postal (1974). As necessary background, we include discussion on the formal nature of derivations within RG.

## Properties of DOs in Kinyarwanda

VERB AGREEMENT

A verb agrees only with a Su, not with a DO or an Oblique (nonterm):

(1)         *Yohani y- ∅- iish-e    impysisi mw-ishyamba.*
            John   he-past-kill-asp hyena   in- forest
            'John killed a hyena in the forest.'

POSITION

The Su precedes the verb; the DO and Obl follow. The DO precedes the Obls:

(2)         **Yohani y- ∅- iish-e    mw-ishyamba impysisi.*
            John   he-past kill-asp in- forest     hyena

CASE MARKING

Su and DO are not case-marked or constructed with a preposition, whereas Obls do take prepositions.

PRONOMINALIZATION

The subject agreement prefix functions as the unmarked subject proform. DOs are pronominalized by an infix which immediately precedes the verb root and agrees in noun class with the controller:

(3)              a. *Yohani y- a- kubis- e    abagore.*
                    John   he-past-strike-asp women
                    'John struck the women.'

                 b. *Y- a- ba- kubis- e.*
                    he-past-them-strike-asp
                    'He struck them.'

Oblique NPs cannot be pronominalized in this way. In some cases they can be pronominalized by the use of an independent form of the pronoun following the preposition:

(4)              a. *Yohani yanditse ibaruwa n-    ikaramu.*
                    John   wrote    letter   with pen
                    'John wrote a letter with the pen.'

                 b. *Yohani yanditse ibaruwa na    yo.*
                    John   wrote    letter   with it
                    'John wrote a letter with it.'

Further, locative NPs like 'forest' in (1) cannot be directly pronominalized (although they can be promoted to object status and then pronominalized, a process we discuss on p. 110):

(5)  *Yohani yishe  impysisi mw-.
     John   killed hyena   in-it
     'John killed a hyena in it.'

REFLEXIVIZATION

DOs are reflexivized by inserting an invariant -i- in the DO pronominal slot in the verb:

(6)  Yohani y- ∅-  i-  kubis-e.
     John  he-past-refl-strike-asp
     'John struck himself.'

Obls cannot be reflexivized directly, even in those few cases where this might seem semantically possible, because there is no independent reflexive pronoun:

(7)    a. Yohani yashyize ibiryo mu bana.
          John   put      food   in child
          'John put food in the child.'

       b. Yohani yashyize ibiryo muri we.
          John   put      food   in   him
          'John put food in him.'

In (7b) the pronoun we 'him' cannot be understood to be coreferential with the subject Yohani.

PASSIVIZATION

DOs passive to Su in a "usual" way. The old DO moves to a preverbal position, and triggers subject agreement. The old Su is demoted to oblique (nonterm) status. Its occurrence is optional, and, if present, it is constructed with a preposition in postverbal position and does not trigger any agreement on the verb. The verb takes a passive nonfinal suffix -w-:

(8)    a. Yohani y- a-  kubis-e    abagore.
          John   he-past-strike-asp women
          'John struck the women.'

       b. Abagore ba-  a-   kubis-w-  e   (na Yohani).
          women   they-past-strike-pass-asp (by John)
          'The women were struck by John.'

Nonterms do not passivize:[2]

(9)      *Isyamba ry-∅-  iish-w-  e   impysisi (mu) (na Yohani).
         forest   it- past-kill-pass-asp hyena  (in)  (by John)
         'The forest was killed a hyena in by John.'

RELATIVIZATION

   Both Su and DO relativize. RCs formed on subjects place a high tone on the
verb root and, for Class 1 nouns only, the subject agreement prefix has a special
form:

(10)     N-a-   bon-ye umugabo w- a-   kubís- e   abagore.
         I- past-see- asp man      rel-past-strike-asp women
         'I see the man who struck the women.'

RCs formed on DOs mark the verb root with a high tone, but do not otherwise
change the verb morphology:

(11)     N-a-   bon-ye abagore Yohani y- a-   kubís- e.
         I- past-see- asp women John    he-past-strike-asp
         'I saw the women who John struck.'

Oblique NPs cannot be relativized directly.[3]

(12)       *ikaramu Yohani y- andíka ibaruwa [na   (yo)].
           pen      John   he-write letter  [with (it)]
           'the pen that John wrote the letter [with (it)].'

---

[2] We should note, however, that there is a very restricted class of locatives that can passivize
more or less directly. In all examples the verb is otherwise intransitive. The promoted locative retains
its locative marking and the subject-verb agreement becomes impersonal, taking ha-, which is
morphologically invariant (examples from Kimenyi, in preparation):

   (i)  Umukoobwa y- iica-ye  kuu ntebe.
        girl         she-sit- asp on  chair
        'The girl is sitting on the chair.'

   (ii) Kuu ntebe h- iica-w-  e   n- umukoobwa.
        on  chair imp-sit- pass-asp by-girl
        'The chair is sat on by the girl.'

[3] In footnote 2 above we mentioned a small class of locatives which undergo a kind of partial
passivization (locative marker retained on NP, verb impersonal). These NPs may also directly
relativize, although the analysis is problematic, because a locative suffix is optionally present on
the verb. This could be interpreted as indicating that the locative has first been promoted to DO
status, an operation that is independently justified in the language (see p. 106) and then relativized, which would somehow allow that the promotion to object marker could be deleted. As
in the passive case, the "promoted" NP retains its locative marking, but here the verb retains its

There is also a class of cleft constructions in KR which discriminates Su and DO from the nonterms in the same way as do RCs. For further discussion of clefts in KR see Kimenyi (in preparation).

### The Categories IO and Benefactive in Kinyarwanda

In this section we will show that surface NPs which we expect to be IOs or Benefactives present the characteristic properties of DOs in KR. We further show that a given sentence may present more than one NP with the DO properties. On pp. 106–117 we argue that this surface-based analysis also represents the basic or underlying sentence pattern.

The paradigm case of IOs, in languages which have this category, is represented by the recipient NP in active sentences whose main verbs are verbs like *give*, *send*, *show*, and *tell*. We use the term RECIPIENT (R) to designate the SEMANTIC relation which such NPs bear to the verb. Similarly, the term BENEFACTIVE (B) designates the semantic relation which *for*-NPs bear to their verb in sentences like *Mary danced for the children*, *Mary cut the meat for Harry*, etc. It is clear that these semantic relations are distinct. The R and B NPs in sentences like *John sent the letter to Mary (R) for Bill (B), who was ill* clearly are semantically related to the action expressed by the verb in different ways.

PROPERTIES OF RECIPIENT NPs

*Coding Properties: Verb Agreement, Case Marking, Position.* Like DOs, R's occur in postverbal position, without a case marker (or preposition); they do not trigger verb agreement:

(13)             a. *Yohani y- oher-er-eje  Maria ibaruwa.*
                   John   he-send-R-asp Mary letter
                   'John sent a letter to Mary.'

There is a clear preference for the R to precede the DO, but the alternate order is possible:

(13)             b. *Yohani y- oher-er-eje  ibaruwa Maria.*
                   John   he-sent-R-asp letter    Mary
                   'John sent a letter to Mary.'

---

normal agreement with its subject (examples from Kimenyi, in preparation):

(i)  *Umugore a-  ryaam-ye  mu gitaanda.*
     woman  she-lie-   asp in bed
     'The woman is lying in bed.'

(ii) *Mu gitaanda umugore a-  ryaam-ye- (mo).*
     in  bed      woman  she-lie-   asp-(loc)
     'The bed in which the woman is lying.'

If both the DO and the R are animate, however, the R must precede the DO:

(14)                    *Umuhungu y- a-    oher-er-eje umwana umugore.*
                        boy         he-past-send-R-asp child      woman
                        'The boy sent the woman to the child.'
                        *'The boy sent the child to the woman.'

Note further that the verb obligatorily carries a nonfinal suffix which is under-lying /ir/ and which may be realized by phonologically conditioned variants—[ir], [i], [er] (as above), or [e]. These suffixes as used above indicate that there is a R present in the clause.

*Pronominalization.*   Like DOs, the postverbal R pronominalizes with an infix between the tense marker and the verb root. Both the R and the DO can be pronominalized in this way in the same sentence:

(15)            a. *Yohani y- a-   mw-oher-er-eje ibaruwa.*
                   John   he-past-her-send-R-asp letter
                   'John sent her the letter.'

                b. *Yohani y- a-   y-oher-er-eje Maria.*
                   John   he-past-it-send-R-asp Mary
                   'John sent it to Mary.'

                c. *Yohani y- a-   yi-mw-oher-er-eje.*
                   John   he-past-it- her-send-R-asp
                   'John sent it to her.'

Note that both of the infixed pronouns can also represent animate class objects:

(16)                    *Yohani y- a-   mu- mw- oher-er-eje.*
                        John   he-past-him-him-send-R-asp
                        'John sent him to him.'

Further, the order of the pronominal forms within the verb is fixed, the (non-reflexive) DO pronoun preceding the (nonreflexive) R pronoun, although the morphological shape of the pronouns is not distinct. Sentences which contain one full NP unmarked after the verb and an infix pronoun are structurally ambiguous:

(17)    *Yohani y- a-   mw-oher-er-eje umugore.*
        John   he-past-her-send-R-asp woman
        'John sent her to the woman.' **or** 'John sent the woman to her.'

*Reflexivization.*   R's reflexivize in the same way as DOs:

(18)                    *Yohani y- a-   yi- oher er-eje ibaruwa.*
                        John   he-past-refl-send-R-asp letter
                        'John sent himself a letter.'

Further, it is possible to have both a reflexive form and a DO pronoun infixed in the verb together:

(19)                    *Yohani y- a-    yi- y-oher-er-eje.*
                        John   he-past-refl-it-send-R-asp
                        'John sent it to himself.'

*Passivization.*   Both the DO and the R passivize in the same way:

(20)    a. *Yohani y- ∅-    oher-er-eje Maria ibaruwa.*
           John   he-past-send-R-asp Mary  letter
           'John sent a letter to Mary.'

        b. *Ibaruwa y-∅-    oher-er-ej- w-   e    Maria (na Yohani).*
           letter   it-past-send-R-asp-pass-asp Mary  (by John)
           'The letter was sent to Mary by John.'

        c. *Maria y-   ∅    oher-er-ej- w-   e    ibaruwa (na Yohani).*
           Mary  she-past-send-R-asp-pass-asp letter     (by John)
           'Mary was sent a letter by John.'

We note that Passive cannot apply twice to the same verb. Once we have passivized on the DO, for examples, we cannot then again passivize on the R, and vice versa. Note further that the R suffix *-ir-* remains on the verb under passivization.

*Relativization.*   Finally, R's relativize in the same way as DOs, and in a given sentence both the DO and the R relativize:

(21)    a. *N-a-   bon-ye  ibaruwa Yohani yohér-er-eje Maria.*
           I- past-see- asp letter   John   sent- R-asp Mary
           'I see the letter that John sent to Mary.'

        b. *N-a-   bon-ye  Maria Yohani yohér-er-eje ibaruwa.*
           I- past-see- asp Mary  John   sent- R-asp letter
           'I see Mary to whom John sent a letter.'

(If the R is a common noun, Relativization applies in the same way.)

On the surface, then, R's exhibit the full range of syntactic properties of DOs. The only difference—to be discussed in the next section—is the obligatory presence of the *-ir-* suffix on a verb which has an R NP among its arguments.

PROPERTIES OF BENEFACTIVES

*Coding Properties.*   With regard to verb agreement, case marking, and position, Benefactive NPs follow the paradigm of Recipients exactly.

(22)                    *Maria y- a-   tek- e- ye  abana    inkoko.*
                        Mary  she-past-cook-B-asp children chicken
                        'Mary cooked a chicken for the children.'

Thus B's do not trigger verb agreement. They do occur postverbally without a preposition. Most commonly they precede the DO, but, as with R's, the alternate order is possible. Note that the suffix -e- is the same suffix which occurs when an R is present. A verb may not take two such suffixes and, in fact, cannot be constructed with both an R and a B NP:

(23)                 *Yohani y- ∅-   oher- er- er- eje Bill Maria ibaruwa.
                     John   he-past-send-R-B- asp Bill Mary  letter
                     'John sent a letter to Mary for Bill.'

A simple sentence like (24) is ambiguous (or vague) according to whether *Mary* is understood to be a B or an R:

(24)                 Yohani y- ∅-   oher- er-  eje Maria ibaruwa.
                     John   he-past-send-R/B-asp Mary letter
                     'John sent a letter to/for Mary.'

Note further that B's occur easily with verbs which are otherwise intransitive:

(25)              a. Maria y- a-   byin- ye.
                     Mary she-past-dance-asp
                     'Mary danced.'

                  b. Maria y- a-   byin- i- ye umugabo.
                     Mary she-past-dance-B-asp man
                     'Mary danced for the man.'

In regard to the other DO-like properties of B's, they passivize, pronominalize, reflexivize, and relativize exactly like R's. Below we illustrate Passive, but dispense with repetition of the other properties:

(26)       a. Inkoko y-a-  tek- e- w-  e   abana   (na Maria).
              chicken it-past-cook-B-pass-asp children (by Mary)
              'The chicken was cooked for the children by Mary.'

           b. Abana  ba- a-  tek- e- w-  e   inkoko (na Maria).
              children they-past-cook-B-pass-asp chicken (by Mary)
              'The children were cooked a chicken (for) by Mary.'

## Generating the Double Object Constructions in KR

In this section we sketch some basic properties of derivations of sentences within a Relational Grammar (RG) framework, in order to present our analysis of KR and to contrast it with the view in Perlmutter and Postal (1974). We shall be particularly concerned with the relation between grammatical categories and coding rules—case marking, verb agreement, and linear ordering—since part of our analysis of KR involves case marking. To our knowledge this relation has not been explicitly studied within RG.

Our formulation of underlying structures and the transformations which operate on them derives largely from Perlmutter and Postal (1974), but also draws on Johnson (1974b). Our proposals differ from those of Perlmutter and Postal and of Johnson in several respects concerning formalism and the basic nature of underlying structures. This difference is motivated, in part but not entirely, by the need to make explicit in underlying structure the information needed by case-marking rules. (Here and elsewhere we use CASE MARKING to refer to the morphological means used to indicate the grammatical or semantical relation between surface NPs and their verbs.)

## DERIVATIONS IN RELATIONAL GRAMMAR

The underlying structure of a sentence in RG will be called a RELATIONAL STRUCTURE (RS). It is to RSs that transformations apply initially, and so RSs are the equivalent in this theory of base phrase markers in e.g. the Standard Theory. A relational structure $RS$ consists of a DOMAIN, $D$, of objects, and of two sets of RELATIONS, $R_g$ and $R_s$, defined on $D$. $D$ is a finite set consisting of exactly one active verb and of one or more (occurrences of) noun phrases. The unique verb in any domain $D$ will be referred to as $V_D$, the MAIN VERB of $D$.[4] $R_g$ is a set containing the grammatical relations[5] which NPs in the domain $D$ bear to $V_D$. Thus $R_g$ will have members like '$Su(x, V_D)$', '$DO(y, V_D)$' etc., indicating that the noun phrase $x$ bears the subject relation to the verb, etc. The only relations which may be mentioned here are Su, DO, and IO. Finally, $R_s$ will be the set of nongrammatical relations which NPs in the domain bear $V_D$. It will thus include elements like INST($z, V_D$) and GOAL-LOC($w, V_D$). It is important to include such relations in the underlying structures of a RG

---

[4] It is allowed that the NPs in a domain $D$ be themselves relational structures, although we shall not discuss such structures explicitly in this article. E.g. the RS underlying *John thinks that Fred left* would have *thinks* as its $V_D$ and two NPs in its domain—*John* and the RS of *Fred left*. Like other NPs, as we discuss immediately above, sentential NPs may bear both grammatical and semantic relations to the $V_D$. Thus the NP (*that*) *Fred left* above would be a grammatical DO of *think*. Semantically it might be in, say, the CONTENT relation to *think*, indicating that it expresses the content of the thought.

Using this formalism, then, we have natural definitions of CLAUSEMATE and BE IN A HIGHER CLAUSE THAN. Thus two NPs are CLAUSEMATES just in case they are members of the same domain. And $X$ IS IN AN IMMEDIATELY HIGHER CLAUSE THAN $Y$ just in case $Y$ is in the domain of some NP—$Z$—and $Z$ and $X$ are clausemates. Clearly, then, a notion equivalent to COMMAND can be defined on the underlying structures in RG. Note, however, that the formalism would have to be extended to represent structures for sentences containing two verbs, like *John came early and left late*, as well as for sentences containing the serial verb constructions discussed above.

[5] The term grammatical RELATION is perhaps slightly inaccurate in the framework of Perlmutter and Postal (1974), since they require that an NP bearing such a relation to a given verb be unique (if there is any at all). Such "relations," then, are more accurately referred to as (partial) FUNCTIONS defined on the set of domains. The term relation is more accurate in our proposals, however, since we allow in principle that more than one NP may bear a given relation to the verb of a given domain.

because many transformations will be sensitive to them—e.g. in many Bantu languages there will be rules promoting instrumentals or locatives to DO or Su status. The rules must be able to distinguish among the NPs which do not bear a grammatical relation to the verb, for only one particular NP can undergo the rule that promotes instrumentals to DO, etc. Similarly, case-marking rules (including the insertion of pre- and postpositions) will obviously be sensitive to what types of nonterm an NP is.

Note that the nongrammatical relations are semantically specific. To know that an NP in a given simple sentence is an instrumental, a goal-locative, etc., is to know how that NP is semantically related to the verb. Thus $R_s$ is the set of SEMANTIC relations which NPs in $D$ bear to $V_D$. Note further that the NPs which bear grammatical relations to the verb also bear semantic relations to them, but that the semantic relation is not unique for any given grammatical relation. Thus a subject may be an AGENT, or an EXPERIENCER, or simply some sort of NEUTRAL, as in *John is fat*. As we shall illustrate shortly, however, the semantic relation a subject or DO bears to its verb must also be referenced in the statement of various transformations; thus that information will also be included in the underlying relational structures. It will be required that every NP in the domain bear some semantic relation to the verb of the domain. Further, in general this semantic relation will not change throughout the course of a derivation (unless, perhaps, the NP is deleted—a topic we do not discuss here), although the grammatical relation the NP bears to the verb may change.

We note that the inclusion of this set of semantic relations among the primitive elements in the underlying structures for sentences, and allowing that some NPs can bear both grammatical relations and semantic relations to their verb, is not part of the original proposal by Perlmutter and Postal (1974).

We shall now exemplify our definition by means of a simple English sentence (ignoring a great many problems such as the representation of tense and aspect, cross-reference, and quantification). We then propose a relational definition of the Passive transformation and illustrate how it would operate in the simple case.

(27)    A relational structure $RS$ for *John cut the meat with a knife* is a set $\{D, R_g, R_s\}$, where:

$D = \{cut_V, John_N, meat_N, knife_N\}$
$\quad +\text{act}$

(Clearly the $V_D = $ 'cut' in this case)
$\quad\quad\quad\quad\quad +\text{act}$

$R_g = \{\text{Su}(John, V_D), \text{DO}(meat, V_D)\}$

$R_s = \{\text{Agent}(John, V_D), \text{Patient}(meat, V_D), \text{Inst}(knife, V_D)\}$

In this view, Passive is an operation which converts one relational structure, $\{D, R_g, R_s\}$, to another, $\{D', R'_g, R'_s\}$. The input relational structure must meet three conditions: first, its verb, $V_D$, must be marked $+\text{active}$; second, some noun phrase in the domain $D$ must bear the DO relation to $V_D$; and, third, a distinct noun phrase must bear the Su relation to $V_D$. The derived relational structure differs from the input structure in the following ways: First, its domain, $D'$, is identical to $D$ except that $V_{D'}$ is marked as $+$passive rather than $+$active; second, the noun phrase which bore the DO relation to $V_D$ now bears the Su relation to $V_{D'}$; and, third, the noun phrase which bore the Su relation to $V_D$ bears no grammatical relation to $V_{D'}$. The semantic relations in the derived structure are identical to those of the input structure.

Somewhat more formally, we might represent Passive as follows:

(28)        PASSIVE: $\{D, R_g, R_s\} \rightarrow \{D', R_g', R_s'\}$ where

$$D: \{ \quad V, n_1, n_2, \ldots, n_k\} \rightarrow \{ \quad V, n_1, n_2, \ldots, n_k\}$$
$$\quad\quad +\text{act} \quad\quad\quad\quad\quad\quad\quad +\text{pass}$$

$$R_g: \{\text{Su}(n_i, V_D), \text{DO}(n_j, V_D), X\} \rightarrow \{\text{Su}(n_j, V_D), X\}$$

$$R_s: \{Y_1, Y_2, \ldots, Y_m\} \rightarrow \{Y_1, Y_2, \ldots, Y_m\}$$

CONDITION: $n_i \neq n_j$

Remarks on the definition of Passive:

1. The statement of the rule could be simplified by taking advantage of the Relational Annihilation Law (RAL), which guarantees that the subject NP in the input structure will not bear any grammatical relation to the verb in the output structure. Thus this information would not have to be included explicitly in the statement of the transformation. (But, as we show below, the Kinyarwanda data will force a reconsideration of the RAL.)

2. The Passive rule as we have given it is intended to be universal. It is the same transformation in every language which has a passive. Of course, language-particular rules will assign the appropriate passive morphology on the verb, thereby eliminating the feature $+$passive. Similarly, language-particular rules will assign the appropriate case marking and position to the demoted subject. Note that an advantage of taking semantic relations as basic in relational structures is that we can, in effect, define DEMOTED SUBJECT (of an activity verb—and similar definitions would work for other subclasses of verb) to be an NP which bears the AGENT relation to the derived verb but does not bear the Su relation to it. It is this phrase which will be marked with *by* in English. We do not need then a special category for demoted terms (CHÔMEURS, in the terminology of Perlmutter and Postal 1974), nor do we need any special non-grammatical relations which demoted terms would have to bear to their verbs (as used in Johnson 1974b). Similarly, a demoted DO can be defined, in the paradigm case, as an NP which bears the Patient relation but not the DO relation to the verb. Note that the positioning and marking of demoted DOs in English is different from those of demoted Su's (e.g. only the latter take a preposition; and there are order restrictions, e.g. *Mary was given the stamp by John*, *\*Mary was given by John the stamp*).

3. Languages will, of course, vary considerably in regard to the contexts in which Passive can apply. In Tagalog and Malagasy, for example, Passive may not apply if the DO is indefinite (and in Tagalog it must apply if the DO is definite). It is to be expected that taking semantic relations as basic in relational structures will allow us to state, on a language-particular basis, at least certain fairly general restrictions on Passive. E.g. if the Su is not an agent, and the DO is not a patient, it is often the case that Passive will not apply. [Recall the list of verbs (*suit, resemble*, etc.) in English which do not passivize. They are all verbs whose subjects are not agents and whose DOs are not patients.]

The one condition we have stated in the rule is designed to prevent Passive from applying to the structure underlying e.g. *John cut himself*, which appears correct since *John was cut* does not have that meaning. This condition on Passive appears extremely general, but even here is perhaps not universal. Thus in Modern Greek, in addition to an active sentence type with an overt reflexive pronoun, truncated Passives are used to indicate a reflexive (but somewhat accidental) action—a usage which presumably goes back to the use of the "middle" voice in Classical Greek:

(29)         a. *O  Yianis xtipise ton anθropo.*
                art John   struck  the man

             b. *O  Yianis xtipise ton eaftó tu.*
                art John   struck  the self   his
                'John struck himself (intentionally).

(30)         a. *O  Yianis xtipiθike apo ton anθra.*
                art John   +pass    by  the man
                          strike
                'John was struck by the man.'

             b. *O  Yianis xtipiθike.*
                art John   +pass
                          strike
                'John struck himself (accidentally).'

## CONSTRAINTS ON DERIVATIONS IN RG

*Constraints on Underlying Structures.* In addition to the constraints on the form of relational structures inherent in the definition, certain other "meta" constraints will have to be given. For example, we want to require that each NP in a domain (of a simplex sentence) bear some semantic relation to the verb. Further, on the strong generative view we have been characterizing we would have to require that no more than one NP bear a given grammatical relation to its verb. And we might want to require that one NP always bear the Su relation to its verb, etc.

*Constraints on Transformations.* The transformations which apply to relational structures are not externally ordered, with one exception: Those transformations which alter the termhood status of NPs are required to operate cyclically. In addition, certain other transformations—such as Reflexivization and perhaps Relative Clause Formation—are held to be universally cyclic. (The latter transformation, of course, will operate on a cycle higher than that determined by the verb whose NP is relativized.)

Note further that RG will need rules to introduce the CODING PROPERTIES—linear ordering, case marking, and verb agreement—as none of these is present in the initial stage of a relational structure. The ordering of these rules relative to the cyclic ones poses some problems, and is not universally statable. Example in Achenese (Lawler 1975) passive verbs agree only with the underlying subject, not the derived subject. Thus in that language verb agreement must apply, presumably, before term-changing rules (or else agreement is subject to a global constraint), not after them. In Kapampangan (Mirikitani 1972), on the other hand, passive verbs agree with both the underlying and the derived subject, so presumably agreement applies both before and after the term-changing rules, but in such a way that cycle-initial agreement (with the active subject) is not lost when subject agreement applies again after Passive. In Chicewa, on the other hand, active verbs agree with subjects and, optionally, with DOs. In passive sentences, however, the verb subject agrees with the derived subject, but optionally retains its object agreement, and so agrees twice with the same surface NP:

(31)[6]    a. *John o- ma- (chi)-lim- a    chi-manga.*
              John he-habit-it   -farm-indic corn
              'John farms corn.'

           b. *chi-manga chi-ma- (chi)-lim- idw- a    (ndi John).*
              corn        it- habit-it- farm-pass-indic by John
              'Corn is farmed by John.'

Thus in Chicewa it appears that object agreement applies before Passive—and is not lost afterward—and that subject agreement applies after Passive.

In Palauan (Foley 1975) active verbs agree only with DOs. (This is the case in the perfective. In the imperfective active verbs agree with nothing.) Passive verbs, however, still OBJECT-agree with the patient, even though it is a derived subject, and, further, they now also agree with the demoted subject!:

(32)       a. *A ngalek a s- il- seb- iy$_i$ a  blai$_i$.*
              art child    perf-post-burn-it$_i$ art house$_i$
              'The child had burned down the house.'

---

[6] Examples from Lee Trithart (personal communication).

b. *A blai$_i$   a le$_j$-   s-   il-   seb-   iy$_i$ a   ngalek$_j$.*
art house$_i$   pass  perf-past-burn-*it$_i$* art child$_j$
      3 sg$_j$-
'The house had been burned down by the child.'

Presumably verb agreement in Palauan must apply both before and after term-changing rules, and the later application is subject to a global condition. (Perhaps both subject and object agreement apply precyclically, and some late rule deletes the subject-verb agreement in actives. But the existence of such a a rule would have to be motivated.)

In the languages with which we are concerned here, English and KR, it seems most natural to require that verb agreement, as well as linear ordering and case-marking rules, apply after the term-changing rules: It is clear that they must apply after term-changing rules in any event (since verbs agree only with derived subjects, for example), and, if they were to also apply before the term-changing rules, then the later application would have to be made more complex so as to assure that the effect of the earlier application was lost (in distinction e.g. to the Kapampangan and Palauan cases).

In the literature on RG with which we are familiar, we have not seen an explicit formulation of the rules which introduce the coding properties (position, verb agreement, and case marking). Because our analysis of KR will require that these rules have certain properties, however, here we wish to establish, on universal grounds, certain general relations between coding properties—specifically case marking—and grammatical relations in order that our particular analysis of KR be seen to reflect the general case and not appear peculiar to KR.

## SOME GENERAL RELATIONS BETWEEN GRAMMATICAL RELATIONS AND CODING PROPERTIES, IN PARTICULAR CASE MARKING

Very generally speaking, there is an extremely poor correlation between the coding properties and grammatical relations. For example, it is almost never the case that an NP takes a certain case marking if, and only if, it bears a certain grammatical relation to its verb. Thus:

*Fact 1.* In many languages, NPs which bear different relations to their verbs are case marked in the same way. Several patterns of this sort recur in many languages and thus are not accidental.

CASE 1. Many languages, such as Hindi and Spanish, case mark IOs and certain definite DOs in the same way. (We are not claiming here or in what follows to give a thorough description of the case-marking conditions in any particular language.) Here are examples from Hindi (Saeed Ali and Boyd Mikailovsky, personal communication):

(33)                          a. *Rām-ne rādha-ko chiṭhī bhējī.*
                                 Ram-erg Rada-dat letter sent
                                 'Ram sent Radha a letter.'

        b. *Rām-ne murgī- ko mārā.*
          Ram-erg chicken-acc kill
          'Ram killed the chicken.'

CASE 2. In many ergative languages subjects of transitive verbs are marked in the same way as are instrumentals, e.g. Gugu-Yalanji (Hershberger 1964), or even as are genitives, e.g. Eskimo (Woodbury 1975).

CASE 3. In many languages, such as English, IOs and goal-locatives are marked in the same way (*to*).

CASE 4. In many languages agent NPs in passive sentences are marked like instrumentals (Russian) or locatives (English, French). For further discussion of this property of case marking see Starosta (1973).

*Fact 2.* NPs which bear the same relation to their verbs in sentences of somewhat different structural types may be case marked in different ways. One of the most widespread cases is that of ergative languages, in which subjects of transitive sentences take one case marker (the ergative) and those of intransitive sentences take another (often zero). Such languages are widely represented in several of the major language families of the world (Australian, Caucasian, and Amerindian). For illustrative purposes compare (34a) and (34b) below from Hindi:

(34)        a. *Wah    ro rahā    thā.*
            he (nom) cry be (past, imperfective)
            'He was crying.'

        b. *Us-        ne aurat- ko    mārā.*
            he (oblique)-erg woman-acc/dat hit
            'He hit the woman.'

   Hindi illustrates a second type of variation. For the subject to take the ergative marker, not only must the sentence be transitive, but it must also be perfective. Compare:

(35)        a. *Wah    kitāb likh rahā    thā.*
            he (nom) book write be (past, imperfective)
            'He was writing a book.'

        b. *Us-        ne kitāb likhī.*
            he (oblique)-erg book wrote (perfective)
            'He wrote a book.'

(Note that in (35b) the verb agrees with the DO *kitab* 'book', whereas in (35a) it agrees with the subject *wah* 'he'.) In fact, many languages are ergative only in certain tenses or aspects. Georgian, for example, is ergative only in the aorist.

Other types of examples here would include languages like Russian and certain other Slavic languages in which DOs are marked accusative in affirmative sentences but genitive in negative sentences; and languages like Mojave (Munro 1974) and Wappo (Li and Thompson 1975), in which the subject case marking present in main clauses is lost in certain types of subordinate clauses. Below are examples from Wappo (Sandra Thompson, personal communication):

(36)                a. *Ce kew-i    ew toh- ta?.*
                       that man-subj fish catch-past
                       'That man caught a fish.'

                    b. *Ah ce   kew ew toh-  ta? hatiskhi?.*
                       I    that man fish catch-past know
                       'I know that that man caught a fish.'

We might note that facts 1 and 2 above are paralleled by similar facts concerning verb agreement. Thus, in some languages, NPs bearing different relations to the verb will trigger the same agreements, and NPs bearing the same relation to verbs in different sentences may have different verb agreements. Both cases are illustrated by languages like Abaza and Jacaltec, in which subjects of transitive verbs trigger one type of verb agreement and subjects of intransitives and DOs of transitive verbs trigger another type. Examples from Jacaltec (Craig 1975) follow:

(37)                a. *X- $\emptyset_i$-cam no'   cheh.*
                       asp-it-die  class. horse
                       'The horse died.'

                    b. *X- $\emptyset_i$-s$_j$- watx'e na$_j$ te'    ngah.*
                       asp-it-he-make  he$_j$ class. house$_i$
                       'He made a house.'

*Fact 3.*   The case marker that an NP carries may also depend on its underlying semantic relation to the verb or on its inherent semantic features. As we have already seen, subjects of transitive perfective sentences in Hindi may take an ergative marker *-ne* [example (34)]. But they take this marker only if they are semantically AGENTS. If they are experiencers, as in (38) below, they are not marked as ergative, but rather are unmarked:[7]

(38)                *Ram (*-ne) Radha-ko     bhula.*
                    Ram  (-erg) Rada-acc/dat forgot
                    'Ram forgot Rada.'

[7] Boyd Mikailovsky (personal communication) points out to us, however, that the class of such verbs is very small, perhaps being restricted to 'forget'. Most verbs which would take experiencer subjects, like *jānnā* 'to know', cannot be constructed in the perfective, and since perfectivity is another prerequisite for ergativity, would not be present in an ergative format in any case.

Similarly, in many languages [e.g. Hindi, Spanish, Hebrew (Givón 1975), and Malagasy (Keenan 1975a)] definite animate DOs are case marked differently from indefinite inanimate DOs. (The relative importance of definiteness versus animacy is not exactly the same in these languages.):

(39)  a. *Rām-ne  murgī-∅ mari.*
         Ram-erg chicken killed
         'Ram killed a chicken.'

      b. *Rām-ne  murgī- ko      mārā.*
         Ram-erg chicken-dat/acc killed
         'Ram killed the chicken.'

Animacy is more clearly a factor in Gugu-Yalanji (Hershberger 1964), in which transitive subjects take one case marking if animate and another (the instrumental) if inanimate:

(40)  a. *Dingkar-angka      kaya kunin.*
         man-   erg animate dog  hit
         'The man hit the dog.'

      b. *Kalka-bu           kaya kunin.*
         man- erg inanimate  dog  hit
             (= instrument)
         'The spear hit the dog.'

A third type of case concerns case marking on DOs in Finnish. A given DO may be marked in the partitive case if it is only partially affected by the action of the verb, but may be marked in another case if it is affected more totally (example from Raimo Antilla, personal communication):

(41)  a. *Vien  poja-t        kouluun.*
         take-I boy- nom/-pl school
                    acc
         'I am taking the boys to school.'

      b. *Vien  poiki-a       kouluun.*
         take-I boy- part-pl school
         'I am taking some of the boys to school.'

In general, then, case marking in surface structure may depend on (i) the surface grammatical relation the NP bears to its verb, (ii) the underlying semantic relation that it bears to its verb, and (iii) its inherent semantic properties. Note further:

*Fact 4.* Case marking may affect the verb. Given that one of the major parameters expressed by case marking concerns the syntactic-semantic relation an NP bears to its verb, it would not be surprising if case marking were marked both on the verb and on the noun, or even on the verb alone. In fact, there are instances of both situations.

CASE 1.   In the examples below from Hungarian (Katalin Radics, personal communication), the locative postposition on the noun is matched by the locative prefix on the verb; clearly, case is marked on both the verb and the noun:

(42)   a. *Janos ra- ∅- te- tt-  e      a  kalap-ot  az  asztal-ra.*
          John  on-it-put-past-3sg 3sg the hat-  acc the table- on
          'John put the hat on the table.'

       b. *Janos ala-  ∅- te- tt-  e      a  kenyeret az  asztal-ala.*
          John  under-it-put-past-3sg 3sg the bread    the table- under
          'John put the bread under the table.'

Similarly, in Homeric Greek, although we have not found instances of a case marker occurring simultaneously on both the verb and the NP, we do find markers which occur sometimes on the noun and sometimes on the verb. E.g. the particle *en/eni* may occur as a preposition (43a), as a postposition (43b), or as a verbal prefix. In all uses it governs the dative case of the noun:

(43)[8]   a. *en spéssi*
             in caves (dat)

          b. *elēmō̜        éni trṓōn*
             populace (dat) in   of-Trojans
             'among the Trojans'

          c. *pa̧idos   gar mŷtʰon pepnyménon **én**-tʰeto   tʰymō̂.*
             of-child for word   thought-out **in-** placed spirit (dat)
             'for the thoughtful word of her son lodged in her mind'

CASE 2.   In the examples below from Machiguenga (Snell and Wise 1963) the semantic relation that the major NPs bear to their verb is marked only on the verb (where it is marked at all):

(44)   *I- kʸisa-  ši-   ta- ka- ro no- šinto    hoa.*
       he-be angry with  vb-refl-her my-daughter John
                  ref. to
       'John was angry with my daughter.'

(45)   *I- kʸisa-  ko        ta- ka- ro no- šinto    hoa.*
       he-be angry-because of vb-refl-her my-daughter John
       'John was angry because of my daughter.'

---

[8] Examples from E. J. W. Barber (personal communication).

(46)   a. *I- tog-an- ta- iga-ka- ro$_i$ ača$_i$ camairinci.*
           3-cut-inst-vb-pl- refl-it  axe field
           'They cut the field with an axe.'

       b. *O- pašit- an- ta- k$^y$e- na-      ro$_i$ no- šinto$_i$      o-  bašikaro.*
           she-cover-inst-vb-nrefl-for me-her  my-daughter her-blanket
           'She covered my daughter with her blanket for me.'

       c. *I-  tog-an- ta- k$^y$e- ne- ri    no- ačane i-  camaire.*
           he-cut-inst-vb-nrefl-ben-him my-axe   his-field
           'He cut his field for him with my axe.'

In general, then, full NPs carry no marking in Machiguenga. Among the approximately 150 sentences cited in Snell and Wise (1963), only one noun marker is recorded: a generalized locative postposition -k$_A$ (remarkable, because Machiguenga is a verb-initial language, and such languages are usually prepositional). The normal way to indicate semantically specific relations that NPs bear to verbs is to mark the verb, as in our examples. It is worth noting that these markers are present whenever there is a NP in the sentence which bears the semantically specific relation to the verb, regardless of the surface grammatical relation it bears. Thus, when semantically instrumental NPs are passivized to subject, and so trigger the prefixal agreement, the instrumental marker -an- is still present. Compare:

(47)   a. *No-kamarang-an- ta- ka seri.*
           I- vomit-     inst-vb-refl tobacco
           'I vomit by means of tobacco.'

       b. *O-kamarang-an- t- a-  gani seri.*
           it- vomit-     inst-vb-refl-pass tobacco
           'Tobacco is an emetic.' (more literally, 'Tobacco is vomited by oneself.')

We further note that instrumental NPs (the NPs discussed most extensively in Snell and Wise 1963, which we might expect to be nonterms) do not seem to differ much in their behavior from P(atient) NPs. Note that while the Inst triggers the suffixal agreement on the verb in (46a), it is the P which triggers it in (46b). The Inst is still present, however, and still requires the instrumental case marker on the verb. In (46c) neither the P nor the Inst triggers the suffixal agreement, as benefactives usurp that slot (in the third person). Similarly, we have already noted that Insts may passivize to subject; so also may P's, in which case the Inst is still unmarked and the case marker is still present on the verb:

(48)           *O-tog-an- t- a-  gani camairinci ača.*
               it$_i$-cut-inst-vb-refl-pass field$_i$       axe
               'The field was cut down with an axe.'

Snell and Wise cite further examples which show that the Causee in causative sentences can trigger the suffixal agreement, and that Causees and Recipients, as well as P's and Inst's, can passivize to subject. These data provide prima facie evidence that Machiguenga tolerates more than one (Direct) Object in surface, although more data than present in Snell and Wise would be needed to substantiate this claim.

Machiguenga does appear to illustrate more fully than our other examples a type of case-marking typology that we shall call VERB CODING. The extreme form such a typology would take would be a language in which the case of NPs is never marked on the NP, but only on the verb. Machiguenga fails to realize this typology in the most extreme form since certain locative NPs may carry case marking.

We shall now argue that Kinyarwanda illustrates a verb-coding typology, although to a somewhat lesser extent than Machiguenga in the sense that fewer NPs can have the "case" marked only on the verb.

## Two Proposals for a Relationally Based Analysis of Kinyarwanda

We are concerned here with the derivation of sentences in KR like (13a), repeated from above, which appear to have two DOs on the surface:

(13)                    a. *Yohani n- oher-er-eje Maria ibaruwa.*
                           John   he-send-R-asp Mary  letter
                           'John sent Mary a letter.'

On what we shall call the Promotional Analysis (PA), represented in Perlmutter and Postal (1974), the underlying structure of (13a) would be as follows: The domain would consist of the verb 'send' (here and elsewhere, for ease of reference, we use English rather than KR morphemes), and three NPs—'John', 'Mary', and 'letter'. In the set of grammatical relations, $R_g$, they would bear the Su, DO, and IO relations, respectively, to 'send'. In the set of semantic relations, $R_s$, they would bear the AGENT (A), PATIENT, and RECIPIENT relations to 'send'. (13a) would be derived by a Dative transformation in which 'Mary' comes to bear the DO relation to 'send' and 'letter' ceases to bear any grammatical relation to 'send'. The -ir- marker on the verb would be a surface reflex of the fact that Dative had applied, just as the -w- suffix on the verb is a reflex of Passive.

On the analysis we propose, which we shall call the Two Objects Analysis (TOA), the underlying structure of (13a) would be as in the PA, except that both 'Mary' and 'letter' would stand in the DO relation to 'send' and no NP will bear the IO relation to 'send'. No Dative rule is needed to generate (13a). Coding rules, of course, are needed in both approaches. In ours they will position DOs indifferently in immediate postverbal position, subject to the constraint that if there are two animate DOs the R will precede the P. This is a semantic or role-based constraint of the sort that we have already seen is necessary to impose on coding rules in general.

The two analyses, the PA and the TOA, make rather different predictions about KR. We shall outline these differences and argue that TOA is superior both in terms of overall simplicity and in terms of capturing generalizations about KR:

1.   PA is prima facie more complicated than TOA in that it requires distinguishing three grammatical relations rather than just two, and in that it requires that KR have a Dative rule. There is no evidence, however, that KR has a Dative rule. The primary motivation for such a rule in English (or in any other language for which there is asserted to be a Dative rule) is that the language presents pairs of sentences like *John gave Mary the book* and *John gave the book to Mary* in which the corresponding NPs present the same semantic relations to the verb and in which similar distributional and selectional restrictions are exhibited. The Dative rule represents those generalizations. If both the dative and the nondativized sentences were generated independently, then the similarity in privileges of occurrence and selectional restrictions would be accidental.

In KR, however, there are no "undativized" sentences. It is not possible on the surface to present an R as an object of a preposition. This is perhaps surprising, since in some related Bantu languages (see Trithart 1975 for examples from Chicewa) R's can be introduced by the goal-locative preposition *ku*. But in KR, an NP, even if animate, must be interpreted as goal-locative when it follows *ku*. Thus in (49) below the phrase *kwa Maria* must be interpreted to mean 'Mary's place' and not simply 'Mary' herself.

(49)          *Yohani y- ohere-je   ibaruwa kwa Maria.*
              John    he-send- asp letter    to   Mary
              'John sent a letter to Mary's house.'

The primary generalizations that Dative is designed to capture in English, then, simply do not exist in KR. Analogous claims hold for Benefactives. That is, it is not possible to construe a B with a preposition in KR. The closest preposition is *kubera*, which most accurately translates as 'because of'. Thus (50) does not mean that the action was done FOR Mary, but only BECAUSE of her—that is, Mary is some sort of indirect cause:

(50)          *Yohani a- ra- andik-a   kubera Maria.*
              John    he-pres-write- asp because Mary
              'John is writing the letter because of Mary.'

There is, however, another possible, if unobvious, source for benefactive DOs—namely, as possessor NPs. Thus (51) below has, in addition to the expected meaning, a benefactive reading:

(51)   *Yohani y- a- buz-e   inzu   ya Maria.*
       John    he-past-buy-asp house of Mary
       'John bought Mary's house' **or** 'John bought a house for Mary.'

Furthermore, there is a transformation which promotes possessors of DOs
to DO status; this transformation does introduce the -*ir*- affix on the verb:

(52)      *Yohani y- a-   gur- i- ye  Maria inzu.*
          John   he-past-buy-R-asp Mary  house
          'John bought Mary's house.' **or** 'John bought Mary a house.'

Possessor-Promotion cannot be a general source for benefactive DOs,
however, since the sentences it generates necessarily contain three NPs (the
Su, the derived DO, and the old head of the possessive construction). Thus
this transformation cannot generate derived DOs in sentences which are otherwise intransitive, as in (25b), repeated below:

(25)              b. *Maria y- a-   byin- i- ye  umugabo.*
                     Mary  she-past-dance-B-asp man
                     'Mary danced for the man.'

On the TOA, however, such sentences pose no problem. Their underlying
structures simply contain an NP which bears the DO relation to the verb and
also bears the (semantic) BENEFACTIVE relation to the verb. (Recall that it is a
general property of terms that a given term, like Su, may express many different
semantic relations (AGENT, EXPERIENCER, etc.) to the verb in different sentences.

Also, note that in sentences generated by Possessor-Promotion the former
possessed NP does not behave like a DO. That is, it cannot passivize to subject,
relativize, etc. Thus from (52) we cannot form (53) or (54) and preserve the
possessive reading. [(53) and (54) are acceptable, however, on the benefactive
reading.]:

(53)              *\*Inzu  Yohani y- a-   gúr- i- ye  Maria*
                  house John   he-past-buy-B-asp Mary
                  'the house of Mary's that John bought'

(54)              *\*Inzu  y-a-   gúr- i- w-   e   Maria (na Yohani).*
                  house it-past-buy-B-pass-asp Mary  (by John)
                  'The house of Mary's was bought by John.'

Thus Possessor-Promotion does not generate sentences with two apparent DOs
and so is not the source for the benefactive DOs in sentences like (13a).

So far, then, TOA is to be preferred to PA on the grounds that PA requires
the existence of two transformations for which the primary motivation is
lacking.

**2.**  PA and TOA differ in a second respect in regard to the analysis of (13a)
('John sent Mary a letter'). Namely, PA claims that, in the output of Dative,

'letter' bears no grammatical relation to the derived verb. Thus it should not have any of the properties characteristic of DOs in general. But, as we have seen on pp. 91–94, both the unmarked NPs after the verb appear to have all the properties characteristic of DOs in simple cases: both relativize, passivize, reflexivize, etc. It would appear, then, that 'letter' still does bear a DO relation to the verb and that, on the PA, the Relational Annihilation Law is violated, since the DO 'letter' was not demoted after Dative promoted the IO 'Mary' to DO status.

Some, but not all, of these data, however, can be expressed without relinquishing the PA, although only at the cost of considerable complication in the grammar. Consider for illustrative purposes the fact that both 'Mary' and 'letter' can passivize. We repeat the relevant examples for convenience of reference:

(13)           a. *Yohani yoher-er-eje Maria ibaruwa.*
                  John    send- R-asp Mary  letter
                  'John sent the letter to Mary.'

(20)           b. *Ibaruwa yoher-er-ej- w-  e   Maria (na Yohani).*
                  letter    sent- R-asp-pass-asp Mary  (by John)
                  'the letter was sent to Mary by John.'

               c. *Maria yoher-er-ej- w-  e   ibaruwa (na Yohani).*
                  Mary  sent- R-asp-pass-asp letter    (by John)
                  'Mary was sent the letter by John.'

(20c) can be easily generated on the PA by the simple application of Passive to the output of Dative. And (20b) can be generated by applying Passive first to 'letter', when it is still a DO, and then applying Dative, endowing the passive verb with a derived DO. Since the transformations in the cycle are unordered, both orders of application are possible.

But there are strong objections to this approach: First, recall that only terms in KR can relativize. But we do get relative clauses in which the P(atient) NP has been relativized and the R(ecipient) NP is present in surface as a DO:

(21)           a. *Nabonye ibaruwa Yohani yohér-er-eje Maria.*
                  I-saw    letter   John   sent- R-asp Mary
                  'I saw the letter that John sent Mary.'

To account for this fact (preserving the generalization that only terms relativize) in the same way that the Passive facts above were accounted for, the PA would have to claim that 'letter' in (21a) was relativized when it was a DO, and then that Dative was applied. But 'letter' is relativized on a cycle higher than that determined by 'send'. Thus promotion of the supposed IO to DO could not be a strictly cyclic rule in violation of the cyclicity assumption. (See p. 86.)

PA could simply abandon the generalization that only terms relativize, and say that only terms or demoted terms relativize. But this latter generalization is also not correct; e.g. demoted subjects do not relativize:

(55)         *umugabo abagore ba- a-   kúbis- w-  e   (NA)
             man      women  they-past-strike-pass-asp (by)
             'the man whom the women were struck by'

Furthermore, there are object-creating rules in the language which do force the demotion of the old object, and that old object does not relativize (nor does it have any of the other properties of DOs). E.g. there is a rule which we call LOC which promotes locatives to DO status as in (56a-b) below, where they relativize, passivize, and otherwise behave as DOs should in KR:

(56)      a. Yohani y- ∅-   iish-e    impyisi mw-ishyamba.
             John   he-past-kill-asp hyena in- forest        **Loc** ⇒
             'John killed a hyena in the forest.'

          b. Yohani y- ∅-   iish-e-   mo ishyamba impyisi.
             John   he-past-kill-asp-loc forest      hyena      **Pass** ⇒
             'John killed-in the forest a hyena.'

          c. Ishyamba ry-∅-   iish-w-  e-  mo impyisi (na Yohani).
             forest      it- past-kill-pass-asp-loc hyena   (by John)
             'The forest was killed-in a hyena by John.'

          d. Ishyamba Yohani y- ∅-   iish-e-   mo impysis.
             forest      John   he-past-kill-asp-loc hyena
             'The forest that John killed-in a hyena.'

However, once the locative has been promoted to DO, as in (56b), the former DO becomes a nonterm, and can, for example, no longer relativize or passivize:

(57)      a. *Nabonye impiyisi Yohani y- ∅-   iish-e-   mo ishyamba.
             I-saw     hyena    John   he-past-kill-asp-loc forest
             'I saw the hyena that John killed-in the forest.'

          b. *Impyisi y-∅-   iish-w-  e-  mo ishyamba (na Yohani).
             hyena   it-past-kill-pass-asp-loc forest      (by John)
             'The hyena was killed-in the forest by John.'

Thus on this approach the conditions of relativization would have to specify that not only terms, but certain former terms created in certain ways (e.g. by Dative) but not in others (e.g. by Passive or Loc), can relativize. In our opinion, this unnecessarily complicates the statement of the conditions on relativization. In the TOA both the P and the R in (13a) are DOs and so relativization applies without problems. In (56b) the locative is a derived DO and the former DO, 'hyena', simply bears no grammatical relation to the verb and so does not undergo relativization. And the generalization that only terms relativize is preserved.

Second, PA cannot adequately account for Object Pronoun Incorporation (OPI). Recall that nonterms do not take their pronouns infixed in the verb. But it is easy to have a patient pronoun infixed and a full NP recipient present:

(58)              *Yohani y- a-   y-oher-er-eje  Maria.*
                  John   he-past-it-send-R-asp Mary
                  'John sent it to Mary.'

Surely the infixed pronoun -*y*- still bears the DO relation to the verb. And clearly 'Mary' is present, on the PA, as a derived DO. So, again, the sentence appears to present two DOs and the Relational Annihilation Law would appear to have failed.

PA could perhaps argue here that once OPI has applied the verb somehow becomes intransitive and does not really have a DO. (This is the case that would be made for Reflexivization.) Then another NP [e.g. the supposed IO in the underlying structure for (58)] would be free to be promoted to DO status. But this analysis is objectionable on several grounds (quite aside from the fact that we find no basis for saying that pronominal DOs are not "really" DOs). For one thing, OPI cannot take place on the cycle determined by the verb of the clause in which the NPs to be pronominalized occur, for the controller of the pronominalization will be specified on a higher cycle. Thus if the promotion of the putative IO occurs after OPI then, again, this process must not be strictly cyclic. Further, this approach creates problems in the generation of sentences like 'John sent it to her' (15c)—cases where the controller of the R is reached before the controller of the P. This will yield an intermediate stage at which we have (correctly) 'John sent her the letter'. But at this stage, initially, 'letter' is a nonterm since it has been demoted by Dative. It must now be re-promoted to DO status! In other words, we have a DO which is demoted and then repromoted to DO, but we have no evidence of the stage at which it was a nonterm. Such a rule is totally opaque, and seems motivated solely by the desire to preserve the "no more than one DO at a time" hypothesis. It is certainly difficult to see how children would acquire such a rule (but then again it's difficult to see how children acquire any rules).

Note further that the repromotion problem is not limited to the case concerning OPI. Even to generate a relative clause like 'the letter that Mary was sent', as in (59) below, we must either relativize 'letter':

(59)              *ibaruwa Maria y-  ∅-   ohér-er-ej-  w-   e*
                  letter   Mary  she-past-send-B- asp-pass-asp
                  'the letter that Mary was sent'

when it is an original DO (assuming the generalization that only terms relativize), in which case Dative and Passive must apply on the lower cycle after relativization has applied on the higher cycle (a gross violation of strict cyclicity), or we must allow that 'letter' in 'Mary was sent the letter' be repromoted from nonterm status to DO again.

So far then, it seems to us that the comparison of the PA and the TOA weighs heavily in favor of TOA, for none of the problems cited above arise in the TOA. For instance, Passive applies exactly as we originally defined it. It selects any NP bearing the DO relation to the verb, makes it a Su in the derived sentence, and makes the former subject cease to bear any grammatical relation to the verb. The conditions of Relative Clause Formation are not problematic. The only condition we need (of concern here) is that whenever the structural description is met, the lower (see footnote 4) NP must be a term (i.e. Su or DO). The cyclicity of the promotion rules is not endangered since, because we have multiple DOs in any case, there is no need to fiddle the derivation so that the right NP is a DO at the right time. And OPI is not problematic, since any NP which is a DO may undergo it. And since sentences may have more than one DO there is no problem saying that an object pronoun is still a DO.

**3.**    There is a third point of comparison between the two approaches, however, which, on the basis of data so far presented, would appear to favor the PA over the TOA. In the TOA we need two ways to get the /ir/ marking on the verb. On the one hand, it arises by a kind of case-marking rule (to be discussed below), and, on the other hand it is introduced transformationally during Possessor-Promotion. In the PA, however, the verb is marked /ir/ only if an NP has been promoted to DO. Thus PA appears to give a uniform analysis of the source of /ir/ marking.

Unfortunately, further data show that there is no uniform source for /ir/ marking. Thus, in addition to signalling the presence of an underlying recipient or benefactive, /ir/ also signals optionally the presence of locatives. And these locatives need not be present as surface DOs. They may occur obliquely, carrying a preposition and not triggering any of the operations which are sensitive to DO-hood:

(60)                    *Umugabo a- ra-   andik-ir-a    ku meeza.*
                        man         he-pres-write- L-asp on table
                        'The man is writing on the table.'

On either approach we need two sources for -ir- marking, and in this respect neither approach is to be preferred to the other. We would like to stress, however, that regarding -ir- marking as a kind of case marking is natural in the sense that its properties resemble those of coding properties in other languages. Thus we want to say that a verb in underlying structure gets marked -ir- obligatorily when it has a R or a B NP, and optionally when it has a locative.

In marking case partially or wholly on the verb, then, KR resembles Homeric Greek, Hungarian, and Machiguenga. In using the same case marker for different semantic roles KR resembles most, if not all, languages. In making case marking dependent on underlying semantic role KR resembles Hindi, Gugu-Yalanji, and Finnish. (See pp. 100–101.) In the marking of verb agreement KR resembles Kapampangan, in which verbs agree with underlying agents regardless of whether they are surface subjects, and Palauan [example (32)], in which verbs agree with underlying patients, regardless of whether they are surface DOs. And finally, in sometimes case marking for DOs and sometimes not, KR resembles Hindi, Spanish, Hebrew (Givón 1975), and Malagasy (Keenan 1975a), in which DOs are sometimes marked and sometimes not.

**4.** A final point of comparison between PA and TOA concerns a very general constraint on promotion transformations, first enunciated in Perlmutter and Postal (1974). We will show that, on the PA but not on the TOA, KR violates this otherwise well-motivated constraint. The constraint, called the Advancee Tenure Law (ATL) in Perlmutter and Postal (1974), applies only to ADVANCEMENT rules. Advancement rules are promotions which affect only NPs in the domain of a given verb. Thus rules which promote DOs, IOs, and Obl's to Su are advancement rules. So also are rules which promote IOs and Obl's to DO. On the other hand, Possessor-Promotion, mentioned earlier, is not an advancement rule. (This rule, recall, converts sentences like *John took Mary's clothes* to *John took Mary the clothes*, promoting an underlying possessor to DO. But the underlying possessor is not in the domain of *took*. The only NPs in its domain are *John* and *Mary's clothes*.)

The ATL states, in effect, that a term derived by an advancement rule cannot be demoted by any other advancement rule (on any cycle). In fact, to the best of our knowledge, the ATL can be generalized as follows: *No derived term of any sort can be demoted by an advancement rule.*

The ATL receives very substantial support from many languages. E.g. in Tagalog and in Malagasy (Keenan 1972 and 1975a) basically any major NP in a clause can be advanced to subject. But once one NP has been so advanced no others can be.

On both the PA and the TOA, KR possesses several advancement to DO rules. We have already mentioned Loc, which converts locatives to DO. Another rule, Inst, which converts instrumental NPs to DOs, is illustrated below:

(61)     a. *Yohani yandit-se   ibaruwa n-   ikaramu.*
            John    wrote- asp  letter   with-pen
            'John wrote the letter with the pen.'

         b. *Yohani yandik-ish- ije  ikaramu ibaruwa.*
            John    wrote- inst-asp pen       letter
            'John wrote-with the pen the letter.'

Further, the derived DO clearly behaves as a DO should in KR, e.g. it passivizes and relativizes:

(62)       *Ikaramu y-andik-ish- ij-  w-   e   ibaruwa (na Yohani).*
           pen        it-write-inst-asp-pass-asp letter     (by John)
           'The pen was written-with a letter by John.'

(63)       *Nabonye ikaramu Yohani y- ∅-   andik-ish- ije ibaruwa.*
           I-saw     pen      John  he-past-write-inst-asp letter
           'I saw the pen that John wrote-with a letter.'

In addition, on the PA, but not on the TOA, there is a rule which converts IOs to DOs. On the PA, the ATL clearly predicts that no two of these rules can apply on the same cycle, for such a rule would necessarily demote a DO that was derived by an advancement rule (assuming the Relational Annihilation Law). The TOA does not necessarily make this prediction, since it allows multiple DOs and therefore does not require that a derived DO be demoted when something else has been promoted to DO status. And in fact, although there are severe constraints on the permissible combinations of derived DOs (see Kimenyi, in preparation, for discussion), it is possible to get sentences in which more than one DO has been derived:

(64)   a. *Yohani y- a-   andits-e   ku meza n-   ikaramu.*
          John    he-past-write- asp on table with-pen       ⇒ **Loc**
          'John wrote on the table with the pen.'

       b. *Yohani y- a-   andits-e-  ho ameza n-   ikaramu.*
          John    he-past-write- asp-loc table  with-pen       ⇒ **Inst**
          'John wrote on the table with the pen.'

       c. *Yohani y- a-   andik-iish-ije- ho ameza ikaramu.*
          John    he-past-write- inst-asp-loc table   pen
          'John wrote on the table with the pen.'

We note that (64c), like its English translation, is ambiguous according to whether 'table' is merely the locus of the action or actually receives the writing, as in the sense of INSCRIBE. The sentences which have undergone Loc above [(64b) and (64c)] have only the inscribe sense.

## CONSEQUENCES FOR UNIVERSAL GRAMMAR

The facts cited in the previous section argue, persuasively, we feel, in favor of the TOA over the PA. And this in turn supports our original suggestion that the Relational Hierarchy—*Su > DO > IO > nonterm*—merely stipulates a set of possible grammatical relations out of which a language may choose. But a language is not obliged to opt for all of these relations; in particular, IO may be lacking, as in KR. Further, we have supported the nonuniqueness claim that a language may present more than one NP in a given grammatical relation, e.g. the DO relation, to its verb.

Thus in a RG for any language we will require a specification of which particular grammatical relations it uses and what the minimum and maximum number of permissible NPs of any given relation are in an arbitrary sentence. Indeed, these two facts can be incorporated in a single statement. Thus the min-max pairs for English would be: $Su(1, 1)$; $DO(0, 1)$; $IO(0, 1)$; $OBL(0, \infty)$.[9] That is, any sentence (in underlying structure) must have at least one Su and at most one Su; possibly zero DOs and at most one, etc. The min-max pairs for KR might be: $Su(1, 1)$; $DO(0, 2)$; $IO(0, 0)$; $OBL(0, \infty)$. (We discuss the status of two as the max number for DOs in KR below.)

Accepting our case as proven for the moment, the consequences of allowing more than one NP to bear the same grammatical relation to a verb are perhaps less severe than expected. Although we have not investigated all the constraints imposed on RG in Perlmutter and Postal (1974), the principle consequence of the nonuniqueness hypothesis seems to affect only the Relational Annihilation Law. Thus, if a language allows more than one DO and it promotes an NP to DO in a sentence containing only one DO, does the original DO necessarily get demoted or not? It seems to us that the RAL simply has no prediction to make here. Perhaps the original DO's relation is taken over, in which case there is a demotion to nonterm status, or perhaps it is the available DO relation which is now filled. Note that even in Perlmutter and Postal (1974) it is necessary to allow that an advancement to DO not create a nonterm in cases where the original sentence did not have a DO to begin with. Thus the application of Inst in (65a) could not create a nonterm:

(65)  a. *Yohani y- a- hiin-  ze n- isuka.*
     John  he-past-cultivate-asp with-hoe
     'John cultivated with the hoe.'

    b. *Yohani y- a- hiing-  iish- ije isuka.*
     John  he-past-cultivate-inst-asp hoe
     'John cultivates-with the hoe.'

Further, it appears that KR illustrates both possibilities. We have already shown that when Loc applies to an already transitive sentence the old DO becomes a nonterm. When Inst applies to a transitive sentence, however, the promoted NP acquires the DO properties, as already exhibited in (61)–(63), and the former DO retains its DO properties. Thus from (66a), generated by Inst, we can passivize and relativize the old DO:

(66)  a. *Yohani yandik-ish- ije ikaramu ibaruwa.*
     John  wrote- inst-asp pen  letter
     'John wrote-with a pen a letter.'

[9] '$\infty$' means 'unbounded'.

b. *Ibaruwa y-andik-ish- ij- w- e ikaramu (na Yohani).*
   letter    it-write- inst-asp-pass-asp pen      (by John)
   'The letter was written-with a pen by John.'

c. *Nabonye ibaruwa Yohani y- andik- ish- ije ikaramu.*
   I-saw    letter    John    he-wrote-inst-asp pen
   'I saw the letter that John wrote-with a pen.'

We might then have to abandon the RAL in light of the KR facts. This would mean that for each promotion rule we would have to specify whether or not an NP gets demoted. However, abandoning the RAL totally does not seem warranted, i.e., even in KR it still applies unequivocally to advancement to subject rules. We would like to suggest, as an hypothesis for further research, a weaker version of the RAL—the Weak Relational Annihilation Law (WRAL). To state it we will first define the VALENCE of a grammatical relation $X$ to be the maximum number of full NPs which can simultaneously bear the relation $X$ to a given verb in a RELATIONALLY PRIMITIVE sentence. A sentence is relationally primitive just in case no term-changing rules are involved in its derivation.

**The Weak Relational Annihilation Law**

*If, in a given language, L, application of a promotion to X rule exceeds the valence of X in L, then one of the X's is demoted to nonterm status.* The WRAL still requires, then, that promotion to subject rules in KR demote the old subject, since the valence of Su is one, and if the old subject were not demoted then the derived sentence would have two subjects. On the other hand, promotion to DO rules in KR need not demote old DOs, since these rules need not result in exceeding the valence of DO, which is two. In this sense the WRAL is a kind of weak structure-preserving constraint, a point made in Kimenyi (in preparation). An advancement-to-DO rule can result in two DOs only if the language independently allows two DOs. The WRAL is clearly much weaker than the RAL, however, since it allows that a promotion-to-$X$ rule demote an old $X$ even if the valence of $X$ is not exceeded. This is in fact what Loc does in KR.

The WRAL seems to us largely correct for KR. Of the many ways we might expect to be able to generate a sentence with more than two full NP DOs (and KR has at least two more promotion to DO rules than we have considered here), all are generally blocked in one way or another. Note, however, that most of the expected derivations satisfy WRAL vacuously. That is, if a sentence like (67a) below already has two DOs, then it is not generally the case that a promotion to DO rule applies demoting one of the former DOs:

(67)        a. *Y- a- andik-i- ye Maria ibaruwa n- ikaramu.*
               he-past-write- R-asp Mary letter    with-pen
               'He wrote a letter to Mary with the pen.'

b. *Y- a-    andik-ish- ir- ije ikaramu Maria ibaruwa.
he-past-write- inst-R-asp pen    Mary letter
'He wrote-with the pen a letter to Mary.'

Rather, some constraint prevents the promotion rule from applying. The WRAL (and the RAL) in nowise rule out such constraints. In fact, the Advancee Tenure Law is one presumably universal such constraint. Thus, to take a simple case, if the input structure to an advancement to Su rule were met, but the current Su were derived, then the advancement rule would be prevented from applying.

Furthermore, even acknowledging that we have not pursued in depth the various ways in which more than two DOs might be created, we must note one case that may violate even the WRAL. Namely, if some of the NPs bearing the DO relation to the verb are pronominal then we easily get more than two DOs. Note the following example, taken from Kimenyi (in preparation):

(68)    Y- a-    yi-ki-bi-ba-    andik-iish- ir- ije- ho.
he-past-it- it- it- them-write- inst-B-asp-loc
'He wrote it on it with it for them.'

Such a sentence has clearly had two underlying DOs; it evidences two promotions to DO, namely, Inst and Loc. A considerably more detailed investigation of the constraints on such multiple-promotion-to-object rules is being undertaken in Kimenyi (in preparation), and we refer the reader to that source for further consideration of these problems.

## CONCLUSION, AND AN ALTERNATE HYPOTHESIS

We have argued that unmarked Patient and Recipient-Benefactive NPs in Kinyarwanda share an overwhelming number of syntactic properties and hence should not be considered to bear distinct grammatical relations to the verb, but rather should be viewed as subtypes of the same grammatical relation. If P and R-B NPs do not bear distinct grammatical relations to the verb, then the Promotional Analysis is a fortiori incorrect. And, we have argued, the Two Objects Analysis is preferable.

However, as Peter Cole (personal communication) has pointed out, there is an alternative to the TOA which is also prima facie plausible. Namely, we regard unmarked P and R-B NPs as bearing DO and IO relations to the verb, respectively, and simply note that in KR their transformational properties are almost identical. But there are, of course, two differences. The IO shows a strong preference for preceding the DO and it triggers the -ir- marking on the verb. The -ir- marking can be regarded as a dative or an IO case marker, but on the verb, not on the NP.

Concerning case marking, however, we cannot regard the -*ir*- marker as coding the grammatical relation of IO. We have already seen [example (62)] that -*ir*- may signal the presence of a locative which is not a DO. Furthermore, Alessandro Duranti (personal communication) has pointed out to us some cases of verbs—e.g. 'want', 'like', and 'win'—which lexically select R-B subjects, as in (69):

(69)            *Yohani y- a-   tsiind-i-   ye igiheembo.*
                John   he-past-win-  R-B-asp award
                'John won the award.'

This is clear evidence that -*ir*- does not code grammatical relations but only semantic relations: If an R-B is present, regardless of its grammatical role, mark the verb with -*ir*-.

Note further that sentences like (69) passivize, as in (70):

(70)            *Igiheembo cy-a-   tsiind-i-   w-   e   na Yohani.*
                award     it- past-win-  R-B past-asp by John
                'The award was won by John.'

Thus, if the R-B subject in (69) were derived by an advancedment rule, (90) would be a further violation of the Advancee Tenure Law. And since the ATL is well-motivated we have further support that -*ir*- is not a reflex of an advancement to subject rule.

Consequently, the putative DO and IO on the alternate hypothesis do not differ with regard to grammatical case marking, and part of the apparent support for that hypothesis is nonexistent. The grammatical case marking of the two NPs is identical, namely, zero. Thus we are left with only the word-order difference in basic sentences to distinguish DOs and IOs on the alternate hypothesis. And, in the face of the overwhelming syntactic similarity of P and R-B NPs, this difference is not great enough to warrant making a distinction in grammatical category. A minor difference in coding properties (position, verb agreements, and case marking) can be naturally attributed to subcategory differences between NPs bearing the same grammatical relation to the verb. We have already indicated that in Hindi, for example, different subclasses of subject NPs differ in case marking (ergative versus unmarked) and in control of verb agreement (ergative NPs do not trigger subject agreement on the verb, while unmarked subjects normally do). Further examples where subcategories of a given grammatical relation bear different positions are not hard to find. For example, in Hungarian (Katalin Radics, personal communication) definite DOs follow the verb and trigger object agreement. Indefinite nonspecific DOs precede the verb and do not trigger object agreement:

(71)                    a. *a   férfi ver-i    az asszony-t.*
                           the man hit-3sg 3sg the woman-acc
                           'The man is hitting the woman.'

b. *a férfi néhány asszony-t ver-ø.*
the man some woman-acc hit-3sg
'The man is hitting some woman.'

Thus linearization rules which place different subcategories of NPs bearing the same grammatical relation to the verb in different positions are not unnatural, and the alternate hypothes is largely unsupported relative to the Two Objects Analysis which we have proposed.

## ACKNOWLEDGMENT

We wish to thank Alexandre Kimenyi, not only for having served as our informant, but for substantive contributions concerning the theoretical claims we have made. We also thank him for having made available his unpublished papers on Kinyarwanda.

## REFERENCES

Craig, C. (1975) *Jacaltec Syntax: A Study of Complex Sentences*, unpublished Doctoral dissertation, Harvard University, Cambridge, Massachusetts.

Foley, B. (1975) "Comparative Austronesian Syntax and Linguistic Theory," presented at Linguistics Colloquium, University of California, Los Angeles, California.

Givón, T. (1975) "Promotion, Accessibility and the Typology of Case Marking," unpublished paper, preliminary draft, University of California, Los Angeles, California, and Stanford University, Stanford, California.

Hershberger, H. (1964) "Case-Marking Affixes in Gugu-Yalanji," in R. Pittman and H. Kerr, eds., *Papers on the Languages of the Australian Aborigines*, Australian Institute of Aboriginal Studies, Canberra.

Johnson, D. (1974a) "Prepaper on Relational Constraints on Grammars," unpublished paper, Mathematical Sciences Department, IBM Thomas J. Watson Research Center, Yorktown Heights, N.Y.

Johnson, D. (1974b) "On Relational Constraints on Grammars," unpublished paper, IBM Thomas J. Watson Research Center, Yorktown Heights, N.Y.

Keenan, E. L. (1972) "Relative Clause Formation in Malagasy (and Some Related and Some Not So Related) Languages," in P. Peranteau, J. N. Levi, and G. C. Phares, eds., *The Chicago Which Hunt: Papers from the Relative Clause Festival*, Chicago Linguistic Society, University of Chicago, Illinois.

Keenan, E. L. (1975a) "Remarkable Subjects in Malagasy," to appear in C. Li (ed) *Subject and Topic*, Academic Press, New York.

Keenan, E. L. (1975b) "Towards a Universal Definition of 'Subject'," to appear in C. Li, ed., *Subject and Topic*, Academic Press, New York.

Kennan, E. L. and B. Comrie (1972 and to appear) "Noun-Phrase Accessibility and Universal Grammar," presented to the 1972 Annual Meeting, Linguistic Society of America; to appear in *Linguistic Inquiry*.

Kimenyi, A. (in preparation) *Topics in the Relational Grammar of Kinyarwanda*, chs 1–3, Doctoral dissertation, University of California, Los Angeles, California.

Lawler, J. (1975) "On Coming to Terms in Achenese: The Function of Verbal Dis-Agreement," in R. E. Grossman, L. J. Sam, and T. J. Vance, eds., *Papers from the Parasession on Functionalism*, Chicago Linguistic Society, University of Chicago, Chicago, Illinois.

Li, C. and S. Thompson (1975) "Subject and Word Order in Wappo," unpublished paper, University of California, Los Angeles, California.

Mirikitani, L. (1972) "Kapampangan Syntax," *Oceanic Linguistics* No. 10.

Munro, P. (1974) *Topics in Mojave Syntax*, unpublished Doctoral dissertation, University of California, San Diego, California.

Schachter, P. (1974) "A Non-Transformational Account of Serial Verbs," *Studies in African Linguistics*, Supp. 5.

Snell, B. and R. Wise (1963) "Noncontingent Declarative Clauses in Machiguenga (Arawak)," *Studies in Peruvian Indian Languages* 1, 103–145 [Summer Institute of Linguistics, University of Oklahoma, Norman, Oklahoma].

Starosta, S. (1973) "The Faces of Case," *Language Sciences* No. 25, 1–14 [Research Center for the Language Sciences, Indiana University, Bloomington, Indiana].

Trithart, L. (1975) "Relational Grammar and Chicewa Subjectivization Rules," in R. E. Crossman, L. J. Sam, and T. J. Vance, eds., *Papers from the Eleventh Regional Meeting of the Chicago Linguistic Society*, University of Chicago, Chicago, Illinois.

Woodbury, A. (1975) *Ergativity of Grammatical Processes: A Study of Greenlandic Eskimo*, unpublished Master's essay, University of Chicago, Chicago, Illinois.

# CLAUSE UNION AND GERMAN ACCUSATIVE PLUS INFINITIVE CONSTRUCTIONS

*WAYNE HARBERT*
University of Illinois

This chapter will be concerned with two groups of suspected Clause Union predicates in German—the causative/concessive verb *lassen*[1] and certain verbs of perception, including *sehen* 'to see', *hören* 'to hear', and *fühlen* 'to feel'. These groups are the most common members of the class of predicates which occur exclusively with accusative plus simple infinitive (AcI) complements.[2,3]

[1] *Lassen* is neutral with respect to the causative/concessive parameter—a feature it shares with a large number of Clause Union causatives in other languages. In the absence of a disambiguating context,

> *Er ließ ihn kommen.*

may mean either 'he permitted him to come' or 'he made him come'.

[2] 'Simple infinitive' will be employed here to refer to infinitives which are not preceded by the preposition *zu*, which generally marks infinitives in Equi-produced complements in German.

Other verbs which take only AcI complements are *haben* 'to have', with stative complements indicating position.

> *Er hat ein Pferd im Stalle stehen.*
> 'He has a horse standing in the stall.'

and *machen* 'to make/cause', which is highly restricted, and which no longer seems to be a productive causative in German.

In addition, there is a group of verbs which occur with both AcI complements and *NP + zu + infinitive* complements. These include *helfen* 'to help', *lehren* 'to teach', and *heißen* 'to order'. The choice between the two types depends on the "weight" of the complement:

> *Ich lehre ihn singen.*
> 'I teach him to sing.'
> *Ich lehre ihn, die Lieder Schuberts zu singen.*
> 'I teach him to sing the songs of Schubert.'

[3] Historically, a number of other verbs—notably speech act predicates and verbs of mental action—occurred with AcI complements. These constructions were most likely produced by a rule

(1)                    *Ich ließ ihn kommen.*
                       'I let him come.'


(2)                    $Ich \begin{Bmatrix} sah \\ h\ddot{o}rte \end{Bmatrix} ihn\ kommen.$

                       'I $\begin{Bmatrix} saw \\ heard \end{Bmatrix}$ him come.'


In previous studies, attempts have been made under the influence of surface similarities to assign a common derivation to the AcI complements of both of these groups. Bierwisch (1963), for example, claimed that all of these verbs take complements of the form $NP_i\ [_sNP_iVP]$ with subsequent Equi-deletion of the embedded subject. Ebert (1972) proposed that both *lassen* and the verbs of perception take sentential objects, with subsequent Raising of the embedded subject into direct-object position. Clément (1971) also supported Subject-to-Object Raising (SOR) as the process involved in producing AcI complements with verbs of perception. Reis (1973) argued that neither an Equi analysis nor a SOR analysis accounts for the behavior of *lassen* complements: she suggested rather that a diacritic complementizer is inserted on complements of *lassen*. This complementizer triggers deletion of the embedded S-node and the consequent collapsing of matrix and embedded clauses.[4] Reis assumed that arguments like those ruling out Equi with *lassen* are applicable to the verbs of perception, for whose complements she proposed the same derivation.

It will be seen below that, while the application of clause-bounded rules shows that collapsing has occurred in both cases, the arguments presented by

---

of Subject-to-Object Raising, and are generally attributed to Latin influence. While Latin may have been the original source for SOR in German, the frequent occurrence of the rule in German literature spanning a period of several centuries leaves little doubt that it had become nativized.

The rule of SOR in German virtually disappeared from the grammar during the eighteenth and nineteenth centuries, although it is still possibly necessary to account for vestigial complements (with obligatory copula deletion) in sentences like:

> *Er findet das Klima angenehm (\*sein)* ∼
> *Er findet $_s$[das Klima ist angenehm]$_s$*
> 'He finds the climate (to be) comfortable.'

Reis claims, however, that these cases as well involve Null-Complementizer Insertion.

[4] Null-Complementizer Insertion as described by Reis, Clause Union as discussed by Comrie (1973), and Verb Raising as discussed by Aissen (1974a and 1974b) are apparently divergent analyses of the same process—a process through which two clauses merge as a consequence of the erasure of a branching S-node. The relative merits of the three analyses will not be considered here. It should be noted, however, that there are substantially different claims involved in the three positions. Reis, for example, views Null Complementizer Insertion as a cyclic rule, while Aissen, in (1974b), argues that Verb Raising is precyclic.

Reis against an Equi analysis of *lassen* complements do not retain their validity when applied to the verbs of perception. Moreover, there are numerous differences in behavior between the complements of the two groups with respect to other rules which place in question the possibility of assigning them a common derivation. Evidence will be presented in support of the position that Equi is involved in the derivation of AcI complements of verbs of perception, but not of those of *lassen*. Since clause-bounded rules apply down into complements of both types, it is necessary to reject the claim in Aissen (1974a) that such rules can operate down into infinitive complements produced through Verb Raising, but not down into those produced through Equi or SOR.[5] Consequently, the application of clause-bounded rules does not provide a sufficient basis on which to distinguish between cases of Verb Raising and cases of Equi or SOR.

Arguments of other types—including those presented by Reis (1973)—will be seen to leave little doubt that *lassen* is a member of the cross-linguistic class of Verb Raising or Clause Union causatives discussed in Aissen (1974a and 1974b) and in Comrie (1973). Neither Aissen nor Comrie considers *lassen* as a member of this class, and its addition promises to contribute to the understanding of Clause Union.

The last sections of this chapter will consider the significance of *lassen* complements with respect to Aissen's (1974a and 1974b) claims about the order of constituents in verb-raising constructions, the problem discussed by Comrie concerning whether 'extended movement' of a subject displaced by clause union, or passivization, is responsible for agent phrases in sentences like the French:

(3)         *Paul fait arrêter Anne par les gendarmes.*
            'Paul has Anne arrested by the police.'

and the arguments made by Aissen (1974b) for the precyclic application of Verb Raising.

## EVIDENCE FOR UNDERLYING BISENTIALITY

Most of the arguments for the bisentential origin of sentences containing *lassen* with an AcI complement involve considerations of simplicity. The following two arguments are adapted from Aissen (1974a).

---

[5] Evidence leading to the same conclusion also appears in Gothic. Gothic reflexivization was clause-bounded, and could only be triggered by the cyclic subject. It could, however, operate down into SOR complements, as in this phrase from Luke (19:27) (Streitberg 1971:157):

> *þaiei ni wildedun mik þiudanon ufar sis$_i$*
> 'who did not want me to rule over themselves'

AcI complements of *lassen* are fully productive, in that there are no restrictions on the predicates which can occur in the infinitive slot so long as they are semantically compatible with the notion of causation/permission:[6]

(4)                              *\*Ich ließ ihn ein Säugetier sein.*
                                 'I let him be a mammal.'

In view of this unrestricted productivity, the alternative to the bisentential analysis—namely that for every verb $X$ in the lexicon which takes $n$ arguments and which is compatible with causation there is a compound verb *Xlassen* which takes $n + 1$ arguments—would be highly uneconomical.

For every grammatical string of the form *lassen* + $NP_i$ [*Accusative*] + $V_k$ [*Infinitive*] there must be a corresponding grammatical sentence of the form $NP_i$ [*Nominative*] $V_k$:[7]

(5)                        a. *\*Er läßt die Idee Torte essen.*
                              'He lets the idea eat cake.'

                           b. *\*Die Idee ißt Torte.*
                              'The idea eats cake.'

The selectional restrictions holding between the accusative object and the infinitive in (5a) are the same as those holding between the subject and the verb in (5b). This fact would also require an extra statement in a grammar in which *lassen* + *AcI* constructions were viewed as underlyingly simplex.

The bisentential analysis also affords an explanation of case assignment in embedded complements. In *lassen* constructions containing more than one object, the object corresponding to the underlying subject in a bisentential analysis takes accusative case, as required by *lassen*, while other objects appear in cases determined by the infinitive:

(6)                        a. *Laß mich dir helfen!*
                                        dat V[+dat]
                              'Let me help you.'

                           b. *Er läßt den Sohn meiner gedenken.*
                                            gen      V[+gen]
                              Literally, 'He causes his son to remember me.'

---

[6] The embedded verb in AcI complements of verbs of perception must be [-stative]. Otherwise, there are no restrictions on the class of predicates which can appear in these either, so long as the predicate is compatible with the mode of perception indicated by the matrix verb.

[7] Exceptions to this are idioms of which *lassen* is an essential part:

> *Er läßt sich sehr gehen.*
> 'He really lets himself go.'
> *\*Er geht sehr.*

c. *Lassen Sie mich Ihr Freund werden.*[8]
          nom     V[+nom]
   'Let me become your friend.'

This pattern, which follows automatically from cyclic application of case marking in the bisentential analysis, would have to be accounted for by lexical redundancy rules in a compound verb analysis.

Semantic considerations favoring a sentential source for AcI constructions with verbs of perception are buttressed by the fact that such constructions alternate and are partially synonymous with corresponding full sentential complements:

(7)         a. *Ich hörte ihn sich erschießen.*
               'I heard him shoot himself.'

            b. *Ich hörte, daß er sich erschoß.*
               'I heard him shoot himself'

                            **or**

            'I heard that he shot himself'

## EVIDENCE FOR SURFACE SIMPLICITY

The application of clause-bounded rules provides abundant evidence that all elements of AcI constructions are superficially members of the matrix clause. The following examples involve Reflexivization, Topic Preposing, and various object-mixing phenomena, all of which are clause-bounded processes in German.

### Reflexivization[9]

(8)         $Er_i \begin{Bmatrix} sah \\ ließ \end{Bmatrix}$ *den Diener zu* **sich**$_i$ *kommen.*

         'He$_i$ $\begin{Bmatrix} saw \\ caused \end{Bmatrix}$ the servant to come to himself$_i$.'

---

[8] Some speakers also accept:

        *Lassen Sie mich Ihren Freund werden.*
                acc

in which the case of the embedded object is determined by the matrix rather than by the embedded verb. Such sentences, however, are generally held to be archaic.

[9] There are some rather complex restrictions on reflexivization into AcI constructions, some of which are discussed by Reis. It is possible, for example, to reflexivize in such constructions across an intervening NP down into an optional prepositional phrase, but not into a dative NP:

        *Er$_i$ sah die Frau neben sich$_i$ stehen.*
        'He saw the woman stand(ing) next to him.'
        *Er$_i$ sah das Mädchen sich$_i$ zulächeln.*
        'He saw the girl smile at him.'

**Topic Preposing**

(9)                          *Laut hörte ich ihn singen.*
                             'I heard him sing loudly.'

**Scrambling**

Reflexive objects, as well as other objects, normally occur in postverbal position in German. Under certain conditions, however—including Topic Preposing and the consequent movement of the subject to postverbal position, or the movement of the verb to clause-final position in subordinate clauses—the reflexive object usually precedes the subject:

(10)           a. *Der Mann$_i$ erschoß **sich**$_i$ plötzlich.*
                  'The man suddenly shot himself.'

               b. *als **sich**$_i$ der Mann$_i$ plötzlich erschoß*
                  'when the man suddenly shot himself'

The exact nature of this process is not relevant to the present discussion. What is of importance is, first, that this inversion can apply in AcI constructions, mixing elements of the matrix and embedded clauses:

(11)           a. *Die Frauen$_i$ haben sich$_i$ das gefallen lassen.*
               b. *Jahrelang haben sich$_i$ die Frauen$_i$ das gefallen lassen.*
                  'For years the women let themselves be pleased by
                  (= put up with) that.'

and, second, that this type of inversion cannot operate to invert a subject and a reflexive object when the latter belongs to a noun phrase + *zu* + *infinitive* complement (compare, however, Ebert 1975 on the varying degree of "clausiness" exhibited by *zu* + *infinitive* phrases with respect to such processes):

(12)           *\*als **sich**$_i$ ihm der Mann$_i$ befahl, zu erschießen*
               'when the man ordered him to shoot himself'

The rule is therefore clause-bounded, and provides further evidence for the surface simplicity of sentences like (11b).

**Object Movement**

A similar argument for surface simplicity is provided by the fact that, under certain conditions, pronominal objects of embedded simple infinitives are obligatorily moved leftward over elements of the matrix sentence. This is illustrated by the following examples, in which the underlined elements belong to the embedded sentence while the negative *nicht* belongs logically to the matrix sentence:

(13)  a.  *Ich* $\begin{Bmatrix} sah \\ ließ \end{Bmatrix}$ ***es ihn** nicht **machen**.*

'I didn't $\begin{Bmatrix} \text{see} \\ \text{make} \end{Bmatrix}$ him do it.'

b.  *\*Ich* $\begin{Bmatrix} sah \\ ließ \end{Bmatrix}$ *nicht **ihn es machen**.*

Again, this rule cannot apply between full sentential complements or between NP + *zu* + *infinitive* complements and the matrix sentence:

(14)  *Ich befahl ihm, **es nicht zu tun**.*

(14) can mean only 'I ordered him not to do it' (with the negative belonging to the embedded rather than the matrix S), and not 'I didn't order him to do it'.

In German simple sentences, pronominal objects occur before nominal objects:

(15)  a.  *Ich gab ihm das Buch.*
           dat acc
           'I gave him the book.'

b.  *Ich gab es   dem Mann.*
           acc *dat*
           'I gave it to the man.'

The same relative order exists between the accusative object of *lassen* and a reflexive dative object of the embedded infinitive:

(16)  a.  *Ich lasse mir solches Benehmen nicht gefallen.*
           dat acc
           Literally, 'I don't let such behavior please me.'

b.  ***Ich lasse es   mir** nicht gelallen.*
           acc dat
           'I don't let it please me.'

Such movement of dative reflexive objects over accusative nominal objects cannot operate out of *zu* + *infinitive* complements, again demonstrating that the rule involved is clause-bounded, and that both the accusative object and the embedded dative object are parts of the same clause at the time of its application. (Dative reflexive object fronting is also blocked, however, in AcI complements of verbs of perception; cf. Bierwisch 1963:131. This seems to indicate that verb of perception constructions are not as simplex as are *lassen* constructions.)

Ebert (1975) provides further evidence for the simplex structure of such sentences in the form of their behavior with respect to Extraposition and VP–Pied Piping.

## MOTIVATION FOR DISTINCT DERIVATIONS

Evidence has been presented above that elements of German AcI constructions are superficially members of the matrix clause, and that at one point they were members of an embedded clause. It remains to be determined what rule or rules mediate between these two stages. There are three possibilities offered by transformational grammar: (i) Equi NP-deletion, (ii) SOR—with subsequent pruning of the S-node (possibly as a consequence of some other rule, like *zu* Complementizer Deletion, which triggers pruning of the resultant non-branching S-node according to a universal convention),[10] and (iii) Clause Union/Verb Raising.

Reis argues convincingly that the first possibility must be ruled out in regard to *lassen*. Her most compelling arguments are based on sentences like the following:

(17)            a. *Er läßt meiner* [*vom   Sohn*] *gedenken.*
                         gen      agent phrase V[+gen]
                   'He causes me to be remembered by the son.'

                b. *Er läßt* [*an               mir*] [*von   niemand*]
                         prepositional phrase  agent phrase
                   *herumnörgeln.*
                   V[+prepositional phrase]
                   'He doesn't let me be grumbled at by anyone.'

                c. *Er läßt mir* [*von   Paul*] *helfen.*
                         dat  agent phrase V[+dat]
                   'He lets me be helped by Paul.'

---

[10] Pruning of this sort does in fact occur in German. Infinitive complements of the verbs *helfen*, *lehren*, and *heißen* discussed in footnote 2 appear on the basis of Passive Equivalence and other tests to be derived through Equi. If these complements are long, then the complementizer *zu* is retained. If, on the other hand, the complement consists only of the embedded subject and verb, *zu* is deleted. Application of the Extraposition and VP–Pied Piping tests discussed by Ebert (1975) shows that S-node pruning has occurred in the complements without *zu*, but not in those with *zu*. In order to avoid the counterintuitive claim that infinitive complements of these verbs are produced by one rule if the complement is "heavy" and by another if it is "light", it must be assumed that Equi followed by complement deletion does result in erasure of the embedded S-node and consequent simplex surface structure.

Reis argues against the insertion and subsequent deletion of *zu* (with consequent pruning) in complements of verbs of perception and of *lassen*, partly on the ground that *zu* never surfaces as a complementizer with these verbs. In the case of the verbs of perception, however, there is evidence (to be discussed below) that Equi does play a role in the derivation of their complements. Since *zu* appears as a complementizer on complements of all other Equi verbs in German, it does not seem farfetched to claim that it is inserted with the verbs of perception as well—especially since, as the preceding paragraph shows, there is independent motivation for a *zu*-deletion rule.

Equi is incapable of accounting for such sentences. First of all, such an analysis would require that *lassen* take matrix objects with a wide range of cases and prepositions, the choice of which would be determined in all instances by the object case taken by the embedded verb. Second, in German the victim of Equi must be a subject. The dative object *mir* in (18), which is fronted but not made subject by Impersonal Passive, cannot be erased when embedded under an Equi verb like *beabsichtigen* 'to intend':

(18)    *Mir wird*          [*von   ihm*]   *geholfen.*
        dat  passive auxiliary   agent phrase  verb[+dat]
        'I am helped by him.'

(19)    *\*Ich$_i$ beabsichtige, $\emptyset_i$ von ihm geholfen zu werden.*
        'I intend to be helped by him.'

This condition on Equi would therefore block the grammatical sentences in (17) if Equi were involved in their derivation.

Reis's arguments against SOR with *lassen* center around the fact that, by itself, SOR cannot explain the behavior of all elements of **lassen** + *AcI* complements, not just of the embedded subject, as members of the matrix clause with respect to clause-bounded rules. It appears, however, that the same examples which she introduces as evidence against an Equi derivation also provide substantive evidence against a SOR derivation.

By definition, SOR applies to raise the embedded subject into matrix direct object position. The embedded subject in the sentences in (17) does not appear as a direct object, however, but rather as an oblique agent phrase.

If it is assumed that the embedded subject has been demoted to agent phrase by some rule applying on the embedded cycle, then SOR must be ruled out in such sentences for the following reason: Only accusative objects in German are eligible for promotion to subject. The embedded verbs in (17) take objects in cases other than accusative, and these objects are consequently incapable of being promoted to fill the subject slot vacated by Subject-to-Agent-Phrase Demotion. On the matrix cycle, therefore, SOR could not operate to raise the embedded subject into matrix object position, since the embedded sentence would be subjectless at that point, having lost its original subject on the embedded cycle, and having no NP eligible to replace it:

(17)            c.'  *Er läßt* [*Paul mir          helfen*]. *subject demotion*
                     Paul me [+dat] help    ⇒

                *Er läßt* [*mir von Paul helfen*].
                     me [+dat] agent phrase

*Mir* cannot be promoted to subject (*ich*) because it is dative. SOR cannot apply because there is no embedded subject.

If, on the other hand, it is assumed that the agent phrase is not created on the embedded cycle, then, in order to maintain an NP-Raising analysis at all, it would be necessary to claim that German has a Subject-to-Agent Phrase Raising rule [next to the SOR rule required by sentences like (1)]. Such an analysis is not only complicated, but unlikely on other grounds.

Neither Reis's argument against Equi nor the argument presented above against SOR with *lassen* complements can be extended to the verbs of perception, however, since crucial examples parallel to those in (17) do not occur with these verbs. Agent phrases are not permitted in AcI complements of verbs of perception:

(20)        *Ich höre über ihn von vielen Leuten sprechen.*
            'I hear him talked about by many people.'

This restriction renders Reis's anti–SOR–Equi arguments for *lassen* inapplicable to verbs of perception by ruling out possible examples involving these verbs with complements which (i) have no embedded subject; (ii) could not have had an embedded subject at the point at which SOR or EQUI would apply; and (iii) meet other conditions on AcI complements with verbs of perception (including the condition that the complement be -stative). Condition (ii) must be mentioned because the agentless counterpart of sentence (20) is grammatical:[11]

---

[11] There are restrictions on such 'agentless passive' AcI constructions with verbs of perception—significantly, restrictions not shared by *lassen*—which I have not been able to isolate fully. First, *verb of perception* + *AcI* constructions are never ambiguous in the way that *lassen* complements are: *Ich lasse ihn rufen* can mean either 'I let him call/cry', or 'I let him be called' (with deletion of the indefinite agent). *Ich höre ihn rufen*, on the other hand, can only mean 'I hear him call/cry'.

A possible explanation for this fact is that there is a transderivational constraint blocking deletion of the underlying subject of a verb of perception complement if the embedded S also contains an accusative object which may be interpreted as an underlying subject:

(i)                    *Ich ließ die Fahne nähen.*
                       'I let the flag be sewn.'
                       *Ich sah die Fahne nähen.*

Those few instances in which such a constraint would not be valid (e.g. *Ich höre ein Lied singen* 'I hear a song being sung') may be viewed as residual formulae from the period—extending well into the nineteenth century—in which both active and passive readings (with subject loss) were possible. The following example comes from Adelung (eighteenth century), cited in Grimm and Grimm (1885: Volume 10, 1:138):

(ii)                   *Ich habe ihn taufen sehen.*
                       'I saw him be baptized.'

The problem with the transderivational constraint analysis is that deletion is sometimes blocked from occurring even when there is no accusative object in the complement which could be interpreted as subject:

(iii)        a.        *Er ließ [mit sich] reden.*
                       prepositional phrase
                       'He let himself be talked to.'

             b.        *Ich hörte mit ihm reden.*

(21)                    *Ich höre über ihn sprechen.*

The infinitives in sentences like (17) and (21) are frequently referred to as passive infinitives, although it is not clear whether passivization is involved in their derivation. Of the three characteristics of passive sentences—past participial form of the embedded verb, presence of the passive auxiliary, and the agent phrase with the preposition *von*—the first is ruled out with all AcI complements. The latter is permitted only in AcI complements of lassen.[12]

In both (22a) and (22b) it is apparent on semantic grounds that an underlying indefinite subject has been deleted in the course of the derivation:

(22)                    a. *Ich lasse ein Lied singen.*
                           'I let a song be sung.'

                        b. *Ich höre ein Lied singen.*
                           'I hear a song being sung.'

The problem is one of finding a motivated explanation for such a loss, since there is no process in German which deletes indefinite subjects directly. One possibility is that in all such cases the subject is demoted to the role of agent phrase by Passive or some other rule. Indefinite agent phrases are deleted obligatorily in German. According to this analysis, Passive applies in the embedded complement of (22), leaving:

(22)          c. *Ich* $\begin{Bmatrix} lasse \\ höre \end{Bmatrix}$ $_S$*[ein Lied wird von einem gesungen]*

----

[12] There are sentences in which both *von*-phrases and past participles can occur in complements of some verbs of perception. (cf. Bierwisch, 1963:132):

(i)              *Ich fühlte mich* [*von   ihm*]   *betrogen.*
                                 agent phrase past participle
                 'I felt myself deceived by him.'

(ii)             *Er sah sich* [*von   allen*]   *verlassen.*
                             agent phrase past participle
                 'He saw himself abandoned by everyone.'

There are a number of reasons for viewing these instances as something other than sentences containing AcI complements which have undergone passivization. First of all, as Clément notes, they do not share the direct perception meaning of the corresponding active AcI constructions; rather, they allow only an interpretation involving 'intellectual' (= indirect) perception, and therefore can only be paraphrased by means of sentences with full sentential complements. The corresponding AcI complement is, in fact, often ungrammatical:

(iii)            **Ich fühlte ihn mich betrügen.*
                 'I felt him deceive me.'

Moreover, the predicates which can occur in the two types of complements are subject to different restrictions. Participial complements of these verbs of perception can be [+stative].

The agent is then deleted, Raising applies, the past participle is converted to infinitive form (a process which occurs under other circumstances in German), and the passive auxiliary *werden* is deleted.

This analysis seems quite probable with *lassen* AcI complements, since sentences like (22d), with definite agent phrases, are also possible:

(22)        d. *Er ließ sein neues Lied vom berühmten Sänger singen.*
               'He let his new song be sung by the famous singer.'

The alternation of $\emptyset$ indefinite agent and *von*-phrase definite agent is precisely that found in normal passive sentences. A serious difficulty arises in connection with the verbs of perception, however, in that not even definite *von* phrases can occur in their complements. There is, therefore, no evidence that Passive or any process involving subject-to-agent demotion has ever occurred. To argue for such a derivation would involve placing an ad hoc restriction on agent demotion such that it could apply in such sentences only if the evidence of its application were subsequently erased by Indefinite Agent Deletion.

An alternative, and much simpler, analysis is that the indefinite object of *hören*, etc., is deleted on the matrix cycle by the independently motivated rule of Indefinite Object Deletion found in (23) (cf. Bierwisch, 129):

(23)                     $Ich\ esse\ \begin{Bmatrix} *etwas \\ \emptyset \\ Torte \end{Bmatrix} gern.$

                         'I like to eat $\begin{Bmatrix} *something.' \\ \emptyset.' \\ Torte.' \end{Bmatrix}$

In an Equi analysis, (22b) would therefore have a derivation like:

*Ich höre man* $_s$*[man ein Lied singen]* $\Rightarrow$
*Ich höre man* $_s$*[$\emptyset$ ein Lied singen]* through Equi, $\Rightarrow$
*Ich höre $\emptyset$* $_s$*[$\emptyset$ ein Lied singen]* through Indefinite Object Deletion.

Both the SOR and the Clause Union analyses are likewise compatible with the Indefinite Object Deletion approach.

Finally, the deletability of the subject of AcI complements with verbs of perception is subject to an apparent transiderivational constraint (discussed in footnote 11), while with *lassen* it is not. This fact is accounted for if the constraint is associated only with a single deletion process—that of Indefinite Object Deletion.

Sentence (21), therefore, does not argue against SOR or Equi with verbs of perception, since there is no reason for assuming that the lower S was subjectless at the end of the embedded cycle. Thus, Reis's most compelling arguments against Equi with *lassen* fail to apply to the verbs of perception. The arguments that remain against Equi/SOR analyses are those based on considerations of simplicity. By itself, neither Equi nor SOR can explain the operation of clause-bounded rules down into the complements of verbs of perception, since they both produce structures in which only the matrix object, and not NP elements of the infinitive complement, is subject to such rules. Some other rule would also have to apply to prune the embedded S. Clause Union, on the other hand, produces simplex surface structures directly. However, if facts can be found which are explained by the more complex derivation but not by the simpler one, then such considerations have no force.

As mentioned earlier, there is evidence that *lassen* and verb of perception AcI complements are not to be derived in the same way, and, specifically, that Equi does play a role in the derivation of verb of perception complements. Among the differences between the complements of the two groups are the restrictions on passive infinitives with verbs of perception, including their inability to contain agent phrases, and the failure of dative reflexive object fronting to occur in verb of perception complements.

There is another set of differences which is best explained by assuming Equi in the derivations of AcI complements of verbs of perception. Such complements cannot be formed when the subject of the embedded S is an essential part of an idiom or a dummy pronoun.[13] Compare:

(24) a.  *Es geht dir gut.*
         'It goes well with you.'

　　 b.  *\*Ich sehe es dir gut gehen.*
         'I see that it goes well with you.'

　　 c.  *Laß es dir gut gehen!*
         'Let it go well with you.' (= 'Have a good time!')

(25) a.  *Es wird ihm heiß.*
         'It's becoming hot for him.'

　　 b.  *\*Er fühlte es sich heiß werden.*
         'He felt it becoming hot for him.'

---

[13] One troublesome exception to this rule is the meteorological *es*, which can occur with the verbs of perception:

> *Ich sah es schneien.*
> 'I saw it snow.'

Meteorological pronouns also seem to be a problem in English, where the apparent Equi verb *make* can occur with meteorological infinitive complements:

> *The magician made it snow.*

Moreover, there is no evidence for the transformational insertion of these pronouns. It might therefore be speculated that such pronouns are not dummies, but have a psychologically real referent.

c. (?)*Ich ließ es ihm heiß werden.*[14]
   'I let it become hot for him.'

(26) a. *Der Teufel reitet ihn.*
     'The devil's riding him.' = 'He's behaving crazily.'

   b. *\*Ich sehe ihn den Teufel reiten.*
      'I see him behaving crazily.'

(27) a. *Das Herz fiel mir in die Hosen.*
     'My heart fell into my pants.' = 'My heart was in my throat.'

   b. *\*Ich fühlte das Herz mir in die Hosen fallen.*

Neither SOR nor Clause Union provides a natural explanation for these facts (as is demonstrated by the ability of *lassen* to occur with dummy pronouns and essential chunks of idioms as objects). On the other hand, Equi does, since its statement requires coreference—and dummy pronouns and chunks of idioms are necessarily noncoreferential.

Clément and Ebert based their arguments for a SOR derivation of AcI complements with verbs of perception primarily on the partial synonymy of sentences like:

(28)                          *Ich höre, daß er weint.*
                              'I hear that he is crying.'

                          **or**

                              'I hear him crying.'

(29)                          *Ich höre ihn weinen.*
                              'I hear him crying.'

Clément argues that SOR can apply to constructions like (28) to produce those like (29) only if three conditions are met. First, the embedded verb must be [-stative], blocking sentences like:

(30)                          *\*Ich sehe das Kind Fieber haben.*
                              'I see the child having fever.'

Second, it cannot be passive, blocking:

(31)                          *\*Ich sehe ihn (vom Hund) gebissen werden.*
                              'I see him being bitten (by the dog).'

Finally, the actions in the matrix sentence and in the embedded sentence must be simultaneous, ruling out sentences like:

[14] Not all speakers, however, accept this sentence.

(32)     *Ich sehe ihn gekommen sein.
         'I see him to have come.'[15]

According to Clément, the simultaneity condition blocks Raising if the complement contains temporal adverbs or tense markers which differ from those in the matrix sentences.

Simultaneity, however, is not sufficient to account for the possible difference in meaning between (28) and (29). (29) is appropriate only if the actor was perceived directly in the process of performing the action. It can be true only if *ich höre ihn* 'I hear him' is also true. (28), on the other hand, is neutral for the many speakers who accept the indicative mood in the direct discourse readings of such sentences, with regard to whether the action itself or a report of the action is perceived. Depending on context, (28) can indicate either direct or indirect perception.

Both the unambiguous direct perception meaning of (29) and the neutrality of (28) with respect to the source of the perception can be accounted for if it is assumed that verbs of perception can appear either with complements of the form $NP$—$S$ or with sentential complements alone. In the former case Equi must apply, producing sentences like (29). In the latter case, Equi cannot apply, resulting in sentences like (28). (28) can be synonymous with (29) on one of its interpretations simply because of the fact that the source of the perception is not specified by a nominal object. Direct perception is therefore not excluded as a possible reading.[16]

---

[15] Both the nonstativity condition and the simultaneity condition are the results of added constraints in the grammar of New High German:

   *Ich horte in wol den ersten sin.* [*Biterolf,* thirteenth century, line 5164, cited in Behagel 1923: Volume 3, 327]
   'I heard him to be the first.'

   *den man sihit gewunnen han* [*Nibelungenlied,* thirteenth century, line 973:4, cited in Behagel 1923: Volume 3, 325]
   'whom one sees to have won'

Cases like the latter seem to suggest that the verbs of perception were at least sometimes SOR predicates in the earlier stages of the language.

[16] The ambiguity of full sentential complements of verbs of perception is not limited to whether the perception was direct or indirect. Indirect perception readings are multiply ambiguous.

(i)     *Ich sehe, daß er zu viel ißt.*
        'I see that he eats too much.'

would be appropriate in any of the following situations:

   I observe him eating too much.
   I notice that he is getting fat.
   I find that there is no food left for me.

When the matrix sentence is augmented by an object, this ambiguity is resolved:

(ii)    *Ich höre von seiner Schwester, daß er weint.*
        'I hear from his sister that he cries.'

One diachronic phenomenon seems to support the Equi analysis of AcI complements of verbs of perception against the SOR analysis proposed by Clément. The disappearance of AcI complements with verbs of mental action and speech act predicates, which can be assumed on the basis of semantic considerations to have been produced by SOR, did not affect AcI constructions with *lassen* or the verbs of perception (cf. Footnote 3). This fact can be accounted for as a consequence of the loss of SOR from the grammar (or a restriction of SOR to a unitarily characterizable set of cases in which the embedded verb is the copula *sein*, subsequently deleted in the derivation)—if it is accepted that AcI complements with *lassen* and the verbs of perception are produced by rules other than SOR.

## EVIDENCE FOR *LASSEN* AS A CLAUSE UNION CAUSATIVE

If, as the above evidence suggests, Equi is the source for AcI complements with verbs of perception, and if clause-bounded rules can operate down into such complements, then the claim (Aissen 1974a: 14) that ". . . not only do clause-bounded transformations not apply down into embedded S's, they also do not apply down into the remnants of embedded S's which have been reduced by rules like raising into object position [or] EQUI-NP DEL . . ." must be rejected. Further examples, from Gothic and German, are cited in footnotes 5 and 10; they also show that simplex surface structure is only a necessary, not a sufficient, basis for a Clause Union analysis. Therefore other evidence showing that *lassen* is a Clause Union causative must be found.

Such evidence might take two forms. First, there are arguments like those on pp. 128–130 above which show that SOR and Equi cannot be involved in the derivation of *lassen* complements. Second, if *lassen* is a Clause Union causative, one would expect its complements to behave in ways characteristic of the complements of such causatives in other languages. Among the notable cross-linguistic properties of Clause Union causatives are the restrictions on the transformations which can apply in their complements. No transformations are permitted which affect verbal morphology, including those which introduce periphrastic verb forms (Aissen, 1974a).[17] *Lassen* exhibits this property. Not only the passive auxiliary, but tense auxiliaries as well, are blocked from occurring in its complements.[18]

Finally, as Comrie notes, the embedded subject in such complements is displaced by the matrix subject during Clause Union; it moves down a universal case hierarchy *Subject—Direct Object—Indirect Object* . . . to the next available slot—that of the direct object case. If this slot is already occupied by an

---

[17] Aissen (1974b) makes the stronger claim that no cyclic transformation may apply in the embedded sentence. The latter claim is the subject of some controversy. At least the former, however, seems to be universally true.

[18] All AcI complements in German, not only *lassen* complements, are subject to this constraint.

embedded direct object, then the subject assumes the case of the indirect object, and so on down to the case of oblique objects.[19]

On the surface, German *lassen* constructions do not seem to follow this pattern, since (with the exception of the agent phrases occurring in passive infinitive constructions) the embedded subject appears as an accusative no matter how many arguments the embedded verb has:

(33)     *Ich ließ **ihn** kommen.*
          'I let him come.'

(34)     *Ich ließ **ihn** das Kind besuchen.*
          'I let him visit the child.'

(35)     *Ich liess **ihn** dem Kind das Buch geben.*
          'I let him give the child the book.'

There is evidence, however, that the surface case marking in these sentences obscures, rather than reflects, underlying grammatical relationships. In earlier stages of the language the embedded subject in infinitive phrases after *lassen* did in fact surface in the dative case—the case of the indirect object:

(36)          *wenn Sie mir wissen lassen*[20]
                   dat
               'if you let me know'

---

[19] The theoretical ideal of subject displacement is realized, according to Comrie, in only a few languages, including Turkish. In other languages, the following deviations are found: (i) The inability of an embedded subject to be demoted below a certain point on the case hierarchy; (ii) 'Doubling up' of NPs on certain positions on the case hierarchy; and (iii) 'Extended movement'—movement down the hierarchy further than is necessary. Possibilities (ii) and (iii) will be discussed below in relation to *lassen* complements.

Cole (1975) presents arguments from Hebrew showing that displacement of the embedded subject is not the only possibility for reassignment of grammatical relations in the wake of Clause Union. Hebrew has Clause Union constructions in which both embedded subject and embedded object surface as accusative objects. (The embedded direct object may also appear optionally as an oblique NP.) Cole shows, however, that in such cases only the underlying embedded subject is treated as a surface direct object with respect to various matrix transformations, while the accusative object corresponding to the underlying embedded direct object behaves like a displaced NP. Furthermore, if it is assumed that of the two accusative NPs only the underlying embedded subject is a surface direct object, the unmarked order of objects in such constructions can be accounted for. Cole argues that the matter of which NP is displaced during Clause Union is determined by two competing cross-linguistic principles—the Place-holder Principle, according to which an NP tends to remain in its original role, and the Accessibility Hierarchy, according to which NPs lower on the Heirarchy of grammatical relations tend to be displaced by NPs higher on the hierarchy. Where the Placeholder Principle dominates, as in Turkish, the embedded subject is displaced. Where the Accessibility Hierarchy dominates, as in Cole's Hebrew examples, the embedded subject displaces another, lower, NP. Arguments similar to those presented by Cole will be introduced below, showing that Clause Union in German is of the Turkish type.

[20] Lessing, eighteenth century, cited in Grimm and Grimm (1885: Volume 6, 232).

It is possible that the change to accusative case took place on analogy to the accusative objects of *lassen* 'to leave, abandon'. However, the fact that other verbs (including *lehren* 'to teach', which once occurred with dative of person and accusative of object) now appear with double accusatives indicates that this change was part of a more general process.[21] *Lehren* also provides evidence that the accusative case marking is a superficial matter. When the "second" accusative object of *lehren* is passivized, the first appears in the dative case:

(37)             a. *Ich lehrte ihn die Sprache.*
                    'I taught him the language.'

                 b. *Die Sprache wurde ihm gelehrt.*
                                        dat
                    'The language was taught to him.'

If *lassen* is a Clause Union causative, then it is to be expected that the embedded subject of its complement, in spite of its consistent accusative marking, will behave in predictable ways with respect to matrix transformations. Comrie's theory concerning the orderly displacement of the embedded subject makes the prediction that the subject of an embedded intransitive verb will act like a direct object of the matrix sentence, while the subject of a transitive verb will act like an indirect object. German passivization makes precisely this distinction.

Reis (1973) noted that the subject of an intransitive verb embedded under *lassen* is passivizable on the matrix cycle,[22]

(38)             a. *Man ließ ihn warten.*
                    'One let him wait.'

                 b. *Er wurde warten gelassen.*
                    'He was allowed to wait.'

while subjects of transitive verbs are not passivizable in the matrix sentence in German:

(39)             a. *Man ließ die Kinder Torte essen.*
                    'One let the children eat cake.'

                 b. *\*Die Kinder wurden Torte essen gelassen.*

[21] The two verbs are not entirely parallel, however, since many speakers still put the animate object of *lehren* in the dative case. Among young speakers this use of dative seems to be growing. The subjects of *lassen* complements never appear as dative objects.

[22] The passivizability of such NPs varies cross-dialectically. Helbig and Heinrich (1972) claims that no NP of an AcI complement can be passivized in the matrix sentence. Most of my informants, however, found such passivization acceptable.

Accusative objects are freely passivizable. Thus, the grammaticality of (38b) is predicted by the Clause Union approach. Dative objects are not passivizable. Moreover, the Impersonal Passivization in sentences like (18) is not allowed when the sentence contains an accusative object. Therefore, the ungrammaticality of (39b) is also explained by Clause Union.

A problem arises, however, in that not only the embedded subject in (39a), but also the embedded direct object, fails to passivize:

(39)        c. *Torte wurde die Kinder essen gelassen.

In this respect, German differs from the "paradigm" case of Turkish, in which both subjects of embedded intransitives and objects of embedded transitives are capable of passivization. One possible solution to the German problem might be to assume that the embedded direct object (as well as the embedded subject) is somehow displaced to a nonpassivizable grammatical role, and that its accusative marking reflects its former role. Such a solution would be rather arbitrary, however, in view of the fact that, in most languages with verb raising causatives, the displacement of the embedded subject (or, as in Hebrew, of the embedded direct object) is explained by the assumption that another element assumes its role. A claim of mutual displacement in German would therefore lack cross-linguistic support.

Moreover, as observed by Reis, "lassen passives with passive complement subjects seem to be better than those involving active complement subjects, especially if the complement objects are still present (1973: 521)." In other words, embedded direct objects are more readily passivizable on the matrix cycle than are embedded transitive subjects. For Reis:

(40)                  *Er wird töten gelassen.

is more grammatical on the reading 'he is caused to be killed' than on the reading 'he is caused to kill'. Although my informants did not concur on this example, they did find (41a) measurably better than (41b):

(41)     a. ??Das Verfahren wurde mir mitteilen gelassen.
              'The procedure was caused to be communicated to me.'

         b. *Ich wurde das Verfahren mitteilen gelassen.
              'I was caused to communicate the procedure.'

And when presented with a theoretically ambiguous sentence like:

(42)                  *Er wird schlagen gelassen.

and asked to paraphrase it, even those informants who found both readings of (40) equally bad paraphrased (42) as 'he is caused to be hit' rather than 'he is caused to hit'. Thus, while direct objects of transitive verbs in *lassen* complements are not as readily passivizable as are subjects of intransitives, they are, as Clause Union predicts, more readily passivizable than are subjects of transitive verbs.

Further evidence for the claim that the embedded subject of a transitive *lassen* complement becomes an indirect object upon Clause Union is found in the order of objects. When the direct object in German is pronominal, it precedes the indirect object. Otherwise, it follows the indirect object:

(43)                a. *Ich gab ihm das Buch.*
                          IO  DO
                       'I gave him the book.'

                    b. *Ich gab es   dem Mann.*
                          DO IO
                       'I gave it to the man.'

                    c. *Ich gab es   ihm.*
                          DO IO
                       'I gave it to him.'

The order of the underlying subject and direct object of *lassen* complements reflects the same pattern, with some restrictions:

(44)                a. *Ich ließ ihn  das Wort sagen.*
                          him the word
                       'I let him say the word.'

                    a′. *\*Ich ließ das Wort ihn  sagen.*
                          the word him

                    b. *Ich ließ **es ihn** sagen.*
                          it  him
                       'I let him say it.'

                    b′. *?Ich ließ **ihn es** sagen.*
                          him it

                    c. *Ich ließ es einen Assistenten sagen.*
                          it an    assistant
                       'I let an assistant say it.'

                    c′. *?Ich ließ einen Assistenten es sagen.*
                          an    assistant   it

(44b′) and (44c′) exhibit an acceptable, but marked, emphatic order of objects. Note that the more usual order of (44b) and (44c) entails the movement of the pronominal embedded direct object across the embedded subject.

The order of the object NPs in (44) is explainable if it is assumed that the underlying embedded subject has become an indirect object in spite of its surface case marking. Word order, as well as behavior with respect to matrix transformations, appears to be useful in recovering underlying grammatical relations, and many of the apparent instances of 'doubling' in Comrie's treatment may yet turn out to be simply matters of surface case marking, as in German.[23]

In summary, the following evidence exists that Clause Union is involved in the derivation of *lassen* complements:

1.   Such complements meet the necessary condition of simplex surface structure.

2.   They satisfy the restrictions characteristic of Clause Union causatives on transformations which affect verbal morphology.

3.   The Clause Union approach correctly predicts that intransitive subjects of *lassen* complements behave like direct objects with respect to matrix transformations, that embedded transitive subjects behave like indirect objects, and that embedded direct objects are more readily accessible to matrix passivization than are embedded transitive subjects.

4.   The Clause Union approach affords a motivated explanation for the relative ordering of embedded transitive subjects and embedded direct objects in *lassen* complements.

Aissen makes two claims concerning the linear ordering of elements in Verb Raising constructions which are, in the case of German, conflicting. The first of these is that "in all three language types, SOV, SVO, and VSO, the embedded verb ends up contiguous to the matrix verb (1974a: 122)." In Spanish and French, both SVO languages, this condition requires that the embedded verb move across nominal elements of the embedded sentence, while in Maori, a VSO language, no such reordering occurs. Aissen concludes on the basis of this pattern that the process involved is one of raising the verb from the embedded sentence and attaching it to the matrix verb. Her second claim is that, if a causative verb is a verb-raising causative, then it behaves like an auxiliary verb.

*Lassen* meets the second condition, but not the first. Both *lassen* and auxiliary verbs normally occur as the second element of the sentence, while all nonfinite verbs occur clause-finally. An auxiliary verb and its dependent infinitive are

[23] As noted in Footnote 19, Cole has demonstrated that double accusative marking in Hebrew Clause Union constructions is also a superficial matter. Only the accusative object corresponding to the original embedded subject behaves like a direct object. In Hebrew, unlike German, the double accusative marking can be explained naturally. The original direct object is assigned its accusative case on the lower cycle. During Clause Union, this direct object is displaced by the embedded subject, while optionally retaining its previous case marking. The new direct object, in the meantime, is re-marked according to its new role. Such an analysis will not work in German because all available evidence indicates that the embedded subject, not the embedded object, is displaced.

adjacent only if the embedded sentence happens to lack other NPs, adverbs, etc.:

(45)                             a. *Ich kann kommen.*
                                    'I can come.'

                                 b. *Ich **kann** mit euch **kommen**.*
                                    'I can come with you.'

Adjacency is usually blocked with *lassen*, since its complement must always contain at least one NP argument.

The requirement that the causative and embedded verbs be adjacent seems to exist only in those languages in which auxiliaries and dependent nonfinite verbs are normally adjacent. Where a different placement of auxiliaries and infinitive forms is the rule, as in German, then the Clause Union causative and the dependent infinitive will not be adjacent. Toman (1975) observes that Clause Union constructions in Czech also fail to meet the adjacency requirement, but that in that language they do pattern as *auxiliary* + *infinitive* constructions. The proper generalization, therefore, seems to be the 'behavior as auxiliary' condition. This condition, moreover, seems to be a manifestation of the still more general fact that the order of elements in Clause Union constructions is parallel to that in simple sentences.

As seen above, the surface order of the NPs of *lassen* complements is similar to that exhibited by simple sentences [cf. sentences (16) and (44)]. Aissen notes that the same is true of French. A subject of a transitive complement embedded under *faire* becomes an indirect object, and as such must appear to the right of the embedded direct object:

(46)                             **J'ai fait lire à Jean le livre.*
                                    'I made Jean read the book.'

One of the explanations she considers for this reordering is that Verb Raising raises the verb and its accusative object, moving both as a unit over the embedded subject. In German, however, such a rule would not work, since the relative order of the embedded object and embedded subject depends on whether the embedded object is a noun or a pronoun. To repeat previous examples:

(44)                             a'. **Ich ließ das Wort ihn  sagen.*
                                                        him
                                    'I let him say the word.'

                                 b. *Ich ließ **es ihn** sagen.*
                                              it  him
                                    'I let him say it.'

The order of elements in VR constructions in a given language is the same as that in simple sentences. As an alternative to trying to incorporate this information into the rule itself, thereby sacrificing its cross-linguistic validity, Aissen (1974a) mentions the possibility that there is a transderivational rule which effects the necessary changes. She questions, however, whether limiting a rule in terms of target output is possible in a standard transformational model. But such problems cease to be problems if, as Toman and others suggest, the base of the grammar consists of labelled grammatical relations without linear ordering, rather than linear configurations which define grammatical relations. In such a model, Clause Union would erase the embedded S-node and trigger the demotion of the embedded subject to its new grammatical role. Subsequently, language-specific linearization rules—like the ones in German placing infinitives in clause-final position and ordering direct and indirect objects—would apply to the simplex output of Clause Union. This approach allows a cross-linguistically valid formulation of Clause Union in terms of the changes in grammatical relations which it effects, and explains the parallels between the order of elements in Clause Union constructions and the order of elements in simple sentences.

## *LASSEN* COMPLEMENTS AND EXTENDED MOVEMENT

In a number of languages with Clause Union causatives, it is possible for the embedded subject to surface as an oblique NP agent phrase even when some of the positions above oblique in the Accessibility Hierarchy remain vacant [cf. sentence (3)]. German is one such language. The embedded subject may appear as the object of the preposition *von*, or as $\emptyset$ if it is indefinite.

Comrie considers two possible explanations for such cases. According to the first, the agent phrase is a relic of passivization in the embedded sentence—or at least that portion of Passive involving the demotion of the subject to the agent phrase. The second analysis views the agent phrase in such sentences as a consequence of 'extended movement' of the embedded subject during Clause Union all the way down the hierarchy to the role of oblique NP. The fact that the case marking or prepositions of such NPs correspond to those of passive agent results from a general principle that a NP demoted to oblique, regardless of the rule involved, always ends up in the same case.

Comrie rejects the first analysis on the basis of facts like the following:

1. Finnish subjects embedded under causatives can surface as adessive case NPs, even though Finnish has no passive constructions with agents in the adessive case.

2. In Turkish, the embedded subject can surface as an object of the agentive preposition *tarafİndan* only if the embedded S contains both a direct and an indirect object (i.e. only if the next role available to the demoted subject is

that of oblique object). In normal passivized sentences in Turkish, however, the underlying subject becomes an object of *tarafIndan* even though the sentence lacks an indirect object. At least in Turkish, therefore, the view that Clause Union demotion of the subject is responsible seems more plausible.

There are two facts which indicate that the passivization analysis is, at least for German, the correct one. First, the restrictions on the predicates which can occur as passive infinitives (with or without agent phrases) in *lassen* complements are largely coextensive with those on predicates which allow passivization.

Certain transitive verbs in German do not allow passivization; nor can these verbs appear as passive infinitives under *lassen*. Compare (47a–b) with (47c–d):

(47)   a. *\*Das Buch wird*                 [*von    Kindern*] $\begin{Bmatrix} gehabt. \\ bekommen. \end{Bmatrix}$

   passive auxiliary  agent phrase     past participle

   'The book is $\begin{Bmatrix} \text{had} \\ \text{gotten} \end{Bmatrix}$ by children.'

   b. *\*Das Buch$_i$ läßt sich$_i$ nicht* [*von Kindern*] $\begin{Bmatrix} haben. \\ bekommen. \end{Bmatrix}$

   'The book doesn't let itself be (= can't be) $\begin{Bmatrix} \text{had} \\ \text{gotten} \end{Bmatrix}$ by children.

   c. *Das Buch wird von Kindern verstanden.*
   'The book is understood by children.'

   d. *Das Buch$_i$ läßt sich$_i$ nicht von Kindern verstehen.*
   'The book doesn't let itself (= can't be) understood by children.

There is also a large class of intransitive verbs in German which can be passivized, with insertion of a dummy subject *es*. (For reasons of focus, such constructions rarely contain definite agent phrases, and, since indefinite agents are obligatorily deleted, they are usually agentless.) The same verbs can appear as passive infinitives with *lassen*:

(48)                    a. *Es wird* $\begin{Bmatrix} gelaufen. \\ getanzt. \\ geschlafen. \end{Bmatrix}$

   'It is $\begin{Bmatrix} \text{run.'} \\ \text{danced.'} \\ \text{slept.'} \end{Bmatrix} = $ 'One $\begin{Bmatrix} \text{runs.'} \\ \text{dances.'} \\ \text{sleeps.'} \end{Bmatrix}$

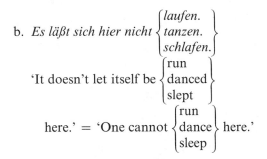

b. *Es läßt sich hier nicht* { *laufen.* / *tanzen.* / *schlafen.* }

'It doesn't let itself be { run / danced / slept }

here.' = 'One cannot { run / dance / sleep } here.'

One condition on such intransitive passives is that the underlying subject must be animate. The same condition applies to intransitive passive infinitives in *lassen* complements:

(49)  a. *\*Es wird geblüht.*
'It is bloomed.'

b. *\*Es läßt sich blühen.*
'It lets itself be bloomed.'

Among those intransitive verbs which do take an animate subject, there are some which cannot be passivized. Nor can these occur as passive infinitives with *lassen*:

(50)  a. *\*Es wird gekommen.*
'It is come.'

b. *\*Es läßt sich nicht kommen.*
'It doesn't let itself be come.'

Finally, sentences in which intransitive verbs occur with free accusatives cannot be passivized, nor can such intransitive verbs occur as passive complements with *lassen*:

(51)  a. *Er stirbt den Tod fürs Vaterland.*
            acc
'He dies the (=a) death for the fatherland.'

b. *\*Der Tod fürs Vaterland wird **von ihm** gestorben.*
   nom             by him
'A death for the fatherland is died by him.'

c. *Er läßt ihn den Tod fürs Vaterland sterben.*
     him
'He lets him die a death for the fatherland.'

    d. *\*Er läßt den Tod fürs Vaterland **von ihm** sterben.*
                                            by  him
              'He lets a death for the fatherland be died by him.'

Such parallels can be accounted for by assuming that passive infinitive constructions with *lassen* actually do involve passivization, and that the agent phrases arise through passivization.

Alternatively, it could be argued that the restriction on nonpassivizable verbs is in fact a restriction preventing all subject-demotion processes, including extended movement as well as passive demotion, from applying to their subjects. Such a claim will not stand without further modification, however, since in the "normal" Clause Union construction of (51c) the embedded subject is demoted (although not to oblique) without producing an ungrammatical sentence. The restriction would therefore have to be one blocking only the demotion of the subjects of these verbs to the role of oblique NP.

Moreover, as noted above, the embedded subject of a *lassen* complement normally shows up as an accusative marked NP rather than as an oblique agent, even when all roles above oblique NP are filled. Since the output of "normal" movement of the embedded subject down the hierarchy is not an oblique NP even when the positions above oblique are occupied, there is all the less reason for suspecting that agent phrases in *lassen* complements result from extended movement.

The second argument for a passive rather than an extended movement analysis concerns the source of the reflexive pronoun *sich* in sentences like (52c):

(52)        a. *Man tanzt hier nicht* ⇒
            'One doesn't dance here.'

        b. *Es wird (\*von einem* ⇒ ∅) *hier nicht getanzt.*
            'It isn't danced here.'

        c. *Es$_i$ läßt **sich**$_i$ hier nicht tanzen.*
            'It does not let itself (=can't be) danced here.'

        d. *Er$_i$ läßt **sich**$_i$ nicht so behandeln.*
            'He doesn't let himself be treated like that.'

The only apparent source for this *sich* is the *es* inserted as subject into intransitive passive sentences like (52b), with subsequent reflexivization parallel to that in (52d). In turn, the *es* in (52b) may come from one of two sources. Either it is inserted by a subrule of the Object Promotion half of Passive reading, *scan the sentence for nominativizable NP to make subject. If there is none, insert es;* or it is introduced by the rule inserting *es* into the initial position of sentences without initial subjects, as in:

(53)        a.   *Die folgenden Leute werden sprechen* ⇒
                 'The following people will speak.'

            b.   *∅ werden die folgenden Leute sprechen* ⇒
                 'The following people will speak.'

            c.   *Es werden die folgenden Leute sprechen.*
                 'The following people will speak.'

In either case, the Extended Movement analysis fails to explain the presence of the pronoun in (52c). The first possible source for it, that of insertion by Object Promotion on the embedded cycle, requires that both Subject Demotion and Object Promotion apply prior to Clause Union. The Extended Movement hypothesis claims, on the other hand, that demotion of the subject is a consequence of Clause Union. The second possible source, that of *es* insertion into vacated initial-subject position, is also incompatible with the Extended Movement analysis, since according to this analysis demotion of the embedded subject would occur only through Clause Union, and the vacated subject slot would immediately be filled by the matrix subject, leaving no need for *es*-insertion to apply. (If *es* insertion is postcyclic, this analysis fails.)

The Passive analysis, therefore, appears preferable to the Extended Movement analysis in German because it explains why nonpassivizable verbs should also not be able to occur as passive infinitives with agent phrases in *lassen* complements, and because it offers an explanation for the presence of *sich* in intransitive complements like that in (52c).

## *LASSEN* COMPLEMENTS AND PRECYCLICITY

As noted on p. 137 above, Clause Union causative constructions are universally characterized by restrictions on the set of transformations which can apply on the embedded cycle. The nature of these restrictions, as well as an explanation for them, remains a matter of dispute.

In her dissertation Aissen (1974a) suggested that the constraint blocks any transformations which affect verbal morphology from applying (including those which create periphrastic verb forms). In her article on Verb Raising (1974b), Aissen makes the stronger claim that no cyclic transformation may apply in Verb Raising complements—although she notes that some speakers of French do allow reflexivization on the embedded cycle. The explanation she offers for the claimed failure of cyclic transformations to apply in these complements is that Verb Raising is a precyclic rule.

In German the application of most cyclic rules, including (possibly) Reflexivization, and Equi, does not shed any light on the problem of whether Clause Union is in fact precyclic, since they may be triggered by subjects, direct objects, or indirect objects.[24] Reflexivization in (54), therefore, could have been triggered by *ihn* either while it was still the underlying embedded subject or subsequent to its transformation into matrix object:

(54)                                        *Ich ließ ihn$_i$ über* **sich**$_i$ *reden.*
                                            'I let him talk about himself.'

Some evidence does exist in German, however, which seems to indicate that the precyclic hypothesis is wrong. First of all, either of the two rules which could account for the presence of *sich* (deriving from *es*) in sentences like (52c)—Object Promotion and Initial *es*-Insertion—would have to apply prior to Clause Union, since Clause Union destroys their structural description, and both of them are cyclic. The cyclicity of Object Promotion has been established in a great number of languages; it seems to be universal. Initial *es*-Insertion must also be at least cyclic, since it is ordered after Object Promotion, Number Agreement, and Extraposition [cf. (53)].[25]

In addition, as seen in example (6), the case of an object of the verb embedded under *lassen* is determined by that verb, while the (surface) case of the embedded subject is assigned to it by *lassen*. Case marking must therefore apply both before and after Clause Union; yet, as demonstrated by its application after Passive, case marking must be a cyclic rule. Again, this fact provides evidence that the precyclic hypothesis cannot be correct.

## ACKNOWLEDGMENTS

Research for this paper was conducted within the framework of the Illinois Project on Universals of Grammatical Organization and Rule Interaction, National Science Foundation grant SOC75–00244. I would like to thank Peter Cole, Irmengard Rauch, and Paul Roberge for their helpful comments on and criticisms of earlier versions of this paper.

[24] In Bierwisch (1963), as in traditional treatments, reflexivization is regarded as being triggered by subjects only. If this is true, then the cyclicity of Clause Union appears indisputable. There is evidence, however, that German reflexivization can be triggered by direct objects—and sometimes, at least, by indirect objects, as in the following example:

> *Ich erzählte ihm eine Geschichte von sich selbst.*
> 'I told him a story about himself.'

[25] Both of these rules are relation creating, and it has been claimed by Postal and others that relation-creating rules are essentially cyclic.

Postal (1974) also maintains that there are no abdication rules. All demotions must be triggered by the replacement of the demoted element. If this claim is correct, then object promotion must precede demotion. The latter therefore cannot be precyclic, as Aissen claims. Keenan, however, argues that the universal aspect of the passivization transformation is that of demotion: "In several languages PASSIVE can demote a Su[bject] without promoting anything else" [1975:347].

# REFERENCES

Aissen, J. (1974a) *The Syntax of Causative Constructions*, unpublished Doctoral dissertation, Harvard University, Cambridge, Massachusetts.

Aissen, J. (1974b) "Verb Raising," *Linguistic Inquiry* 5, 325–366.

Behagel, O. (1923–1932) *Deutsche Syntax*, 4 vols., Carl Winter Universitätsverlag, Heidelberg.

Bierwisch, M. (1963) *Grammatik des deutschen Verbs*, Akademie Verlag, Berlin.

Clement, D. (1971) "Satzeinbettungen nach Verben der Sinneswahrnehmung im Deutschen," in Dieter Wunderlich, ed., *Probleme und Fortschritte der Transformationsgrammatik*, (Max Hueber Verlag,) Munich.

Cole, P. (1975) "Verb Raising in Modern Hebrew," presented at the Summer Meeting of the Linguistic Society of America.

Comrie, B. (1973) "Causatives and Universal Grammar," unpublished paper, University of Cambridge, Cambridge.

Ebert, R. (1972) *On Predicate Complementation in Geiler's Seelenparadies*, unpublished Doctoral dissertation, University of Wisconsin, Madison, Wisconsin.

Ebert, R. (1975) "Subject Raising, the Clause Squish, and German *scheinen*-Constructions," in R. E. Grossman, L. J. Sam, and T. J. Vance, eds., *Papers from the Eleventh Regional Meeting of the Chicago Linguistic Society*, University of Chicago, Chicago, Illinois.

Grimm, W. and J. Grimm (1885) *Deutsches Worterbuch*, revised by Morris Heyne, Verlag von S. Hirzel, Leipzig.

Helbig, G., and G. Heinrich (1972) *Das Vorgangspassiv*, VEB Verlag Enzyclopädie, Leipzig.

Keenan, E. L. (1975) "Some Universals of Passive in Relational Grammar," in R. E. Grossman, L. J. Vance, eds., *Papers from the Eleventh Regional Meeting of the Chicago Linguistic Society*, University of Chicago, Chicago, Illinois.

Postal, P. (1974) "Report of Work Done as Part of the MSSB Workshop on Constraints on Grammars," duplicated, IBM Thomas J. Watson Research Center, Yorktown Heights, New York.

Reis, M. (1973) "Is There a Rule of Subject-to-Object Raising in German?", in C. Corum, T. C. Smith Stark, and A. Weiser, eds., *Papers from the Ninth Regional Meeting of the Chicago Linguistic Society*, University of Chicago, Chicago, Illinois.

Streitberg, W. (1971) *Die Gotische Bibel*, 6th ed., Carl Winter Universitätsverlag, Heidelberg.

Toman, J. (1975) "Clause Union in Czech," unpublished paper.

# ON RELATIONAL CONSTRAINTS ON GRAMMARS

*DAVID E. JOHNSON*
*IBM Thomas J. Watson Research Center*

## INTRODUCTION

The fundamental problem of theoretical linguistics can be taken to be the precise characterization of the essential properties of human language, i.e. the construction of a comprehensive, general theory of the structure and organization of language or, more simply, a universal grammar.[1] Within the broad problem of developing an empirically adequate universal grammar, one can isolate the following fundamental questions:

1. THE EXISTENCE QUESTION: *What syntactic rules can occur in natural languages?*
2. THE SELECTION QUESTION: *Given a universal set of possible syntactic rules, what rules can (or must) a given language 'select'? I.e., are there any conditions on which rules will appear in particular languages?*

---

[1] In this study I will ignore the complications created by the phenomenon of ergativity. It is argued in Johnson (to appear and in preparation) that ergativity can be adequately accounted for within the present type of system.

The following abbreviations are used: A = absolutive; acc = accusative; BEN = benefactive; CH = chômeur; COM = comitative; comp = complementizer; dat = dative; DO = direct object (of); dc = direct object chômeur marker; do = direct object marker; E = ergative; ind = indefinite; INS = instrumental (of); inm = instrumental voice marker; IO = indirect object (of); io = indirect object marker; nm = noun marker; OO = oblique object (of); oo = oblique object marker; pr = purposive marker; prt = particle; S = subject (of); sc = subject chômeur marker; S-ch = subject chômeur; sm = subject marker; tns = tense; trans = transitive; vm = voice marker.

Data and claims referencing Chung (to appear), Keenan (to appear), Keenan and Comrie (to appear), Lawler (this volume), and Schachter (to appear) are from the unpublished versions of these papers.

151

In one form or another, both of these questions have been discussed in the linguistic literature. Bach (1971), for instance, states:

> The strongest hypothesis about transformations that seems worth considering is that there is a fixed finite list of transformations available for any language. Of course, this cannot be literally true if we maintain the definition of transformation that is currently accepted. What I would ultimately look for would be a general definition of "major transformations" such that we could divide the transformations of each language into major transformations from such a universal list and much more severely limited minor transformations or "housekeeping" rules. In the meantime, however, a good working hypothesis would be that transformations such as question rules, topicalizations, subject-formation, relative clause, subject-raising, imperatives, and so on, would have to be chosen from a fixed list. We could then make predictions like this: given certain structural features of a language, its relative clause rule will have such and such features, it will (or will not) have a topicalization rule, and so on [p. 154].

> Question movement will occur only in SVO and VSO languages, never in (deep) SOV languages [p. 164].

Until very recently, however, little attention has been given to determining how grammatical relations bear upon these questions.[2]

Perlmutter and Postal (forthcoming) and Johnson (1974b) have advanced a number of hypotheses, crucially dependent upon grammatical relations, that restrict the class of possible rules (the Existence Question), and Perlmutter and Postal (forthcoming), Keenan and Comrie (to appear) and Johnson (1974a and 1974b) have discussed relational constraints that restrict the rules a language might "pick" (the Selection Question). But this type of investigation is in its infancy.[3] It is the purpose of this paper to examine certain aspects of the role that grammatical relations play in restricting the type and selection of syntactic rules. The major point to be argued is that there are a number of universal principles referring to grammatical relations at work in natural languages which have the effect of substantially limiting the rules which particular languages may have. The theoretical viewpoint adopted is that of Relational Grammar (RG). The choice is not arbitrary, since this framework both encourages one to look for such regularities and provides the theoretical underpinnings necessary for stating them in a principled manner. For the benefit of those who are not familiar with RG, a very brief overview is provided in the following section.[4]

---

[2] Cf. Chomsky (1973); Keenan and Comrie (to appear); Johnson (1974a, 1974b, and in preparation); Perlmutter (1968); Perlmutter and Postal (forthcoming); Postal (1969, 1974a, 1974b, and 1975); and Ross (1974).

[3] By 'relational constraint' I simply mean any principle or condition which crucially refers to grammatical relations.

[4] The facts discussed in this paper indicate that information concerning grammatical relations must be universally present at nonunderlying as well as at underlying derivational levels. Since transformational grammar does not provide a principled way to refer to grammatical relations (at any level), it cannot, in general, state relational constraints in a theoretically adequate manner. For specific arguments that transformational grammar is fundamentally inadequate in its treatment of grammatical relations, see Johnson (1974a, 1974b, and in preparation) and Perlmutter and Postal (forthcoming).

## OVERVIEW OF RELATIONAL GRAMMAR

This section contains a very sketchy overview of Relational Grammar as the present writer currently conceives of it.[5] I do not intend to present a justification of Relational Grammar here. Many arguments supporting its basic tenets can be found in Perlmutter and Postal (forthcoming); Johnson (1974a, 1974b, and in preparation), Postal (1974a and 1975), and Pullum (1975a; see also Pullum's chapter in this volume).

### General Viewpoint

The fundamental tenet of Relational Grammar is that grammatical relations such as 'subject of' and 'direct object of' play a central role in the syntax of natural languages, i.e. they are the proper units for the description of many aspects of clause structure at various derivational levels and figure directly in the statement of numerous grammatical rules and universal principles which govern the structure and organization of the syntax of natural languages. Relational Grammar posits these grammatical relations as primitives in linguistic theory. This contrasts with the position of standard transformational grammar, which views such relations as definable in terms of the constituent structure notions of 'dominance' and 'precedence.'[6]

### Some Specifics

#### DEFINITIONS AND NOTATION

RG posits a fixed, universal set of primitive 'pure' grammatical relations $GR = \{subject\text{-}of(S), direct\text{-}object\text{-}of(DO), indirect\text{-}object\text{-}of(IO)\}$ and a set of 'impure' grammatical relations such as INSTRUMENTAL, LOCATIVE, and BENE-FACTIVE, which, unlike the pure relations, have independent semantic content.[7]

---

[5] In the early 1970s a number of independent observations and discoveries by Comrie, Keenan, Morgan, Perlmutter, Postal, and Ross sparked an ever-growing awareness in the linguistic community that grammatical relations play a central role in the syntax of natural languages. In 1972 Perlmutter and Postal (in a number of lectures) first proposed and presented arguments that transformational generative grammar should be replaced by a theory of Relational Grammar. The present account presents only the very broadest (and consequently oversimplified) outline of Relational Grammar. This overview rests heavily upon the views of Perlmutter and Postal as I understand them but also reflects my own thinking on the subject. (See Perlmutter and Postal, forthcoming, for a definitive account of their conception of Relational Grammar; cf. Johnson 1974a, 1974b, to appear, and in preparation.)

[6] See Johnson (1974b) for a detailed criticism of the Chomskyan approach to defining grammatical relations. Cf. Keenan (1976) and Perlmutter and Postal (forthcoming). Keenan (1976) proposes to define the notion 'subject of' in terms of a conglomeration of more primitive syntactic and semantic properties. For criticism of this approach, see Johnson (to appear and in preparation).

[7] The terms 'pure' and 'impure' are taken from Perlmutter and Postal (forthcoming). Perlmutter and Postal also posit many other primitive grammatical relations, e.g. 'conjunct of', 'precedes', and 'flag of' (the relation which prepositions, postpositions, and cases bear to their arguments). These will not be discussed here.

An NP which holds an impure grammatical relation will be termed an OBLIQUE OBJECT (OO). Following Perlmutter and Postal (forthcoming), NPs holding pure relations will be referred to as TERMS. Subject and direct object relations will be referred to as NUCLEAR RELATIONS; and, correspondingly, subjects and direct objects will be called NUCLEAR TERMS. A primitive grammatical relation of general (nondesignated) dependency, the X RELATION, is also postulated. If $a$ bears a designated grammatical relation to $b$, $GR_i(a, b)$, then $a$ is generally dependent on $b$, or, simply dependent on $b$, $X(a, b)$. However, the converse does not necessarily hold, i.e. $X(a, b)$ does not imply $GR_i(a, b)$.

In RG, a clause (at a given derivational level) is viewed as consisting basically of a predicate ($V$) and a number of nominal arguments, each of which bears exactly one grammatical relation to the governing $V$. Like transformational generative grammar, RG involves a multilevel theory of clause structure, and thus the characterization of a particular sentence necessitates the specification of the relational structure of that sentence at various derivational levels. For example, in *Max was hit by John with a balloon*, *Max* is the initial direct object and the cyclic subject of *hit*; *John* is the initial subject and the cyclic 'subject chômeur' of *hit*, and *a balloon* is both the initial and cyclic instrument of *hit*.[8] The initial and cyclic levels of this sentence are related by the relation-changing rule of Passive, which creates a derived subject from a direct object. This "advancement" has the effect of putting the input subject in CHÔMAGE. This change in grammatical relations is held to be the fundamental, universal property of passivization. Linear order and changes in verbal and nominal morphology are considered to be language-specific side effects (to use Perlmutter and Postal's terminology).

As a first approximation, the universal aspect of Passive can be represented in relational terms as follows:

(1)                    Passive (in relational terms) (DO → S)

        a.  $DO(A, V_i) \rightarrow S(A, V_i)$
        b.   $S(B, V_i) \rightarrow X(B, V_i)$

As mentioned above, various language-specific parameters such as verbal and

---

[8] The terms 'initial' and 'cyclic' are due to Postal, who defines a 'cyclic subject (of C)' as "the subject of C at the end of the (sub)cycle determined by C" and an 'initial subject (of C)' as "the first subject that C has in a derivation" (1976:156). The latter usually corresponds to the subject in base structure, except in cases where new compound verbs are created by rules like Predicate Raising. These definitions are carried over to the other grammatical relations. In a more detailed treatment the question of the level at which a particular relation holds between an NP and a V becomes of paramount importance.

CHÔMEUR, French for 'unemployed', is the Perlmutter-Postal term for an NP whose grammatical relation has been usurped by virtue of the application of some relation-changing rule. A subject that has been put in CHÔMAGE is a s(ubject)-CHÔMEUR; more generally, an NP whose grammatical relation G has been usurped is a G-CHÔMEUR. A chômeur of a given $V$ bears the $X$ relation to that $V$.

nominal morphology must be specified for each language which has the process of passivization, i.e. the rule in (1) is a rule schema out of which language-particular rules can be constructed.

Grammatical rules fall into two broad classes: those that do not alter grammatical relations, such as Pronominalization, Case Assignment, and Verb Agreement, and those that do, such as Passive, Dative Movement, and Subject-to-Object Raising. Under the Perlmutter-Postal conception of Relational Grammar, there are three types of relation-changing rules: Promotions, Deletions, and Clause Unions (Predicate Raisings). Promotions fall into three classifications: INSERTIONS, ASCENSIONS, and ADVANCEMENTS. Insertions involve the insertion of a 'dummy' NP or the replacement of a given NP of a clause bearing a grammatical relation $GR_i$ to the verb of that clause with a dummy NP; examples are the rules of *It*-extraposition and *there*-insertion in English. Ascensions involve the replacement of some NP, the HOST, which is a term of a given clause, by another NP which is part of the host. Examples of Ascensions in English include Quantifier Floating (e.g. *all of the men are here → the men are all here*) and Subject-to-Object Raising.[9]

To elaborate slightly and informally, in the case of Subject-to-Object Raising, the subject ($A$) of a host subordinate clause ($H$) which bears the direct object relation to the verb ($V$) of a superordinate clause assumes the direct object relation to $V$. Concomitantly $A$ ceases to bear the subject relation to the governing verb in $H$ and, furthermore, $H$ ceases to bear the direct object relation to $V$. Not all of these facts must be stated in the rule, however, since much of the reassignment of grammatical relations is performed automatically by general relational principles. In particular, the fact that $A$ ceases to bear the subject relation to the lower verb and the fact that $H$ ceases to bear the direct object relation to the higher verb are automatic consequences—they result from the application of two general relational principles:

1. THE UNIQUE DEPENDENCY PRINCIPLE: *When an NP assumes a grammatical relation, it ceases to bear any other grammatical relation.*

2. THE RELATIONAL ANNIHILATION PRINCIPLE (Perlmutter and Postal, forthcoming): *When an NP, $NP_i$, assumes the grammatical relation G borne by another NP, $NP_j (i \neq j)$, then $NP_j$ ceases to bear G and in* CHÔMAGE.

For instance, in *John believes Bill to be ill* (from *John believes that Bill is ill*), *Bill* (the former subject of the embedded clause, *Bill is ill*, which bore the direct object relation to the higher verb believe) has assumed the direct object relation to believe. Consequently, by these two principles, *Bill* ceases to be the subject of the embedded clause and the embedded clause ceases to bear the direct object relation to *believe* and is a DIRECT OBJECT CHÔMEUR.

---

[9] See Postal (1976) for a relational account of Quantifier Floating contrasted with a transformational account of this phenomenon and Postal (1974b) for a detailed discussion of Subject-to-Object Raising.

Advancements are cases where a given NP which holds a grammatical relation $GR_i$ to $V_j$ assumes another grammatical relation $GR_j$ to $V_j$; where $GR_j <$ $GR_i$ on the Relational Hierarchy: $S < DO < IO < OO$ (see below).[10] Two well-known examples of advancements are Passive and so-called Dative Movement (indirect object advances to direct object). Notice that it follows from the Relational Annihilation Law (RAL) that the subject of the input clause to Passive becomes a SUBJECT CHÔMEUR, i.e. (1b) need not be stated in the rule itself. Similarly, the direct object of the input clause to Dative Movement automatically becomes a direct object chômeur. E.g. the derivation of *John gave Mary a book* would involve the following:

(2)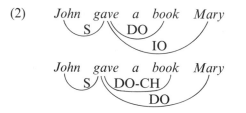

[by (IO → DO) and RAL]

A number of universal principles refer to the Relational Hierarchy (Perlmutter and Postal, forthcoming):

(3)                        The Relational Hierarchy

$$S < DO < IO < OO$$

where if $A < B$, $A$ is said to 'have precedence over' or to 'outrank' $B$.

A central principle of RG which makes crucial use of the Relational Hierarchy (RH) is the Reranking Law (Perlmutter and Postal, forthcoming):

(4)   THE RERANKING LAW: *A rule that alters the status of an NP with respect to termhood must increase the rank of that NP.* DEFINITION OF RANK: *within a structure* Q, *a constituent* A *outranks a consituent* B *if* A *unilaterally 'commands'* B; *or, if* A *and* B *command each other and* A *is higher in the RH than* B. *Elements not in* Q *have zero rank in* Q.[11]

---

[10] Note that all advancements are clause-internal; ascensions can be clause-internal (e.g. Quantifier Floating) or cross-clause (e.g. Subject-to-Object Raising).

[11] What is meant here is the relational analogue of the constituent structure notion 'command'. Essentially the same principle, independently discovered, was presented in Johnson (1974b: Chapter 5, "The Usurpation Principle." All rules either move NPs up the AH or raise NPs into a superordinate clause (where the AH refers to the Keenan-Comrie Accessibility Hierarchy; cf. below on relational constraints). Also independently discovered and presented in Johnson (1974b: Chapter 5) was the X-RATING CONVENTION: any NP whose grammatical relation is usurped is x-rated, which is the analogue in the system described there to the Perlmutter-Postal Relational Annihilation Law.

RG posits many other universal principles which substantially reduce the number of possible grammars compatible with linguistic theory. Several examples taken from Perlmutter and Postal (forthcoming) follow:

(5)　a.　THE RELATIONAL SUCCESSION LAW: *An NP promoted by an ascension rule assumes the grammatical relation borne by the host out of which it ascends.*

　　　b.　THE AGREEMENT LAW: *Only terms can trigger verbal agreement.*

　　　c.　THE REFLEXIVIZATION LAW: *Only terms can trigger reflexivization.*

　　　d.　THE COREFERENTIAL DELETION LAW: *Only terms can trigger coreferential deletion.*

Other universal relational principles will be the major topic of the subsequent discussion.

## RELATIONAL CONSTRAINTS

### Primacy Conditions

Several years ago, Ross (1974) proposed the following as a universal principle:

(6)　THE PRIMACY CONSTRAINT: *Subjects have primacy over objects, and no rule works more freely for objects than for subjects.*

An early example illustrating the primacy constraint was the rule of Raising. At the time that Ross first proposed that Primacy Constraint, it seemed that if a language could raise subjects to object status then it could also raise them to subject status. More recent work, however, has shed doubt on this claim; in particular, it appears that Japanese and Latin allow Subject-to-Object, but not Subject-to-Subject, Raising (Ross 1974). Other examples include Equi and Reflexivization; the Primacy Constraint predicts that, to quote Ross, "any language allowing non-subjects to control Equi or to antecede reflexives should also allow subjects to" (1974:574). These predictions appear to be borne out. (Examples are given on pp. 166–168.)

At about the same time, Keenan and Comrie (to appear) surveyed the relative clause formation (RCF) strategies in over forty languages and found that the following cross-linguistic generalization holds:

(7)　ACCESSIBILITY TO RELATIVE CLAUSE FORMATION: *If, by means of RCF, a language can relativize an NP holding position X on the Accessibility Hierarchy (AH), then it can relativize NPs holding positions higher than X on the AH: S ≥ DO ≥ IO ≥ OO ≥ Possessor-NP ≥ Object of Comparative Particle.*

Keenan and Comrie also claimed (but did not substantiate) that the AH holds for other "focusing" operations such as Wh-Question Formation and Clefting. The evidence from their RCF data indicates that, in certain cases, Ross's general notion of primacy must be refined to take into account primacy relations among nonsubjects as well as between subjects and nonsubjects. It is apparent, however, that the same basic generalization is lurking under both of these principles. Moreover, the Keenan-Comrie AH bears a striking resemblance to the Perlmutter-Postal RH, which was established in part from very different considerations, e.g. the statement of the Reranking Law, as well as from their discovery that certain rules, e.g. Quantifier Floating (which applies only to terms) and Dummy Insertion (which applies only to nuclear terms) conform to the RH: i.e. in a language $L$, if a term $T_i$ can float quantifiers or undergo Dummy Insertion, then any term $T_j$, $j < i$ on the RH, can float quantifiers or undergo Dummy Insertion. Johnson (1974a and 1974b) presented evidence that advancements to subjecthood also conform to the RH; Moravcsik (1974) has found that the same restriction holds in regard to verb agreement.[12]

It should be noted in passing that the '$<$' of the Perlmutter-Postal RH is not logically equivalent to the '$\geq$' of the Keenan-Comrie AH. The symbol '$<$' of the RH is a theoretical term which has no direct interpretation such as 'as accessible to'. The notion 'as accessible to RCF' is easily definable on the RH (ignoring the positions not held in common): If $A < B$ on the RH, then $A \geq B$ on the AH. Notice that other definitions would be logically possible: e.g. if $A < B$ on the RH, then $B \geq A$ on the AH; and it is even conceivable that the two might have no principled relationship to each other. The fact that the AH and the RH have the same relative ordering for all positions that they have in common provides impressive empirical support for the universality of the ranking $S < DO < IO < OO$.[13] Such remarkable cross-linguistic consistency in the ranking of NPs with respect to different grammatical phenomena helps to motivate and provide meaning for the theoretical terms S, DO, and IO in RG, since these primitive syntactic terms gain their significance not by direct interpretation, but rather by virtue of their participation in a complex system of principles which govern the behavior of NPs that bear these relations.

Determining the exact manner and extent to which primacy conditions hold in natural languages is, from the viewpoint of universal grammar, a fundamental problem. The rest of this paper will be largely devoted to a further consideration of this topic.

---

[12] This phenomenon has been called 'line drawing' by Perlmutter and Postal (forthcoming).

[13] It should be stressed that the RH and the AH refer to both underlying and nonunderlying grammatical relations, i.e., they assume that grammatical relations are well-defined at other than the 'deep structure' level (cf. Chomsky 1965:253–258, and Johnson 1974b:Chapter 2). Also, notice that, since the languages investigated differ in word order, the differential relativizability of constituents could not be attributed to left-right order asymmetry without sacrificing the cross-linguistic generalizations embodied in the hierarchies.

### The Advancement-to-Subject Chaining Constraint

As briefly noted in the previous section, Johnson (1974a and 1974b) presented evidence that what can be advanced to subjecthood in particular languages obeys the following principle:

(8)  THE ADVANCEMENT-TO-SUBJECT CHAINING CONSTRAINT (ASC): *If a language* L *can advance NPs holding position* B *on the RH to subjecthood, then for any position* A, *if* A $<$ B, *then* L *can also advance NPs holding* A *to subjecthood.*

For the sake of concreteness, illustrative data supporting the ASC are given in (9)–(11); their relevant aspects are summarized in (12):

(9)  Languages having only (**DO** → **S**):

    a.  French

        (i)  *Marie a   donné le  livre  à  Jacques.*
           Mary  has given the book io Jack
           'Mary gave the book to Jack.'

        (ii)  *Le livre a  été  donné à  Jacques par Marie.* (**DO** → **S**)
           The book has been given io Jack    sc  Mary
           'The book was given to Jack by Mary.'

        (iii)  *\*Jacques a  été  donné le  livre* (*par Marie*). (**IO** → **S**)
           Jack    has been given the book (sc Mary)
           'Jack was given the book (by Mary).'

    b.  German[14]

        (i)  *Er hat ihm      Bücher gegeben.*
           he has him (dat) books  given
           'He gave books to him.'

        (ii)  *Bücher wurden ihm     von mir gegeben.* (**DO** → **S**)
           books  were   him (dat) sc  me given
           'Books were given to him by me.'

---

[14] German may be classified wrongly here, since sentences such as:

(i)  *Er hat es geschenkt bekommen.*
    he has it presented received
    'He has been presented it.'

(ii)  *Er hat es gegeben gekriegt.*
    he has it given    received
    'He has been given it.'

could well be cases of (*IO* → *S*) rather than of IO Deletion, as tentatively assumed here.

    (iii) *Er wurde von mir Bücher gegeben. (**IO** → **S**)
       He was    sc  me  books  given
       'He was given books by me.'

  c. Albanian

    (i)   *Gjergji          ja      dha  librin          Jonit.*
       George-def-nom to-him-it gave book-def-acc John-def-dat
       'George gave the book to John.'

    (ii)  *Libri        ju-dha              Jonit        prej*
       book-def-nom to-him-passive-give John-def-dat sc
       *Gjergjit.* (**DO** → **S**)
       George-def-dat
       'The book was given to John by George.'

    (iii) **Joni*         ju-dha         librin         (*prej Gergjit*).
       John-def-nom was given the book-def-acc (by  George)
       (**IO** → **S**)
       'John was given the book by George.'

(10)  Languages having (**DO** → **S**) and (**IO** → **S**):

  a. Japanese[15]

    (i)   *John ga Mary ni hon   o   atae-ta.*
       John sm Mary io book do give-past
       'John gave a book to Mary.'

    (ii)  *Hon  ga John ni (yotte) Mary ni atae-rare-   ta.* (**DO** → **S**)
       book sm John sc        Mary io give-passive-past
       'A book was given to Mary by John.'

    (iii) *Mary ga John ni (yotte) hon   o   atae-rare-   ta.* (**IO** → **S**)
       Mary sm John sc        book do give-passive-past
       'Mary was given a book by John.'

  b. Sanskrit

    (i)   *Rāmah          Nalāya       pustakam       dadāti.*
       Rama-nom-sing Nala-dat-sing book-acc-sing gives
       'Ram gives the book to Nala.'

    (ii)  *Rāmena Nalāya   pustakah   diyate.* (**DO** → **S**)
       Rama-sc Nalah-dat book-nom give-passive-tense
       'The book is given to Nala by Ram.'

    (iii) *Nalah      Ramena pustakam dāpyate.* (**IO** → **S**)
       Nala-nom Rama-sc book-acc cause-give-passive-tense
       'Nalah is being given the book by Ram.'

[15] Data from Kuno (1973).

(11)   Languages having (**DO** → **S**), (**IO** → **S**), and (**OO** → **S**):

    a.  Malagasy[16]

        (i)  *Atolo-dRasoa*        *an-dRakoto ny  vary.* (**DO** → **S**)
           is offered by Rasoa to Rakoto  the rice
           'The rice is offered to Rakoto by Rasoa.'

       (ii)  *Toloran-dRasoa*     *ny  vary Rakoto.* (**IO** → **S**)
           is offered by Rasoa the rice  Rakoto
           'Rakoto is offered the rice by Rasoa.'

      (iii)  *Nividy  ny  vary ho an'ny ankizy   ny  vehivavy.*
           bought the rice  for the    children the woman
           'The woman bought the rice for the children.'

      (iv)  *Novidin'ny*     *vehivavy ho an'ny ankizy   ny*
           bought by the woman  for the    children the
              *vary.* (**DO** → **S**)
              rice
           'The rice was bought for the children by the woman.'

       (v)  *Nividianan'ny  vehivavy ny  vary ny  ankizy.* (**OO** → **S**)
           bought by the woman  the rice  the children
           'The children were bought the rice by the woman.'

      (vi)  *Nividy  ny  vary amin'ny vola    ny  vehivavy.*
           bought the rice  with the money the woman
           'The woman bought the rice with the money.'

      (vii)  *Nividianan'ny  vehivavy ny  vary ny  vola.* (**OO** → **S**)
           bought by the woman  the rice  the money
           'The money was used by the woman to buy the rice.'

    b.  Cebuano[17]

        (i)  *Nagpalit    ang babaye ug  saging.*
           vm + buy sm  woman ind banana
           'The woman bought some bananas.'

       (ii)  *Gipalit     sa babaye  ang saging.* (**DO** → **S**)
           vm + buy sc  woman sm  banana
           'The bananas were bought by the woman.'

      (iii)  *Gisulat     ni Go. Abaya ang sulat kanila para kang*
           vm + write sc Mr. Abaya sm  letter them  for   prt
             *Perla.*
             Perla
           'The letter was written to them by Mr. Abaya for Perla.'

---

[16] Data from Keenan and Comrie (to appear) and Keenan (1972b).
[17] Data from Bell (1974a).

(iv) *Sulatan      sila  ni Go. Abaya ug  sulat alang kang*
write + vm they sc Mr. Abaya ind letter for    prt
        *Perla.* (**IO → S**)
        Perla
        'They were written a letter by Mr. Abaya for Perla.'

 (v) *Sulatan      ni Go. Abaya si   Perla ug  sulat.* (**BEN → S**)
        write + vm sc Mr. Abaya sm Perla ind letter
        'Perla will be written a letter by Mr. Abaya.'

(vi) *Gipalitan         sa babaye  any bata' ug*
        vm + buy + vm sc woman sm  boy   ind
        *saging.* (**OO → S**)
        bananas
        'The woman bought some bananas from the boy.'

(vii) *Gilaba       niya   kining ma-ayong sabon.* (**OO → S**)
        vm + wash he/she this   good       soap
        'He/she washed (clothes) with this good soap.'

(12)                    Direct Subject-creating Advancements

| Language | Advancement of | | |
|----------|----|----|----|
|          | DO | IO | OO |
| *French:*   | *yes* | *no*  | *no*  |
| *German:*   | *yes* | *no*  | *no*  |
| *Albanian:* | *yes* | *no*  | *no*  |
| *Japanese:* | *yes* | *yes* | *no*  |
| *Sanskrit:* | *yes* | *yes* | *no*  |
| *Malagasy:* | *yes* | *yes* | *yes* |
| *Cebuano:*  | *yes* | *yes* | *yes* |

**The Nuclear Chaining Constraint**

There exist a number of rules which create derived DOs, e.g., (*IO → DO*), (*BEN → DO*), (*INS → DO*), (*COM → DO*). The following examples illustrate some of the rules in the Advancement-to-DO family:

(13)    Luganda

a. *John yatta     enkonko     n'ekiso.*
        John killed a chicken with a knife
        'John killed a chicken with a knife.'

b. *John yattisa        ekiso   enkonko.* (**INS → DO**)
        John killed-with a knife a chicken
        'John killed a chicken with a knife.'

c. *John yattira      mukazi   enkonko.* (**BEN → DO**)
        John killed-for a woman a chicken
        'John killed a chicken for a woman.'

(14)    Indonesian[18]

    a. *Ali mentjutjikan badja ini  buat                 saja.*
       Ali laundered    shirt  the for (the use of ) me
       'Ali laundered the shirt for me.'

    b. *Ali mentjutjikan saja badja ini.* (**BEN → DO**)
       Ali laundered    me  shirt  the
       'Ali laundered the shirt for me.'

    c. *Ali membelikan buku  itu  untuk                 saja.*
       Ali bought       book the for (the benefit of ) me
       'Ali bought the book for me.'

    d. *Ali membelikan saja buku itu.* (**BEN → DO**)
       Ali bought       me  book the
       'Ali bought me the book.'

    e. *Ali memberikan buku  itu  kepada saja.*
       Ali gave         book the to    me
       'Ali gave the book to me.'

    f. *Ali memberikan saja buku  itu.* (**IO → DO**)
       Ali gave         me  book the
       'Ali gave me the book.'

(15)    English

    a. *John gave the book to Mary.*
    b. *John gave Mary the book.* (**IO → DO**)
    c. *John bought the book for Mary.*
    d. *John bought Mary the book.* (**BEN → DO**)
    e. *John played three games of chess with Max.*
    f. *John played Max three games of chess.* (**COM → DO**)

(16)    Dyirbal[19]

    a. *Bayi  ɲalŋga  ŋada wugali ŋamundu.* (**IO → DO**)
       nm-A child-A I     gave  breast-dc
       'I gave the child my breast.'

    b. *Balan dugumbil  baŋgul yaɽaŋgu baŋgu  yuguŋgu balgan.*
       nm-A woman-A nm-E  man-E    nm-ins stick-ins hit
       'The man hit the woman with the stick.'

    c. *Bala  yugu    baŋgul yaɽaŋgu bagalman bagun*
       nm-A stick-A nm-E    man-E    hit + inm nm-dat
         *dugumbilgu.* (**INS → DO**)
         woman-dat
       'The man hit the woman with the stick.'

---

[18] Data from MacDonald and Soejono (1967).
[19] Data from Dixon (1972).

Without having investigated a large number of languages in detail, I would like to hypothesize that the rules in the Advancement-to-DO family also form a RELATIONAL CHAIN, e.g., if a language can derive DOs from instrumentals, then it can also derive DOs from IOs:

(17)  ADVANCEMENT-TO-DO CHAINING CONSTRAINT: *For any language* L, *if* (OO → DO) *is in* L *for some* OO, *then* (IO → DO) *is also in* L.

The Advancement-to-S and Advancement-to-DO Chaining constraints can be collapsed. First, some useful definitions will be introduced. In a rule of the form $(GR_i → GR_j)$, the relation $GR_i$ will be termed the CANDIDATE RELATION and NPs that hold this relation will be referred to as CANDIDATES. The relation $GR_j$ will be termed the TARGET RELATION and NPs that hold this relation will be referred to as TARGETS. For example, in $(DO → S)$, the $DO$ relation is the candidate relation and the $S$ relation is the target relation. Notice that the Reranking Law restricts PERMISSIBLE candidate-target relation pairs, e.g. $(DO → S)$ but not $(S → DO)$ is permissible. The following generalization can now be stated:

(18)  THE NUCLEAR CHAINING CONSTRAINT (NCC): *If a language* L *can advance NPs holding grammatical relation* A *to* C, *then, for any permissible candidate relation* B *such that* B < A, L *can also advance NPs holding* B *to* C.

(N.B.: the phrase 'permissible candidate relation' ensures that $C < B$.)

### The Predictive Power of Relational Constraints: Some Examples

Combined with relational constraints on possible rules such as those proposed by Perlmutter and Postal (forthcoming) and by Johnson (1974b), conditions such as the NCC substantially limit the types of languages compatible with linguistic theory. Consider the following putative universal:

(19)  THE TARGET UNIQUENESS PRINCIPLE (TUP):[20] *No language can have two advancement rules that have the same candidate relation but different target relations.*

Together the TUP and the NCC make a number of predictions. For instance, it is predicted from the fact that Japanese has $(IO → S)$ that it does not have

---

[20] This principle was inspired by the Advancee Laziness Law, proposed by Perlmutter and Postal: *An NP undergoing advancement will advance to the lowest point in the hierarchy permitted by universal and language-particular conditions.* For example, given a rule of the form 'Advance IO', the IO will advance to DO unless there is a language-particular condition forbidding advancements to DO in general, or advancements of particular constituent types to DO.

($OO \rightarrow DO$) for any OO. The reasoning is as follows: suppose that Japanese does have ($OO \rightarrow DO$). Then by the NCC it is predicted that it has ($IO \rightarrow DO$), which contradicts the TUP, since it is known independently that it has ($IO \rightarrow S$). Hence, Japanese must not have ($OO \rightarrow DO$). To take a different example, consider Bahasa Indonesian, which has ($IO \rightarrow DO$). By the TUP, it is predicted that it does not have ($IO \rightarrow S$) and, hence, from the NCC, that it does not have ($OO \rightarrow S$) for any OO.

More generally, limiting our attention to advancements to S and DO, the TUP and the NCC predict that there are only eight possible language types which create nuclear terms:

(20)    Language Type                        Example

$OO, IO, DO \rightarrow S$              *Malagasy, Kalagan, Cebuano*

$IO, DO \rightarrow S$                    *Japanese*

$DO \rightarrow S$                          *Hindi*

$OO, IO \rightarrow DO$                  *?*

$IO \rightarrow DO$                        *?*

$IO \rightarrow DO, DO \rightarrow S$    *?*

$OO, IO \rightarrow DO, DO \rightarrow S$    *Indonesian, Shona*

*None*                                       *?*

Since there are, a priori, thirty-two possible language types, the NCC and the TUP eliminate three-fourths of the logical possibilities.[21]

**Double Chains**

As noted by Ross (1974), Reflexivization[22] and Coreferential Deletion rules also manifest primacy behavior. However, Ross's observation is oversimplified in two respects which are important here: (i) as noted earlier, he did not refine

[21] The situation is oversimplified here in that 'OO' is considered a unitary grammatical relation. Strictly speaking, there is no rule ($OO \rightarrow DO$), but a set of rules: ($BEN \rightarrow DO$), ($INS \rightarrow DO$), etc. This oversimplification will be carried through the rest of this chapter.

With this oversimplification, the number of language types with respect to advancement rules is calculated as follows: There are three advancement-to-S rules—($OO, IO, DO \rightarrow S$)—and two advancement-to-DO rules—($OO, IO \rightarrow DO$). Without any constraints on which rules a language can have, i.e. taking all possible combinations into account, there are $2^3 = 8$ types of advancement-to-S families and $2^2 = 4$ types of advancement-to-DO families. Multiplying these together gives the number of logically possible families involving both types of rules, namely, 32.

[22] In the discussion that follows, only clause-internal reflexivization will be discussed. Furthermore, many other parameters will be ignored. These parameters include possible deletion of a coreferential clausemate, verb morphology, and reflexivization of genitives (e.g. *John sold his own book*). There are a number of languages, such as Cebuano, which allow sentences of the form:

(i)    *Himself$_i$ could not be controlled by him$_i$.*

The ultimately crucial problem of characterizing at what levels various rules apply will not be discussed (cf. Footnote 28). In many other languages, such as English, linear sequencing also seems

the notion of Primacy so as to distinguish among nonsubjects; and (ii) he did not point out that both controllers and victims of such rules could form relational chains. Examples of variation along both the controller and victim parameters of (clause-internal) Reflexivization rules [examples (21)–(23)] and Coreferential Deletion rules [examples (24)–(26)] are given below:

(21)   Indonesian (Malay).[23] Only direct objects can be reflexivized (nonemphatic, "true" relexive form):

   a.   *Saja (me)- lihat diri saja dalam air.*
        I     trans-see  self my  inside water
        'I saw myself in the water.'

   b.   *\*Sjahirir men- tjerita-kan  sesuatu tjerita kepada diri-nja.*
        Sjahirir trans-tell-  BEN a      story  to       himself
        'Sjahirir told a story to himself.'

(22)   German. In general, nonsubject NPs can be reflexivized under subject (and only subject) control:

   a. *Der Mann$_i$ liebt  sich$_i$.*
      The man    loves himself.

   b. *Johannes$_i$ redete mit  Maria$_j$ über  sich$_i$,\*$_j$.*
      John        spoke with Maria about himself.

   c. *Der Mann$_i$ verkaufte den Sklaven$_j$ an sich$_i$,\*$_j$.*
      The man    sold       the slave     to himself.

(23)   English. In general, nonsubject NPs can be reflexivized by higher ranking NPs:

   a. *John loves himself.*
   b. *John sold the book to himself.*
   c. *John talked to Mary about himself.*
   d. *John sold the girl to herself.*
   e. *John talked to Mary about herself.*
   f. *John crossed the wire over itself.*
   g. *Mary received a present from herself.*

---

to play a part:

   (ii)  a.   *John talked to Mary about herself.*
         b.   *\*John talked about herself to Mary.*

It is not the purpose of this paper to characterize exhaustively all constraints on reflexivization; thus many important areas will be ignored (cf. Jacobson 1975; Johnson, in preparation; Perlmutter and Postal, forthcoming).

   [23] Data from Chung (1976a).

My data on Coreferential Deletion rules are sparse but it appears that in Vietnamese (Truitner 1972) and in Dyirbal (Dixon 1972) DOs can be Equi victims and that in Bahasa Indonesian only Ss and DOs can be Equi controllers (Chung 1976a):

(24)   Vietnamese.[24] S and DO can delete:[25]

   a. *Kim moũn    John danh.*
      Kim wanted John hit
      'Kim wanted John to hit her.'

   b. *Kim moũn    danh John.*
      Kim wanted hit    John
      'Kim wanted to hit John.'

(25)   Dyirbal.[26] S and DO can delete:

   a. *Bayi yaṛa     baŋgul gubiŋgu mundan baŋgun dugumbiṛu balgali.*
      nm-A man-A nm-E gubi-E brought nm-E  woman-E  hit + pr
      'The man was brought by the gubi to be hit by the woman.'

   b. *Baḷan dugumbil  baŋgul yaṛaŋgu wawun   ŋayinbagu walmbilŋaygu.*
      nm-A woman-A nm-E man-E  fetched girls-dat  get up + ŋay + pr
      'The man fetched the woman to get the girls up.'

(26)   Indonesian.[27] Only S and DO can control deletion:

   a. *Dia meng-endarai mobil itu  supaja dia dapat mentjoba-nja.*
      he  trans-drive   car   the comp he  can   trans-try-it
      'He drove the car so that he could test it.'

   b. *Mereka mem-beli ikan itu supaja (ikan itu) dapat di-      masak*
      they   trans-buy fish the comp  fish  the  can   passive-cook
      *oleh saja.*
      by   me
      'They bought the fish so that it could be cooked by me.'

   c. *Dia meng-endarai mobil itu  untuk men- tjoba-nja.*
      he  trans-drive   car   the for   trans-try- it
      'He drove the car to test it.'

---

[24] Data from Truitner (1972).

[25] These may not be valid examples of the coreferential deletion of a DO, since they may result from a general rule of Pronoun Deletion. Coreferential Object Deletion also occurs in certain environments in English:

   (i)   *The chicken is ready for you to eat.*
   (ii)  *Pumpkins are fun to look at.*
   (iii) *Rex is too dumb for Mary to train.*

[26] Data from Dixon (1972).
[27] Data from Chung (1976a).

d. *Mereka mem- beli ikan itu untuk dapat di-      masak oleh saja.*
   they      trans-buy fish the for    can   passive-cook by   me
   'They bought the fish to (be able to) be cooked by me.'

e. *Saja mem- bawa surat itu kepada wanita  itu supaja dia dapat*
   I     trans-bring letter the to       woman the comp  she can
   *mem- batja-nja kepada anak      nja.*
   trans-read- it   to      children-her
   'I brought the letter to the woman so that she could read it to
   her children'

f. **Saja mem- bawa surat itu  kepada wanita  itu untuk dapat*
   I     trans-bring letter the to       woman the for    can
   *mem- batja-nja kepada anak-   nja.*
   trans-read- it   to      children-her

Focusing on Reflexivization, English is very free in terms of both controllers
and victims. In contrast, Indonesian is as strict as a language can be and still
have Reflexivization—there is only one possibility. German is similar to
Indonesian in that it is strict with controllers (S only), but similar to English
in that it is relatively free with its victims. The slim data I have found suggest
that Coreferential Deletion rules follow the same basic pattern. For example,
Vietnamese and Dyirbal allow DO victims in cases where English and Indonesian would prohibit them. English and Indonesian contrast in that only the
former allows IOs to control deletion. Although not very abundant, these
facts, in conjunction with the previous evidence that grammatical processes
tend to form relational chains, naturally suggest the following hypothesis:

(27)   THE DOUBLE CHAINING CONSTRAINT (DCC): *Both controllers and
       victims of clause-internal Reflexivization rules and Coreferential
       Deletion rules conform to the RH, i.e. they range over a continuous
       segment of the RH.*

The DCC, along with the following relational principles,[28] generates a
restricted set of theoretically permissible language types and thus constitutes

---

[28] Throughout this chapter I have consistently ignored the very important problem of stating
at what derivational stage such constraints hold. In fact there is some language-specific variation
in this area. For instance, Lawler (this volume) argues that in Achenese verb agreement is triggered
by initial subjects (contrasting with the more typical situation of cycle-final subject agreement):

(i)  Achenese

     a. *Gopnyan ka  gi-  com lon.*
        she        perf she-kiss me
        '*She (already) kissed me.*'

an empirical hypothesis about the nature of human language:

(28)    a.   THE REFLEXIVIZATION LAW:[29] *Only terms can trigger Reflexivization.*

        b.   THE COREFERENTIAL DELETION LAW:[30] *Only terms can trigger Coreferential Deletions.*

        c.   THE CLAUSEMATE CONTROLLER CONSTRAINT: *If* A *controls* B *in a clausemate Reflexivization rule, then* A $<$ B.

---

     b. *Lon ka   gi- com le- gopnyan.*
       I    perf she-kiss by-her
       'I've already been kissed by her.'

and, as discussed by Bell (1974a and 1974b), Cebuano optionally allows initial, noncyclic subjects to trigger reflexivization:

(ii)    a.   *Nagbantay ako sa akong kaugalingon.*
         look after I    oo my    self
         'I look after myself.'

        b.   *Bantayan      nako ang akong kaugalingon.*
         look after-vm me   sm my    self
         'Myself will be looked after by me.'

        c.   *\*Nagbantay ang akong kaugalingon kanako.*
         look after sm my    self        me
         'Myself looked after me.'

Cases of initial terms triggering coreferential deletions have also been reported, e.g. in Tagalog (cf. Schachter 1976).

It has been claimed that such examples present a problem for RG in that (i) they indicate that nonterms can control grammatical processes claimed to be restricted to term controllers by RG and/or (ii) they indicate that the notion 'subject of' is not a primitive notion as assumed by RG (since "typical" subject properties are distributed over various NPs in a given clause (cf. Keenan 1976 and Schachter 1976). These conclusions are seen to be unwarranted once the crucial notion 'level/stage of derivation' is taken into consideration. Consider the examples from Cebuano (iia–c). Only (iic) is ungrammatical, and it is just this case in which the reflexivization trigger cannot be construed naturally as a subject of the relevant clause at any derivational level. This difference in behavior between languages like English, German, and Indonesian, on the one hand, and languages like Tagalog. and Cebuano, on the other, can be sensibly interpreted to indicate that the relevant relational constraints hold at different derivational levels in these two types of languages. More generally, with a multilevel conception of derivations, it makes no sense, strictly speaking, to say, for example, that *A* is the 'subject of clause *C*'; rather, one must specify that *A* is the 'subject of *C* at level *L*'. It appears quite clear that many languages allow noncyclic, initial terms to control a variety of processes such as Reflexivization, Equi-NP-Deletion, and Verb Agreement. (Cf. Bell, 1974a and 1974b; Lawler, this volume; Perlmutter and Postal, forthcoming; Pullum 1975b; and Schachter 1976). The description of such phenomena causes no real problem for multilevel linguistic theories (such as RG); in fact, such theories are "made to order" for such phenomena and gain indirect support from such facts. What remains to be determined is the exact type and range of such phenomena, e.g. whether there are interactions among them such that if a language *L* triggers a process $P_1$ with initial triggers, then it also triggers $P_2$

The DCC, the Reflexivization Law, and the Clausemate Controller Constraint generate the following language types:

(29)                    Clausemate Reflexivization Language Types

        a. *None*
        b. *S/DO*
        c. *S/IO; S/DO*
        d. *S/OO; S/IO/ S/DO*
        e. *DO/IO; S/IO; S/DO*
        f. *DO/OO; DO/IO; S/OO/ S/IO; S/DO*
        g. *IO/OO; DO/OO; DO/IO; S/OO; S/IO; S/DO*

Without these relational conditions there would be 226 possible language types.[31] Thus the DCC and principles (28a) and (28c) substantially reduce the number of language types compatible with linguistic theory along the dimension of Reflexivization.

Turning to Coreferential Deletions, if the weakest assumption regarding potential victims is employed, namely, that they can go as low as the OO slot on the RH, then the DCC and the Coreferential Deletion Law (28b) allow the

---

with initial triggers, etc., and what combinations of conditions which can be defined within multi-level derivational theories actually occur.

Reflexivization in Samoan appears to provide a counterexample to (28c). Chapin (1970) gives the following examples, in which it appears that a DO can optionally reflexivize an S:

(iii)   a. *Sa sogi loane ie  ia lava.*

       tns cut  John $\begin{Bmatrix} \text{sm} \\ \text{sc} \end{Bmatrix}$ he reflexive

       'Himself cut John.'

**or perhaps**

       'Himself (was) cut by John.'

      b. *Sa Sogi e  loane ia lava.*

       tns cut  sm John he reflexive

       'John cut himself.'

It is possible that such sentences as (iiia) result from passivization and are basically the same as the Cebuano example (iib), except that there is no passive verbal morphology (which does sometimes occur, e.g. in Achenese). A second consideration is the fact that Samoan is an 'ergative' language and as such, while it might be a true counterexample to (28c) as stated, suggests a weakening of (28c) which would allow for 'subject reflexivization' in ergative languages only. For further discussion, see Johnson (to appear and in preparation).

   [29] Taken from Perlmutter and Postal (forthcoming).

   [30] Taken from Perlmutter and Postal (forthcoming).

   [31] The calculations are as follows: There are four possible controllers and four possible victims: $S$, $DO$, $IO$, and $OO$. Hence, there are $2^4 = 16$ possible controller sets, e.g. $\{\emptyset\}$, $\{S\}$, $\{S, DO\}$, etc., and 16 victim sets. Ignoring all controller-victim pairs in which one member is empty, e.g. $(S, \emptyset)$ and $(\emptyset, DO)$, we have $(15 \times 15) + 1 = 226$ logically possible controller-victim sets.

following thirteen possibilities:

(30)  Coreferential Deletion Language Types

     a. *None*
     b. *S/S*
     c. *S/DO; S/S*
     d. *S/IO; S/DO; S/S*
     e. *S/OO; S/IO; S/DO; S/S*
     f. *DO/S; S/S*
     g. *DO/DO; DO/S; S/S*
     h. *DO/IO; DO/DO; DO/S; S/S*
     i. *DO/OO; DO/IO; DO/S; S/OO; S/IO; S/DO; S/S*
     j. *IO/S; DO/S; S/S*
     k. *IO/DO; IO/S; DO/DO; DO/S; S/DO; S/S*
     l. *IO/IO; IO/DO; IO/S; DO/IO; DO/DO; DO/S; S/IO; S/DO;*
       *S/S*
     m. *IO/OO; IO/IO; IO/DO; IO/S; DO/OO; DO/IO; DO/DO;*
       *DO/S; S/OO; S/IO; S/DO; S/S*

As in the case with Reflexivization, if there were no conditions on permissible controller-victim pairs there would be 226 possible language types.[32] If the three groups of language types—(27), (29), and (30)—are considered together, then there are $8 \times 7 \times 13 = 728$ possible language types given the relational constraints and $32 \times 226 \times 226 = 1,634,432$ possible language types without any of these constraints (with very few rules having been taken into consideration). Thus, it can be concluded that primacy conditions play a significant role in limiting the number of possible natural language types.[33]

## The Continuous Segment Principle

Ross's Primacy Constraint is very strong in that it refers to all rules but too weak in that it distinguishes only subjects from nonsubjects and is vague with respect to controllers and victims. On the other hand, the principles proposed here are weaker than the Primacy Constraint in that they refer to specific types of rules: The NCC refers to advancement rules and the DCC refers to rules which have controllers and victims, such as Reflexivization and Coreferential Deletion rules. However, the principles proposed do make finer distinctions among various relationally determined NPs. Ross's constraint states that

---

[32] My reasoning here is the same as that in Footnote 31.

[33] From the standpoint of language acquisition, one can see why such constraints might exist. Without strong assumptions such as these regarding what particular grammars can be like, a child, on the basis of a limited amount of primary data, would have a hard time constructing a grammar of the language he is attempting to learn since there would be a tremendously large number of possible grammars compatible with the primary data.

subjects are always more accessible than are nonsubjects. There is good evidence that this claim is too strong, e.g. Tough Movement, Indefinite-NP Deletion, Noun Incorporation, and Cross-clause Reflexivization (at least in Italian, cf. Napoli 1974) apply to NONSUBJECTS BUT NOT TO SUBJECTS, either universally or idiosyncratically:[34]

(31)         a. Tough Movement
                  i. *John is easy for Mary to please.*
                  ii. **John is easy to please Mary.*
             b. Indefinite NP Deletion
                  i. *The man was hit.*
                  ii. **Hit the man.* [on reading equivalent to (i)]

The NCC and the DCC bear a close resemblance to each other—the same basic phenomenon underlies both. The only difference is that rules like Reflexivization which involve coreference have two entities that can range over the RH, controllers and victims. The fact that the same basic phenomenon crops up again and again in a wide variety of grammatical processes (including Advancements, Insertions, Verb Agreement, and rules involving coreference such as Reflexivization, Coreferential Deletions, and Relativization) suggests that all rules which refer to grammatical relations form relational chains. Thus,

---

[34] These facts raise the following questions: Which 'upper bounds' on relational chains are universally determined and which are determined by particular languages? For example, Indefinite-NP Deletion is clearly language-specific since a number of languages allow the deletion of subjects, e.g. Dyirbal:

(i)    *Balan dugumbil  balgan.*
       nm-A woman-A hit
       'Someone hit woman.'

and Eskimo (Swadesh 1944):

(ii)   *Tiyianiaq takuvoq.*
       fox-A    see
       'Someone saw the fox.'

and with respect to Noun Incorporation some languages allow certain subjects to incorporate, e.g. Mohawk:

(iii)  *Ka + ?sreht + hu?syi.*
       it + car + black
       'The car is black.'

Another problem which arises within this general area is how to determine whether certain rules are inherently insensitive to the RH. Notice that a relationally insensitive rule would not violate the Primary Constraint; it would also seem, however, that linguistic theory should have more to say about such rules. Pronominalization and NP-Internal Concord appear to be examples of rules that are intrinsically insensitive to grammatical relations. No solution to these problems will be sought here.

we are led to postulate a universal principle covering all these cases:

(32)   THE CONTINUOUS SEGMENT PRINCIPLE (CSP): *No rule* R *can apply to a noncontinuous segment of the RH, i.e., if* R *applies to NPs holding grammatical relations* U *and* W *on the RH* (U < W), *then, for all* V *on the RH such that* U < V < W, R *can apply to NPs holding* V.

The term 'applies' as used in (32) is imprecise; it is meant to cover both controllers and victims as well as advancee candidates, agreement triggers, etc. In the following section certain aspects of the previous discussion are formalized in order to remove this imprecision and to allow the statement of other generalizations.

## Formalization of Some Relational Constraints[35]

At the level of universal grammar, it will be assumed that there are, among others, the following two relation-changing rule schemata:

(33)     Subject-creation Schema:
$GR_i(NP_m, V_n) \rightarrow S(NP_m, V_n)$

(34)     Do-creation Schema
$GR_j(NP_m, V_n) \rightarrow DO(NP_m, V_n)$
(where $GR_i$ and $GR_j$ are variables over $\{S, DO, IO, OO\}$ and
$NP_m$ and $V_n$ refer to arbitrary NPs and Vs, respectively)

The basic idea is that languages can "construct" rules from these schemata by applying various relational principles and filling in certain language-specific details such as morphological changes associated with the schema in question. One thing that a language "choosing" a schema such as (33) must do is to specify values for the variable $GR_i$, i.e. it must specify what the candidate relations are to be. For example, in English the only candidate relation for $GR_i$ in (33) is DO; in Japanese both IO and DO are permissible values. To be more precise, the following definitions are introduced:

(35)   a. *A variable (relational) component of a rule (schema) is any string of the form* $G(NP, V)$, *(where* G *is any variable over* $\{S, DO, IO, OO\}$, *e.g.* $GR_i$ *and* $GR_j$ *in (33) and (34), respectively, and NP and V refer to variables over* NPs *and* Vs, *respectively).*

[35] Inspiration for the concept of a 'relation-changing rule of grammar' which is developed in this section has come from Bach (1965 and 1971), Lakoff (1972), and Postal (1971). For a more detailed development of this conception, see Johnson (in preparation). Cf. Andrews (1973) and Keenan (1972a).

b. *Let* R *be a rule schema with a variable* (*relational*) *component*
$GR_i(NP_m, V_n)$. *Then, the* BOUNDS *for that component of* R *in*
L *are the two grammatical relations assigned as values of* $GR_i$,
*either universally or by* L *when it* "*selects*" R. *Suppose* A *and*
B *are the bounds for a given component of* R, *and that* A < B
*on the RH. Then,* A *is the* U(*pper*) B(*ound*) *and* B *is the*
L(*ower*) B(*ound*) *for that component. If* A = B, *then* A *is both*
*the* UB *and the* LB.

Moreover, it is assumed that any grammatical process which is sensitive to
grammatical relations in the sense being discussed here is to be formulated
universally in terms of variable components. For instance, Clausemate Reflexivization in universal grammar would have two variable components, one
ranging over controllers and one ranging over victims. Below several relational
principles which use these definitions are given:

(36)   a. THE BOUNDARY CONDITION: *All variable components of a rule* R
          *in* L *must be assigned a* LOWER BOUND *and an* UPPER BOUND *by*
          L, *unless they are assigned universally.*

       b. THE ADVANCEMENT UPPER BOUND CONDITION: *Subject-creation*
          *and DO-creation* CANNOT *have language-particular upper*
          *bounds.*

       c. THE CONTINUOUS SEGMENT PRINCIPLE (REVISED): *Let* $GR_i(NP_m,$
          $V_n$) *be an arbitrary variable component of a given rule* R *in an*
          *arbitrary language* L. *If* A *is the upper bound and* C *is the lower*
          *bound assigned to* $GR_i$, *then, for each* B *on the RH such that*
          A < B < C, B *is a possible value for* $GR_i$. (*N.B.:* This
          formulation will apply to BOTH controllers and victims in
          double chains, assuming that both are universally represented
          in terms of a variable component.)

On the basis of these assumptions and definitions, the Reranking Law can be
viewed as a general principle which assigns universal UBs to variables over
candidate relations in advancement rules. The Advancement Upper Bound
Condition guarantees that no language will assign its own UB to an advancement schema which would undercut the universal UB assigned by the Reranking
Law.

   Given the possibility of selection or nonselection of (33) and (34), the principles in (36), in conjunction with the Reranking Law and the Advancee
Laziness Law, will generate exactly the language types given in (20). For
instance, if a language picks rule schema (33) and not (34) and in accordance
with (36a) and (36b) assign the IO relation as the LB, then the CSP, (36c), and
the Reranking Law require that the language have ($IO \rightarrow S$) and ($DO \rightarrow S$).

This is the case in Japanese. It should be stressed that, for instance, $(IO \rightarrow S)$ is not itself a rule of Japanese grammar insofar as it does not specify various language-specific parameters such as the verbal and nominal morphology and rule government associated with the relational change. In fact, more than one rule of grammar in a given language can make use of a given schema, e.g. reflexive passives and "ordinary" passives. (See Perlmutter and Postal, forthcoming, and Chung 1976b).

We thus arrive at a rather abstract conception of the notion 'relational rule of grammar'. Universal grammar must provide, among other things, a set of rule schemata and a set of principles which govern the "use" of these schemata by particular languages in the "construction" and "application" of particular rules. Some of these universal principles are, I believe, the Reranking Law, the Relational Annihilation Law, the Boundary Condition, and the CSP. A concrete, although over simplified, example from Japanese may help to clarify this particular conception of the notion relational rule of grammar:

(37)    a. Universal Schema: Subject-creation:

$$GR_i(NP_m, V_n) \rightarrow S(NP_m, V_n)$$

      b. Language-specific Schema: Japanese Subject-creation:

$$GR_i(NP_m, V_n) \rightarrow S(NP_m, V_n)$$

Language-specific Parameters

(i) $LB = IO$

(ii) *Verbal Morphology:* $V$ + ***rare***

(iii) *Chômeur Morphology:* *Chômeur* ***ni*** (***yotte***)

      c. Language-specific Rules ['Instantiations' of (b)]:

i. $IO(NP_m, V_n) \rightarrow S(NP_m, V_n)$

Language-specific Parameters

(a) *Verbal Morphology:* $V$ + ***rare***

(b) *Chômeur Morphology:* *Chômeur* ***ni*** (***yotte***)

ii. $DO(NP_m, V_n) \rightarrow S(NP_m, V_n)$

Language-specific Parameters

(a) *Verbal Morphology:* $V$ + ***rare***

(b) *Chômeur Morphology:* *Chômeur* ***ni*** (***yotte***)

The construction of rule (37b) follows from the selection of (37a) and the application of universal principles, which, among other things, state that an LB must be assigned and that the associated morphology must be specified. (37c) represents the actual 'rule instantiations' that are applied in specific derivations. (37c) does not have to be listed in the grammar of Japanese since these instantiations are derivable from (37b) by universal principles. That is, the grammar of Japanese must only state (i) that schema (33) has been selected and (ii) what the language-specific parameters are. Given this, we can say that a stage in a derivation $D_2$ is derivable from a stage $D_1$ by means of (37b) if there is an instantiation of (37b) which takes $D_1$ into $D_2$ (in conjunction with universal principles of rule application, e.g. the Relation Annihilation Law).

This rather abstract conception of relational rules (i.e. any rule which is sensitive to grammatical relations) appears to permit an adequate formulation of the Continuous Segment Principle, namely (36c).[36,37]

## ACKNOWLEDGMENTS

I am grateful to Fred Damerau, Jagdish Jain, Warren Plath, and Paul Postal for their many helpful comments and suggestions on this paper. I am also greatly indebted to the pioneering work of E. Bach, B. Comrie, E. Keenan, J. Morgan, D. Perlmutter, P. Postal, and J. Ross, whose insights,

[36] The basic claim throughout this chapter is NOT that a given term $T_i$ will trigger or undergo some process if $T_j$ does, where $i < j$, in every derivation or even in every derivation type. The claim being advanced here is weaker, namely, that if there exist derivations that allow $T_i$ to trigger or undergo process $P$, then there exist derivations (perhaps disjoint with the first set) that allow $T_j, j < i$, to trigger or undergo $P$. Thus, for example, a given language $L$ could well allow IOs but not DOs to trigger verb agreement in $X\ V\ DO\ IO\ Y$ structures, without violating any of the claims put forth here. As an example, consider Equi. It is not being claimed that in any PARTICULAR derivation if Equi can apply under DO control, then it can also apply under subject control, i.e. it is not claimed that (ia–b) are ambiguous:

(i)   a. *John forced Bill to leave.*
      b. *John permitted Bill to leave.*

The semantics of the main verb apparently affect potential controllers in particular derivations. The claim being made is roughly as follows: If syntactic Equi under DO-control is allowed for some verbs specifying semantically an "anaphoric connection" (cf. Postal 1971) between a DO and a complement NP, then syntactic Equi under subject control will, in general, be allowed for verbs specifying semantically an anaphoric connection between a subject and a complement NP. To illustrate, no language could accept such sentences as (i) and reject all such sentences as (ii):

(ii)  a. *Bill wanted to leave.*
      b. *John promised Bill to leave.*

The same remarks hold for the other types of rules. Such "local priorities" are a separate issue. (Cf. Moravcsik 1974 and Johnson, in preparation.)

[37] I have come across the following potential counterexample to the CSP, more specifically to the ASC. English has such constructions as:

(i)   a. *Mary takes good pictures (photographs well).*
      b. *This barn houses one hundred cows.*
      c. *This plane flies three hundred people.*

which, if derived by the same rule, would violate the ASC and CSP since (ia) involves the advancement of a DO to subject and (ib–c) involve the advancement of LOCATIVE to subject. There appear to be no similar cases, however, which involve the advancement of IO to subject: *\*Mary sells easily* (=*one can sell things to Mary easily*). Characteristic of this type of sentence are (i) no special verbal morphology, (ii) inability to take a subject-chômeur (*\*Mary takes good pictures by Peter/everyone*), and (iii) some sort of generic meaning. I do not know what to make out of these constructions.

observations, and hypotheses are used throughout. This paper is basically a generalization and refinement of some of the observations in Keenan and Comrie (to appear) and Ross (1974), based upon independent results within the framework of Relational Grammar established by Perlmutter and Postal (forthcoming) and Johnson (1974a, 1974b, and in preparation). Any errors are, of course, my own. In addition, I would like to thank the following people for supplying data on various languages discussed in the text: Albanian: Jerry Morgan; French: Paul Postal; German: Ladislav Zgusta and E. O. Lippmann; Mohawk: Paul Postal; and Sanskrit: Mrs. Panharipande and Tej Bhatia.

# REFERENCES

Andrews, A. (1973) "Agreement and Deletion," in C. Corum, T. C. Smith-Stark, and A. Weiser, eds., *Papers from the Ninth Regional Meeting of the Chicago Linguistic Society*, University of Chicago, Chicago, Illinois.

Bach, E. (1965) "On Some Recurrent Types of Transformations," in C. Kreidler, ed., *Georgetown University Monograph Series on Languages and Linguistics* 18, 3–18.

Bach, E. (1971) "Questions," *Linguistic Inquiry* 2, 153–166.

Bell, S. J. (1974a) "Some Notes on Cebuano and Relational Grammar," unpublished paper, M.I.T.

Bell, S. J. (1974b) "Two Consequences of Advancement Rules in Cebuano," in E. Kaisse and J. Hankamer, eds, *Papers from the Fifth Annual Meeting*, North Eastern Linguistic Society, Harvard University, Cambridge, Massachusetts.

Chapin, P. (1970) "Samoan Pronominalization," *Language* 46, 366–378.

Chung, S. (1976a) "An Object-creating Rule in Bahasa Indonesian," *Linguistic Inquiry* 7, 41–88.

Chung, S. (1976b) On the Subject of Two Passives in Indonesian. In C. Li, ed., *Subject and Topic*, Academic Press, New York.

Chomsky, N. (1965) *Aspects of the Theory of Syntax*, M.I.T. Press, Cambridge, Massachusetts.

Chomsky, N. (1973) "Conditions on Transformations," in S. R. Anderson and P. Kiparsky, eds., *A Festschrift for Morris Halle*, Holt, Rine-hart and Winston, New York.

Dixon, R. M. W. (1972) *The Dyirbal Language of North Queensland*, Cambridge University Press, Cambridge.

Jacobson, P. (1975) "Crossover and About Movement in a Relational Grammar," in C. Cogen, et. al., eds., *Proceedings of the First Annual Meeting, of the Berkeley Linguistic Society*, University of California, Berkeley, California.

Johnson, D. E. (1974a) On the Role of Grammatical Relations in Linguistic Theory," in M. W. La Galy, R. A. Fox, and A. Bruck, eds., *Papers from the Tenth Regional Meeting of the Chicago Linguistic Society*, University of Chicago, Chicago, Illinois.

Johnson, D. E. (1974b) *Toward a Theory of Relationally-based Grammar*, unpublished Doctoral dissertation, University of Illinois, Urbana, Illinois.

Johnson, D. E. (to appear) "Ergativity in Universal Grammar," IBM Research Report, IBM Thomas J. Watson Research Center, Yorktown Heights, N.Y.

Johnson, D. E. (in preparation) *An Essay on Universal Grammar*.

Keenan, E. L. (1972a) "On Semantically Based Grammar," *Linguistic Inquiry* 3, 413–462,

Keenan, E. L. (1972b) "Relativization in Malagasy," In P. Peranteau, J. N. Levi, and G. C. Phares, eds., *The Chicago Which Hunt: Papers from the Relative Clause Festival*, Chicago Linguistic Society, University of Chicago, Chicago, Illinois.

Keenan, E. L. (1976) Towards a Universal Definition of 'subject of'," in C. Li, ed., *Subject and Topic*, Academic Press, New York.

Keenan, E. L. and B. Comrie (to appear) "Noun Phrase Accessibility and Universal Grammar," *Linguistic Inquiry*.

Kuno, S. (1973) *The Structure of the Japanese Language*, M.I.T. Press, Cambridge, Massachusetts.

Lakoff, G. (1973) "Fuzzy Grammar and the Performative/Competence Terminology Game," in

P. Peranteau, J. N. Levi, and G. C. Phares, eds., *Papers from the Eighth Regional Meeting of the Chicago Linguistic Society*, University of Chicago, Chicago, Illinois.

Lawler, J. (this volume) "A Agrees with B in Achenese."

MacDonald, R. and D. Soejono (1967) *Indonesian Reference Grammar*, Georgetown University Press, Washington, D.C.

Moravcsik, E. (1974) "Object-Verb Agreement," *Working Papers in Language Universals* 15, Stanford University, Stanford, California, 25–140.

Napoli, D. J. (1974) "Reflexivization across S Boundaries in Italian: Semantic Conditions on a Syntactic Process," presented at the Annual Meeting, Linguistic Society of America.

Perlmutter, D. and P. M. Postal (forthcoming) *Relational Grammar*.

Postal, P. M. (1969) "On the Surface Verb 'Remind'," *Linguistic Inquiry* 1, 37–120.

Postal, P. M. (1971) "The Method of Universal Grammar," in Paul Garvin, ed., *Method and Theory in Linguistics*, Mouton, The Hague.

Postal, P. M. (1974a) "Observations on Structure Preservation," unpublished paper, IBM Thomas J. Watson Research Center, Yorktown Heights, N.Y.

Postal, P. M. (1974b) *On Raising*. M.I.T. Press, Cambridge, Massachusetts.

Postal, P. M. (1976) "Avoiding Reference to Subject," *Linguistic Inquiry* 7, 151–181.

Pullum, G. K. (1975a) "Squibs on Relational Grammar," Nos. 1–6, unpublished papers, University College, London.

Ross, J. R. (1974) "There, There, (There, (There, (There, . . .)))," in M. W. La Galy, R. A. Fox, and A. Bruck, eds., *Papers from the Tenth Regional Meeting of the Chicago Linguistic Society*, University of Chicago, Chicago, Illinois.

Schachter, P. (1976) "The Subject in Phillippine Languages: Topic, Actor, Actor-Topic or None of the Above?," in C. Li, ed., *Subject and Topic*, Academic Press, New York.

Swadesh, M. (1944) "South Greenlandic (Eskimo)," in *Viking Fund Publications in Anthropology* 6, New York.

Truitner, N. (1972) "Passive Sentences in Vietnamese," in P. Peranteau, J. N. Levi, and G. C. Phares, eds., *Papers from the Eighth Regional Meeting of the Chicago Linguistic Society*, University of Chicago, Chicago, Illinois.

# THE OBJECT RELATIONSHIP IN CHI-MWI:NI, A BANTU LANGUAGE

*CHARLES W. KISSEBERTH*

*MOHAMMAD IMAM ABASHEIKH*

University of Illinois

## INTRODUCTION

Until very recently, most analyses of Bantu grammar have been analyses of the morphological structure of the various Bantu languages. This is not surprising. The complex morphology of these languages offers a stimulating field of investigation. Furthermore, most of the linguists investigating Bantu languages have not been native speakers of the languages in question. The limitations that this situation imposes for transformational approaches to syntactic analysis hardly require mention. Nor, in many cases, is there even a substantial body of texts available for examination.

As a result of the situation outlined above, every area of Bantu syntax is still almost totally unexplored. The problem of grammatical relations is in no way an exception to this statement. In this study we examine the grammatical relationships exemplified by one verbal construction—the so-called APPLIED or PREPOSITIONAL verb—in Chi-Mwi:ni, a Bantu language closely related to Swahili which is spoken in the city of Brava in Somalia.[1] More particularly, we examine certain patterns of linguistic form that are generally regarded as being

[1] Chi-Mwi:ni has generally been treated as a dialect of Swahili, but there are extensive differences at the morphophonemic, morphological, and lexical levels. We prefer to regard Chi-Mwi:ni as a separate, although closely related, language. There are important syntactic differences (for example, in the structure of relative clauses) between Chi-Mwi:ni and Swahili, but the full extent of these differences has not yet been determined. The only published works on Chi-Mwi:ni, prior to our own investigation (which is still in progress), are two short articles: Whiteley (1965) and Goodman

179

characteristic of the 'object' of the verb in Bantu languages with the purpose of determining whether there is, in fact, a NP in applied verbal constructions that, on the basis of these patterns, can be identified unequivocally as the object. We will show that, while in a certain range of cases there is a single NP in applied verbal constructions that displays all the characteristics of the object of the verb, in yet other cases no one NP has all the properties commonly associated with the object: two different NPs each exhibit features that are typically restricted to the object. In such cases, the label 'object' cannot be applied exclusively to a single NP. The factors that determine whether a single NP will posses all the characteristics of the object, or whether two different NPs will share these characteristics, will be shown to be basically semantic in nature. In other words, the syntactic relationship 'object of the verb' in Chi-Mwi:ni is inextricably tied up with semantic contrasts.

## BACKGROUND

Certain background information about Chi-Mwi:ni grammatical structure will facilitate discussion. First, it should be noted that grammatical relations are not formally marked on nouns in any way. Thus a noun such as *chibu:ku* 'book' will have the same shape whether it is functioning as subject, as in (1):[2]

(1)                                    *Chibu:ku chibe:le.*
                                       book   is lost
                                       'The book is lost.'

or as "principal object," as in (2):

(2)                                    *Wa:na   wachiboze+e chibu:ku.*
                                       children stole        book
                                       'The children stole the book.'

or as a "subsidiary object," as in (3):

(3)                                    *Wa:na   wamboze+e mwa:limu chibu:ku.*
                                       children stole      teacher    book
                                       'The children stole the book from the teacher.'

(The terms "principal" and "subsidiary" are dealt with below.)

A distinction can be made, however, between what we refer to as an 'un-marked' NP and a 'marked' NP. A NP is unmarked if it is neither preceded

---

(1967). The latter writer refers to the language as Bravanese. A small part of the material that we have collected on the language appears in Kisseberth and Abasheikh 1974a, 1974b, 1974c, and 1974d).

[2] Since this chapter is concerned exclusively with aspects of Chi-Mwi:ni syntax, we have provided no discussion of the transcription system utilized and no explanation of the various morphophonemic alternations that can be observed in the data cited. The interested reader should consult our papers cited in footnote 1.

by a preposition nor suffixed by the locative suffix -*ni*. Thus in (3) above, both *mwa:limu* 'teacher' and *chibu:ku* 'book' are unmarked NPs. Compare (4) and (5) below:

(4)          *Mwa:na ţinziɫe: ṇama ka: chisu.*
             child     cut      meat with knife
             'The child cut the meat with a knife.'

(5)          *Ja:ma mɫeseɫe mwa:na hafisa:ni.*
             brought child       office-locative
             'Jama brought the child to the office.'

In (4), *ṇama* 'meat' is an unmarked NP, but *chisu* 'knife' is marked, being preceded by the preposition *ka* 'with'. Similarly, in (5), *mwa:na* 'child' is an unmarked NP, but *ha:fisa* 'office' is marked, being suffixed with the locative -*ni*.

A second point that requires comment is that Chi-Mwi:ni displays the typical Bantu phenomenon of noun classes, where a noun class is defined in terms of (i) the class prefix (CP) that appears on the noun itself and (ii) the pattern of agreement that the noun governs. Consider, for example, a noun such as *chiguwo* 'rag, cloth'. This noun can be analyzed into two parts: the CP *chi-* and the noun stem -*guwo*. The CP *chi-* occurs in a great many nominal forms (*chiti* 'chair', *chisiwa* 'island', *chiga:ri* 'cart', *chire:za* 'razor', and so on). The noun stem -*guwo* can occur with other CPs besides *chi-*; for example, *ziguwo* 'rags, cloths' and *nguwo* 'clothes'.

A variety of items must agree with the noun to which they are grammatically linked. For example, adjectives modifying nouns must be assigned an agreement prefix (AP), the shape of which is determined by the noun. For example, the noun *chiguwo* requires that the AP *chi-* be prefixed to the adjective stem, whereas *ziguwo* requires *zi-* and *nguwo* requires *n-* (which assimilates to the point of articulation of a following stop). The AP that is assigned to items other than adjectives is not always identical in shape to the AP that is assigned to an adjective. For example, the interrogative particle -*mpʰi* 'which?' must have an AP which agrees with the noun that it modifies. In the case of *chiguwo* and *ziguwo*, the AP used is the same as occurs with adjective stems: *chiguwo chi:mpʰi* 'which rag?' and *ziguwo zi:mpʰi* 'which rags?'. In the case of *nguwo*, however, we find the AP *zi-*rather than the *n-* that occurs before adjectives: *nguwo zi:mpʰi* 'which clothes?' (as compared with *nguwo ni:ngi* 'many clothes'). The preceding example serves to illustrate another important point: The AP that a noun determines is not necessarily phonologically identical with the CP of the noun itself.

A noun class is determined, then, by BOTH the CP of the noun and the pattern of agreement that the noun governs. Two nouns that have the "same" CP (in terms of phonological shape) do not always govern the same pattern of agreement. Compare in this respect the nouns *muti* 'tree' and *muke* 'woman'. These nouns have a CP with the shape *mu-*. They differ, however, in that in certain instances the AP that these nouns govern is not the same. For example, a finite verb in Chi-Mwi:ni typically must have an AP that agrees with the subject of the verb. We refer to this particular AP as the subject prefix (SP). The SP for *muti* is *u-*, as in *muti u-burbushiłe* 'the tree fell', whereas the SP for *muke* is null, as in *muke ∅-teteme:łe* 'the woman shivered'.

A third dimension that is sometimes used to identify the class to which a noun belongs involves the systematic pairing between singular and plural forms. A noun like *muti* (i.e. a noun with the CP *mu-* that requires the SP *u-*) generally has a corresponding plural form with the CP *mi-*. Thus the plural of *muti* is *miti* 'trees'. A noun like *muke* (i.e. a noun with the CP *mu-* that requires a null SP) generally has a plural form with the CP *wa-*. Thus the plural of *muke* is *wake* 'women'.

In addition to the SP, a verb in Chi-Mwi:ni may also have another AP; this second AP is determined by the object of the verb, and thus we will refer to it as the object prefix (OP). Although the SP is an obligatory element, in general the OP may or may not appear on a verb. The OP often functions as a device for signalling definiteness, as the examples in (6) illustrate:[3]

(6)                     a. *Nu:ru ∅-somełe chibu:ku.*
                           SP read        book
                        'Nuru read a book.'

                        b. *Nu:ru ∅-chi-somełe chibu:ku.*
                           SP OP read        book
                        'Nuru read the book.'

Both the SP and the OP may occur either with or without an overt controller NP present in the sentence. In other words, the NP that determines the shape of the SP or OP may itself be omitted from the surface form of the sentence. When the controller NP is omitted, the AP has much the same effect as an anaphoric pronoun, as in (7b):

(7)                     a. *Wake   wa-mw-osheze  mwa:na.*
                           women SP OP washed child
                        'The women washed the child.'

                        b. *Wa-mw-oshe:ze.*
                           SP  OP washed
                        'They washed him/her.'

---

[3] In the course of this chapter we will cite many examples where an OP occurs on the verb. The reason for this is that we are concerned here with grammatical relations, and the ability to govern an OP on the verb is a characteristic feature of the (principal) object in Chi-Mwi:ni and other Bantu languages. The reader should be warned, however, that an OP is not as commonly used with inanimate objects as the text might suggest. An OP is generally present when a human being functions as object, but generally not when an inanimate functions as object.

In most instances, the SP and the OP required by a given noun class will be identical phonologically. In (8) we list the main noun classes in Chi-Mwi:ni (numbered in accordance with the general practice in Bantu linguistic descriptions) together with the SP and the OP that they govern. The SP and the OP are first given in their morphophonemic representation. Due to the operation of various morphophonemic rules, in many cases the SPs and the OPs are pronounced in a form that differs from their basic shape; therefore, we list the main morphophonemic variants of each of the prefixes immediately after the morphophonemic representation. The reader is referred to Kisseberth and Abasheikh (forthcoming) for a detailed discussion of the rules that govern these variations. The purpose of this chart is simply to help the reader in parsing the many examples cited in the text.

| (8) | Noun Class | | Example | SP | OP |
|---|---|---|---|---|---|
| | 1: | 1 sg. | *mi* 'I' | /ni/: n, m, ŋ | same as SP |
| | | 2 sg. | *we* 'you' | ∅ | /xu/: x |
| | | 3 sg. | *ye* 'he, she' | | |
| | | | *muke* 'woman' | ∅ | /mu/: mw, m |
| | | | *mwa:na* 'child' | | |
| | 2: | 1 pl. | *si* 'we' | /chi/: ch, sh | same as SP |
| | | 2 pl. | *ni* 'you' | /ni/: n | same as SP |
| | | 3 pl. | *wo* 'they' | | |
| | | | *wake* 'women' | /wa/ | same as SP |
| | | | *wa:na* 'children' | | |
| | 3: | | *muti* 'tree' | /u/: w | same as SP |
| | 4: | | *miti* 'trees' | /ya/ | same as SP |
| | 5: | | *ijiwe* 'stone' | /i/: y | same as SP |
| | 6: | | *majiwe* 'stones' | /ya/ | same as SP |
| | 7: | | *chiguwo* 'rag' | /chi/: ch, sh | same as SP |
| | 8: | | *ziguwo* 'rags' | /zi/: z, s | same as SP |
| | 9: | | *nu:mba* 'house' | /i/: y | same as SP |
| | 10: | | *nu:mba* 'house' | /zi/: z, s | same as SP |
| | 11: | | *luti* 'stick' | /li/: l | same as SP |

## CHARACTERISTICS OF THE OBJECT

In the literature on Bantu languages, the "object" of the verb in Bantu languages is most often identified on the basis of three properties: (i) it is the NP that controls the OP that may appear on the verb; (ii) it is the NP that (in neutral contexts at least) immediately follows the verb; and (iii) it is the NP that may be promoted to subject via the syntactic process of Passivization. Bantu languages appear to differ with respect to whether just one NP in a clause may have any or all of these characteristics or whether more than one NP can share these characteristics. If one considers only morphologically simple (i.e. nonderived) verbs in Chi-Mwi:ni, it seems to be the case that in a given clause there will be only one NP displaying the features cited above. This NP is always unmarked—that is, it is neither preceded by a preposition nor suffixed with the locative -ni.

There may be more than one unmarked nonsubject NP in a clause. In his pioneering work on Bantu syntax, C. M. Doke (1938) refers to the unmarked NP that controls the OP and that normally follows immediately after the verb as the PRINCIPAL OBJECT of the verb. Doke refers to any other unmarked nonsubject NPs as SUBSIDIARY OBJECTS.[4] In order to illustrate this distinction between principal and subsidiary objects, consider the following Chi-Mwi:ni sentence:

(9)                   *Wa:na  wa-m-bozełe  mwa:limu zibu:ku.*
                      children SP OP stole   teacher     books
                      'The children stole the books from the teacher.'

In (9), the OP on the verb agrees with *mwa:limu* (a 3 sg. Class 1 noun). If the verb in (9) were to have an OP agreeing with *zibu:ku* (a Class 8 noun), an ungrammatical sentence would result, regardless of the relative ordering of *mwa:limu* and *zibu:ku*:

(10)                  *\*Wa:na wa-zi-bozełe* $\begin{cases} mwa:limu\ zibu:ku. \\ zibu:ku\ mwa:limu. \end{cases}$
                                SP OP

Thus, of the two unmarked nonsubject NPs in (9), only *mwa:limu* can control the OP. In Doke's terminology, *mwa:limu* is the principal object, while *zibu:ku* is a subsidiary object.

It will be noted that, not only does *mwa:limu* control the OP in (9), it also occurs in the position immediately after the verb. (9) represents the normal word order: No special emphasis is placed on either *mwa:limu* or *zibu:ku*. Although we have not made an intensive study of sentence stress in Chi-Mwi:ni, it appears that in neutral sentences the rightmost word in the verb phrase is more heavily stressed than are preceding words. Stress is generally on the penultimate syllable of a word, but under various conditions may be on the last syllable. In (9), *zibu:ku* is stressed more heavily than *mwa:limu*. If *zibu:ku* is placed before *mwa:limu*, a grammatical sentence results only if *zibu:ku* bears

---

[4] Cf. Doke (1938:418).

heavier stress than *mwa:limu*. Thus (11) is well-formed:

(11)                  *wa:na wa-m-bozele zibú:ku mwa:limu.*
                      SP OP
                      'The children stole **books** from the teacher.'

where the stress mark on *zibu:ku* indicates that it is more heavily stressed than
the following word(s) in the verb phrase, contrary to the usual situation. The
effect of moving a subsidiary object into position after the verb is to put special
emphasis on it.

The principal object not only governs the OP and immediately follows the
verb in the normal word order, it is also able to be made the subject of a passive
construction. (12) is the passive variant of (9):

(12)                  *Mwa:limu ∅-bozela      zibu:ku na wa:na.*
                      teacher   SP was stolen  books  by children
                      'The teacher had some books stolen (from him)
                      by the children.'[5]

In (12), *mwa:limu* is the subject of the passive verb *bozela*. The noun *zibu:ku*
cannot be the subject of this passive verb; (13) is ungrammatical:

(13)                  \**Zibu:ku zi- bozela      mwa:limu na wa:na.*
                      books  SP were stolen teacher     by children
                      'The books were stolen from the teacher by the
                      children.'

It is the presence of *mwa:limu* in a sentence such as (9) that prevents *zibu:ku*
from functioning as the principal object of the verb and thus being eligible for
passivization. For a sentence such as (14) is well-formed:

(14)                  *Wa:na  wa-zi- bozele zibu:ku.*
                      children SP OP stole   books
                      'The children stole the books.'

That is, the verb 'steal' (*-bo:l-* is the underlying representation of the verb root)
can take either one unmarked nonsubject NP, as in (14), or two such NPs, as
in (9). When *zibu:ku* occurs as the only unmarked nonsubject NP, as in (14),
then it controls the OP on the verb and can also be made the subject of a passive

---

[5] Many of the passive sentences cited in the text have no word-for-word equivalent in English.
In such cases we have attempted to construct an English sentence that conveys as far as possible
the essential grammatical relationships observable in the Chi-Mwi:ni example.

construction. (15) is the passive variant of (14):

(15)                        *Zibu:ku zi- bozela        na wa:na.*
                           books  SP were stolen by children
                           'The books were stolen by the children.'

Apparently, then, the ungrammaticality of (13) is the direct consequence of the
fact that when *-bo:ł-* 'steal' has two unmarked nonsubject NPs the indirectly
affected NP (*mwa:limu*) functions as the principal object, while the directly
affected NP (*wa:na*) is relegated to the role of subsidiary object.

The behavior of *-bo:ł-* is typical of verbs that allow two unmarked nonsubject
NPs. (16) illustrates the behavior of the verb *-p-* 'give':

(16)                        *Ni-m-pełe   Ja:ma kujá.*
                           SP OP gave          food
                           'I gave Jama food.'

The noun *Ja:ma*, a proper name, controls the OP in (16); an ungrammatical
sentence results if the verb agrees with *kuja* (a Class 9 noun):

(17)                        **Ni- 'i-pełe Ja:ma kujá.*

Not only does *Ja:ma* control the OP in (16), it is also located immediately after
the verb in the unmarked word order. Furthermore, *Ja:ma* can be passivized,
while *kuja* cannot be:

(18)                        *Ja:ma ∅-pela:       kuja na: mi.*
                           SP was given food by  me
                           'Jama was given food by me.'

(19)                        **Kuja   i-pela      Ja:ma na: mi.*
                           food SP was given         by  me
                           'Food was given to Jama by me.'

*Ja:ma*, a NP indirectly affected by the verb, exhibits the behavior of the
principal object, while *kuja*, the NP directly affected, functions as the subsidiary
object. In the preceding examples the NP indirectly affected refers to a human
being, but this is not always the case. When an inanimate NP is the indirectly
affected NP, we find that it too functions as the principal object, though with
one variation in behavior:

(20)                        *Ałi ∅-pashiłe chiga:ri o:liyo.*
                           SP applied  cart   oil
                           'Ali oiled the cart.'

In (20), *chiga:ri* is the indirectly affected NP, while *o:liyo* is directly affected.
*Chiga:ri* exhibits the expected behavior of a principal object. It can control the

OP on the verb 'apply' (-*pak*- is the underlying representation of this verb), whereas *o:liyo* cannot:

(21)                                     *Ali ∅-sh-pashile chiga:ri o:liyo.*
                                          SP OP

(22)                     *\*Ali ∅-i-pashile* $\begin{cases} chiga:ri\ o:liyo. \\ o:liyo\ chiga:ri. \end{cases}$

*Chiga:ri* can be passivized, but *o:liyo* cannot be:

(23)                             *Chiga:ri sh-pashila o:liyo na Ali.*
                                          SP

(24)                             *\*o:liyo i-pashila chiga:ri na Ali.*
                                          SP

The one essential point of difference between (20) and the examples cited earlier in (9) and (16) has to do with word order. It is possible to move *o:liyo* next to the verb in (20) without thereby putting particular emphasis on it:

(25)                             *Ali ∅-pashile o:liyo chiga:ri.*

(25) is pronounced like (20)—that is, with the expected stress pattern whereby the rightmost word in the verb phrase is more heavily stressed than are preceding words. Of course, a sentence like (26) is also possible, where *o:liyo* has heavier stress than *chiga:ri*:

(26)                             *Ali ∅-pashile o:liyo chiga:ri.*
                                 'Ali applied **oil** to the cart.'

But in (26) special emphasis is being placed on *o:liyo*, which is not true in (25).

To summarize what has been shown in this section, if a morphologically simple verb allows two unmarked nonsubject NPs, the indirectly affected NP will function as principal object and the directly affected NP as a subsidiary object. The principal object controls an OP on the verb and can be passivized. The principal object occurs immediately after the verb in the normal word order, although if the principal object is inanimate the subsidiary object may also occur immediately after the verb.

## THE "APPLIED" VERB

Let us turn now to the main topic of this paper: what is traditionally referred to by Bantuists as the applied or prepositional form of the verb. In Chi-Mwi:ni, this verbal form is characterized by the occurrence of a suffix -*il*-, which has several variant forms: *-el-*, *-il-*, *-el-*, *-iłiz-*, and *-ełez-*. The morphophonemic principles governing the selection of the correct shape of this suffix are given in Kisseberth and Abasheikh (1974b); being rather complex, they are not repeated here. In order to make clear to the reader that a given verbal form is an applied verb, we will capitalize the applied suffix whenever it occurs in our transcriptions.

The semantic functions of the applied verb in Chi-Mwi:ni are varied; we restrict ourselves to three primary uses. We label these uses as (i) benefactive, (ii) indirective, and (iii) instrumental. The benefactive use will be dealt with first.

### The Benefactive Applied Verb

The benefactive use of the applied verb can be illustrated by considering the following pair of sentences:

(27)          a. *Hamadi ∅-pishiłe cha:kuja.*
                        SP cooked      food
                 'Hamadi cooked food.'

              b. *Hamadi ∅-wa-pikILile         wa:na cha:kuja.*
                        SP OP cooked-APPL children     food
                 'Hamadi cooked food for the children.'

In (27a) *cha:kuja* is the principal object of this verb 'cook' (which has *-pik-* as the underlying form of the verb root). *Cha:kuja* may govern an OP, as shown by (28):

(28)                    *Hamadi ∅-sh-pishiłe cha:kuja.*
                                 SP OP
                        'Hamadi cooked the food.'

Furthermore, *cha:kuja* may become the subject of a passive construction based on (27a):

(29)                    *Cha:kuja  sh-pishila      na Hamadi.*
                                 food SP was cooked by
                        'The food was cooked by Hamadi.'

Turn now to (27b). In this sentence *wa:na* 'children', not *cha:kuja*, governs the OP on the verb (*wa:na* is a 3 pl. Class 2 noun and thus requires the OP *-wa-*). A sentence such as (30), where *cha:kuja* controls the OP, is ungrammatical:

(30)                    **Hamadi ∅-sh-pikILile wa:na cha:kuja.*
                                 SP OP

Placing *cha:kuja* next to the verb in (30) would in no way render the sentence acceptable.

*Wa:na* can also be made the subject of a passive variant of (27b), whereas *cha:kuja* cannot be. Consequently, (31) is well-formed, but (32) is not:

(31)      *Wa:na   wa-pikILila*          *cha:kuja na Hamadi.*
          children SP was cooked-APPL     food by
          'The children had food cooked for them by Hamadi.'

(32)      *\*Cha:kuja sh-pikILila wa:na na Hamadi.*
          SP
          'Food was cooked for the children by Hamadi.'

It is apparent, then, that *wa:na*, not *cha:kuja*, is the principal object in (27b). Word order confirms this, since *wa:na* is located immediately after the verb in the normal word order.

At this point let us introduce some terminology that will be of use in our discussion of the applied verb. We will refer to the verb in (27a), which lacks the applied suffix, as the 'basic' form of the verb. The verb in (27b) will be referred to as the 'applied' form. What we are terming here as the basic form may itself be morphologically complex, but this possible complexity is irrelevant to the present discussion. The basic form of the verb is converted into the applied form by the addition of the suffix *-il-* (in one of its surface shapes). The applied form of the verb typically allows the occurrence of an unmarked nonsubject NP that the basic form of the verb does not allow. In (27b) this "extra" NP is *wa:na* 'children'. We refer to this extra NP as being 'dependent' upon the applied form. That is, this NP could not occur in the sentence (as an unmarked NP) except by virtue of the fact that the verb is in its applied rather than its basic form. In the case of the benefactive applied, we refer to this extra NP as the 'beneficiary'. The NP that is dependent on the applied verb (the beneficiary, in the present case) typically functions as the principal object of the verb. We have seen that *wa:na* in (27b) governs the OP on the applied verb, can be passivized, and occurs immediately after the verb in the normal word order. The principal object of the basic verb, *cha:kuja* in (27a), ceases to be the principal object when the verb is in the applied form. We will say that the object of the basic verb is 'displaced' when the verb is put into the applied form. In (27b) *wa:na* will be said to have displaced *cha:kuja*. Displaced NPs function as subsidiary objects (in Doke's terms); that is, they remain unmarked, but do not exhibit the properties of the principal object.

Additional examples of benefactive applied verbs are cited in (33)–(34):

(33)      a.   *A:sha ∅-y-andishile: xati.*
                SP OP wrote    letter
               'Asha wrote the letter.'

      b.  *A : sha ∅-mw-andikILile   Nu : ru xati.*
             SP OP wrote-APPL        letter
             'Asha wrote the letter for Nuru.'

      c.  *Nu : ru ∅-andikILila :        xati   na A : sha.*
             SP was written-APPL letter by
             'Nuru had the letter written (for him) by Asha.'

      d.  *\*Xati y-andikILila          Nu : ru na A : sha.*
             letter SP was written-APPL        by
             'The letter was written for Nuru by Asha.'

(34)      a.  *Ja : ma ∅-i-tiłanziłe : nama.*
             SP OP cut     meat
             'Jama cut the meat.'

      b.  *Ja : ma ∅-sh-tiłangILile chija : na    nama.*
             SP OP cut-APPL small child meat
             'Jama cut the meat for the small child.'

      c.  *Chija : na    sh-tiłangILila :    nama na Ja : ma.*
             small child SP was cut-APPL meat by
             'The small child had the meat cut (for him)

      d.  *\*nama i-tiłangILila       chija : na    na Ja : ma.*
             meat SP was cut-APPL small child by
             'The meat was cut for the small child by Jama.'

In each of these examples it can be seen that the NP that is dependent on the applied form of the verb is the NP that governs the OP on the applied verb [cf. the (b) sentences], and can be passivized [cf. the (c) sentences]. The NP that is displaced by the dependent NP cannot be passivized [cf. the (d) sentences]. The normal word order, illustrated by the (b) sentences in (33)–(34), has the dependent NP occurring after the verb before the displaced NP. If the displaced NP is placed immediately after the verb, it must bear heavier stress than does the dependent NP, as in (35):

(35)          *A : sha ∅-mw-andikILile : xáti Nu : ru.*
             'Asha wrote a **letter** for Nuru.'

The beneficiary in a benefactive applied construction is generally a human NP, since actions are typically performed for the benefit of human beings, not inanimate objects. Nevertheless, one can find instances of benefactive applied constructions where an inanimate NP functions as the beneficiary:

(36)          *Ja : ma ∅-łetELele      sufuriya iyi  shfiniko.*
             SP brought-APPL pan     this lid
             'Jama brought a lid for this pan.'

The normal word order is that given in (36), with *sufuriya iyi* preceding *shfiniko*. This word order suggests that *sufuriya iyi* is the principal object. The evidence provided by passivization supports this view, since it is possible for *sufuriya iyi*, but not *shfiniko*, to passivize:

(37)  *Sufuriya iyi   i-łetElela*          *shfiniko na Ja:ma.*
      pan     this SP was brought-APPL lid       by
      'This pan was brought a lid by Jama.'

(38)  *\*Shfiniko chi-łetELela*          *sufuriya iyi   na Ja:ma.*
      lid        SP was brought-APPL pan       this by

Furthermore, *shfiniko* cannot control an OP on the applied verb, confirming that it has been displaced by *sufuriya iyi*:

(39)         *\*Ja:ma ∅-chi-łetELele sufuriya iyi shfiniko.*

Moving *shfiniko* next to the verb in (39) would not alter its ungrammaticality at all. A sentence such as (40), where *sufuriya iyi* controls the OP, is well-formed:

(40)         *Ja:ma ∅-i-łetELele sufuriya iyi shfiniko.*
             SP OP

The reader is reminded, however, that in Chi-Mwi:ni the OP is used to definitize a NP, and that it is much more common when the NP is human than when it is not.

In (36) the beneficiary is inanimate and the NP that it displaces is also inanimate. The displaced NP can, however, be human, as in (41):

(41)         *Nu:ru ∅-patILile   ga:rı shuʃe:ri.*
             SP got-APPL car    driver
             'Nuru got a driver for the car.'

The beneficiary in (41) is, again, the principal object. The normal word order is for *ga:ri* 'car' to precede *shufe:ri* 'driver'. Furthermore, *ga:ri* can be made the subject of a passive variant of (41):

(42)         *Ga:ri i-patILila*          *shufe:ri na Nu:ru.*
             car    SP was gotten-APPL driver   by
             'The car was gotten a driver by Nuru.'

A sentence like (43) is also well-formed, but is the passive counterpart of (44) rather than of (41):

(43)         *Shufe:ri ∅-patILila*          *ga:ri na Nu:ru.*
             driver   SP was gotten-APPL car    by
             'The driver had a car gotten (for him) by Nuru.'

(44)                        *Nu:ru ∅-m-patILile     shufe:ri ga:ri.*
                            SP OP got-APPL driver    car
                            'Nuru got a car for the driver.'

In (44) *shufe:ri* is the beneficiary and *ga:ri* is the displaced NP, in contrast to
(41), where the roles are reversed.

The data in this section have shown that the applied verb can convey the
notion of performing the action specified by the basic verb for the benefit of
someone or something. The reader may well be wondering whether a benefactive notion can be conveyed by using the basic verb plus a preposition in
front of the beneficiary NP. The preposition that one might expect to be used
in such a fashion in Chi-Mwi:ni would be *ka* (which has a variety of uses, two
of which will be noted below in the course of discussing the indirective and the
instrumental applied verbs). But sentences like those in (45) are not well-formed
(in the intended interpretation):

(45)                a.  *\*Hamadi ∅-pishile cha:kuja ka wa:na.*
                        SP cooked       food for children
                        'Hamadi cooked food for the children.'

                    b.  *\*A:sha ∅-andishile: xati  ka Nu:ru.*
                        SP wrote       letter for
                        'Asha wrote a letter for Nuru.'

                    c.  *\*Ja:ma ∅-tilanzile: nama ka  chija:na.*
                        SP cut          meat for child
                        'Jama cut the meat for the small child.'

Thus, although the benefactive applied verb conveys a "prepositional" notion,
this notion cannot be conveyed in Chi-Mwi:ni through the use of a preposition.
It must be expressed by the applied form of the verb.

## The Indirective Applied Verb

We turn now to a consideration of the indirective use of the applied verbal
form. Note the following pair of sentences:

(46)                a.  *Nu:ru ∅-chi-lesele  chibu:ku.*
                        SP OP brought book
                        'Nuru brought the book.'

                    b.  *Nu:ru ∅-m-letELele       mwa:limu chibu:ku.*
                        SP OP brought-APPL teacher        book
                        'Nuru brought the book to the teacher.'

*Chibu:ku* is the principal object of the basic verb in (46a), as can be seen from the fact that it can control an OP on the verb [cf. (46a)] and that it can be passivized [cf. (47)].

(47)        *Chibu:ku chi-łesela      na Nu:ru.*
                 book     SP was brought by
                 'The book was brought by Nuru.'

But in (46b) *mwa:limu* is the principal object, as can be seen from the fact that it governs the OP on the verb and is located immediately after the verb in the normal word order. Furthermore, *mwa:limu* can be passivized:

(48)        *Mwa:limu ∅-łetELela      chibu:ku na Nu:ru.*
                 teacher    SP was brought-APPL book  by
                 'The teacher was brought the book by Nuru.'

*Chibu:ku*, which functions as the principal object in (46a), ceases to have this function in (46b). It cannot control the OP on the applied verb. (49) is ill-formed:

(49)        *\*Nu:ru ∅-chi-łetELele mwa:limu chibu:ku.*
                 SP OP

Moving *chibu:ku* into position after the verb in (49) does not make the sentence grammatical. Nor can *chibu:ku* in (46b) be passivized:

(50)        *\*Chibu:ku chi-łetELela mwa:limu na Nu:ru.*
                 SP
                 'The book was brought to the teacher by
                 Nuru.'

Notice that the verb 'bring' (which has -łe:t- as the underlying verb root) allows one unmarked nonsubject NP. By adding the applied suffix to this basic verb, we get a verbal form that allows two unmarked nonsubject NPs. *Mwa:limu* in (46b) is the NP that is dependent on the applied verb, and once again we see that the dependent NP is the NP that functions as principal object. *Chibu:ku*, which is the principal object of the basic verb in (46a), is displaced in (46b), in which it functions as a subsidiary object. We have labeled the applied verb in (46b) as 'indirective'; this term is intended to indicate that the action expressed by the basic verb is directed toward someone or something. We shall refer to the NP that is dependent upon the indirective applied verb as the 'indirect' NP. In (46b) *mwa:limu* is the indirect NP, and *chibu:ku* is the NP that it displaces.

Additional examples of the indirective applied verbal construction are given in (51)–(52) below:

(51)        a.   *A:sha ∅-y-andishiłe: xati.*
                   SP OP wrote   letter
                 'Asha wrote the letter.'

  b. *A : sha ∅-mw-anḏikILile Nu : ru xaṯi.*
    SP OP wrote-APPL  letter
    'Asha wrote a letter to Nuru.'

  c. *Nu : ru ∅-anḏikILila :  xaṯi na A : sha.*
    SP was written-APPL letter by
    'Nuru had a letter written (to him) by Asha.'

  d. *\*Xaṯi y-anḏikILila  Nu : ru na A : sha.*
    letter SP was written-APPL  by
    'The letter was written to Nuru by Asha.'

(52)   a. *Mwa : na ∅-ṯawañize ma : yi.*
     child SP spilled water
     'The child spilled water.'

    b. *Mwa : na ∅-m-ṯawañIŁIZe Ałi ma : yi.*
     child  SP OP spilled-APPL water
     'The child spilled water on Ali.'

    c. *Ałi ∅-ṯawañIŁIZa  ma : yi na mwa : na.*
     SP was spilled-APPL water  by child
     'Ali had water spilled on him by the child.'

    d. *\*Ma : yi ya-ṯawañIŁIZa  Ałi na mwa : na.*
     water  SP was spilled-APPL by child
     'Water was spilled on Ali by the child.'

The (a) sentences in (51)–(52) have a basic verb that allows one unmarked
nonsubject NP. The (b) sentences show that the addition of the applied suffix
allows an additional unmarked NP to occur; this extra NP is the one that we
are calling the indirect NP. The (c) sentences show that this indirect NP can be
passivized, while the (d) sentences show that the NP displaced by the indirect
NP cannot be.

  In some (but not all) cases, a nonapplied verb in conjunction with the preposition *ka* may function similarly to the indirective applied verb. Thus (53)
below is equivalent in meaning to (51b):

(53)       *A : sha ∅-anḏishiłe : xaṯi  ka Nu : ru.*
        SP wrote  letter to
        'Asha wrote a letter to Nuru.'

Unlike (51b), (53) cannot also be understood as meaning that Asha wrote a
letter FOR Nuru. The preposition *ka* does not convey a benefactive notion.
However, (53) is still ambiguous. While *ka Nu : ru* can mean 'to Nuru', it is also
interpretable as 'at Nuru's place'.

In (53) *xati* functions as the principal object, as the examples in (54) make clear:

(54)       a.   *A:sha ∅-y-andishile: xati ka Nu:ru.*
                SP OP wrote    letter to Nuru
                'Asha wrote the letter to Nuru.'

           b.   *Xati y-andishila       ka Nu:ru na A:sha.*
                letter SP- was written to       by
                'The letter was written to Nuru by Asha.'

           c.   *(Ka) Nu:ru ∅-andishila:   xati   na A:sha.*
                SP was written letter by
                'Nuru was written a letter by Asha.'

(54a) shows that *xati* can govern an OP on the verb; (54b) that *xati* can be passivized; and (54c) that *Nu:ru* cannot be passivized, regardless of whether or not the preposition *ka* precedes it.

Not all indirective applied verbs have an equivalent sentence involving the basic verb plus the preposition *ka*. Consider, for instance, (55) and (56):

(55)                    *Ni-m-tumile Ja:ma ka Nu:rú.*
                        SP OP sent        to
                        'I sent Jama to Nuru (to tell
                         Nuru something).'

(56)                    *Ni-m-tumILile     Nu:ru Ja:má.*
                        SP OP sent-APPL
                        'I sent Jama to Nuru (to get him).'

Although in both (55) and (56) Jama is being sent and Nuru is his destination, the two sentences are given different interpretations as to the purpose of the sending—in one case it is to inform Nuru, in the other case it is to get him.

(57) and (58) provide another example where the two kinds of constructions are not equivalent in meaning:

(57)                    *Mwa:limu ∅-lesele chibu:ku ka Nu:ru.*
                        teacher   SP brought book   to
                        'The teacher brought the book to Nuru's place.'

(58)                    *Mwa:limu ∅-m-letELele      Nu:ru chibu:ku.*
                        teacher   SP OP brought-APPL       book
                        'The teacher brought the book to Nuru.'

In (57) *ka Nu:ru* is interpreted as 'to Nuru's place' rather than simply as 'to Nuru', whereas in (58) *Nu:ru* is the recipient (and is not necessarily at his home when he gets the book).

Because of examples such as those in (55)–(56) and (57)–(58), it is difficult to view the indirective applied verb as simply a VARIANT of the corresponding basic verb plus the preposition *ka* before the indirect NP. While the benefactive applied verb never has an equivalent construction involving the basic verb plus a preposition, the indirective applied verb sometimes has such an equivalent— but not always.

## The Instrumental Applied Verb

The third principal use of the applied verb stem is to convey the concept of performing an action by means of an instrument. This use can be illustrated by examining the following pair of sentences:

(59)             a.  *Nu:ru Ø-tiłanziłe: nama ka:  chisu.*
                     SP cut        meat  with knife
                     'Nuru cut the meat with a knife.'

                 b.  *Chisu, Nu:ru Ø-tiłangILile: nama.*
                     knife,        SP cut-APPL   meat
                     'The knife, Nuru cut meat with (it).'

In (59a) the NP that refers to the means by which the cutting is accomplished is preceded by the preposition *ka*; the verb is in its basic form. In (59b), on the other hand, the instrument is no longer preceded by the preposition *ka* and the verb is in its applied form. (We cite the instrumental applied verb with the instrument topicalized due to the fact that this verbal form is typically used when the instrument is the topic, what the sentence is "about." See below.) (59a) and (59b) are equivalent in terms of meaning, and in general it is the case that, for every basic verb that can occur with a *ka*-instrumental phrase, there is a corresponding applied verb which allows the instrument to occur unmarked. In other words, the situation here is different from the situation described on p. 192 above, where we saw that a benefactive applied verb could not be replaced by the basic verb plus a preposition and have the same meaning, and also different from the situation described on pp. 194–196, where we saw that an indirective applied verb sometimes, but not always, had an equivalent sentence involving the basic verb and a preposition. The instrumental applied verb always has a corresponding sentence involving the basic verb plus *ka*.

Nevertheless, the instrumental applied construction is not equivalent in all respects to the basic verb plus *ka*. The instrumental applied verb is limited in its occurrence to contexts where the instrument is the topic or, least, presupposed (not asserted). As evidence for this claim, we can cite several re-strictions on the instrumental applied construction that seem to reflect this contextualization. First consider the process of topicalization, whereby a NP is extracted from its original position in the sentence and fronted. (59b) shows us that an instrument in an applied construction can be topicalized. But other nonsubject NPs cannot be topicalized when the verb is in the instrumental applied form:

(60)                    *_Nama, Nu:ru ∅-ti̱langILile: chisu._
                        meat        SP cut-APPL   knife

In contrast, the benefactive applied verbal construction permits both the beneficiary and an NP displaced by a beneficiary to topicalize:

(61)          a. _Mwa:na, Nu:ru ∅-m-ti̱langILile: nama._
                 child            SP OP cut-APPL  meat
                 'The child, Nuru cut the meat (for him).'

              b. _nama, Nu:ru ∅-m-ti̱langILile mwa:na._
                 meat         SP OP cut-APPL  child
                 'The meat, Nuru cut for the child.'

Similarly, the indirective applied verbal construction permits both the indirect NP and also the NP that it displaces to topicalize:

(62)          a. _Nu:ru, A:sha ∅-mw-and̲ikILile: xati̱._
                                 SP OP wrote-APPL letter
                 'Nuru, Asha wrote him a letter.'

              b. _xati̱, A:sha ∅ mw and̲ikILile  Nu:ru._
                 letter        SP OP wrote-APPL
                 'The letter, Asha wrote it to Nuru.'

   A second restriction showing that the instrumental applied verb is contextually limited involves question formation. One cannot question the instrument, if the instrumental applied verb is used. Thus (63) is ill-formed:

(63)                    *_Nu:ru ∅-ti̱langILi:lé-ni    nama?_
                        SP cut-APPL    what meat
                        'What did Nuru cut the meat with?'

One can, however, question the NP displaced by the instrument:

(64)                    _Nu:ru ∅-ti̱langILi:lé-ni    chisu?_
                        SP cut-APPL    what knife
                        'What did Nuru cut with the knife?'

If one wishes to question an instrument, the basic verb, rather than the applied verb, must be used:

(65)                        *Nu:ru Ø-ṯiḻanziḻe ká   ni    ṉama?*
                            SP cut        with what meat
                            'What did Nuru cut the meat with?'

In comparison, the benefactive applied verbal construction allows both a beneficiary and an NP displaced by a beneficiary to be questioned:

(66)              a. *Nu:ru Ø-m-ṯiḻangILile   ná:ni ṉama?*
                     SP OP cut-APPL who   meat
                     'Who did Nuru cut the meat for?'

                  b. *Nu:ru Ø-m-ṯiḻangILi:lé-ni     mwa:na?*
                     SP OP cut-APPL  what child
                     'What did Nuru cut for the child?'

Similarly, the indirective applied verb allows both the indirect NP and the NP it displaces to be questioned:

(67)              a. *Nu:ru Ø-m-ḻetELele        ná:ni chibu:ku?*
                     SP OP brought-APPL who    book
                     'To whom did Nuru bring the book?'

                  b. *Nu:ru Ø-m-ḻetELe:lé-ni      mwa:limu?*
                     SP OP brought-APPL what teacher
                     'What did Nuru bring the teacher?'

   Further evidence of the restricted use of the instrumental applied verb is provided by relativization. When an unmarked NP in a relative clause is identical to the head noun of the relative clause, the unmarked NP is simply deleted. A NP that is preceded by a preposition cannot be so deleted; it must be replaced by a 'pro' form. If the relative verb is in the instrumental applied form, it is possible for the instrument to be deleted under identity with the head noun. (68) is a well-formed relative construction:

(68)   *chisu cha  Nu:ru Ø-ṯiḻangILilo: ṉamá*
       knife RM      SP cut-APPL   meat
       'the knife that Nuru cut the meat with'

       (RM = relative marker, consisting of an agreement prefix plus -*a*)

It is not possible, however, to have a relative construction where the NP displaced by the instrument is deleted under identity with the head noun.

(69)             *nama ya Nu:ru ∅-tiłangILilo: chisú
                meat RM      SP cut-APPL  knife
                'the meat that Nuru cut with the knife'

In order to get a well-formed relative clause, it is necessary to put the verb in its basic form and to have the preposition *ka* precede the instrument:

(70)             nama ya Nu:ru ∅-tiłanziło ka:  chisú
                meat RM      SP cut       with knife
                'the meat that Nuru cut with the knife'

The above data show that, if the relative verb is an instrumental applied verb, the relative clause provides information about the instrument rather than about the NP that the instrument displaces.

Compare the benefactive applied verb. Both the beneficiary and the NP displaced by the beneficiary can be deleted under identity with the head noun of a relative construction:

(71)        a.  mwana wa Nu:ru ∅-m-tiłangILilo: namá
                child   RM      SP OP cut-APPL  meat
                'the child who Nuru cut the meat for'

            b.  nama ya Nu:ru ∅-m-tiłangILilo  mwa:ná
                meat RM      SP OP cut-APPL child
                'the meat that Nuru cut for the child'

Similarly, both an indirect NP and the NP that it displaces can be deleted under identity with the head noun of a relative construction:

(72)        a.  mwalimu wa Nu:ru ∅-m-łetELelo        chibu:kú
                teacher  RM      SP OP brought-APPL  book
                'the teacher to whom Nuru brought the book'

            b.  chibuku cha Nu:ru ∅-m-łetELelo        mwa:limú
                book    RM      SP OP brought-APPL teacher
                'the book that Nuru brought to the teacher'

Yet another restriction on the instrumental applied verb involves sentence stress. It was pointed out above that the most neutral stress pattern appears to be one where the rightmost word in the verb phrase is more heavily stressed than are preceding words. This stress pattern would be used, for example, if the entire verb phrase is part of what is being asserted in the sentence and no special emphasis is being given to a particular element in the verb phrase. When we examine instrumental applied verbs we find that a sentence containing such a verb cannot be pronounced with a neutral stress pattern. Both (73a) and (73b) are inappropriate sentences:

(73)          a. *Nu:ru ∅-<u>ti</u>langILile: <u>n</u>ama chísu.
               SP cut-APPL    meat   knife
               'Nuru cut the meat with a knife.'

         b. *Nu:ru ∅-<u>ti</u>langILile: chisu <u>n</u>áma.
               'Nuru cut the meat with a knife.'

This absence of a neutral stress pattern for sentences containing an instrumental applied verb fits in with the observation that such verbs are used only when the instrument is presupposed and not asserted. This observation also seems to be involved in the explanation for the fact that only (74a), not (74b), is grammatical:

(74)          a.   Nu:ru ∅-<u>ti</u>langILile: <u>n</u>áma chisu.
               'Nuru cut the **meat** with a knife.'

         b. *Nu:ru ∅-<u>ti</u>langILile: chisu <u>n</u>ama.
               'Nuru cut the meat with a **knife**.'

(74a) asserts that it was meat that was cut with a knife. The instrument is presupposed here, and the sentence is well-formed. But (74b) asserts that a knife was used to cut the meat; this sentence is ill-formed, since the instrument cannot be asserted, but rather must be presupposed, if the instrumental applied verb is used. To render (74b) acceptable, the verb must be put in its basic form, with *ka* placed in front of the instrument:

(75)                Nu:ru ∅-<u>ti</u>lanzi<u>l</u>e ka: chísu <u>n</u>ama.
               'Nuru cut the meat with a **knife**.'

    Benefactive applied verbs behave quite differently from instrumental applied verbs, since it is possible to utilize the neutral stress pattern:

(76)                Nu:ru ∅-m-<u>ti</u>langILile mwa:na <u>n</u>áma.
               'Nuru cut the meat for the child.'

In addition, both (77a) and (77b) are well-formed:

(77)          a.   Nu:ru ∅-m-<u>ti</u>langILile: <u>n</u>áma mwa:na.
               'Nuru cut the **meat** for the child.'

         b.   Nu:ru ∅-m-<u>ti</u>langILile mwá:na <u>n</u>ama.
               'Nuru cut the meat for the **child**.'

The indirective applied verb behaves like the benefactive. Thus (78) is pronounced with the neutral stress pattern:

(78)        *Mwa:na ∅-m-tawañIŁIZe Aŧi ma:yi.*
            child   SP OP spilled-APPL  water
            'The child spilled water on Ali.'

And both (79a) and (79b) are well-formed:

(79)        a. *Mwa:na ∅-m-tawañIŁIZe má:yi Aŧi.*
               'The child spilled **water** on Ali.'

            b. *Mwa:na ∅-m-tawañIŁIZe Áŧi ma:yi.*
               'The child spilled water on **Ali**.'

At this point, let us return to (59a) and (59b)—which we repeat below for the reader's convenience—and look at these sentences from the point of view of grammatical relations.

(59)        a. *Nu:ru ∅-tiŧanziŧe: nama ka: chisu.*
            b. *Chisu, Nu:ru ∅-tiŧangILile: nama.*

In (59a) *nama* functions as the principal object of the verb. It can control an OP:

(80)        *Nu:ru ∅-i-tiŧanziŧe: nama ka: chisu.*
                  SP OP

and can be passivized:

(81)        *nama i-tiŧanzila  ka:  chisu na Nu:ru.*
            meat SP was cut with knife by
            'The meat was cut with a knife by Nuru.'

However, in (59b) *nama* no longer functions as the principal object of the verb. One piece of evidence in support of this claim is the observation that the instrumental applied verb cannot have an OP in agreement with *nama*:

(82)        *\*Chisu, Nu:ru ∅-i-tiŧangILile: nama.*

A second piece of evidence that *nama* is not the principal object of the instrumental applied verb comes from the fact that it cannot be passivized:

(83)        *\*Chisu, nama i-tiŧangILila na Nu:ru*

We have given evidence that *nama* is not the principal object in (59b). What about *chisu*? Has it assumed the role of principal object (as we would expect, on the basis of comparison with beneficiary and indirect NPs)? The data provided by object agreement might lead one to the conclusion that *chisu* is not the principal object, since (84) is ungrammatical:

(84)                          *Chisu, Nu:ru ∅-sh-tilangILile: nama.
                                    SP OP

That is, the instrumental applied verb may not agree with the instrument *chisu*. No OP is possible in this particular example, since we have already seen that *nama* cannot control the OP either. (But see the following section.)

While word order is generally a useful criterion for determining what the principal object of a verb is, it is not very helpful in the case of the instrumental applied verb. Above we showed that when a sentence is pronounced with the neutral stress pattern the principal object precedes the subsidiary object. The problem, of course, is that instrumental applied verbs cannot be pronounced with the neutral stress pattern—cf. (73).

There is, however, one significant point in favor of considering the instrument to be the principal object in (59b), namely, it can be passivized:

(85)             Chisu sh-tilangILila:      nama na Nu:ru.
                 knife  SP was cut-APPL meat by
                 'The knife was used to cut the meat by Nuru.'

This ability of the instrument to be passivized would certainly seem to count heavily in favor of considering the instrument to be the principal object in an instrumental applied construction, given that the NP displaced by the instrument in (59b), *nama*, has no objectlike characteristics at all. (But, again, see the following section.)

It is perhaps of some interest to note that at least one native speaker's reaction to a sentence like (85) is that this structure invites an interpretation whereby the subject of the passive applied verb, *chisu*, is understood as a beneficiary; but, since it is improbable that meat would be cut for the benefit of a knife, the sentence is readily understood in an instrumental rather than a benefactive sense.

## COMPLICATIONS

### Object Agreement

The question of grammatical relations in instrumental applied verbal constructions is not as simple as the discussion of (59b) above might indicate. (59b) represents the typical situation when the NP that is displaced by an instrument is inanimate. Some additional examples are given in (86):

(86)             a.  Muke      ∅-pezele: nṯhi ka lpe:lo.
                     woman SP swept    floor with broom
                     'The woman swept the floor with a broom.'

b.   *Lpe:ɬo, muke    ø-pelELe:    nt̲ʰi.*
broom woman SP swept-APPL floor
'The broom, the woman swept the floor with
(it).'

c.   **Lpe:ɬo, muke ø-i-pelELe: nt̲ʰi.*
            SP OP

d.   *Lpe:ɬo l-pelELa:        nt̲ʰi na: muke.*
broom SP was swept-APPL floor by woman
'The broom was used to sweep the floor by
the woman.'

e.   **Lpe:ɬo, nt̲ʰi i-pelELa         na: muke.*
broom floor SP was swept-APPL by woman
'The broom, the floor was swept with (it) by
the woman.'

(86a) has a basic verb plus the preposition *ka* in front of the instrument. (86b) has the applied form of the verb, with the instrument (not preceded by *ka* now) topicalized. (86c) shows that the NP displaced by the instrument cannot control an OP. (86d) shows that the instrument can be passivized, while (86e) shows that the NP displaced by the instrument cannot be passivized.

A somewhat different situation obtains when the NP displaced by an instrument is animate. Such an NP continues to be able to govern an OP on the applied verb. Consider the examples in (87):

(87)       a.   *Aɬi ø-m-d̲urile    Hamad̲i.*
              SP OP pricked
          'Ali pricked Hamadi.'

       b.   *Si:nd̲anu, Aɬi ø-m-d̲urILile        Hamad̲i.*
          needle       SP OP pricked-APPL
          'The needle, Ali pricked Hamadi with (it).'

       c.   **Si:nd̲anu, Aɬi ø-i-d̲urILile Hamad̲i.*

In (87) the basic verb has an OP agreeing with *Hamad̲i*. In (87) the verb is in the applied form, but the OP still is governed by *Hamad̲i*. (87) is ill-formed; that is, the applied verb may not have an OP agreeing with the instrument, *si:nd̲anu*.

An additional example, parallel to (87), is given in (88):

(88)          a.   *Haɬi:ma ø-m-bishiɬe mwi:zi.*
               SP OP hit    thief
           'Halima hit the thief.'

      b.   *Luti, Hali:ma ∅-m-bigILile    mwi:zi.*
          stick          SP OP hit-APPL thief
          'The stick, Halima hit the thief with (it).'

      c.   *Luti, Hali:ma ∅-1-bigILile mwi:zi.*

The (a) sentence gives the verb in its basic form; the (b) sentence reveals that the applied verb has an OP agreeing with the human NP that the instrument displaces; the (c) sentence shows that the instrument cannot control an OP on the applied verb.

We have claimed that the pattern illustrated in (87)–(88) is characteristic of animate nouns. So far, all the examples cited involve Class 1 and Class 2 nouns. Class 1 and Class 2 nouns consist entirely of human nouns, but there are human nouns that belong to other classes. In Chi-Mwi:ni diminutives are Class 7 or Class 8 nouns. (Recall that noun classes in Bantu languages are typically paired, one class being singular, the other plural; Class 7 nouns are singular, Class 8 are plural.) The noun *mwa:na* 'child' has the diminutive form *chija:na*, while *wa:na* 'children' has the diminutive form *zija:na*. Most commonly, a noun such as *chija:na* governs an OP that has the shape appropriate to a Class 1 noun—namely, *-m-*; it is possible, however, to use the OP *-chi-*, the shape that a Class 7 noun would be expected to require. In either case, if *chija:na* is displaced by an instrument, it still governs the OP:

(89)          *Si:ndanu, Ali ∅-$\begin{Bmatrix} m \\ chi \end{Bmatrix}$-durILile    chija:na.*

          needle      SP  OP  pricked-APPL child
          'The needle, Ali pricked the child with (it).'

Animals generally belong to Class 9 or Class 10. (These two classes have the same CP in both the singular and the plural—either *-n-*, which assimilates the point of articulation of a following stop, or ∅.) A Class 9 or Class 10 noun referring to an animal—*mbwa* 'dog/dogs', for instance—exhibits a peculiar agreement pattern, different from inanimate Class 9 and Class 10 nouns. *Mbwa* 'dog' requires the OP *-m-*, which is the OP that a Class 1 (human) noun requires. *Mbwa* 'dogs', on the other hand, most frequently occurs with the *-zi-* OP, the OP that a Class 10 noun generally requires. However, the *-wa-* OP can also be used; *-wa-* is the OP typically limited to Class 2 nouns.

When a noun such as *mbwa* (singular or plural) is displaced by an instrument, it still controls the OP:

(90)          *Si:ndanu, Ali ∅-$\begin{Bmatrix} zi \\ wa \end{Bmatrix}$-durILile:    mbwa.*

          needle      SP  OP  pricked-APPL dogs
          'The needle, Ali pricked the dogs with (it).'

To summarize, an animate noun that is displaced by an instrument retains a certain objectlike character in that it controls an OP on the instrumental applied verb. The instrument does not have this ability.

## Passivization

The natural question to ask at this point is, What about passivization? When the noun displaced by an instrument is animate, is it the instrument that passivizes—or is it the displaced NP? Let us first consider, displaced human nouns belonging to Class 1 and Class 2:

(91)       a.  *Luti l-bigILila      mwi:zi na Hali:ma.*
              stick SP was hit-APPL thief    by
              'The stick was used to hit the thief by Halima.'

       b.  ?*Luti, mwi:zi ∅-bigILila      na Hali:ma.*
              stick thief  SP was hit-APPL
              'The stick, the thief was hit with (it) by Halima.'

       c.  *Luti   ∅-bigILila      mwi:zi na Hali:ma.*
              stick SP was hit-APPL thief    by
              'The stick, the thief was hit with (it) by Halima.'

In (91a) it can clearly be seen that the instrument can passivize even when the noun displaced by the instrument is human. (91b), while of doubtful grammaticality, is a much better sentence than the (e) sentence in (86), for example. (91c) is a perfectly well-formed sentence. Note that in both (91b) and (91c) the displaced NP, *mwi:zi*, has been passivized and that it controls the SP on the passive applied verb. The only difference between the marginal sentence (91b) and the fully grammatical (91c) is word order. In (91b) *mwi:zi* is located in preverbal position, whereas in (91c) it occupies the position immediately after the verb (which, incidentally, is not an uncommon position in Chi-Mwi:ni for a subject to occupy when it is not the topic of the sentence).

The sentences in (92) below are parallel to those in (91):

(92)       a.  *Si:ndanu i-durILila*          *Hamadi na Ali.*
              needle    SP was pricked-APPL        by
              'The needle was used to prick Hamadi by Ali.'

       b.  ?*Si:ndanu, Hamadi ∅-durILila*      *na Ali.*
              needle           SP was pricked-APPL by
              'The needle, Hamadi was pricked with (it) by Ali.'

       c.  *Si:ndanu ∅-durILila*       *Hamadi na Ali.*
               needle  SP was pricked-APPL      by
              'The needle, Hamadi was pricked with (it) by Ali.'

The (a) sentence demonstrates that the instrument can be passivized; the (b) and (c) sentences show that a human being displaced by an instrument can also be passivized, though the sentence that results is fully grammatical only if the subject is in postverbal position. It should be emphasized that the instrument in the (c) sentence must be topicalized in order for the sentence to be well-formed.

It was shown in the preceding section that inanimates displaced by an instrument cannot be passivized. This is true regardless of word order. Consider (93):

(93)   a.   *Chiguwo sh-pangulILa        sabu:ra      na mwa:limu.*
           rag       SP was wiped-APPL blackboard by teacher
           'The rag was used to wipe the blackboard by the teacher.'

       b.   **Chiguwo, sabu:ra      i-pangulILa        na mwa:limu.*
           rag        blackboard SP was wiped-APPL by teacher
           'The rag, the blackboard was wiped with (it) by the teacher.'

       c.   **Chiguwo i-pangulILa        sabu:ra      na mwa:limu.*
           rag       SP was wiped-APPL blackboard by teacher
           'The rag, the blackboard was wiped with (it) by the teacher.'

The instrument can be passivized [cf. (93a)], but the inanimate noun that it displaces cannot be, no matter how it is positioned: before the verb [as in (93b)] or after the verb [as in (93c)].

We have seen so far that human nouns—of Class 1 and Class 2—can be passivized. Not all human nouns however, behave in this fashion. Consider (94):

(94)       a.   *Luti l-bigILila          chija:na na Hali:ma.*
               stick SP was hit-APPL child      by
               'The stick was used to hit the child by Halima.'

           b.   *Luti ∅-bigILila          chija:na na Hali:ma.*
               stick SP was hit-APPL child      by
               'The stick, the child was hit with (it) by Halima.'

           c.   **Luti chi-bigILila          chija:na na Hali:ma.*
               stick SP was hit-APPL child      by
               'The stick the child was hit with (it) by Halima.'

Recall that a noun like *chija:na*, which can be identified as a Class 7 noun, shows ambiguous behavior with respect to the OP. It can control either the OP *-m-*, like a Class 1 (human) noun, or the OP *-chi-*, like a Class 7 noun. *Chija:na* behaves similarly with respect to the SP. That is, it commonly occurs with a ∅ SP, like a Class 1 noun, but may also occur with the *-chi-* SP, like a Class 7 noun. Note now that (94b) is well-formed, but that (94c) is not. In (94b) *chija:na* controls the ∅ SP, while in (94c) it controls the *-chi-* SP. Thus *chija:na* can be passivized just in case it is being treated as a Class 1 noun. When it behaves like a Class 7 noun, as in (94c), passivization is disallowed.

The evidence provided by *chija:na* suggests that only nouns that behave parallel to Class 1 and Class 2 nouns (with respect to the SP or OP they govern) are capable of being passivized when displaced by an instrument. Further evidence in favor of this view is provided by Class 9 and Class 10 nouns referring to animals. Recall that a noun such as *mbwa* requires the *-m-* OP, just like a Class 1 noun, when functioning as a singular noun. It also requires the same SP as a Class 1 noun—namely, $\emptyset$. When *mbwa* functions as a plural, however, it generally requires the OP *-zi-*, characteristic of Class 10 nouns. It also requires the *-zi-* SP, again characteristic of a Class 10 noun. Now, note the data in (95) and (96):

(95)      a. *Luti l-bigILila:*     *mbwa na Hali:ma.*
           stick SP was hit-APPL dog  by
           'The stick was used to hit the dog by Halima.'

      b. *Luti $\emptyset$-bigILila:*     *mbwa na Hali:ma.*
           stick SP was hit-APPL dog  by
           'The stick, the dog was hit with (it) by Halima.'

(96)      a. *Luti l-bigILila:*     *mbwa na Hali:ma.*
           stick SP was hit-APPL dog  by
           'The stick was used to hit the dogs by Halima.'

      b. *\*Luti zi-bigILila:*     *mbwa na Hali:ma.*
           stick SP was hit-APPL dogs  by
           'The stick, the dogs were hit with (it) by Halima.'

(95b) is well-formed, where *mbwa* 'dog' is passivized; (96b) is ill-formed, where *mbwa* 'dogs' is passivized. The difference would seem to be a consequence of the fact that *mbwa* 'dog' requires the SP appropriate to Class 1 nouns, while *mbwa* 'dogs' requires the SP appropriate to Class 10 nouns.

It is only Class 1 and Class 2 nouns displayed by an instrument that are susceptible to passivization. A NP displaced by a beneficiary or an indirect NP cannot be passivized, regardless of word order. Consider benefactive constructions first. Given a sentence like (97):

(97)          *Ja:ma $\emptyset$-m-someshELEZe Nu:ru wa:na.*
              SP OP taught-APPL     children
              'Jama taught the children for Nuru.'

it is possible to passivize the beneficiary; thus (98) is well-formed:

(98)          *Nu:ru $\emptyset$-someshELEZa*   *wa:na  na Ja:ma.*
              SP was taught-APPL children by
              'Nuru had the children taught (for him) by Jama.'

If *wa:na*, rather than *Nu:ru*, controls the SP, as in (99) below, a grammatical sentence results—but *wa:na* is now interpreted as the beneficiary:

(99)      *Wa:na wa-someshEŁEZa      Nu:ru na Ja:ma.*
     children SP were taught-APPL
     'The children had Nuru taught (for them) by Jama.'

Thus (99) cannot be regarded as a passive variant of (97), but rather of (100):

(100)      *Ja:ma ∅-wa-someshEŁEZe wa:na      Nu:ru.*
     SP OP taught-APPL children
     'Jama taught Nuru for the children.'

No manipulation of the word order of (99) will result in a sentence where *wa:na* is understood as the displaced NP rather than as the beneficiary. In particular, (101)—which superficially looks similar to (91)—cannot be so interpreted:

(101)      ?*Nu:ru wa-someshEŁEZa      wa:na    na Ja:ma.*
     SP was taught-APPL children by
     'Nuru, the children had him taught (for them) by Jama.'

(101) is of doubtful grammaticality; but in any case it cannot be understood as a passive variant of (97). In (101) *wa:na* can be interpreted only as the beneficiary.

Turning to indirective applied constructions, we find again that a Class 1 or Class 2 human NP displaced by an indirect NP cannot be passivized. A sentence such as (102):

(102)      *Ałi ∅-m-tumILile      Nu:ru wa:na.*
     SP OP sent-APPL      children
     'Ali sent the children to (get) Nuru.'

allows the indirect NP to be passivized:

(103)      *Nu:ru ∅-tumILila      wa:na    na Ałi.*
     SP was sent-APPL children by
     [No close English equivalent exists. (103) means the same thing
       as (102).]

If *wa:na*, rather than *Nu:ru*, controls the SP, as in (104), a grammatical sentence results—but now *wa:na* is interpreted as the indirect NP:

(104)      *Wa:na wa-tumILila      Nu:ru na Ałi.*
     children SP were sent-APPL      by

In (104) *Nu:ru* is being sent to *wa:na*, whereas in (102) it is the opposite. Thus (104) cannot be viewed as a passive variant of (102), but rather of (105):

(105)              *Ali ∅-wa-tumILile    wa:na   Nu:ru.*
                   SP OP sent-APPL children
                   'Ali sent Nuru to the children (to get them).'

Again, no manipulation of the word order will convert (104) into a sentence that can be interpreted analogously to (102). (106) is of doubtful grammaticality, but in any case it can only be interpreted as meaning that *wa:na* is the indirect NP:

(106)              *?Nu:ru wa-tumILila        wa:na    na Ali.*
                   SP was sent-APPL children by

Thus (106) is not a passive variant of (102).

## Passivization Again

There is yet another situation which allows a displaced Class 1 or Class 2 noun to be passivized in an instrumental applied construction. Examine the data in (107):

(107)      a   *Li·kopi luti   la Hali:ma ∅ m bigILile    mwi:zi?*
               where is stick RM         SP OP hit-APPL thief
               'Where is the stick that Halima used to hit the thief?'

           b.  *Li:kopi luti   l-bigILila          mwi:zi?*
               where is stick SP was hit-APPL thief
               'Where is the stick that was used to hit the thief?'

           c.  *Li:kopi luti   la    mwi:zi ∅-bigILi:lá?*
               where is stick RM thief SP was hit-APPL
               'Where is the stick that the thief was hit with?'

In each of the examples in (107) *luti* is the head noun of a relative construction. In Chi-Mwi:ni relative clauses follows the head noun; they are introduced by a relative marker (RM), except that the RM is absent when the head noun is immediately followed by the main verb of the relative clause. (This occurs most commonly when the subject of the relative clause is deleted under identity with the head noun.) In (107a) the RM *la* occurs between the head noun, *luti*, and the subject of the relative clause, *Hali:ma*. In (107a), on the other hand, the instrument in the relative clause has been passivized into subject position (and hence controls the SP on the relative verb) and deleted under identity with the head noun. Hence no RM occurs in (107b).

The most interesting sentence is (107c), where it will be noted that the head noun *luti* is again followed by the RM *la*. This time the subject of the relative clause is *mwi:zi* 'thief' (as can be seen by the ∅ form of the SP on the relative verb). *Mwi:zi* has gotten into subject position via passivization. (107) shows that when the verb is in the instrumental applied form, two different NPs can passivize: The instrument [as in (107b)] and the Class 1 or Class 2 noun displaced by the instrument [as in (107c)].

An inanimate NP displaced by an instrument cannot be passivized in circumstances similar to (107c). Note (108):

(108)      a.  *Li:kopi lpeło    la:  muke     ∅-pelELo:     nt$^h$i?*
               where is broom RM woman SP swept-APPL floor
               'Where is the broom that the woman used to
                 sweep the floor?'

           b.  *Li:kopi lpeło    l-pelELa:                  nt$^h$i?*
               where is broom SP was swept-APPL floor
               'Where is the broom that was used to sweep the
                 floor by the woman?'

           c.  *\*Li:kopi lpeło    la:  nt$^h$i  i-pelE:lá?*
               where is broom RM floor SP was swept-APPL
               'Where is the broom that the floor was swept
                 with by the woman?'

Animate nouns that govern the same agreement prefixes as Class 1 and Class 2 nouns may be passivized. Thus *mbwa* 'dog' can passivize, but *mbwa* 'dogs' cannot. Contrast (109a) with (109b):

(109)      a.  *Li:kopi luti   la:  mbwa ∅-bigILi:lá?*
               where is stick RM dog SP was hit-APPL
               'Where is the stick that the dog was beaten with?'

           b.  *\*Li:kopi luti   la:  mbwa zi-bigILi:lá?*
               where is stick RM dogs  SP were hit-APPL
               'Where is the stick that the dogs were hit with?'

It must be emphasized, again, that it is only Class 1 and Class 2 nouns displaced by an INSTRUMENT that exhibit the behavior of (107). A Class 1 or Class 2 noun displaced by a beneficiary cannot be similarly passivized:

(110)      a.  *Ukopi   munt$^h$u wa   mwa:limu ∅-m- someshELEZa*
               where is man      RM teacher  SP OP taught-APPL
               *wa:ná?*
               children
               'Where is the man who the teacher taught the children
                 (for him)?'

b. *Ukopi munt<sup>h</sup>u ∅- someshEŁEZo wa:ná?*
where is man  SP was taught-APPL children
'Where is the man who had the children taught (for him)?'

≠ c. *?Ukopi munt<sup>h</sup>u wa wa:na wa-someshELE:zá?*
where is man  RM children SP were taught-APPL
'Where is the man who the children had taught (for them)?'

In (110b) the beneficiary in the relative clause is passivized into subject position and then deleted under identity with the head noun. Whether or not (110c) is a well-formed sentence, it cannot be considered a passive variant of (110a). (110c) can be interpreted only as specifying *wa:na* as a beneficiary, whereas in (110a) *wa:na* can be interpreted only as the displaced NP.

Similar observations hold for indirective applied verbs. A Class 1 or Class 2 noun displaced by an indirect NP cannot be passivized in a situation parallel to (107c):

(111)  a. *Ukopi munt<sup>h</sup>u wa Ali ∅-m-tumILilo wa:ná?*
where is man  RM SP OP sent-APPL children
'Where is the man whom Ali sent the children to?'

b. *Ukopi munt<sup>h</sup>u ∅-tumILila wa:ná?*
where is man  SP was sent-APPL children

≠ c. *?Ukopi munt<sup>h</sup>u wa wa:na wa-tumILi:lá?*
where is man  RM children SP were sent-APPL

In (111b) the indirect NP in the relative clause is passivized into subject position and then deleted under identity with the head noun *munt<sup>h</sup>u* 'man'. (111c) is of uncertain grammaticality, but in any case it cannot be interpreted as a passive variant of (111a). In (111c) *wa:na* must be understood as the indirect NP, whereas in (111a) *wa:na* must be interpreted as the NP displaced by the indirect NP.

## Instruments Co-occurring with Beneficiaries and Indirect NPs

We have not as yet exhausted the complications that the instrumental applied construction causes for a systematic account of grammatical relations in Chi-Mwi:ni. To get at the additional complexities, consider the following problem: Suppose that one wishes to include, in a single clause, both a beneficiary and an instrument; or both an indirect NP and an instrument; or both a beneficiary and an indirect NP. How is this done? We will begin to answer this question by examining (112):

(112)  *Muke ∅-wa-fulILe wa:na nguwo ka sa:buni.*
woman SP washed-APPL children clothes with soap
'The woman washed clothes for the children with soap.'

Note that the verb in (112) is in the applied form, with the beneficiary *wa:na* located immediately after the verb, and the displaced NP *nguwo* following the beneficiary. The instrumental phrase *ka sa:buni* 'with soap' follows the displaced NP. This represents the normal word order.

The preposition *ka* is obligatory in (112). If it is omitted, the resulting sentence is ill-formed:

(113)     *Muke     ∅-wa-fulILe          wa:na   nguwo sa:buni.
          woman SP OP washed-APPL children clothes soap

Thus in (112) *wa:na* is unequivocally the principal object of the verb. Not only does it control the OP and immediately follow the verb, but it also can be passivized:

(114)     Wa:na  wa-fulILa:              nguwo  ka   sa:buni na:
          children SP were washed-APPL clothes with soap     by
               muke.
               woman
          'The children had their clothes washed (for them) by
               the woman.'

The instrument, being preceded by a preposition in (112), is clearly not the principal object.

Nevertheless, the following sentence is well-formed:

(115)     Sa:buni s-fulILa              wa:na   nguwo na: muke.
          soap      SP was washed-APPL children clothes by woman
          'The soap was used to wash the clothes for the children by
               the woman.'

In other words, the instrument *sa:buni* can occur in an unmarked form if it is passivized. In (115) we have two different NPs DEPENDENT on the applied verb (that is, occurring in the sentence in an unmarked form by virtue of the presence of an applied verb): *wa:na*, the beneficiary, and *sa:buni*, the instrument. The explanation for why *sa:buni* must occur in a marked form in (112) but occurs in an unmarked form in (115) would appear to involve the observation made on p. 196—namely, the instrumental applied verb is used when the instrument is not asserted, but rather is presupposed or the topic of the sentence.

It is, therefore, not just a passive structure like (115) that permits the instrument to occur in an unmarked form. Topicalization of the instrument also allows the instrument to occur without a preposition:

(116)  Sa:buni, muke     ∅-wa-fulILe          wa:na   nguwo.
       soap      woman SP OP washed-APPL children clothes
       'The soap, the woman washed clothes for the children with (it).'

It is only topicalization of the instrument that allows the instrument to be unmarked. In (117a) the beneficiary is topicalized, and in (117b) the NP displaced by the beneficiary is topicalized; in neither case can the preposition *ka* be omitted:

(117)  a.  *Wa:na, muke    ∅-wa-fulILe:       nguwo ka  sa:buni.*
         children woman SP OP washed-APPL clothes with soap

      b.  *Nguwo, muke    ∅-wa-fulILe        `   wa:na ka  sa:buni.*
         clothes  woman SP OP washed-APPL children with soap

Relativization provides a third context in which the instrument can be grammatically dependent on an applied verb which also has a beneficiary dependent on it. We have already pointed out that unmarked NPs are simply deleted under identity with the head noun of a relative clause. In most cases, an NP preceded by a preposition is replaced by a pronominal form if it is identical to the head noun of a relative clause. There is, however, an exception to this practice. An instrument preceded by *ka* cannot be relativized at all. (118) is ungrammatical:

(118)            *\*chisu cha Nu:ru ∅-tiłanziło: nama ka:  chó*
            knife RM     SP cut      meat with it
            'the knife that Nuru cut the meat with'

To obtain a well formed relative clause, one must use the applied verb.

(119)            *chisu cha Nu:ru ∅-tiłangILilo: namá*
            knife RM     SP cut-APPL  meat
            'the knife that Nuru cut the meat with'

In (119), the instrument in the relative clause has been deleted under identity with the head noun. This deletion is possible because the instrument in the relative clause is unmarked, being grammatically dependent on the applied verb.
    With the above facts in mind, examine (120):

(120)    *sabuni za: muke    ∅-wa-fulILo       wa:na  nguwó*
         soap  RM woman SP OP washed-APPL children clothes
         'the soap that the woman washed the clothes for the
            children with'

A sentence such as (120) arises from the deletion of the instrument in the relative clause under identity with the head noun of the relative clause, but this deletion is possible only if the instrument is in its unmarked form. Thus the instrument in (120) must be grammatically dependent upon the applied verb. The beneficiary, however, is also grammatically dependent on the same verb.

If either the beneficiary or the NP displaced by the beneficiary is deleted under identity with a head noun, the instrument must be preceded by the preposition. Thus (121a) and (121b) would both be ungrammatical if *ka* were omitted:

(121)   a. *wana    wa: muke    Ø-wa-fulILo:          nguwo ka  sa:buni*
            children RM woman SP OP washed-APPL clothes with soap
            'the children who the woman washed clothes (for them) with soap'

        b. *nguwo za:  muke    Ø-wa-fulILo          wa:na  ka  sa:buni*
            clothes RM woman SP OP washed-APPL children with soap
            'the clothes that the woman washed for the children with soap'

So far in this section we have considered only sentences where an instrument occurs in the same clause as a beneficiary. Let us turn now to the case where an instrument occurs in the same clause as an indirect NP:

(122)       *Ali Ø-m-letELele        Nu:ru skuñi    ka   chiga:ri.*
               SP OP brought-APPL          firewood with cart
            'Ali brought firewood to Nuru with a cart.'

Note that the indirect NP, *Nu:ru*, governs the OP on the applied verb and immediately follows the verb. *Skuñi*, the NP displaced by *Nu:ru*, occurs next, followed by the *ka*-instrumental phrase. The indirect NP in (122) can be passivized, further establishing that it functions as the principal object of the verb:

(123)       *Nu:ru Ø-letELela            skuñi    ka   chiga:ri na Ali.*
               SP was brought-APPL firewood with cart        by
            'Nuru was brought firewood with a cart by Ali.'

Although the *ka* cannot be omitted from (122), it is still possible to passivize *chiga:ri*:

(124)       *Chiga:ri chi-letELela            Nu:ru skuñi na Ali.*
               cart       SP was brought-APPL
            'The cart was used to bring Nuru firewood by Ali.'

In other words, if the instrument is the topic (as a subject generally is), then it occurs in its unmarked form. The instrument can occur in an unmarked form only if it is grammatically dependent on an applied verb. Thus the applied verb in (124) has two NPs dependent upon it: *Nu:ru*, the indirect NP, and *chiga:ri*, the instrument.

The instrument can also be topicalized in its unmarked form:

(125)        *Chiga:ri, Ali Ø-m-letELele*        *Nu:ru skuñi.*
            cart        SP OP brought-APPL       firewood
            'The cart, Ali brought firewood to Nuru with (it).'

The instrument cannot be in its unmarked form if the indirect NP is topicalized or if the NP displaced by the indirect NP is topicalized. *Ka* cannot be omitted in either (126a) or (126b):

(126)    a. *Nu:ru, Ali Ø-m-letELele*       *skuñi*    *ka*    *chiga:ri.*
                  SP OP brought-APPL firewood with cart

        b. *Skuñi, Ali Ø-m-letELele*        *Nu:ru ka*    *chiga:ri.*
                  SP OP brought-APPL       with cart

The instrument may be deleted under identity with a head noun in a relative construction, which is possible only if it is in its unmarked form and dependent upon an applied verb:

(127)        *chigari cha Ali Ø-m-letELelo*       *Nu:ru skuñi*
            cart    RM   SP OP brought-APPL       firewood
            'the cart that Ali brought the firewood to Nuru with'

The above data show that both an instrument and an indirect NP can be dependent on an applied verb at the same time. While only the indirect NP can govern an OP on the verb, both the indirect NP and the instrument can be passivized.

We have seen that a beneficiary and an instrument or an indirect NP and an instrument may both be simultaneously linked to an applied verb. Thus both may exhibit at least one property of a principal object—namely, the ability to passivize. A NP that is dependent on an applied verb always has this property (as the examples throughout this chapter have shown). Consider now the co-occurrence of a beneficiary and an indirect NP in the same clause:

(128)        *Hamadi Ø-mw-andikILile*    *mwa:na xati*    *ka A:sha.*
               SP OP wrote-APPL child      letter   to
            'Hamadi wrote a letter for the child to Asha.'

In (128) *mwa:na* is the beneficiary: It governs the OP and follows immediately after the verb. *Xati* is the NP displaced by the beneficiary and follows the beneficiary in the normal word order. The *ka*-indirective phrase comes last.

It is not possible to omit the *ka* from (128):

(129)          **Hamadi ∅-mw-andikILile mwa:na xati A:sha.*

Unlike the instrument, the indirect NP cannot occur unmarked in a passive construction either:

(130)     **A:sha ∅-andikILila        mwa:na xati   na Hamadi.*
          SP was written-APPL child     letter

Only the beneficiary may be passivized; when it is, the indirect NP must still be preceded by a preposition:

(131)     *Mwa:na ∅-andikILila:       xati   ka A:sha na Hamadi.*
          child    SP was written-APPL letter to         by
          'The child had a letter written for (him) to Asha by
             Hamadi.'

Similarly, one cannot topicalize the indirect NP in its unmarked form when a beneficiary occurs in the same clause. (132) is ill-formed:

(132)         **A:sha, Hamadi ∅-mw-andikILile    mwa:na xati.*
                 SP OP wrote-APPL child      letter
              'Asha, Hamadi wrote a letter to her for the child.'

Finally, the indirect NP cannot be deleted under identity with the head noun of a relative construction. (133) is ill-formed:

(133)     **muke   wa Hamadi ∅-mw-andikILilo    mwa:na xati*
          woman RM        SP OP wrote-APPL child      letter
          'the woman who Hamadi wrote a letter to for the child'

To obtain a well-formed relative clause analogous to (133), one must have the preposition *ka* plus a pronominal form:

(134)     *muke   wa Hamadi ∅-mw-andikILilo  mwa:na xati ka:ké*
          woman RM        SP OP wrote-APPL child    letter to her
          'the woman who Hamadi wrote a letter to her for the child'

The main thrust of the examples in this section, then, is to show that, although an applied verb cannot have TWO NPs grammatically dependent on it (i.e. occurring in an unmarked form by virtue of the verb being an applied verb) if the NPs are a beneficiary and an indirect NP, such a double dependency is possible if one of the NPs is an instrument and the other a beneficiary or an indirect NP. When an NP is dependent on an applied verb, it has the ability to passivize—and thus has one of the essential characteristics of the principal object. Consequently, when two NPs are dependent on an applied verb, there are two NPs that have a characteristic feature of the principal object.

## CONCLUSIONS

We have assumed here the correctness of the view that unmarked NPs in a Chi-Mwi:ni clause stand in various syntactic relationships to the verb (in addition to having certain semantic roles in the clause). These syntactic relationships are usually viewed by linguists as being identifiable in terms of certain (clusters of) grammatical properties that are associated with particular relationships. In Bantu linguistics, the relationship of (principal) object of the verb is frequently identified in terms of three grammatical properties: verb agreement, word order, and susceptibility to passivization. When these properties converge on a single NP in a clause, there is little difficulty in deciding that that NP is indeed the object. The Chi-Mwi:ni data unearthed in the present study show, however, that the grammatical properties in question do not converge in an unambiguous fashion in all cases.

We have seen, for instance, that a NP may have one of the relevant characteristics without necessarily having the others; thus an instrument in Chi-Mwi:ni (if dependent on an applied verb) can passivize, but does not control an OP on the verb. Furthermore, whereas usually only one NP in Chi-Mwi:ni can be the principal object of the verb, we find that in certain cases involving instruments two different NPs may exhibit characteristics of the principal object.

One possible reaction to these data is to claim that the notion (principal) object in Chi-Mwi:ni is not discrete—whereby a NP either is or is not the principal object. Rather, one might claim that there are degrees to which a NP participates in the principal object relationship. Under this view, instruments are not as fully principal objects as, say, beneficiaries (since instruments cannot control an OP whereas beneficiaries do). On the other hand, instruments—since they can passivize—do participate in the principal object relationship in part, unlike the NPs displaced by a beneficiary or indirect NP (e.g. *xati* in *A:sha mw-andik-il-il-e Nu:ru xati* 'Asha wrote a letter for/to Nuru'). Notice that the extent to which a NP participates in the principal object relationship is (in Chi-Mwi:ni at least) deeply connected with the semantic role of the NP in the clause.

The Chi-Mwi:ni data might also suggest that more than one NP may participate in the principal object relationship at the same time. In particular, in sentences where both an instrument and a beneficiary or indirect NP depend on an applied verb, both appear to be functioning as principal objects. Of course, we have seen that the beneficiary or indirect NP is more fully a principal object than the instrument. But this does not alter the fact that the instrument (in being able to passivize) undergoes a transformation that is reserved for the principal object.

Whether or not the implications of the Chi-Mwi:ni data mentioned above (the nondiscreteness of grammatical relationships, the possibility of more than one NP being in the same grammatical relationship to the verb) turn out to be supported by additional data, it is clear to us that Bantu languages offer a fertile area for the study of grammatical relations—an area that must be explored thoroughly if a proper understanding of grammatical relationships is to be achieved. The present paper has examined only a small area of the grammar of one Bantu language; it is thus just a beginning.

## REFERENCES

Doke, C. M. (1938) *Text Book of Lamba Grammar*, Witwatersrand University Press, Johannesburg.
Goodman, M. (1967) "Prosodic Features of Bravanese, a Swahili Dialect," *Journal of African Languages* 6, 278–284.
Kisseberth, C. W. and M. I. Abasheikh (1974a) "Vowel Length in Chi-Mwi:ni—a Case Study of the Role of Grammar in Phonology," in M. W. La Galy, R. A. Fox, and A. Bruck, eds., *Papers from the Parasession on Natural Phonology*, Chicago Linguistic Society, University of Chicago, Chicago, Illinois.
Kisseberth, C. W. and M. I. Abasheikh (1974b) "A Case of Systematic Avoidance of Homonyms," *Studies in the Linguistic Sciences* 4.1, University of Illinois, Urbana, Illinois, 107–124.
Kisseberth, C. W. and M. I. Abasheikh (1974c) "The Perfect Stem in Chi-Mwi:ni," *Studies in the Linguistic Sciences* 4.2, University of Illinois, Urbana, Illinois, 123–138.
Kisseberth, C. W. and M. I. Abasheikh (1974d) "On the Interaction of Phonology and Morphology: A Chi-Mwi:ni Example," *Studies in the Linguistic Sciences* 4.2, University of Illinois, Urbana, Illinois, 139–147.
Kisseberth, C. W. and M. I. Abasheikh (forthcoming) "The Morphophonemics of Chi-Mwi:ni Prefixes."
Whiteley, W. H. (1965) "Notes on the Ci-Miini dialect of Swahili," *African Language Studies* 6, 67–72.

# A AGREES WITH B IN ACHENESE:
# A PROBLEM FOR RELATIONAL GRAMMAR

*JOHN M. LAWLER*
*University of Michigan*

## INTRODUCTION

The problem of dealing with verb agreement in a principled way in a generative framework has concerned linguists for some time.[1] At least since the non-publication of Postal (1967), in which some of the basic difficulties were outlined, there have been a number of lively discussions, including Morgan (1972) and Anderson (1974). More recently, work in progress in the development of Relational Grammar (RG) by David Perlmutter and Paul Postal[2] has attempted to provide, for the first time, a treatment of the phenomenon based on independently motivated principles, which, if they turn out to provide predictive

[1] Since this chapter was written, I have ceased to believe that a derivational model such as the one used here is a reasonable vehicle for investigating natural language (see Lawler 1975a for details and reasons). I have chosen, however, to leave the arguments and explication in this paper intact, even though I believe them to be seriously inadequate, for the reason that they are consistent with the usual tradition in which RG operates, and, as such, are stated in a mode relevant to the concerns of those interested in RG. In addition, I have nothing to replace them with at the present time (except for what may develop from the remarks in the concluding section), and do not wish to appear more incoherent than usual. For this intellectual cop-out, I beg the reader's indulgence.

[2] This study is concerned primarily with the ways in which Achenese agreement violates some of the principles that Perlmutter and Postal have proposed as universals of Relational Grammar. As such, it would be in order to cite the literature where these principles are proposed; unfortunately, at the present time Relational Grammar exists in the oral tradition exclusively, which makes sources a little hard to find. I will have reference here to an unpublished compendium of claims and hypotheses generated by Perlmutter, Postal, and Johnson, most of which is contained (if in print at all) in documents which threaten dire penalties for quotation. Much of this study is also due to personal communication from Paul Postal.

accuracy, will be a considerable improvement over—and a crucial weakening[3] of—transformational grammar.

The purpose of this study is to present some data on verb agreement and various syntactic rules in Achenese, an Indonesian language of northwest Sumatra.[4] The workings of Achenese agreement are unusual; they constitute a major counterexample to the treatment of verb agreement originally proposed by Perlmutter and Postal. They have since retreated from the position they originally held (Paul Postal, personal communication), in large part because of the evidence from Achenese. It seems to me to be important to present this data, not only because of its importance to Relational Grammar but because of its intrinsic interest and because it may stimulate some further research along certain lines which I will discuss below.

## AGREEMENT IN ACHENESE

Achenese (Ac) is related, and in many respects similar, to other Indonesian languages, although its phonology is unusual, perhaps due to continuing influence from Mon-Khmer.[5] The feature that will most concern us here is the

[3] I use "weakening" in its nonpejorative sense, the sense used by many linguists in discussing generative phenomena. Basically, all it means is that a theory of language should contain as little in the way of special ad hoc devices as possible. If it can be shown that agreement phenomena stem from independent (possibly perceptual) causes, the devices that in the past have been built into a grammar to account for them are no longer necessary, and the theory becomes simpler to state. It is this beneficial sense of "weakening" that is intended.

[4] Also known as Acehnese, Bahasa Aceh, and Bat$^\theta$a Aceh. There are very few sources of data on Achenese, and none in English on Achenese syntax. The sources I have been able to find are: Djajadiningrat (1934), a large Achenese–Dutch dictionary, whose phonology is not above suspicion; Makam and Burr (1971), a small preliminary English–Achenese and Achenese–English word list; Ishak (1968), a small treatise (in Indonesian) dealing primarily with morphology, on the Indonesian model; and Van Langen (1889), which is not particularly informative, either. Achenese is spoken by approximately two million people; it exists in several dialects. The dialect represented here is that spoken in the village of Montasi in Aceh Besar.

[5] See Collins (forthcoming) for further information on the substratum problem. The notation I use here is relatively phonetic. The system looks like the following:

| Vowels | | | | Consonants | | | | | |
|---|---|---|---|---|---|---|---|---|---|
| | *Oral* | | | | | | | | |
| | F | C | B | | L | D | P | V | G |
| High | i | ɨ | u | Stops vl plain | p | t | c | k | ʔ |
| High mid | e | | o | asp | $p^h$ | $t^h$ | $c^h$ | $k^h$ | |
| Low mid | ɛ | ə | ɔ | vd plain | b | d | j | g | |
| Low | | a | | asp | $b^h$ | $d^h$ | $j^h$ | $g^h$ | |
| | *Nasal* | | | Fricatives (vl) | | $t^\theta$ | | | h |
| High | ĩ | ɨ̃ | ũ | Nasals (vd) plain | m | n | ny | ng | |
| Low | ẽ | ã | õ | asp | $m^h$ | $n^h$ | $ny^h$ | $ng^h$ | |
| | | | | funny | m̃ | ñ | ñy | ñg | |
| | | | | Semivowels (vd) | w | | y | | |
| | | | | Resonants (vd) plain: | l | r | | | |
| | | | | asp: | $l^h$ | $r^h$ | | | |

language's complete system of verbal agreement prefixes, a phenomenon which is present in only fragmentary form in most other Indonesian languages. I should perhaps caution the reader that I use the term AGREEMENT in a broad sense here; there are a number of implications of the Ac phenomena which call the normal senses of this common linguistic term into question. I will discuss some of these difficulties at the end of this chapter. In addition, I should mention that there is no phonological evidence of which I am aware that indicates un-ambiguously that the morphemes I have identified as 'agreement' are indeed prefixes rather than particles. Although their position is fixed with respect to the verb, there is virtually no internal sandhi in Ac that could be used to indicate the absence of a word boundary between these morphemes and the verb itself. The positional evidence that I have found is discussed below; for our present purposes, it makes little difference whether these are phonologically prefixes, although there are some implications that will be discussed later.

The following chart presents the free pronouns and agreement prefixes of Ac:[6]

| Person | Singular | | | Plural | |
|---|---|---|---|---|---|
|  | *Pronoun* | *Prefix* | *Pronoun* | *Prefix* | |
| 1 | *lon* | *lon-* (polite) | *gitanyɔ* | *ta-* (inclusive) | |
|  | *kɛ* | *ku-* (impolite) | *kamɔ* | *mɨ-* (exclusive) | |
| 2 | *drɔn* | *nɨ-* | *drɔnnyɔ* | *nɨ-* (older than speaker) | |
|  | *gata* | *ta-* | *gatanyɔ* | *ta-* (same age) | |
|  | *kah* | *ka-* | *kahnyɔ* | *ka-* (younger) | |
| 3 | *gɔpnyan* | *gɨ-* | *uwn ʔɨjɨun* | *gɨ-* (older or same age) | |
|  | *jih* | *ji-* |  | *ji-* (younger) | |

*Footnote 5 continued*
The following should be noted about this schema. High oral vowels are very high and tense; /ɨ/ is rounded to [ʉ] after labials; high mid vowels are also very high; final vowels diphthongize as follows: /e#/ = [ey]: /o#/ = [ow]; /ɛ#/ = [æy]; /ɔ#/ = [əw]; there are probably several different schwas—at least one appears to represent /ɔ/ around certain nasal consonants; the nasal vowels neutralize the high/low-mid distinction. There is a contrastive aspirated consonant for every plain consonant except [ʔ], [h], [tᶿ], [w], and [y]. /tᶿ/ is an interdental affricate which is a reflex of Proto-Indonesian *s; it patterns as a fricative. Glottal stop represents underlying /k/ finally, and also appears in other positions, where it does not represent /k/; I have chosen to mark it wherever it appears, in the interests of phonetic reality, and to make the data more usable. /pʰ/ is often realized as [ɸ] or [pɸ]. There are three sets of nasals: plain, aspirated, and "funny". These latter are nasal consonants pronounced in the appropriate place with significantly reduced nasal air flow, probably produced by partial closure of the velum; they are slightly longer than ordinary nasals, and do not produce the same allophones of vowels in their enviroment as do the plain nasals. They appear to be reflexes of certain nasal + voiced stop clusters in Proto-Indonesian, but no longer do they consist of a prenasalized stop. They are extremely difficult to produce and detect. Stress is on the last syllable, and normal delivery is at an extremely high rate of speed, with copious fast speech rules operating; I have not even attempted to represent these. As should be evident, the phonology of this language would repay some study.

    [6] I should perhaps remark on the provenance of the categories of person and number represented in this chart. Except for the first person, there is really not a plural for the pronouns, and the first-person plural can profitably be regarded as an extension of the category of person (inclusive = 1

As might be expected from such a complicated paradigm, there are many asymmetries. The first-person-singular pronouns are differentiated, as far as I can tell, by social class, which may represent a weakening of an older register system. This differentiation does not appear in the first-person plural, where inclusive/exclusive is the only operative feature. The second and third persons are differentiated along age lines in both singular and plural. It is clear that the plural is derived from the singular here—*nyɔ* is a demonstrative, meaning 'this'. In the third person, there are only two singular pronouns, as opposed to the three in the second person; *gɔpnyan* is used for those older than the speaker, or of the same age, while *jih* is used for those younger. The third-person-plural pronoun is not differentiated by age itself, although the general third-person prefixes are used with it precisely as in the singular. *Awaʔnyan* actually means 'those people'. In practice, the forms denoting older people are used to indicate respect, and there is undoubtedly a very complex pattern of usage involved; however, the morphological and syntactic facts are sufficient for our discussion.

These prefixes (as I will refer to them from now on, pace the previous remarks) precede all derivational prefixes on the verb (of which only three or four are productive, an extremely small number for an Austronesian language). The prefixes are required, at least in main clauses:

(1)        a. *Lon lon-jaʔ u- pɨkan.*[7]
             I    1s- go to-market
             'I go to the market.'

        b. *Gɔpnyan gɨ- jaʔ u- pɨkan.*
             he (old)  3o-go to-market
             'He goes to the market.'

(2)        a. *Jih      ji- langũ krung*
             he(yng) 3y-swim river
             'He swims the river.'

        b. *Jih ji- mɨ-langũ.*
             he$_y$ 3y-X- swim
             'He swims.' (intransitive)

        c. *Jih ji- pɨ-   langũ anɨʔ agam t$^\theta$i- blah deh krung.*
             he$_y$ 3y-caus-swim child male one-side far river
             'He makes/made the boy swim across the river.'

In the sentences above, note that the agreement prefixes precede the derivational prefixes *pɨ-* 'causative' and *mɨ-* 'X'. (I give no gloss except a place holder

---

and 2; exclusive = 1 and 3). Furthermore, the interplay of persons in Achenese (as in all Austronesian languages) is extremely complex, and even the categorization given here does not begin to measure the range of usages. See Becker and Oka (1973) for further discussion.

   [7] In these examples, I mark prepositions like *u* with a hyphen for the same reason as the inflectional prefixes like *gɨ*. There is similarly no unambigious phonological evidence that these are prefixes, but there is the same regularity in ordering.

for this morpheme because I have nothing to offer; in (2b) it functions like *ber-* in Indonesian, as an intransitivizer, but it has at least three other major functions, one of them as a transitivizer. Luckily, its mysteries do not intrude on the subject of this paper, and I will say no more about it, except to note that it should not be confused with the *mi-* agreement prefix for first-person-plural exclusive, since historically, grammatically, and functionally it is distinct from this homophonous morpheme.) The free pronouns may be deleted in some situations, chiefly contextual, where they have been mentioned in previous discourse; thus (1b) can occur grammatically without *gɔpnyan* as an answer to the question *Hɔ gɔpnyan gɨ-ja?* 'where did he go?'. Ordinarily, however, the free subject is necessary unless special conditions hold. There are a number of particles which indicate aspectlike meanings: *ka* 'perfective', *tingɔh*[8] 'progressive', etc. These must follow the free NP subject and precede the agreement prefix:

(3)          a. *Kamɔ mɨ- pajoh bu.*
             we(ex) 1pex-eat  cooked-rice
             'We eat rice.'

          b. *Kamɔ tingɔh mɨ- pajoh bu.*
             we(ex) prog 1pex-eat  cooked-rice
             'We are eating rice.'

          c. *Kamɔ ka mɨ- pajoh bu.*
             we(ex) perf 1pex-eat  cooked-rice
             'We (already) ate rice.'

Finally, the agreement prefixes may not occur except with predicates that are lexical verbs; adjectives and nouns are ungrammatical with them.

(4)          a. *Gɔpnyan tingɔh *(gɨ-) ʔeh.*[9]
             he₀      prog  (3o-) sleep
             'He is sleeping.'

          b. *Gɔpnyan (tingɔh) (*gɨ-) tingɨt.*
             he₀      (prog)  (3o-) asleep
             'He is (temporarily) asleep.'

          c. *Gɔpnyan (tingɔh) (*gɨ-) mi-tingɨt.*
             he₀      (prog)  (3o-) X-asleep
             'He is (temporarily) sleepy.'

          d. *Gɔpnyan (tingɔh) *(gɨ-)  pi-mi-tingɨt aniʔ manya.*
             he₀      (prog)  (3o-) caus-X- sleepy child tiny
             'He (is making) makes the baby sleepy.'

---

[8] Literally, 'middle', which may explain some of the meaning.

[9] In this study I will use a notation involving parentheses and the usual asterisk for ungrammaticality as follows: *(X) means that X is grammatical, and that its absence is ungrammatical; (*X) means that X is ungrammatical, and that its absence is grammatical.

e. *Gɔpnyan (\*gɨ-) guru    lon.*
  heₒ        (3o-) teacher I
  'He is my teacher.'

In example (4), (a) and (d) require the *gɨ-* prefix to agree with the *gɔpnyan* subject, while (b), (c), and (e) do not allow agreement, since *ʔeh* 'sleep' is a lexical
verb, while *tɨngɨt* 'asleep' is an adjective. The derivational *mɨ-* prefix changes
the meaning to *sleepy* in (4c) but does not change the adjective to a verb; the
causative *pɨ-* in (4d), however, forms a lexical verb again, and the agreement is
required. Finally, the predicate in (4e), a noun phrase, blocks the agreement.
Note that *tɨngəh* does not translate as 'progressive' exactly, since it can be used
with stative predicates, even adjectives; here it means something like 'for the
moment, temporarily'.

   The Ac rule I will call PASSIVE is formed by promoting a direct object to
subject and placing the old subject EN CHÔMAGE[10] in a *le*-phrase[11] following
the verb:

(5)              a. *Gɔpnyan gɨ- nging anɨʔ  agam nyan.*
                   heₒ        3o-see    child male  that
                   'He sees the boy.'

                 b. *Anɨʔ agam nyan gɨ- nging le- gɔpnyan.*
                    child male that  3o-see    by-heₒ
                    'The boy is seen by him.'

(I translate these in present tense; they could just as easily be translated in the
past.)
   Note that the agreement prefix remains the same before and after Passive;
the 3o prefix *gɨ-* is present in both sentences, even though the NP *anɨʔ agam*,
denoting a child, would govern the 3y prefix *ji-* if the verb agreed with it.
Obviously, the agreement on the verb in (5b) is triggered by the underlying
subject *gɔpnyan*, now a chômeur, rather than the cyclic subject *anɨʔ agam*. This
is the problem.

---

   [10] This is an RG term; the literal meaning is 'out of work'. A NP that is EN CHÔMAGE is called
a CHÔMEUR; the word refers to a NP that has been 'demoted' from a status as subject, direct object,
or indirect object to an oblique status by virtue of some rule. Thus English Passive creates a chômeur
in the *by*-phrase, since the underlying subject becomes a nonsubject. We will have occasion to refer
also to the natural class consisting of subject, object, and indirect object—these are called TERMS
in RG (subject and direct object are called PRIMARIES, and direct object and indirect object are
called SECONDARIES). One of the basic tenets of RG is that these grammatical relations are considered to be basic and undefined, and that one can profitably define many rules and processes in
particular a well-defined set of cyclic rules, in terms of them.
   [11] *Le* is cognate to Indonesian *oleh*, which originally meant *do*; this seems fitting and proper
for the marker of an agent, somehow. It is also important to mention that ordinarily the *le*-phrase
cannot be deleted, unlike an English *by*-phrase.

Some further examples:

(6)            a. *Gɔpnyan ka  gɨ- cɔm lon.*
                  she₀        perf 3o-kiss I
                  'She (already) kissed me.'

               b. *Lon ka  gɨ- cɔm le- gɔpnyan.*
                  I     perf 3o-kiss by-she₀
                  'I've already been kissed by her'

(7)            a. *Drɔn nɨ- pajoh bɔh- mamplam.*
                  you₀ 2o-eat    fruit-mango
                  'You eat the mango.'

               b. *Bɔh- mamplam nɨ- pajoh le- drɔn.*
                  fruit-mango    2o-eat    by-you₀
                  'The mango is eaten by you.'

Perlmutter and Postal's original claim, which seems to be supported by evidence from most languages with verb agreement, was that such agreement could only be triggered by terms [i.e. by subjects (Su's), direct objects (DOs), or indirect objects (IOs)], and, further, that these must be cyclic terms of the clause in which the agreement takes place (i.e. the Su, DO, or IO AFTER all cyclic rules have applied within the relevant clause). This clearly implies that the verb should always agree with the derived subject after Passive; instead, as we have seen, in Ac the verb agrees with the original subject, even after Passive. The newer position they take is that agreement must be with EITHER] underlying or cyclic terms, and Ac seems to fit this description, since the agreement is always with underlying subject.

## PASSIVE AS A RELATIONAL RULE

In order to show just what the facts are that have motivated this shift in the theory, we will establish the following points: (i) the NP preceding the verb and governing agreement in an active Ac sentence is the subject of that sentence; (ii) the NP preceding the verb but not governing agreement in a Passive Ac sentence is the subject of THAT sentence; (iii) the rule we call Passive in Ac is NOT a (nonrelationally defined) topicalization rule, which could not be expected to change agreement; (iv) the prefixes in question constitute agreement within the meaning of the act. The first two points amount to a claim that Passive is cyclic, since the typical way of demonstrating subjecthood for a given NP is to show that it feeds certain cyclic rules (normally Raising and Equi) which are defined on subjects only; this has the effect of requiring that any rule (Passive, in this case) which precedes the application of these cyclic rules is itself cyclic. In demonstrating the first two points, we will proceed by following a chain of argument which leads to the conclusion that in Ac either Passive, Equi, and Raising are all contained in the cycle, or there is no cycle. The third point will be investigated by looking at two topicalization rules in Ac which seem to be the most likely candidates for identity with Passive, and showing that they cannot be identified with Passive, although there are some interesting interactions. The final point will be discussed at the end of the paper, and it will be suggested that, while the Ac prefixes do indeed fall in the category of 'agreement', the use of this term commits us to some assumptions which need to be further investigated.

In the RG framework, one of the most interesting and potentially most useful claims is that there is a correlation between rules that are defined in terms of grammatical relations—which are claimed to be cyclic rules only—and those which are not—which for the most part are postcyclic.[12] This is a weaker version of the cyclicity hypothesis: Earlier versions postulated a strict distinction between all cyclic rules, which were all to be defined on the basis of grammatical relations, and all other rules, none of which were supposed to be so defined. The present version allows cyclic rules which are not defined on grammatical relations, but does not allow any postcyclic rules which are so defined. The differences in these hypotheses do not enter into our discussion, since it is clear that both "normal" agreement and the type of agreement encountered in Ac are defined on terms at some stage of the derivation, and therefore must, by either hypothesis, be cyclic processes. Therefore, in discussing the topics listed above, we will concentrate on proving cyclicity for Passive; in RG terms, this will involve showing that Passive is defined upon and changes grammatical relations—in particular, that a nonsubject becomes a subject.

Most of the proofs of cyclicity that have been advanced for rules hinge on the feeding of other rules which are assumed to be cyclic. The entire chain of reasoning is based on the assumption that there is a class of rules which can be stated most simply and with maximum explanatory value if a cycle is postulated. While this assumption has come under close scrutiny lately, and deserves further study in itself, it is not my purpose here to deny it, or even cast doubt upon it. Rather, I will give arguments based on this assumption which show that Passive in Ac is cyclic in that it changes grammatical relations.

Regardless of one's particular allegiance in generative theories, Equi NP Deletion (Equi) and Subject Raising (Raising), however formulated, are universally assumed to be cyclic in theories which have anything like them (so is Passive, but the nature and operation of the Ac Passive is what is at issue here). Various proposed alterations of the rules, such as Postal's (1970) own proposal that Equi simply marks pronouns for later deletion, do not affect their essentially cyclic nature. Although the mysteries of Ac complementation are far from

---

[12] Again, this interpretation is based on the oral tradition and on personal communications, most from Postal. I hope I have not misrepresented the substance of the claim.

solved, the broad outlines appear clear. Ac has two- and three-place predicates with Equi and at least two-place predicates with Raising (in this case, to object position). The status of one-place Raising predicates remains unclear, because, if they exist, they shade off into a class of auxiliaries, adverbs, modals, and aspectual particles which cannot be easily demonstrated to be predicates, for the most part, and which are, unsurprisingly, quite idiosyncratic in their syntactic behavior. Although I am quite prepared to believe that they are predicates, and that they take Raising to subject position, such a claim would require far more in the way of motivation and analysis than I am prepared to give here. In any case, the phenomena involving Raising to object position are quite conclusive.)

To take two-place Equi first, we will consider the predicates *hawa* 'want', *ci* 'try', and *ut$^\theta$aha* 'make an attempt, try'. *Hawa* is not a lexical verb and thus takes no agreement prefix; it also participates in some other constructions which emphasize its nonverbal status. In sentences like (8) below, however, it seems to function as a predicate with a complement, and Equi applies:

(8)      a. *Dɔ ʔto  hawa (ba ʔ)    gi- piret$^\theta$a  uring  agam nyan.*
         doctor want (irrealis) 3o-examine person male  that
         'The doctor wants to examine that man.'

      b. *Uring  agam nyan hawa (ba ʔ) gi- piret$^\theta$a  le- dɔ ʔto.*
         person male  that  want (irr)  3o-examine by-doctor
         'That man wants to be examined by the doctor.'

As can be seen, Passive downstairs feeds Equi upstairs, and the *gi-* in both (8a) and (8b) agrees with *dɔ ʔto*, not *uring agam*. The status of *ba ʔ* is unclear, but it appears to be functioning, in this context at least, as an irrealis marker on the lower S, corresponding to the degree of uncertainty expressed by the speaker as to the eventual outcome. *Hawa* with a *ba ʔ* in the lower S can translate 'wish'. *Ba ʔ* is one of the class of modallike particles mentioned above (in many contexts it seems to translate both deontic and epistemic *should*) which follows the free NP subject and precedes the agreement prefix; normally it does not appear in a main clause, probably due to a constraint requiring the presence of an intensional predicate to indicate the source of uncertainty.

*Ci* 'try' has a well-formedness condition not unlike that on English *try*: It requires Equi. However, while many English speakers find (9a) below acceptable, its best Ac equivalent, (9b), is completely ungrammatical. This is because the constraint on *ci* is apparently on the underlying structure—*ci* requires that the underlying subject of its complement clause be coreferential with its own subject. Given this constraint, it is not surprising to find that the complement of *ci* shows no agreement at all: A bare root is added immediately after *ci*, which bears the agreement prefixes, as in (9c). Note that the attempt to add agreement prefixes here to the lower verb dooms the sentence to ungrammaticality:

(9)  a. *The man tried to be examined by the doctor.*

b. *\*urɨng  agam nyan ji-  ci  gɨ-piretᶿa  le- dɔʔto*
person male that 3y-try 3o-examine by-doctor

c. *Dɔʔto gɨ- ci  (\*gɨ-) piretᶿa   urɨng  agam nyan.*
doctor 3o-try  (3o-) examine person male  that
'The doctor tried to examine that man.'

(9b) is ungrammatical regardless of whether the *gɨ*-prefix is attached to the lower verb.

All of the data on two-place Equi up to this point could be explained on an analysis that treated *hawa* as an adverb or modal (since it is not a surface verb) and *ci* as an auxiliary verb. In both cases, an analysis along lines suggested by the Extended Standard Theory would have no difficulty explaining the places where agreement prefixes occur, since most variants of that theory treat adverbs and modals not as predicates with complements, but rather as constituents of one sort or another of the simplex S itself. Hence, the second predicate would have originated in the same simplex S as the first, and there would have been no complement to start with, and thus no Equi. While this analysis would do violence to the semantics and the logic, it will make the syntax workable, if complicated.

Unfortunately for such an analysis, however, there are also lexical verbs without the restrictions of *ci* which take undeniable complements, and which also take Equi. One such verb is *utᶿaha* 'make an attempt, try'. It is syntactically distinct from *ci* in not requiring deep coreference of subjects, but rather requiring merely that Equi be applicable at the appropriate stage of the derivation; Passive can thus feed Equi. In addition, it does not bind the complement so closely, requiring the usual agreement prefixes on the complement verb. Actually, this is closely related to the possibility of feeding with Passive, since virtually the only sign that Passive has occurred is the presence of the former verb agreement, and disallowing that would produce unacceptable ambiguity. As we shall see, Relativization provides a clear example of the importance of this interaction.

(10)  a. *Dɔʔto gɨ- utᶿaha (baʔ) gɨ- piretᶿa   urɨng   agam nyan.*
doctor 3o-try    (irr) 3o-examine person male that
'The doctor made an attempt to examine that man.'

b. *Urɨng  agam nyan ji- utᶿaha (baʔ) gɨ- piretᶿa   le- dɔʔto.*
person male that 3y-try    (irr) 3o-examine by-doctor
'That man made an attempt to be examined by the doctor.'

Note that in (10a) the agreement prefix *gɨ-*, corresponding to *dɔ ʔto*, is present on both verbs, representing the Equi of an underlying subject, while in (10b) the prefix *ji-*, corresponding to *urɨng agam*, is present on the higher but not the lower verb, representing the Equi of a derived subject, created by Passive. (10) provides clear evidence that Passive feeds Equi, and that therefore it is cyclic if Equi is.

Ac also has three-place predicates with Equi. Two such are *yu* 'ask, request' and *pɨ- ʔingat* 'remind' (literally, 'cause to remember'). Equi from object position can be fed by Passive in both cases. We begin by considering *yu*, which requires Equi:

(11)   a. *Urɨng inəng   nyan ji- yu   dɔ ʔto   (ba ʔ) gɨ- piret⁰a   drɔn.*
          person female that  3y-ask doctor (irr)  3o-examine you₀
          'The woman asked the doctor to examine you.'

       b. *Urɨng inəng   nyan ji- yu   drɔn (ba ʔ) gɨ- piret⁰a   le- dɔ ʔto.*
          person female that  3y-ask you₀  (irr)  3o-examine by-doctor
          'The woman asked you to be examined by the doctor.'

Note that Passive can also occur on the higher cycle:

(12)   a. *Dɔ ʔto ji- yu   le- urɨng   inəng   nyan (ba ʔ) gɨ- piret⁰a   drɔn.*
          doctor 3y-ask by-person female that  (irr)  3o-examine you₀
          'The doctor was asked by the woman to examine you'

       b. *Drɔn ji- yu   le-urɨng   inəng   nyan (ba ʔ) gɨ- piret⁰a   le- dɔ ʔto.*
          you₀  3y-ask by-person female that  (irr)  3o-examine by-doctor
          'You are asked by the woman to be examined by the doctor.'

In (12b) Passive applies twice—once on the lower cycle, producing, after Equi, an intermediate structure not unlike that of (11b), and once on the higher cycle, following Equi. The first application creates the conditions for Equi, and the second destroys them. This is the classic "rule sandwich" argument for cyclicity (although this particular example demonstrates that Equi rather than Passive is cyclic: Passive would have to be assumed to be cyclic for this particular argument to go through alone—the point is that a number of arguments of this type argue collectively for a well-defined set of cyclic rules, and both Equi and Passive belong to this group). Similar arguments will be given below for Raising and Passive. In (11) and (12), we take the woman to be younger than the speaker, while the doctor is older. Note that the prefix *nɨ-*, agreeing with *drɔn*, does not appear at all in (12b), even though *drɔn* is the cyclic subject of both clauses, because it is not the underlying subject of either, and thus cannot govern agreement.

*Pɨ- ʔingat* 'remind' takes either a full S as complement, or an S with subject deleted by Equi from the upstairs object as governor. The former type translates as an English *that*-clause, while the latter translates as an infinitive; the distinction is signalled in Ac by the presence or absence of Equi:

(13)    a.  *Lon lon-pɨ- ʔingat dɔʔto gɔpnyan ka gɨ- pɨretᶿa jih.*
        I   ls- remind  doctor he$_o$     perf 3o-examine he$_y$
        'I reminded the doctor$_i$ (that) he$_i$ had (already) examined
          him$_j$.'

    b.  *Lon lon-pɨ- ʔingat dɔʔto jih ka gɨ- pɨretᶿa le- gɔpnyan.*
        I   ls- remind  doctor he$_y$ perf 3o-examine by-he$_o$
        'I reminded the doctor$_i$ (that) he$_j$ had (already) been
          examined by him$_i$.'

    c.  *Lon lon-pɨ- ʔingat dɔʔto (baʔ) gɨ- pɨretᶿa jih.*
        I   ls- remind  doctor (irr) 3o-examine he$_y$
        'I reminded the doctor to examine him'

In (13a) and (13b), *gɔpnyan* and *dɔʔto* can be coreferential (on one reading, just as in English—the coreferentiality is by no means forced, since *gɔpnyan* could as easily refer to a third individual who had been previously mentioned in discourse), and it is this reading that is intended; thus the indices. The perfective marker *ka* forces there to be no Equi, since the application of this rule would be semantically anomalous with a perfective, producing a sentence like \**I reminded the doctor to have already examined him*. Without the *ka*, however, the sentences are grammatical. Note that Passive can occur downstairs, as in (13b), and that the irrealis marker *baʔ* is optional with Equi, as might be expected. In other cases, the application of Passive downstairs can feed Equi:

(14)    a.  *Lon lon-pɨ- ʔingat jih dɔʔto baʔ gɨ- pɨretᶿa jih.*
        I   ls- remind  he$_y$ doctor irr 3o-examine he$_y$
        'I reminded him$_i$ (that) the doctor$_j$ should examine him$_i$.'

    b.  *Lon lon-pɨ- ʔingat jih jih baʔ gɨ- pɨretᶿa le- dɔʔto.*
        I   ls- remind  he$_y$ he$_y$ irr 3o-examine by-doctor
        'I reminded him$_i$ (that) he$_i$ should be examined by the doctor$_j$.'

    c.  *Lon lon-pɨ- ʔingat jih (baʔ) gɨ- pɨretᶿa le- dɔʔto.*
        I   ls- remind  he$_y$ (irr) 3o-examine by-doctor
        'I reminded him to be examined by the doctor.'

(Note that in (14a) and (14b) the irrealis marker seems to function as a modal.) Finally, Passive can apply freely upstairs after Equi:

(15)    a.  *Dɔʔto lon-pɨ- ʔingat le- lon (baʔ) gɨ- pɨretᶿa jih.*
        doctor ls- remind  by-I  (irr) 3o-examine he$_y$
        'The doctor was reminded by me to examine him.'

b. *Jih lon-pɨ- ʔingat le- lon (ba ʔ) gɨ- pɨretʰa   le- dɔ ʔto.*
   heᵧ 1s- remind   by-I   (irr)  3o-examine by-doctor
   'He was reminded by me to be examined by the doctor.'

(15b) shows once again the cyclic rule of Equi preceded and followed by Passive.

Ac also has two-place Raising predicates; the distinction between these and three-place Equi predicates is controversial, mirroring as it does the well-known dispute summarized (and, to my mind, convincingly settled) in Postal (1974). Lacking the intimate knowledge of the language necessary to construct arguments with garbage NPs like *there*, nonreferential *it*, and idiom chunks, I rely in the following on the meaning of the sentences, and on my informant's reactions to their pragmatic acceptability.

*Dawa* 'consider, claim, argue', unlike three-place predicates like *yu* or *pɨ- ʔingat*, can form objects not representing underlying receivers; this is especially true in the cases with downstairs Passive:

(16)     a. *Gɔpnyan gɨ- pɨ- ʔingat jih ji- cu   lɨmõ nyan.*
            heₒ      3o-remind   heᵧ 3y-steal cow that
            'Heᵢ reminded himⱼ to steal the cow.'

         b. *Gɔpnyan gɨ- dawa     jih ji- cu   lɨmõ.*
            heₒ      3o-consider heᵧ 3y-steal cow
            'Heᵢ considers himⱼ to steal cows.'

(17)     a. *\*Gɔpnyan gɨ- pɨ ʔingat lɨmõ nyan ji- cu   le- jih.*
            heₒ      3o-remind  cow that 3y-steal by-heᵧ
            'Heᵢ reminded the cow to be stolen by himⱼ.'

         b. *Gɔpnyan gɨ- dawa     lɨmõ nyan ji- cu   le- jih.*
            heₒ      3o-consider cow that 3y-steal by-heᵧ
            'Heᵢ considers the cow to be stolen by himⱼ.'

It is difficult to form pairs for contrast between *pɨ- ʔingat* and *dawa*, since the most natural sentences with the latter use *ka* for "sequence of tenses", while this particle is difficult to get with Equi on *pɨ- ʔingat*. Nevertheless, (17a) is quite unacceptable, since it means that the cow is the addressee of the reminder; (17b), however, is fine (although better with *ka* downstairs), and does not involve the cow in the performance of a speech act in any way. Derived objects can also be passivized:

(18)  a. *Hakem gɨ- dawa     jih ka ji- cu   lɨmõ nyan.*
         judge  3o-consider heᵧ perf 3y-steal cow that
         'The judge considers him to have stolen that cow.'

b. *Hakem gɨ- dawa        lɨmõ nyan ka   ji- cu   le- jih.*
   judge   3o-consider cow that  perf 3y-steal by-he$_y$
   'The judge$_i$ considers that cow to have been stolen by him$_j$.'

c. *Jih gɨ- dawa      le- hakem ka   ji- cu    lɨmõ nyan.*
   he$_y$ 3o-consider by-judge   perf 3y-steal cow that
   'He is considered by the judge to have stolen that cow.'

d. *Lɨmõ nyan gɨ- dawa       le- hakem ka   ji- cu    le- jih.*
   cow   that 3o-consider by-judge  perf 3y-steal by-him$_y$
   'That cow is considered by the judge$_i$ to have been stolen by him$_j$.'

(18) provides a "sandwich" argument for Raising and Passive; here again
the rule that is shown to intervene between successive applications is not
Passive, but another rule, Raising. However, it is possible to construct sentences
in Ac where Passive intervenes between two applications of other cyclic rules,
although these require somewhat longer sentences. In (19), below, there are
three clauses: The matrix clause contains *ut$^\theta$aha*, which governs Equi from the
subject, the next lower clause contains *dawa*, which governs Raising to object.
The derivation of (19) requires that Raising occur on the *dawa* cycle, followed
by Passive on the same cycle, followed by Equi on the (higher) *ut$^\theta$aha* cycle:

(19)      *Jih ji- ut$^\theta$aha  ba ʔ gɨ- dawa      le- hakem ji- cu    lɨmõ nyan.*
          he$_y$ 3y-attempt irr  3o-consider by-judge   3y-steal cow that
          'He made an attempt to be considered by the judge to have
              stolen the cow.'

Just as in the (rather cumbersome but grammatical) English translation, Passive
intervenes in the derivation between two cyclic rules. This, together with the
preceding arguments, shows that (at least) Equi, Passive, and Raising are
included in the cycle in Ac, which should surprise no one.

   In order to argue, then, that in Ac Passive is not cyclic, one would have to
contend that Equi and Raising are not cyclic either, or that they do not exist.
Neither is likely to be a welcome alternative to anyone who places any faith
at all in the cyclic principle; the Ac rules of Equi and Raising are too similar
to those of English to allow one to discard them with impunity because they
interact with Passive, a rule that does NOT behave very much like the Passive
of English. If, then, Passive is cyclic, as seems to be the case, and if Ac Equi and
Raising have only subjects as victims—which is common to all Austronesian
languages, not to mention most others—this means that Passive creates a new
subject and demotes the old one. But it is clear that the agreement on the
passivized verb is with the underlying subject in all cases, even though it is
a chômeur after Passive has applied; this is the evidence which led to the re-
statement of the Agreement Law.

## PASSIVES AND FRONTING

One possibility that might be proposed to account for the Ac agreement facts is that Passive might not be, in fact, an ordinary subject-creating rule in Ac (and therefore is probably misnamed here), but rather would insert a 'dummy' NP[13] of some sort, with the consequence that the agreement would remain on the former subject, typically moved to a nonsubject position. The classic example is, of course, English *there*-insertion. This phenomenon is handled by a wrinkle in Perlmutter and Postal's Agreement Law, to the effect that a special relationship obtains between the dummy and the shifted NP subject (which Perlmutter and Postal call IN-LAWS), and that agreement is allowed between the verb and the in-law (shifted) NP, even though the dummy has other properties of a subject, e.g. that of feeding Raising. There is little hope of making this work the same way in Ac, since it is clear that the derived subject after Passive is NOT a dummy (at least not as Perlmutter and Postal define it); it has clear reference and originates as a term in the original active S. There is, however, a phenomenon similar to *there*-insertion in English in which a referential NP functions in some way as a subject but does not govern agreement; as we will see, it is paralleled exactly in Ac, with one significant difference.

(20)   a. *The Constitution entrusts the power to regulate education to the states.*

   b. *The Constitution entrusts the states with the power to regulate education.*

   c. *The power to regulate education is entrusted \*(to) the states (by the Constitution).*

   d. *The states are entrusted \*(with) the power to regulate education (by the Constitution).*

   e. *To the states is entrusted (\*with) the power to regulate education (by the Constitution).*

(20) is a fine example of how RG deals with vexatious problems in satisfying ways, up to a point. (20a) is the base S; subject, direct object, and indirect object are in their normal order. The indirect object is marked by *to*. (20b) is an example of Dative with the indirect object having been promoted to direct object, and the direct object having been put en chômage, and marked (in this

---

[13] In this context, a "dummy" NP is a word filling an NP slot and having some of the properties of a term (in this case, the subject), but without reference, and therefore not possessing all of the properties of a term. Besides *there*, English has nonreferential *it* in *it's raining* and the *it* of Extraposition in *it's obvious he's lying*. In this sense, we will show that the subject of Ac Passive cannot be a dummy, since it originates as a term and keeps its reference throughout the derivation.

case) by the preposition *with*. Note that in (20b) there is no *to* on the dative *states*, a consequence of its promotion. (20c) and (20d) are the respective passives of (20a) and (20b); the necessity of *with* in (20d) shows the feeding of Passive by Dative, and simplifies the Passive into: PROMOTE DO TO SU. (20e), however, presents something of a problem. In this sentence, the indirect object has been fronted, triggering subject–verb inversion; i.e. the subject derived by Passive, *power*, follows the verb, and the verb agrees with it, rather than with the dative that precedes the verb; this can be shown by pluralizing *power*:

(20)   f.   *To the states* $\begin{Bmatrix} is \\ are \end{Bmatrix}$ *entrusted the power* $\begin{Bmatrix} \emptyset \\ -s \end{Bmatrix}$ *to regulate education.*

This is reminiscent of *there*-insertion, the more so since the prepositional phrase *to the states* appears to feed Raising:

(20)   g.   *To the states seems to have been entrusted the power to regulate education (by the Constitution).*

Postal has pointed out (personal communication), however, that *to the states* will not feed B-Raising:

(21)   a.   \**Frank considers to the states to have been entrusted the power to regulate education.*

although the grammaticality increases when the prepositional phrase winds up in a subject position by virtue of later Passive:

(21)   b.   ?*To the states is thought/believed to have been entrusted the power to regulate education.*

In addition, the prepositional phrase does not behave as a subject should with respect to question formation:

(21)   c.   \**Is to the states entrusted the power to regulate education?*

Postal proposes to deal with these data (and others) by an analysis on which the subject of (20e) is a null dummy in-law of *power*. In this view, the fronting of the dative prepositional phrase *to the states* is a topicalization, and there is a constraint on the occurrence of null dummies in English, to the effect that, in surface structure, they must be immediately preceded by topics. Since topics occur only initially, this will explain why (21a) is worse than either (20g) or (21b), and since the topic is NOT the subject, it will explain why (21c) is also bad. This analysis will cover the agreement of *entrust* with *power(s)* under the 'in-law' section of the Agreement Law, since a dummy has been inserted. Moreover, Postal suggests that an independently needed constraint—to the effect that dummies (of whatever type) may only insert in intransitive constructions—explains the fact that Dative Preposing will not work on an active version of (20e). In (22), Passive has not applied, the construction is transitive, and *Constitution* cannot be inverted grammatically:

(22)   \**To the states entrusts the Constitution the power to regulate education.*

Sentences where Passive has applied, however, are intransitive, and dummies can be inserted.

An alternative solution (and one that is less likely to displease) is to claim that the dummy is not null, but *there*, which has been deleted because its function (that of holding open the subject slot) is no longer necessary after the topicalization. Both these analyses, however, result from the necessity in RG of having an identifiable subject present at all stages of the derivation; I will suggest below that this is not an altogether obvious requirement, and may lead to unpleasant consequences (as it has here, for anyone who does not like empty nodes). Further, as we will see, an analogous treatment of Ac phenomena will not work; thus Postal's analysis loses generality.

A rule similar to Dative-Preposing exists in Ac; we will call it Fronting (FR). FR has the effect of moving a NP, not necessarily a term, with its attendant prefixes/prepositions, if any, to the front of the sentence. It is the likeliest candidate for a topicalization rule to identify Passive with; the data below show, however, that it interacts with Passive and must be considered as an independent rule, just as the English data above show that, whatever the formal nature of the Dative Fronting rule, it is not to be identified with Passive, although it interacts with Passive. The subject, IF IT IS A DERIVED ONE (i.e., if Passive has applied), may optionally be inverted to follow the verb—note the similarity with the condition on the English rule above.[14]

(23)   a. *Gɔpnyan ka  gɨ- bre  buku nyan kɨ-kamɔ.*
        he$_o$      perf 3o-give book that to-we$_{ex}$
        'He gave the book to us.'

   b. *Buku nyan ka  gɨ- bre  kɨ-kamɔ le- gɔpnyan.*
        book that perf 3o-give to-we$_{ex}$ by-he$_o$
        'The book was given to us by him.'

---

[14] By this observation I do not intend to claim that the conditions are identical and caused by the same circumstances. Nevertheless, coincidences should always be viewed suspiciously, and it seems possible that the rule producing (20f) may require "unlocking" of the normal word order by Passive before the more opaque word order is created. If true, this type of explanation may also apply to Ac, since the function of Passive—in that language, at least—seems to be to signal that the underlying subject is not the cyclic subject. See Lawler (1975b) for details.

c. ***Kɨ-kamɔ** gɔpnyan ka   gɨ- bre  buku  nyan.*
   to-we$_{ex}$  he$_o$      perf 3o-give book that
   '(It's) **to us** (that) he gave the book.'

   ***Kɨ-kamɔ** buku nyan ka   gɨ- bre  le- gɔpnyan.*
   to-we$_{ex}$  book that  perf 3o-give by-he$_o$
   '(It's) **to us** (that) the book was given by him.'

e. *****Kɨ-kamɔ** ka    gɨ- bre  gɔpnyan buku  nyan.*
   to-we$_{ex}$  perf 3o-give he$_o$       book that
   '(It's) **to us** (that) gave he the book.'

f. ***Kɨ-kamɔ** ka   gɨ- bre  buku  nyan le- gɔpnyan.*
   to-we$_{ex}$  perf 3o-give book that  by-he$_o$
   '(It's) **to us** (that) was given the book by him.'

FR produces strong contrastive stress on the fronted element (indicated here by boldface), and has approximately the meaning of (in this case) 'to *us*, and to no one else (as may have been suggested)'. In example (23), (c), (d), and (f) are ungrammatical with this stress without the *kɨ-*. (23e) is ungrammatical because the underlying subject is inverted, exactly like (21). The important thing to note in (23) is that agreement in ALL cases—active, passive, and fronted—is with the underlying subject, *gɔpnyan*. Incidentally, it might be thought that (23f) represents not a passive, but an alternative fronting, with the subject displaced into a *le*-phrase; an analysis like this could claim that the subject is simply moved, not demoted, and that the *le*-phrase is not a chômeur at all. This claim would be helpful to anyone desiring to identify FR and Passive, since the creation of a *le*-phrase by another rule would be highly suspicious. This analysis is vitiated, however, by the fact that no *le*-phrase can occur unless there is an underlying direct object which can feed Passive. That is, on this analysis, one might expect FR to be able to operate on (24a) to yield (24b); but it cannot, because *ja ʔ* is intransitive, and (24c) is ungrammatical. Therefore, the occurrence of the *le*-phrase has precisely the same cooccurrence restrictions as the Passive.

(24)        a. *Urɨng  agam nyan ji- ja ʔ t$^\theta$ikula ngən-moto.*
               person male  that 3y-go school with-car
               'The man goes to school by car.'

            b. ****Ngən-moto** ji- ja ʔ t$^\theta$ikula le- urɨng   agam nyan*
               with- car   3y-go school by-person male  that
               '(It's) **by car** (that) is gone to school by the man.'

            c. ****T$^\theta$ikula** ji- ja ʔ le- urɨng   agam nyan ngən-moto*
               school 3y-go by-person male  that with-car
               '**School** is gone to by the man by car.'

    d. ***Ngən-moto*** *uring   agam nyan ji- ja ? t$^\theta$ikula*
       with- car   person male that 3y-go school
       '(It's) **by car** (that) he goes to school.'

    e. \****Ngən-moto*** *ji- ja ? uring   agam nyan t$^\theta$ikula.*
       with- car   3y-go  person male that  school

(24d) is grammatical, and is the only way FR can apply to the instrumental (or means) adverbial *ngən-moto* of (24a), since Passive will not apply, and (24b) cannot be derived without it. (24e) is ungrammatical, however, since the subject has been moved after the verb. FR with subsequent subject inversion does not operate on intransitives generally: In Ac, it seems to be restricted to passive sentences, so that this type of inversion only occurs in a sentence with a *le*-phrase. Postal's hypothesis regarding the applicability of dummy-insertion in intransitives clearly does not apply here, and thus loses some of its appeal. Even if he is correct about the English cases, the alternative *there*-deletion analysis I suggested above can explain the same facts without necessarily making any claims about Ac, since *there*-insertion dummies are a language-specific phenomenon, and one would not expect a corresponding situation to obtain in Ac.

    The agreement of verb with underlying subject in (23) is in sharp contra-distinction to the English case, where the agreement in (20e) and (20f) is with the derived subject *power(s)*, the product of Passive. Otherwise, the rules seem to share many properties.

    Not the least of these shared properties is the fact that in Ac Raising can be fed by FR:[15]

(25)  a. *Hakem gɨ- dawa*  ***kɨkamɔ***  *ka gɨ-bre buku nyan le gɔpnyan*
       judge  3o-consider to-we$_{ex}$  perf 3o-give book that  by-he$_o$
       'The judge considers **to us** to have been given the book by him.'

    b. ***Kɨ-kamɔ*** *gɨ- dawa*  *le- hakem ka*  *gɨ- bre buku nyan le- gɔpnyan*
       to- we$_{ex}$  3o-consider by-judge  perf 3o-give book that  by-he$_o$
       '(It's) **to us** (that) is considered by the judge to have been given
       the book by him.'

And there is even a dative Passive to which to compare it: Ac datives may undergo Passive, but they do not drag the *kɨ-*, which is deleted, much like the

---

[15] It is also possible that (25b) results from passivization of the entire object clause followed by FR and Extraposition (or Heavy NP Shift). The details of this analysis are not important here, since the same possibility applies to the corresponding English example. It does raise the possibility, however, that FR is cyclic, which would be interesting from an RG standpoint, since FR operates on nonterms like instrumentals.

*to* of English datives. Whether this means that Dative[16] feeds Passive in Ac is an open question, but it is not relevant here; what is relevant is that the *ki-* is dropped, and, further, that contrastive stress is not grammatical on these derived subjects:

(26)          a.   *Kamɔ ka  gɨ- bre  buku  nyan le- gɔpnyan.*
                   we$_{ex}$   perf 3o-give book that  by-he$_o$
                   'We were given the book by him.'

              b.   \**Kɨ-kamɔ ka gɨ-bre buku nyan le-gɔpnyan.*

              c.   \***Kamɔ** ka gɨ-bre buku nyan le-gɔpnyan.*

Subjects derived from datives by Passive, like any derived subjects, may undergo Raising:

(27)   *Kamɔ gɨ- dawa      le- hakem ka   gɨ- bre  buku  nyan le- gɔpnyan.*
       we$_{ex}$   3o-consider by-judge  perf 3o-give book that  by-he$_o$
       'We are considered by the judge to have been given the book
          by him.'

   Postal proposes an analysis of FR similar to that which he gives for (20e), in which FR is viewed as a pair of rules—Topicalization plus an optional Dummy

---

[16] The existence of an Ac rule of Dative is problematical, since it would be entirely opaque. That is, it would never apply unless the promoted indirect object would be further promoted to subject by some other rule, like Passive. The following sentence is ungrammatical, although (26a) is acceptable:

(i)                    \**Gɔpnyan ka  gɨ- bre  kamɔ buku nyan.*
                       he$_o$        perf 3o-give we$_{ex}$  book that

(i) would be the result of application of a rule of Dative, but no such sentence exists. There are sentences in which an indirect object seems to be promoted to direct object but whether they argue for Dative is doubtful; more likely they are results of incorporation or predicate raising:

(ii)          a.   *Gɔpnyan gɨ- bre  bu           kɨ-kamɔ.*
                   he$_o$        3o-give cooked-rice to-we$_{ex}$
                   'He gave rice to us.'

              b.   *Gɔpnyan gɨ- bre- bu           kamɔ.*
                   he$_o$        3o-give-cooked-rice we$_{ex}$
                   'He gave us rice.'

(iii)                  \**Gɔpnyan gɨ- bre- buku kamɔ.*
                       he$_o$        3o-give-book we$_{ex}$

(iia) is the normal form; (iib) is the form with *bu* appended to the verb, forming a unit meaning *feed*; the indirect object *kamɔ* is then usable without *kɨ-*. That this is idiosyncratic is shown by the ungrammaticality of (iii), where the direct object is not *bu*.

Insertion rule which makes a null dummy subject and inverts the previous (derived) subject. We have seen that, if this analysis is viable at all, it must be restricted to Passive sentences, not just intransitives, as Postal suggests, and that, unlike English, there is no evidence that the dummy could be anything else but a null, since Ac has nothing corresponding formally to the *there* of *there*-insertion—in fact, it has no dummies of any kind. Further, (25) shows that the restriction Postal proposes for the English null dummy does not hold for Ac, since fronted NPs behave exactly like subjects with respect to all types of Raising, and are not restricted to occurring first in a tensed clause. Finally, invoking a dummy of any sort (null or otherwise) to handle FR will NOT explain two facts: (i) FR with inversion can occur ONLY with a subject derived from Passive—i.e. FR must be fed by Passive if inversion occurs; and (ii) the agreement in a sentence with FR, with or without inversion, with or without Passive, is always with the underlying subject, never with the fronted NP (which is consistent with Postal's analysis), and never with the inverted subject (which is not). In the light of these data, I find it hard to accept Postal's treatment of FR; in fact, I believe that the evidence argues for treating Ac Fronting differently from that of English, even though they are similar in many respects, and even though they seem to be pragmatically and functionally almost identical. The dummy analysis of English Fronting seems plausible, but dummies do not seem to buy much in Ac. In any event, we can certainly conclude that FR is not the same rule as Passive in Ac, and no dummy analysis can explain the agreement facts in Passive sentences.

## PASSIVE AND SUBJECT PRECLITIC

In addition to FR, there is an Ac rule which topicalizes subjects and has interesting consequences and interactions with Passive. We will call this rule Subject Preclitic (SPC). There is a double condition on its application: First, the underlying subject must not be present as subject; this may be accomplished through Passive, or through Equi or Raising on the next cycle (which argues against SPCs being cyclic). Second, there must remain an agreement prefix on the verb [this will of necessity have reference to the (absent) underlying subject]. The effect of SPC in these circumstances is to replace the agreement prefix with a free noun or pronoun coreferential to the underlying subject. Some examples:

(28)  a.  *Kamɔ ka  gɨ- nging le- gɔpnyan.* (Passive)
          $we_{ex}$   perf 3o-see    by-$he_o$
          'We were seen by him.'

      b.  *Kamɔ ka  gɔpnyan-nging.* (Passive plus SPC)
          $we_{ex}$   perf $he_o$-    see
          'We were seen by **him**.'

(29)   a. *Gɔpnyan gɨ- utᶿaha   baˀ gɨ- pula   pade.* (Equi)
          heₒ          3o-attempt irr  3o-plant rice-plant
          'He made an attempt to plant rice.'

       b. *Gɔpnyan gɨ- utᶿaha   baˀ gɔpnyan-pula   pade.* (Equi plus SPC)
          heₒ          3o-attempt irr  heₒ-      plant rice-plant
          'He made an attempt to plant rice (himself).'

(30)   a. *Kamɔ gɨ- dawa     le- hakem ka  mɨ-  cu    lɨmõ nyan.* (Raising)
          weₑₓ    3o-consider by-judge perf lpex-steal cow  that
          'We are considered by the judge to have stolen the cow.'

       b. *Kamɔ gɨ- dawa     le- hakem ka   kamɔ-cu    lɨmõ*
          weₑₓ    3o-consider by-judge perf weₑₓ- steal cow
          *nyan.* (Raising plus SPC)
          that
          'We are considered by the judge to have stolen the cow (ourselves).'

Some notes on SPC: There are no agreement prefixes on the verbs in the clauses
where SPC has applied—the prefixes that were there [in the (a) examples of
(28)–(30)] have been replaced with NPs (in this case, pronouns, which are,
naturally, more common than are full nouns).[17] The presence of agreement
prefixes would render the (b) examples ungrammatical. Note also the position
of the particles *ka* and *baˀ* in regard to that of the fronted pronouns: As has
been noted above, there are extremely strong restrictions on the placement of
these particles—they must FOLLOW the subject and PRECEDE the agreement
prefixes—and the cliticized pronouns are definitely in the agreement prefix
position, not that of the subject. Any other order of these pronouns and
particles produces ungrammaticality. In the examples I have indicated this
filling of the prefixal position by a hyphen, but I should repeat that there is no
phonological evidence available to show these clitics to be morphological
prefixes, as differentiated from particles, any more than there is for what we
have been calling agreement prefixes. The same strong restrictions on placement, however, will allow us to consider them just as much prefixes as the others.
Those with stronger commitments to consistent linguistic terminology than the
author may prefer to refer to both types as clitics. Another thing to note in
(28b) is the absence of the *le*-phrase, which is normally obligatory in the passive;
this agent phrase is ungrammatical in a sentence with SPC, which suggests
that in this case, at least, SPC may actually move the NP from the agent

---

[17] Full nouns do, however, occur. Cf:

(i)                          *Urɨng  nyan dɔ ˀto- pɨretᶿa.*
                             person that doctor-examine
                             'That man was examined by the **doctor**.'

phrase.[18] This possibility need not affect our discussion, since the important fact is that the underlying subject NP, or some pronoun coreferential with it, shows up in the agreement prefix position, where it is obviously not a term. In (28b), for example, it is clear that *kamɔ* (the NP promoted by Passive, and raised into the matrix S), rather than *gɔpnyan*, is the cyclic subject of the lower S.

The semantic/pragmatic force of SPC is difficult to convey properly in English translations, but it approximates that of FR for nonsubjects.[19] That is, (28b) is appropriate when one desires to point out some particular individual who did the seeing, so as to make no mistake that it was done by anyone else. I have indicated this as contrastive stress in (28b), but in (29b) and (30b), where there is no NP in English to carry the stress, I have indicated it by the emphatic reflexive, although I have no idea how close these constructions actually are pragmatically. The English translations should be taken as very loose approximations.

Further evidence that SPC is a replacement, rather than a movement plus deletion, comes from the places where it CANNOT apply—any S that lacks an agreement prefix will not undergo SPC. Equi with *ci*, for example, leaves no agreement marker on the lower verb, so SPC cannot apply:

(31)    a.  *Jih ji- ci pula pade.*
            he$_y$ 3y-try plant rice-plant
            'He tried to plant rice.'

        b.  *\*Jih ji- ci jih- pula padę,*
            he$_y$ 3y-try he$_y$-plant rice-plant
            'He tried to plant rice (himself).'

With *ut⁰aha*, however, which leaves an agreement marker [as we have seen in (29)], SPC can apply.

The interaction of SPC and Relativization is particularly revealing. Ac Relativization, like that of Austronesian languages in general, operates on subjects only. The relative marker *nyɛng* follows the head noun and the subject of the clause which follows is deleted under coreference with the head. The

---

[18] I wish to ignore here the entire question of whether SPC is actually a movement rule in any sense. That reason why I want to avoid this issue is that it is a nonissue. If movement rules can be analyzed as *copy* + *delete*, which seems likely, then we could have two analyses in theoretical contrast, which are in actuality identical: (i) the movement rule hypothesis, suggested in the text, which says that the NP is copied into the agreement slot and deleted in its original *le*-phrase slot; and (ii) another analysis which says that the underlying subject is copied into this slot, and that the token of that NP in the *le*-phrase is deleted because it is redundant. Note that both these accounts resolve to *copy* + *delete*, and they are in fact the same account. This reminds one of the classics scholar who spent his life proving that the Iliad and the Odyssey were not written by Homer, but by another Greek of the same name.

[19] FR cannot apply to subjects—that is, there cannot be contrastive stress on a subject, since this would be the only sign that FR had operated.

interesting fact is that normally there is no agreement marker present on the verb in a relative clause:

(32)     a.  *Uri̇ng inəng  nyɛng nging kamɔ ji- ja ? tᶿikula.*
             person female rel    see    we_ex  3y-go school
             'The woman who saw us goes to school.'

         b.  *\*Uri̇ng inəng  nyɛng ji- nging kamɔ ji- ja ? tᶿikula.*
             person female rel    3y-see   we_ex  3y-go school

         c.  *Uri̇ng inəng \*(ji-) ja ? tᶿikula.*
             person female (3y-) go  school

(32a) is grammatical and (32b) is ungrammatical, even though they differ only in the absence or presence of the agreement marker in the relative clause; this agreement marker is required in a matrix clause like (32c), which is ungrammatical without it. The only exception to this restriction is when Passive has applied; then the agreement marker is REQUIRED in the relative clause. In other words, there is never any optionality as to whether there can be an agreement marker in a relative clause. If Passive has not applied, it is forbidden, while if it HAS applied, it is required. This has the odd result that the only agreement markers that show up in relatives are those that do NOT agree with the head, since Passive will leave agreement with the chômeur agent.

If SPC is claimed to work when the underlying subject is absent, as in Equi, then it ought to work in relatives. It does, but only when Passive has applied, since only then is there an agreement prefix to replace. Thus (33a) is grammatical while (33b) is not: (33b) is derived (putatively) from (32a), which has no agreement marker—hence, the application of SPC blocks. (33a), on the other hand, is derived from the passive relative in (33c) which has an agreement marker:

(33)     a.  *Uri̇ng inəng  nyɛng kamɔ-nging ji- ja ? tᶿikula.*
             person female rel    we_ex- see   3y-go school

         b.  *\*Uri̇ng inəng  nyɛng jih- nging kamɔ ji- ja ? tᶿikula.*
             person female rel    she_y-see   we_ex  3y-go school

         c.  *Uri̇ng inəng  nyɛng mi̇- nging le- kamɔ ji- ja ? tᶿikula.*
             person female rel    1pex-see   by-we_ex  3y-go school
             'The woman who was seen by us goes to school.'

Note that (33a) lacks the *le*-phrase of (33c).

While it might be objected that (33a) is a simple example of Relativization of object—rather than a more complex derivation involving Passive and SPC—the position of the aspectual markers, as usual, shows that the NP *kamɔ* is in the agreement slot—rather than in that of the subject NP. Consider (34):

(34)    a.   *Bɔh- mamplam nyɛng tïngɔh mï- pajoh le- kamɔ mangat.*
              fruit-mango   rel    prog  lpex-eat  by-we$_{ex}$ delicious
              'The mangoes that are being eaten by us are delicious.'

        b.   *Bɔh- mamplam nyɛng tïngɔh kamɔ-pajoh mangat.*
              fruit-mango   rel    prog  we$_{ex}$- eat   delicious
              'The mangoes **we** are eating are delicious.'

        c.   *\*Bɔh-mamplam nyɛng kamɔ tïngɔh pajoh mangat.*

        d.   *Kamɔ tïngɔh mï- pajoh bɔh- mamplam.*
              we$_{ex}$ prog lpex-eat   fruit-mango
              'We are eating mangoes.'

(34c) is ungrammatical because of the positions of *kamɔ* and *tïngɔh*, normally exemplified in (34d), which is not, of course, a relative.

Postal (personal communication) has suggested that SPC is in fact a case of subject incorporation (with which I agree), and that it should operate only on transitive subjects after Passive. It is certainly true that that is one environment for its application, but it is equally true that SPC can operate on intransitives, provided the subject has been moved or deleted from its normal position. Naturally, Passive cannot apply to intransitives, but Equi can:

(35)        a.   *Drɔn nï- ut$^{θ}$aha  baʔ nï- jaʔ u- jakarta.*
              you$_{o}$ 2o-attempt irr  2o-go to-Jakarta
              'You tried to go to Jakarta.'

        b.   *Drɔn nï- ut$^{θ}$aha  baʔ drɔn-jaʔ u- jakarta.*
              you$_{o}$ 2o-attempt irr  you$_{o}$-go to-Jakarta
              'You tried to go to Jakarta yourself.'

Postal is correct, however, in pointing out that SPC fits the normal pattern of subject incorporation, particularly in regard to the fact that the underlying subject (the 'launching pad' for incorporation, in Perlmutter and Postal's terminology) cannot appear as subject after incorporation. It is also important to note that incorporated subjects are no longer terms, any more than are the agreement prefixes they replace (and it is extremely clear from all the data that SPC does in fact replace the agreement morpheme with a noun phrase).

We conclude, then, that SPC interacts with Passive in interesting ways, but does not itself create or destroy subjects; that it can be only a replacement rule; and that it does some fairly weird things to our notion of "agreement"— surely this is a strange thing to do with prefixes: Ordinarily in language, in- flectional bound forms and lexical free forms go their separate ways, bound together, of course, with a complex web of cooccurrence restrictions and interactions. It is strange to see a syntactic rule convert one into the other; it raises serious questions about the status of the agreement markers, which we will discuss below.

## AGREEMENT AND THE NOTION OF SUBJECT

There are some interesting reasons for the behavior of the Ac agreement morphemes in relation to Passive, which are discussed elsewhere (cf. Lawler 1975b). What is more interesting for our purposes, however, is the question that arises upon looking closely at the strange behavior of these prefixes, particularly at the phenomenon of replacement by NPs that SPC illustrates. That question is, of course, the one we are left with: Do these morphemes constitute verb agreement in any sense of that term familiar to linguists? If the answer is yes, then it is necessary to allow agreement with underlying terms, as well as with cyclic ones; if the answer is no, then the next question is: What are they? It is clear that they have coreference, in at least the same limited sense as agreement morphemes; it is equally clear that they behave in all other ways like agreement morphemes, and that any analysis that calls them something else because they do not agree with the right NPs is circular and ad hoc, and not worth discussing. It seems that some discussion of what we mean by agreement is in order.

Perhaps the clearest cases of verb agreement are found in languages like German, where in most cases the verb encodes morphologically the information as to the identity of the subject, and where the free NP subject is also required. Thus:

(36)                                    *(Ich) spreche Deutsch.

The verb *spreche* '(I) speak' unambiguously marks the subject as first-person singular, but the free pronoun *ich* 'I' is still required. In Spanish and Latin, on the other hand, there is also encoding of the subject, but free NP subjects are not required if there is sufficient context for determining their identity; in particular, first-person subjects are never required:

(37)                                    (Ego) loquor latine.

(38)                                    (Yo) hablo español.

If they are present, in fact, the sentence takes on a different function, since their use signals emphasis.

These phenomena are easy to account for in a generative framework, by adding rules to delete the free subject NPs which govern agreement with their verbs, but these cases should make us uneasy as to just what we mean by agreement when often there is nothing left to agree with.

Some similarities of Ac agreement with these cases might lead someone concerned for the survival of a stronger Agreement Law to postulate that the morphemes we have been calling agreement are actually not that, but rather are pronouns. Certainly there are plenty of resemblances, syntactic and phonological, to the Ac pronouns. And such an analysis could be made to handle the SPC facts, and even the pragmatic force of SPC (on an analogy with the emphatic use of Romance pronouns) in a satisfying way.

Unfortunately, such an analysis puts one in the position of requiring that ALL Ac sentences with lexical verbal predicates (and NO Ac sentences with lexical nonverbal predicates) contain an additional NP, coreferential with the underlying subject, but not a term at any stage of the derivation. This is strange, not to say unheard of. In addition, there seems to be no way to prevent an analysis like this from being applied to (say) Turkish, where the pronouns would become postclitics on the verb, and would therefore undergo the usual harmonizing. A pronoun analysis of Turkish, however, would have to state that the pronouns were not always coreferential with the underlying subject, but rather with the cyclic subject, and the dilemma would be faced again in a different form. And in any language, including Ac, in which such an analysis is proposed, there would have to be a wealth of pronoun-deletion rules to take care of the places where agreement does not take place. Obviously such an analysis could be advanced for Ac alone, on the grounds that Ac agreement morphemes behave differently from those of other languages, but calling them pronouns (or anything else) does not explain the situation—it gives it a different name, a far different thing, and one which linguists should eschew as an explanatory device.

Another, similar, analysis that might be advanced to account for the behavior of Ac agreement morphemes is that they constitute subject incorporation. In view of the fact that SPC is clearly a subject incorporation rule, there might appear to be some plausibility to this approach. However, this vanishes upon closer examination. First, it is unusual, to say the least, for a language to have TWO such rules—one is rare enough. Second, subject incorporation is typically an optional process (like SPC); if we consider the agreement morphemes as subject incorporations, we make the process obligatory for all verbs (and block it for all nonverbs). Third, unlike SPC, the agreement morphemes can occur (and in many cases MUST occur) with a free NP subject coreferential to them; this is also not usual. Finally, this approach suffers from one of the fatal defects of the prior analysis, namely, there is in principle no way to distinguish this case from any other case of verb agreement, and thus to be forced to say that ALL verb agreement is subject incorporation in any language. While such a view may or may not have anything to recommend itself in solving the difficult problems of agreement, it certainly does not buy us anything in Ac as a way of explaining the behavior of the agreement morphemes.

Having demonstrated that the problem of Ac agreement remains, no matter what tack is taken, I would like to suggest how I think it should be handled.

While there is much that is attractive about RG, I think some serious re-thinking is in order on the nature of agreement (as well as other topics).

Recent work by Ross[20] has demonstrated amply, I believe, the necessity for theories of grammar to handle nondiscrete phenomena in nondiscrete ways. Much of the problem with agreement in RG is derived from a strict adherence to discrete categories like 'term', 'subject', 'agreement', etc. It seems much more likely that such notions are not discrete at all, but consist of clusters of properties[21] shared to greater or lesser degree among the NPs in an S; Austronesian languages are well-known to exploit some of the latitude inherent in this schema.

If we posit such an approach to agreement (restricting ourselves for the moment to agreement with subjects—however that latter term is to be defined), we find ourselves constructing a continuum of agreementlike phenomena. The heuristic model I have been using to attack this problem is the following: Consider a syntagma like (39):

(39)                           $N_1-N_2-V$
                        (order of elements irrelevant)

where $N_1$ represents a noun (phrase) that is relatively more free and $N_2$ one that is relatively less free, and where $N_1$ is coreferential with $N_2$ (I use 'free' here in a notional sense, meaning 'close to the verb'; this may manifest itself as morphological affixation, pronominalization, restriction in choice of lexi-calization as compared to $N_1$, etc.) Obviously, such a schema includes subject incorporations and other nonagreement phenomena, but I suspect we may profit from linking them with agreement in this way. We can then take the known properties of subjects, and check various instances of this syntagma to see how they are distributed. At one end of the continuum are the undoubted cases of agreement, like the German or Spanish cases (note that this proposal is not intended to distinguish between these two phenomena; that appears to be a separate and independently vexing problem), where $N_1$ has virtually all of the properties associated with the notion "subject," and $N_2$ has none. The other end is not so easy to see, but one guess might associate it with sentences such as (40):

(40)                       *My old man, he can do anything.*

where many, if not all, of the properties of "subject" have transferred from $N_1$ to $N_2$. It is interesting to note that the subject properties that have transferred in (40) are largely syntactic, not pragmatic. Tomlin (1975) notes that there is good reason to separate these two large groups of subject properties in order

[20] For example, Ross (1972, 1973, 1974, and 1975). For further discussion of the implications of Ross's work, see Lawler (1975a).

[21] Such as the list composed by Keenan (1974). For further discussion of the concepts involved in subject properties, and particularly of the different types of properties, see Tomlin (1975).

to deal with ergativity; here we may have some more evidence regarding the nature of these properties. On such a scale, Ac would be located somewhere in the middle.

It is, of course, an open question as to whether such a continuum can even be constructed; yet surely it is possible to investigate phenomena along these lines, and undoubtedly we would learn something by doing so. One of the benefits might be an ordered list of the properties associated with the notion "subject" (or several such lists, each giving different types of properties), if there turns out to be a relatively smooth distribution of transfers throughout the continuum. If such a list is possible, we will have a definition of "subject" which is empirically sound and which also provides a weighting of the relative strengths of its constituent parts. On the other hand, we might find large discontinuities in the list, which could tell us something useful about the nature of the properties and their dependencies, or conceivably that some of the properties do not define "subject" so much as something else. (As noted above, there may also be some hope of distinguishing pragmatic notions like "topic" or "theme" from syntactic ones like "subject" by this means.) Finally, it may be that there is considerable chaos in the transfers, which will tell us something useful (though not very pleasant) about our notion of "subject"—namely, that it is very largely a fiction. In addition, a study along these dimensions opens the possibility that some historical changes may be more conveniently explicated in terms of the hierarchy, with, for example, pronouns becoming more like agreement markers, or vice versa.[22]

In the paragraphs above, I have no more than sketched out some speculations about agreement phenomena, broadly defined. I do not expect what may emerge from more serious investigation to resemble these hypotheses, but I do think I have shown that much more serious investigation is in order, and that a rethinking of many of our traditional terms and categories is necessary in order to be able to even recognize the important data, let alone deal with it in a responsible and satisfying manner.

## ACKNOWLEDGMENTS

This chapter derives originally from a field methods class at the University of Michigan in 1974–75; I wish to express my deep appreciation to our informant and guide through the mysteries of Achenese, Drs. Idris Ibrahim, of Syiah Kuala University, Banda Aceh, without whose linguistic sophistication and firm command of English subtleties we would have floundered forever. The hard core of the class, students and other interested parties, contributed much in the way of questions, analysis, corrections, and elicitation of data. In particular, I would like to thank Russ Tomlin, Phil Tedeschi, Roger Mills, Roy Cayetano, and Jeff Dreyfuss for their help. I also wish

[22] See Lawler (1975b) for a discussion of a change which has apparently proceeded along these parameters. Other possible examples are the use of the "copula" *hu/hi* in Modern Hebrew, or the possible derivation of the *i-* predication marker in Melanesian Pidgin from English *he*.

to thank Ann Borkin, Charlie Pyle, Ed Keenan, and Sandy Chung for helpful comments and suggestions, and Elli Hirschey and Katie Feeney for their typing of the manuscript. Paul Postal deserves special credit for noticing the theoretical anomalies in the Achenese Passive, and for encouraging me to describe the data, at the expense of theories, if necessary. Finally, I wish to express here a special sense of gratitude, not limited to this or any other single undertaking, to Pete Becker, without whom not. None of the above are responsible for errors of fact, theory, or analysis in this paper, which are my own exclusively, nor should any of them be construed as agreeing with me.

# REFERENCES

Anderson, S. (1974) "On Dis-Agreement Rules," *Linguistic Inquiry* 5, 445–451.
Becker, A. L. and I. G. N. Oka (1973) "Person in Kawi: Exploration of an Elementary Semantic Dimension" mimeographed, University of Michigan, Ann Arbor, Michigan.
Collins, V. (forthcoming) *The Austro-Asiatic Substratum in Achenese*, Doctoral dissertation, University of California, Berkeley, California.
Djajadiningrat, H. (1934) *Atjehsch–Nederlandsch Woordenboek*, 2 vols., Landsdrukkerij, Batavia.
Ishak, D. (1968) *Tatabahasa Atjeh*, P. T. Sakti, Banda Aceh.
Keenan, E. (1974) "A Subject Properties Check-list," mimeographed, University of California, Los Angeles, California.
Lawler, J. (1975a) "Elliptical Conditionals and/or Hyperbolic Imperatives: Some Remarks on the Inherent Inadequacy of Derivations," in R. E. Grossman, L. J. Sam, and T. J. Vance, eds., *Papers from the Eleventh Regional Meeting of the Chicago Linguistic Society*, University of Chicago, Chicago, Illinois.
Lawler, J. (1975b) "On Coming to Terms in Achenese: The Function of Verbal Dis-Agreement," in R. E. Grossman, L. J. Sam, and T. J. Vance, eds., *Papers from the Parasession on Functionalism*, Chicago Linguistic Society, University of Chicago, Chicago, Illinois.
Makam, I. and R. P. Burr (1971) *An Introductory English-Achenese Achenese-English Dictionary*, manuscript, Fakultas Keguruan, Syiah Kuala University, Banda Aceh.
Morgan, J. (1972) "Verb Agreement as a Rule of English," in P. M. Peranteau, J. N. Levi, and G. C. Phares, eds., *Papers from the Eighth Regional Meeting of the Chicago Linguistic Society*, University of Chicago, Chicago, Illinois.
Postal, P. (1967) "A Agrees With B," In *Linguistic Anarchy Notes*, Series G (Wonders of Excessive Power), No. 1, ditto, IBM Thomas J. Watson Research Center, Yorktown Heights, N.Y.
Postal, P. (1970) "On Coreferential Complement Subject Deletion," *Linguistic Inquiry* 1, 439–500.
Postal, P. (1974) *On Raising*, M.I.T. Press, Cambridge, Massachusetts.
Ross, J. R. (1972) "The Category Squish: Endstation Hauptwort," in P. M. Peranteau, J. N. Levi, and G. C. Phares, eds., *Papers from the Eighth Regional Meeting of the Chicago Linguistic Society*, University of Chicago, Chicago, Illinois.
Ross, J. R. (1973) "A Fake NP Squish," in C. J. N. Bailey and R. Shuy, eds, *New Ways of Analyzing Variation in English*, Georgetown University Press, Washington, D. C.
Ross, J. R. (1974) "There, There, (There, (There, (There, . . .)))," M. W. LaGaly, R. A. Fox, and A. Bruck, eds., *Papers from the Tenth Regional Meeting of the Chicago Linguistic Society*, University of Chicago, Chicago, Illinois.
Ross, J. R. (1975) *Nouniness*, in *Kaigai Eigogaku Ronsoo*, Eichosha, Tokyo.
Tomlin, R. (1975) "Some Implications of Subject Properties, Passive, and Ergative Languages," to appear in *New Ways of Analyzing Variation, Etc*, Georgetown University Press, Washington, D. C.
Van Langen, K. F. H. (1889) *Handleiding voor de Beoefening der Atjehsche Taal*, Martinus Nijhoff, 's Gravenhage.

# WORD ORDER UNIVERSALS AND
# GRAMMATICAL RELATIONS

*GEOFFREY K. PULLUM*
University College London

The assumption on which this study is based is the uncontroversial one that grammars of natural languages have to make explicit the principles governing the order of constituents in sentences, and, further, that the theory of grammar should seek to place the strongest constraints on the set of such principles that can be made consistent with observed facts about attested languages. I assume that general linguistic theory is inadequate to the extent that it fails to provide for the description of situations that do occur, but also to the extent that it provides readily for the description of logically conceivable situations that do not occur. For example, a language (English) is known to exist in which most declarative sentence types have sentence-initial subject NPs, a verbal complex following the subject NP, and postverbal object NPs and other constituents, with 'heavy' constituents and extraposed clauses in sentence-final positions. If a language could quite well exist (i.e. be in natural use in a human community) with the mirror image of this typical constituent order (*heavy constituents— object NPs—verbal complex—subject NP*), then linguistic theory should make available a grammar for such a language; but if it could not, then the theory should make it impossible or extremely awkward to construct a grammar which generates the language.

Within the framework of theory that I shall adopt, namely the offshoot of transformational-generative grammar that is becoming known as Relational Grammar, it seems to be necessary to distinguish two ways in which natural language grammars deal with the determination of constituent ordering. On the one hand, there appear to be a very large number of languages that use surface (or shallow) order as a means of indicating the grammatical roles of constituents without resorting to other devices such as morphological marking. Thus in English, for an NP to be in the immediate postverbal position in superficial structures essentially marks it as a direct object, much as an accusative case inflection would in many other languages.[1] To describe such facts, it would appear to be necessary to have LINEARIZATION RULES in a grammar which directly fix linear order on the basis of properties of syntactic derivations or representations. On the other hand, many languages—if not all—show variation of constituent order that cannot be described in such terms without running the risk of obscuring what is actually happening. Alternative orders are made available, sometimes with merely stylistic associated effects, sometimes with pragmatic consequences (particularly to do with discourse context and 'functional sentence perspective'), and sometimes to ensure a special position in the sentence for some designated element regardless of its grammatical role at earlier stages of the derivation (sentence-initial position for question words, for example). The appropriate device for characterizing such phenomena is probably to permit certain POSTCYCLIC MOVEMENT RULES. I shall tentatively assume that linearization rules assign a basic order to the elements of the clause—an order which is ceteris paribus obligatory, the cetera being postcyclic rules—and that postcyclic movement rules operate to modify this order in ways that may lead to preferred or required positioning of constituents that is not attributable to linearization.

In a transformational grammar of the *Aspects* type (Chomsky 1965) the function of linearization is assigned to the phrase structure rules of the base component that defines the underlying level of syntactic structure. This has a number of disadvantages. First, it implies that there is some single, strict ordering relation between any pair of elements introduced into any deep structure, leaving no possibility of free order at all (since in the *Aspect* theory phrase structure rules are assumed to output only strings, never sets). Second, it introduces into deep structures a relation which is irrelevant to their primary function of defining underlying grammatical relations structure, and which is known to be a language-particular matter rather than a potential universal (since objects follow their verbs in English but precede them in Japanese, to cite an obvious example). Third, it implies that there is no reason to suppose a claim such as SUBJECTS PRECEDE VERBS IN ENGLISH will be true of superficial structures, only that such generalizations will be statable with regard to deep structures. The fact that ALL subject NPs, whether underlying or transformationally derived, precede the verbal complex in English sentences becomes an accident of the system of transformational rules—a huge coincidence instead of a clear principle of sentence organization.

For these and other reasons, attempts have been made in the literature of transformational grammar to free syntax from underlyingly assigned linear

---

[1] This needs qualification, of course, but the general point is surely clear.

precedence relations. Staal (1967) is a monograph-length study which argues that the free word order of Sanskrit supports the abandonment of nonsuperficial linear order. Sanders (1970) also attempts to motivate such an abandonment (though his case may not rest on very secure foundations; cf. Harries 1973:145–149, and Pullum 1974:100n). Peterson (1971) uses evidence from mirror-image rules in English to argue for unordered trees. Hudson (1972) shows that McCawley's (1970) arguments for an underlying VSO order in English are equally applicable to the thesis of an underlying SOV order, and suggests that they should really be interpreted as arguments for NO order in deep structure. None of these investigators suggest replacing linear precedence relations in syntax with more abstract grammatical relations of a different sort; they merely propose that hierarchical constituent structure provides a sufficient basis for the operation of transformational rules.

However, recent work in Relational Grammar involves not simply the abandonment of precedence relations but the introduction into syntax of relations such as SUBJECT OF, DIRECT OBJECT OF, etc., as theoretical primes. Johnson (1974) and Keenan (1976a and 1976b) offer some evidence that the configurational definition of such notions by the use of DOMINANCE in phrase structure trees as the prime (cf. Chomsky 1965:68–74) is not possible on a cross-linguistic basis. Radford (1975a and 1975b) mounts an extended defense of the view that some raising rules must operate on unordered structures and must be able to refer to notions such as 'subject of' without deriving them from any antecedently given properties of syntactic representations. Chung (1976) argues at length that the Dative rule in Bahasa Indonesia cannot be adequately stated and constrained in ordinary transformational terms, but needs a relational statement.

Initial work on developing a syntactic theory employing grammatical relations as primes has been discussed at length by Perlmutter and Postal (unpublished lectures, 1974 Linguistic Institute University of Massachusetts, Amherst) and by Johnson (1974). I am convinced of the necessity of such a theory, and in this study I will assume that provision must be made for syntactic rules that operate in terms of grammatical relations (henceforth, GRs). I cannot hope to argue in detail for this position here (cf. Perlmutter and Postal, in preparation), but I offer a few brief remarks about the theoretical constructs I shall appeal to and the notation I shall be using.

Clauses are described as unordered structures ('relational networks' for Johnson 1974) consisting of a verb and a number (one or more) of NPs associated with the verb. One of these NPs will stand in the relation SUBJECT OF (symbolized in this paper by ①) to the verb. If the verb is transitive in the traditional sense, another NP will bear the relation OBJECT OF (symbolized by ②). With certain types of verbs another NP may stand in the relation INDIRECT OBJECT OF (symbol: ③). Other NPs will bear none of these relations and will be called NONTERMS (Ⓝ), as opposed to the GR-bearing NPs, which will be called TERMS. Clauses may themselves be NPs in higher clauses.

Cyclic rules affect the structure of clauses by changing GRs in ways controlled by general laws, i.e. principles of universal grammar. For example, Passive might be stated as a universal GR-changing rule *Object → Subject* (② → ①). By a general law this would determine that the NP which hitherto bore the relation ① to the verb was stripped of that status to become what Perlmutter and Postal call a CHÔMEUR. A morphological rule in the grammar of English of English would be responsible for marking the passive chômeur with the preposition *by*; only after all cyclic rules had operated (but prior to the operation of any postcyclic rules) would the linearization rule determine the linear position of the phrase thus marked by imposing (roughly) the order ①⌒*V*⌒②⌒③⌒ (Ⓝ, *chômeurs*).[2] The linearization rule thus refers to DERIVED termhood: it is the LATEST NP to be assigned to the ① relation that will take clause-initial position.

The main purpose of the rest of this chapter is to investigate the extent to which constraints can be placed upon rules of linearization in relational grammar, and to relate this investigation to available information on universals of constituent order.

## BASIC WORD ORDER TYPES

The classic modern study of word order universals is Greenberg (1963). Greenberg uses terms such as 'subject', 'object', and 'basic word order' without defining them, and there has been some confusion over interpretation because of this. 'Subject' could mean semantically agentive NP in active sentences, morphologically least marked (e.g. zero case inflection) NP, verbal agreement controlling NP, or various other things.[3] 'Basic' order could mean statistically most frequent order (for some defined subset of sentence types such as main simplex active declaratives), intuitively least marked (i.e. least "special") order, required order when ambiguity is to be avoided, or numerous other things. Greenberg says very little in his paper about terminology, theoretical assumptions, or methodology. I believe, however, that a thoroughly coherent and accurate theoretical interpretation of what Greenberg's generalizations are making claims about can be constructed if we read 'basic word order' as ORDER TO BE

---

[2] I use the locution 'linearization rule' throughout. To be more precise, I view linearization as accomplished by an output condition, but this point does not affect anything to be discussed below.

Notice that in a similarly vague way I talk about 'word order'. The paper is, in fact, exclusively concerned with order of major sentence constituents.

[3] Keenan (1976a) even suggests that "subject" should be understood as a multifactor concept definable (statistically) over these and other parameters.

ASSIGNED BY THE LINEARIZATION RULES (i.e. order defined on representations prior to the first application of a postcyclic transformation), and interpret 'subject' and 'object' as CYCLIC ① and CYCLIC ②, respectively.[4] This links theory and observation inextricably, of course, since now the problem of determining from texts what the basic word order is for some language is inseparable from the problem of constructing an adequate relational grammar for that language; but there must surely be very few linguists who ever believed that fact gathering in a theoretical vacuum could be possible in syntax.

Interpreting Greenberg's S(ubject), V(erb), and O(bject) as I suggest, consider the following passage from Greenberg (1963:61), which has become an important statement of standard wisdom to workers in syntactic typology:

(1)   *Logically there are six possible orders: SVO, SOV, VSO, VOS, OSV, and OVS. Of these six, however, only three normally occur as dominant orders. The three which do not occur at all, or at least are excessively rare, are VOS, OSV, and OVS.*

The locution 'dominant orders' here raises a further difficulty of interpretation, but it is one that I think can be coped with. Greenberg states, "The vast majority of languages have several variant orders but a single dominant one" (1963:61). This suggests very strongly that he is interested in the statistically predominant member of a set of occurring surface orders, yet this cannot be so in any oversimple sense: He surely would not be happy with classifying English as OSV just when it was represented by a corpus containing a massive predominance, for some reason, of topicalizations. The objection to that is expressible in the framework adopted here as an objection that, however many topicalizations are found in any particular corpus, or in discourse in English generally, the OSV order is one determined by a postcyclic rule sensitive to discourse conditions; the optimal grammar for English assigns SVO, not OSV, order at the linearization stage. This leaves only one logically possible type of situation in which there could be serious doubt over how to categorize a given language in Greenberg's typology even if we had a good idea of the structure of its grammar in relational terms. A language could conceivably have a linearization rule that assigned ABC order, and also a postcyclic movement rule $ABC \rightarrow BCA$ which was either obligatory, or favored enough to be involved in the derivation of the vast majority of main, simplex, active, declarative sentences used by speakers. In a situation such as this, it would not be clear how to answer the question, "Is this an ABC language or a BCA language?" Its 'dominant' order (IF this means statistically dominant in some sense) would certainly be BCA, yet its

---

[4] A cyclic $n$ is an NP bearing the relation $n$ to the verb of its clause at the end of the cycle on that clause. Since cyclic rules can change clause membership (e.g. by Raising) there is something to be said about the precise way in which linearization interacts with the cycle. There are arguments I hope to present elsewhere that bear on this, but for present purposes I need not go into them.

'basic' order (interpreted as above) would be ABC. This type of possible situation should be kept carefully in mind as I proceed below to reassess the empirical standing of Greenberg's claim (which, if it is correct, must provide the basic datum for a general theory of linearization in natural language).

I take the existence of languages whose basic orders are SVO (like English or Swahili), SOV (like Japanese or Turkish), and VSO (like Welsh or Samoan) to be beyond doubt. I shall consider the other three types separately in some detail.

### Verb-Object-Subject

It seems to me that in the case of VOS Greenberg's study must be regarded as having had a damaging influence on investigation of word order typology, for it has resulted in an almost universal neglect of the evidence for VOS languages. Although available evidence is far too scanty and far too little research has been done, it is my view that VOS almost certainly has to be admitted to the range of occurring word order types. Members of the Universal Grammar Seminar led by Edward Keenan at King's College, Cambridge, in 1974, determined that VOS order seemed to be dominant in at least Toba Batak, Gilbertese, and Malagasy (Keenan, informant work); Tzeltal (Penny Brown, field study); and Classical Mayan (John Payne, summarizing Knorozov 1963). The list of probable VOS languages may perhaps be lengthened to include Fijian (see Arms 1974); Mezquital Otomi, Tumbala Chol, and Tzotzil (Culicover and Wexler 1974, summarizing an unpublished source); and Coeur d'Alene (Greenberg 1963:88, relying on Reichard 1933).

It is true that nevertheless VOS is excessively rare. It is also true that, in many cases of possible VOS languages, an alternative analysis stands at least a chance of being defended. It is by no means easy to determine just when a candidate is a reasonable one, and linguists can easily differ on this point. For example, Classical Mayan was actually in Greenberg's original sample of languages, but was judged by him to fall into the SVO category. An example cited as typical for transitive sentences by Knorozov (1963:113, Section 33) is:

(2)                          Classical Mayan

                             *U– tup        k'ak'ax      tok.*
                             3sg extinguish lamp-lighter light
                             'The lamp-lighter puts out the light.'

but for some reason Greenberg's study of the language inclines him to regard SVO as the basic order type.

I am aware of at least four different kinds of situations in which there may be grounds for reanalyzing dominant VOS as derived from something else. The first is relevant to the analysis of languages such as Tagalog, which has been wrongly categorized as VOS by Ultan (1969) and Ross (1970:250). Bach

(1974:275n) argues against the VOS category of languages as follows:

> As to the [VOS] type, . . . the languages usually cited are Malayo-Polynesian, especially Philippine languages. Here I believe that the order of constituents is determined by a thematization rule moving the theme to the right, and that it is a mistake to think of this item as the subject. To settle this question it is necessary to have a good language-independent characterization of surface subjects, so far lacking. In any event, these questions must be considered very much open.

While I shall disagree with Bach's implied claim that ALL allegedly VOS languages fall into the theme-final class, he is probably right with respect to Philippine languages, such as Tagalog. The typical situation is illustrated in (3):

(3)  Tagalog

   a. *K-um-ain*  *ang bata nang isda.*
      eat (with *um* infix) det child det  fish
      'The child ate the fish.'

   b. *K-in-ain*  *nang bata ang isda.*
      eat (with *in* infix) det  child det fish
      'The child ate the fish.'

Informants appear to feel that (3a) is a less natural construction to use than is (3b). They accept any order of NPs after the verb, but give those in (3) as unmarked and most natural. The *ang/nang* distinction encodes either subject/nonsubject or theme/nontheme. If the former is correct, the *um/in* distinction is one of voice, and the order in (3b) can be described as VXS, where $X =$ *chômeur*. A not entirely conclusive discussion in such terms of a related language, Cebuano, is given in Bell (1974). This would require the recognition of a type of language in which chômeurs precede all terms, but not the recognition of VOS linearization rules. If the latter (more usual) interpretation of *ang/nang* is correct, *um* must be glossed 'actor is theme' and *in*, 'goal is theme'; both the sentences in (3) could be treated as showing VSO order, which could be assumed to be basic (and which happens to be what Bach has conjectured is the underlying order for all languages).

The second type of situation which may turn out not to support a VOS type is rather different, and would not submit to the reanalysis hinted at by Bach. It is the situation in which a language has fixed VOS word order in only one sentence type: the rhematic type, in which there is no theme or topic, the whole sentence being a presentation of new information. Such a language could not be dealt with in terms of the rightward movement of thematic NPs. From a reading of Browne and Vattuone (1975) and Vattuone (1975), Zenéyze, the Romance language spoken around Genoa, Italy, appears to be a case in point. In Zenéyze, when an NP is thematic, a clitic that agrees with it in number and gender is attached to the verb, as in (4), where the subject *a kataynin* is theme:

(4)                          *A   kataynin, a-  vende i   peši   a  zêna.*
                             the Catherine she-sells   the fishes in Genoa
                             'Catherine sells the fish in Genoa.'

But if nothing in the sentence is theme, this word order is not permitted; the order shown in (5) is required:

(5)                          *U-vende i   peši   a  zêna   a   kataynin.*
                             it- sells   the fishes in Genoa the Catherine
                             'Catherine sells the fish in Genoa.'

   In Vattuone (1975), arguments are presented for an analysis of Zenéyze which treats the VOS order as basic and which derives (4) from an underlying structure approximately like (5) by a rule of Thematization. The clitic *u* on the verb in (5) is the third-person-singular nonfeminine pronoun also found in such logically subjectless verbs as 'to rain' (note *u čøve* 'it is raining'), and Vattuone treats it as being inserted by a late rule into verbs that have no clitic attached. Thus the analysis implies that *a kataynin* is the derived ① of (5) in relational terms, *u* being no more than a postcyclically inserted affix; therefore a VOS linearization rule might be called for. There are reasons, however, to think that the correct analysis does not involve VOS linearization. Even if the claim that *u* is postcyclically inserted were correct, there would be the alternative of analyzing Zenéyze as having SVO basic word order and a rightward movement rule that placed 'new information' subject NPs in sentence-final position, followed by *u*-insertion as a surface structure adjustment; this is exactly what is argued for in the case of *es*-insertion in German by Breckenridge (1975). In this way Zenéyze would be related much more clearly to other languages of Western Europe; (5) almost finds a parallel in the awkward and marginal sentences from German and Romansh given in (6):

(6)              a.  German[5]

                     *??Es stiess   ihn  der Soldat von   der Brücke.*
                     it   pushed him the soldier from the bridge
                     'The soldier pushed him off the bridge.'

                 b.  Romansh[6]

                     *??Igl ei emblidau la  fiasta il   parsun.*
                     it   be forgotten the party the treasurer
                     'The treasurer forgot the party.'

---

[5] Example from Breckenridge (1975:87).
[6] Example from Haiman (1974:132).

But, in fact, it is even more likely that *a kataynin* is NOT the cyclic subject of (5). The clitic *u* could turn out to be the subject, having been inserted by a cyclic rule like the *there* of English *there*-insertion (or the Presentational-*there* Insertion discussed by Aissen 1975). That this is actually so is strongly suggested by the fact that, although verbs agree in number with their cyclic subjects in Zenéyze—so that if the subject of (4) were plural the verb form would be *vendu*—the verb in a rhematic sentence like (5) cannot be plural: The sequence *\*u-vendu* cannot occur. If (5) is produced by a cyclic Dummy-insertion rule, the linearization rule for Zenéyze would appear to be SVO.

The third type of potential VOS language that may be reanalyzable may be illustrated via Tzeltal (a dialect of Chiapas, southern Mexico) and by Cœur d'Alene:

(7)      Tzeltal

*La  y- il   te'tikil mut ta hamal te   ziake.*
past he-see wild    bird in forest the Ziak
'Ziak saw a wild bird in the forest.'

(8)      Cœur d'Alene

*Its-gwitc-əms xʷätsi'   xʷä'äbän.*
he- sees- it    the deer the Ben
'Ben sees the deer.'

These languages normally have the predicate followed by the subject, but show in their verb morphology that this could be argued to result from the application to SVO structures of a rule very much like Right Dislocation in English—a postcyclic rule which moves the subject NP to sentence final position, leaving a pronominal copy behind. The obligatory (or heavily favored) operation of a rule like this could, in fact, realize the situation outlined hypothetically above, bringing about a discrepancy between the basic order (SVO) and the dominant surface order (VOS). This has not been demonstrated to be necessary, but, since it is clearly a possible analysis, until it is ruled out we cannot regard Tzeltal, Cœur d'Alene, or similar languages as showing the need for VOS basic order.

The fourth and final VOS type that might be reanalyzable is the type that shows evidence of resulting from attraction to the verb of the direct object in a VSO basic structure. Fijian may be of this type. John Payne informs me that it seems to be only objects that are indefinite and unmodified that appear immediately after the verb. It might be suggested that, as in Hungarian, such objects undergo a specific process which changes the linear order (SOV instead of SVO in Hungarian). This would explain the fact that (according to Keenan, personal communication) the order $V \frown ② \frown ① \frown (③, Ⓝ)$ appears to be dominant in Fijian: moving the object leftward to the verb in a VSOX structure gives exactly this order, with various oblique NPs after the subject (Arms 1974). Keenan informs me that the same order seems from Silitonga (1973) to be dominant in Toba Batak.

Four attested types of language which give the appearance of being VOS can thus be seen to be potentially amenable to reanalysis in terms of some different basic (or underlying) order. In defense of VOS, it might be said that there is no more reason to do this than to attempt the reanalysis of all SVO languages in terms of VOS basic order. The rarity of the VOS type is a fact about the set of ATTESTED languages, not about the set of NATURAL languages (Sampson 1973), and since this set is undoubtedly skewed by historical, geographical, and political accidents it should not be accorded any more weight than the rarity of gorillas vis-à-vis men. But such a defense is not necessary. There happens to be a case of a language which is quite clearly not amenable to reanalysis along any of the lines which have been discussed. This is Malagasy.

Malagasy (i) is organized by reference to the subject/nonsubject dimension, not the theme/nontheme one; (ii) does not show any evidence of a Dummy-insertion rule causing subject postposing; (iii) has no trace of clitic pronouns or even agreement affixes on verbs; and (iv) has the subject NP in final position in the clause, not in general followed by oblique NPs. Word order after the initial verb in a Malagasy transitive clause is not free (as in many verb-initial languages), but fixed in the sequence $V \frown ② \frown (③, ⑩) \frown ①$, as shown in (9):[7]

(9)          *Nividy  kisoa ho'an ny  ankizy   Rakoto.*
             bought pig   for   the children Rakoto
             'Rakoto bought some pork for the children.'

Malagasy even has this order when the subject NP is a pronoun:

(10)                              *Nividy  kisoa ianao/izy/aho.*
                                  bought pig   you   he  I
                                  'You/he/I bought pork.'

The only significant freedom of word order is a very limited freedom for certain oblique NPs in a complicated sentence to drift to the right:

(11)       a. *Nividy  kisoa ho'an ny  ankizy   tamin'ny Asabotsy aho.*
              bought pig   for   the children on      the Saturday I

           b. *Nividy  kisoa ho'an ny  ankizy   aho tamin'ny  Asabotsy.*
              bought pig   for   the children I   on      the Saturday
              'I bought pork for the children on Saturday.'

---

[7] Malagasy data from Keenan (1976c).

but such rightward drifting of oblique NPs (also known in English: *there was a man talking downstairs in the store-room today at lunch-time to your father*) does not motivate any basic order other than VOS. It would appear from the Malagasy evidence alone that there can be a language with a VOS linearization rule. I conclude that, whatever the outcome of the extensive further research that is clearly needed on the other languages mentioned above, VOS as a basic word order has to be admitted to our typology.

### Object-Subject-Verb

I am aware of four references in the literature to the existence of languages allegedly having OSV as basic word order in one sense or another. Johnson (1974:80) asserts that Dyirbal is "an Australian language that is basically O-S-V"; Keenan (1976b) notes that "Hurrian should also be checked as a possible OSV language" (and cites Stephen Anderson's course at the 1974 Linguistics Institute); Ross (1970:250) states that Guy Carden informed him "that the basic order in Aleut is OSV"; and Rischel (1970:225) posits OSV as the underlying (i.e. deep structure) order for West Greenlandic Eskimo, thus implying that it might be basic in some such sense as mine. (In at least some cases, arguments for deep structure order are potentially valid as arguments for order at the end of the cycle.)

It is remarkable that every one of these languages is well known to have morphological case marking on the so-called ergative pattern, with transitive subjects case marked differently from intransitive subjects, and the latter case marked the same as direct objects. An important issue in linguistic description raises its head immediately because of this fact. Faced with a language having two morphological cases ERGATIVE ($E$) and ABSOLUTIVE ($A$), and having the order $NP_{A'}$ $NP_{E'}$ $V$ in transitive sentences, it is on the face of it possible to argue that $A$ case marking indicates the subject (derived ①) just as it does in intransitive sentences where the order is $NP_A \frown V$. The fact that the semantics of transitive sentences with activity verbs would show the $NP_A$ to be the patient or affected entity would then be taken as straightforward evidence that the correlation *initial* ① = *agent* was not universal. For any language that could be analyzed in this way, $A$-before-$E$ order would NOT indicate that an OSV (i.e. ② $\frown$ ① $\frown$ $V$) type had to be recognized.

I shall call the kind of analysis just sketched, with absolutive as transitive subject, a DEEP ERGATIVE analysis (i.e. an analysis treating the ergative-absolutive type of morphological marking as indicative of a fundamental difference in syntactic organization and semantic-syntactic relations). The issue to be faced in dealing with the evidence for OSV languages is whether the deep ergative analysis is correct for any languages of the world.

I deal first with Dyirbal, an aboriginal Australian language of North Queensland which has been described more fully and accessibly, thanks to

Dixon (1972), than any language of its type. The source of Johnson's categorization of it as OSV (and also of the undiscussed listing of Dyirbal as OSV in Culicover and Wexler 1974:66) is the statement by Dixon (1972:291) that the PREFERRED order of constituents, "more likely to be adhered to if ambiguity would otherwise result," is the order illustrated by the simple transitive sentence in (12):

(12)                 *Bayi      bargan      baŋgul      yaɽaŋgu    ɖurga-ɲu.*
                     (*A* prefix) wallaby (*E* prefix) man       spear-tense
                     'The man is spearing the wallaby.'

Note that word order is not being used here to mark GRs in any way. Word order is free in Dyirbal to an extent that many linguists find it hard to believe (see Dixon's remarks on pp. 107–108), with virtually all words freely reorderable in the clause (contradicting a claim in Chomsky 1965:126, that such a thing is unheard of). What Dixon's description says is that there is a preference for having the $NP_A$ in a sentence to the left of the $NP_E$. This is precisely the kind of fact we would expect to find described by means of postcyclic movement rules with some degree of optionality. It is broadly clear that there is some kind of complementarity between case-marking rules and linearization rules in languages of the world, with some (such as English and Chinese) having virtually no case-assignment rules but fairly strict linearization rules, and others depending significantly on case marking to the virtual exclusion of linearization. One advantage of the framework of relational grammar is that it places case marking and linearization in general at the same point in derivations (the end of the cycle) and thus makes it easier to see how this complementary situation might be characterized—perhaps in terms of a typology of end-of-cycle rule systems. It is very clear that Dyirbal leans toward case marking at the expense of linearization, and might conceivably be best described with only the trivial linearization rule *place constituents in some linear order*. This would admit true free word order languages to the typology (and would still not prevent there from being a favored postcyclic rule that accounts for the frequent preposing of absolutive NPs).

Note also that in (12) the case marking is accordance with an ergative-absolutive system. If the agent NP *yaɽaŋgu* 'man' were to be found as the agent in a sentence with an intransitive verb, it would not take *E* marking, but rather would have the *A* form: *bayi yaɽa*. One might consider the question of whether a deep ergative analysis would be correct for Dyirbal. The answer Dixon gives to this question is yes. In his transformational analysis, Dyirbal is distinctly different from a language like English in the way its syntax is related to semantics, and in the categories by reference to which its syntax is organized. For him, *bayi bargan* is both the underlying and the superficial subject of (12).

It will readily be seen that there are two ways immediately open to anyone who wishes to argue that Dyirbal is NOT an OSV language. Looking at the free word order aspect of Dyirbal grammar, one might say that Dyirbal is not OSV but XYZ—totally free at the level of linearization. Or, looking at the ergativity of the language, one might adopt the deep ergative analysis and argue that the *A* case marks ①, the *E* case marks ②, and the order to be taken as basic is ①⌒②⌒*V*: not OSV but SOV.

Some analyses would, in fact, permit the maintenance of both the claim that there are no OSV languages AND the claim that there are no deep ergative languages, without appealing to the free word order as a mitigating factor. One such analysis would be that of George (1974), an attempt to account for all the sentence types found in Dyirbal on the basis of a straightforward agent-as-deep-subject claim about underlying structures, treating (12) [repeated here as (13a)] as a passive sentence with derived subject marked as theme or topic by means of the *A* case:

(13)  a. *Bayi    bargan    baŋgul    yaɽaŋgu ɖurga-ɲu.*
         (*A* prefix) wallaby (*E* prefix) man      spear-tense

      b. *Bayi    yaɽa baŋgul    bargandu ɖurga-na- ɲu.*
         (*A* prefix) man (*E* prefix) wallaby   spear-*ŋay*-tense

      c. *Bayi    yaɽa bagul    bargangu ɖurga-na- ɲu.*
         (*A* prefix) man (*D* prefix) wallaby   spear-*ŋay*-tense

The other two sentences in (13) are both synonymous with (13a); the meaning in each case is 'the man is spearing the wallaby'. George analyzes (13b) as the result of applying Passive but marking the DEEP subject, not the DERIVED subject, as theme with the *A* case prefix. He sees (13c) as representing something close to underlying structure, with no relation-changing rules applying and with the deep subject marked as theme. The case that Dixon refers to as the dative is assigned to cycle-final ② in George's analysis, and other nonabsolutive NPs are marked with the *E* prefix. In this analysis, the reason for the preferred initial positioning of *A*-marked NPs is seen as simply the universal tendency to prefer initial position for themes. I think this is a very plausible idea (and it is not one that is necessarily incompatible with other analyses).

There are certain problems with George's analysis. As David Johnson has pointed out to me, it predicts wrongly for two-object constructions unless it is modified in some way, and it does not correctly accord with the predictions of Keenan and Comrie (to appear) regarding relativization possibilities. Johnson would incline toward an analysis in which the *E*-marked NP of (13a) is actually the superficial subject, and various facts are explained in terms of the exceptional status of ① that are marked *E* (they do not permit relativization, etc., etc.). In this type of analysis it definitely is the derived ② that is preferably in initial position. Even so, it is very significant that (as R. M. W. Dixon has pointed out to me) the most rigid word-order constraint found in Dyirbal is that subject pronouns should be sentence initial; and it is precisely these that do NOT participate in the $A/E$ case marking system, but rather reflect a nominative/accusative system. The word order principle seems to be, then, that the subject comes first unless it is $E$-marked, in which case it is preferable to have the $A$-marked NP first. Whatever analysis is ultimately shown to be correct for Dyirbal syntax, I think these basic claims will be incorporable into it, and I think it is clear that they cannot be said to support the classification of Dyirbal as an OSV language. If there is a linearization constraint of the usual sort, which is itself doubtful, it is most probably $①⌢②⌢V$, as in most Australian languages.

I turn now to the case of Hurrian, which is linked to the preceding one in that it is the sole language other than Dyirbal for which deep ergativity can at present be argued (according to Anderson 1976). Anderson claims that in both Dyirbal and Hurrian the cyclic rules operate by reference to the ergative-absolutive dimensions, which must be regarded as basic rather than (as in so many other so-called ergative languages, he points out) superficial. Hurrian is an extinct Anatolian language, unrelated to any better-known languages, for which there is a desperate paucity of textual material. Knowledge of Hurrian syntax must be gleaned from the study of a single text: the Mitanni letter, a large tablet containing a diplomatic communication of around 1360 B.C. addressed to Amenophis III by Tushratta, king of Mitanni. It contains fewer than five hundred lines of cuneiform writing, the first seven in Akkadian and the rest in Hurrian. The standard handbook on Hurrian is Speiser (1941), and in this the claim giving rise to the suggestion that Hurrian is OSV can be found set out quite clearly on pp. 205–206. 'Goal-agent-action', in Speiser's terminology, is the normal order in transitive sentences. And, interestingly, Speiser chooses to describe the absolutive as the case denoting the 'grammatical subject', which means that his terminology accords with the deep ergative view. For reasons having to do not with morphology (which probably determined Speiser's position), but with the operation of the cyclic rules, Anderson (1976) claims that the deep ergative analysis is correct. If he were right, Hurrian would be removed from the class of candidate OSV languages; it would be SOV. Anderson offers no evidence at all from Hurrian in the paper referred to, however, and I must confess that I cannot see how he could, given the nature of the available material. The evidence regarding the structure of complex sentences in Hurrian is extremely scanty. Speiser (1941) gives only one or two hints about the possible interpretations of certain constructions that appear to be participial, but the materials seem to contain no potential contexts where Equi, Raising, or other GR-changing rules might have applied. A later grammar, Bush (1964), contains not more information on clause structure, but less. I find it hard to believe that the present state of knowledge of Hurrian could possibly be utilized make a convincing argument that the deep ergative hypothesis is correct, or that it is false. It is just possible that in this passage (1941:212) Speiser is alluding to the deletion of an ergative NP under identity with a preceding NP by a process resembling Participial Equi in English (which would speak against Anderson's claim, since in a deep ergative language Equi would apply only to absolutes):

> When the second verbal element is a participle followed by a connective we get a sub-
> ordinate construction . . . *anzannoḫoẑaf kulliman* Mit. III 51 "I begged saying." In the
> latter instance no personal pronoun appears, since both forms are transitive and the agent
> carries thus over from the first form.

Frankly, however, I am unable to tell. Speiser gives no discussion of the kind of
construction he thinks is illustrated here, nor does he supply a morpheme gloss.
It seems to me that there simply is not sufficient clear evidence available for
Hurrian to justify defense of the controversial claim that unlike any other
language in the world, it is deep ergative.[8]

What can be said about Hurrian is that it is generally verb final, with a certain
amount of free order among NPs. Sentences like (14), for example, occur:

(14)         *ᵐImmuriya- θθ-an   zalamθi tan-  oθ-   a.*
             Immuriya-by-and statue   make-PAST-by him
             'And Immuriya made the statue.'

However, Speiser considers that there is evidence to suggest that (14) involves
a stylistic shift of the agent NP to initial position for emphasis; the translation
should perhaps be 'and it was Immuriya that made the statue'. In his view, (15)
exemplifies a more typical order:

(15)                 *θen-    iff  iθa-θ  tat-  aw.*
                     brother-my me-by loved-by me
                     'I love my brother.'

We have too little information to be able to choose among the various grammars
that could account for this situation. We have no idea whether Hurrian permitted other sentence types, not exemplified in the five hundred lines of diplomatic prose at our disposal, which would shed new light on the case-marking
and syntactic systems. I doubt that the deep ergative hypothesis is correct, and
I believe that it would be just as plausible to treat (14) as reflecting the basic
order as it would be to assume (15) was basic.

Fortunately I do not need to be able to make out any strong case. The question I am interested in deciding is really whether we can find a language for
which an OSV ($②⌢①⌢V$) linearization rule MUST be postulated—i.e. a
language which uses linear order rather than case marking to indicate derived
GRs, and which indicates 'direct object' by placing it to the left of the subject
in a verb-final structure. Since Hurrian clearly uses case marking to distinguish
functions of NPs and has some degree of freedom in constituent order, as (14)

---

[8] It would be perfectly possible for me to be proved wrong on this, of course, by someone able
to extract more from the Hurrian materials than I have been able to. Stephen Anderson informs
me that he hopes to argue for Hurrian as a deep ergative language in Anderson (in preparation).

and (15) show, the answer to that question on the basis of the available evidence really has to be no.

It would be much less reasonable, of course, to take this line if there were any languages better known than Hurrian which had OSV basic order. But, in fact, Hurrian would stand totally alone if we were to categorize it as OSV. The information I have on Aleut, to take the next example, lends no support to any OSV claim. The fairly recent description by Menovščikov (1968) states clearly (p. 403) that there are two types of agent–patient–predicate sentences. The first type has an initial ergative NP, an absolutive NP following, and a verb showing agreement with both of them. This sentence type is said to carry emphasis on the "special status" of the object (absolutive) NP, and the example given has an adjectivally modified absolutive. The second type has the initial (semantically agentive) NP in the absolutive case, the following patient NP also in the absolutive, and the verb agreeing only with the agent. The example given by Menovščikov has a nonspecific, unmodified patient NP. Some sources, however, give details of an OSV construction with case marking *absolutive–ergative*. Clearly it is the existence of this construction that must have given rise to talk of OSV being basic for Aleut. But in a paper brought to my attention by Stephen Anderson, Underhill and Vago (1973) have argued on syntactic grounds that the OSV construction must be derived transformationally from the SOV *absolutive–absolutive* type. Their evidence comes from the morphological characteristics of the verb forms involved, which seem to have pronominal clitic forms attached to them, and from relative clauses, in which the same verb forms appear. Thus, far from representing the basic order of constituents, the OSV construction apparently has to be derived from an underlying SOV order if generalizations are to be captured syntactically and morphologically. In my terms, Aleut probably has a ①⌒②⌒V linearization condition and an optional postcyclic rule that fronts a ②.

This leaves West Greenlandic Eskimo as a possible OSV language. But the arguments given by Rischel (1970) for assuming patient-agent-predicate order in deep structures are extremely weak, and are in any case irrelevant from a relational point of view. All Rischel wants is to be able to predict morphological marking from standard, linearly ordered phrase markers in a maximally simple way. By setting up agent-predicate order for intransitive clauses and patient-agent-predicate order for transitive clauses, this can be accomplished: The initial NP is marked absolute, and any NP with an NP to its left is marked ergative. But, clearly, this approximation of a case-marking principle could be obtained just as simply if transitive clauses had agent-patient-predicate order; the rule would be that an NP immediately to the left of a verb is marked absolutive, while an NP followed by another NP is marked ergative. Regarding the dominant surface order, Rischel is unclear; while he states that (16) is given by Schultz-Lorentzen (1951:12) as "an entirely neutral specimen of Eskimo sentence construction":

(16)     *Puiši piniar-tu-  p          pi- ša-      ra-  a.*
         seal   hunt- doer-sing subj get-pass part-have as-sing obj
         (sing)                                      (sing subj)
         'The hunter caught the seal.'

he also states (p. 225) that "the SOV order may be less marked," by which he
apparently means that agent-patient-predicate order is felt to be more normal.
At any rate, there is no question about the freedom of order in Eskimo. Case
marking according to an ergative system, not word order, is employed to
distinguish GRs. In contradiction to Culicover and Wexler (1974), who pick
up Rischel's remark and list West Greenlandic as an OSV language, there is
no real argument here for the existence of a language with a ② ① V linearization rule. Neither for West Greenlandic, nor for any other free-word-order,
verb-final, ergative language is it necessary to set up an OSV typological
category.

## Object-Verb-Subject

I am aware of only three remarks in the literature that should be examined
with a view to assessing the status of OVS as a possible word order: Greenberg
(1963:88) briefly cites the Siuslaw and Coos languages as "VOS and OVS"
(Bach 1974:275n apparently alludes to this in mentioning OVS); Ross
(1970:250) states, "Ives Goddard [has informed me] that the basic order in
Algonquian is OVS"; and Rood (1971:101) indicates that in Wichita the orders
SOV and OVS are free variants.

Greenberg has kindly informed me that his sources on Coos and Siuslaw
(Lower Umpqua) were Frachtenberg (1922a) and (1922b), respectively. The
chief reason for noting OVS as an occurring order for these closely related
languages (now extinct as far as I know) would seem to be Frachtenberg's
statement (1922a:414) that "the subject of the sentence tends to appear at the
very end, especially in subordinate clauses. The object may either precede the
verb or follow it." I do not find that Frachtenberg's materials support this
generalization in its implication that OVS order is frequent. An examination
of Frachtenberg's grammatical sketches, and of the texts appended to them,
and of the further texts published as Frachtenberg (1913) and (1914), convinces
me that OVS sentences are quite infrequent, although there are examples (such
as the three examples Frachtenberg cites immediately after giving the above
generalization) of fronted oblique case constituents, i.e. Ⓝ V ①. The material
available is not ideal for research on the present topic; it consists of narrowly
transcribed texts of jumbled and half-forgotten folk tales elicited from informants who were, to say the least, not highly qualified for the task, and were
in some cases not strictly native speakers. Neither the quality nor the quantity
of the material suffices for any really significant study. However, clear cases

of SVO order are common enough:

(17)     Coos[9]

*Xyabas  yaptitsa lä  pilik˙is, lä  yees, lä  tcū̜, lä  kʷhanas.*
maggots ate up   his anus    his face  his nose his ears
'Maggots ate up his anus, his face, his nose, his ears.'

(18)     Siuslaw

*Squma "ɫ    kumintc taīɫ inq!aitc.*
pelican then not       live in rivers
'At that time, the pelican did not inhabit rivers.'

It should be clear from (17) alone that we are not dealing with the coding of
GRs by means of the sequence ② *V* ①, which would predict that such a
sentence should be near impossible. SVO could perhaps be the basic order for
these language; however, VOS order is also very common, and could be basic:

(19)     Coos

*La" kwinae^iwat līye iluwe^xtcis lɔx māqatɫ.*
he   looks at it  thy heart      the crow
'The crow knows what you're thinking.' (literally, 'The crow
      looks at your heart.')

(20)     Siuslaw

*Xil xcī    tsīt'ya ants tsimil˙ä.*
work(ed) arrows that muskrat
'Muskrat made arrows.'

If any claim that OVS order had basic status were to be made, one consequence
of that claim would be that orders such as those I have exemplified are derived
by postcyclic rules. Such rules are often, perhaps nearly always, sensitive to
discourse conditions (Hankamer 1974:221), and therefore where a discourse
environment could not be present, i.e. discourse initially, these orders should
not occur; the basic order would be expected. However, the one thing I have
not been able to find in the texts for Coos and Siuslaw is an instance of a text
beginning with an OVS sentence. I conclude that, whatever the basic order for
these languages, there is not a trace of evidence that it is OVS.

The remark attributed to Goddard about Algonquian seems simply to have
been an error.[10] All the Algonquian languages are so highly polysynthetic in

---

[9] Here, as elsewhere, I have modified minor details of transcription and glossing in the presentation of examples from Amerindian languages. The object has been to improve consistency and
typographical uniformity.

[10] The error seems to have been that Ross took a remark about Menomini surface order as a
claim about basic order in Algonquian generally. Ives Goddard has kindly pointed out to me the

their morphology that the GR-indicating function of word order is totally usurped, and it is very hard to find any evidence that a basic order is assigned by linearization rules (or phrase structure rules, or any other device) at all. It may be observed that in the description of Fox given by Jones (1911) word order is not discussed at all; given the nature of Algonquian languages, this is not too surprising an omission. In the text given by Jones I find no clear cases of two full NPs bearing different GRs associated with a verb, but, when full NPs are found, the subject-verb order of (21) and the verb-object order of (22) are apparently quite normal, which does not suggest any basic status for OVS.

(21)    Algonquian (Fox)

*Ma'kwʌn ä'pītci'kawänitc$^i$.*
bear       he-went-in-making-a-trail
'The bear went in making a trail.'

(22)    a. *Amʌtʌnāwātc$^i$*           *ma'kwʌn$^i$.*
           then-they-overtook-him bear-accusative
           'Then they overtook the bear.'

        b. *Ahapʌckinʌnihāwātc$^i$*           *ma'kwʌn$^i$.*
           then-they-put-him-to-lie-on-top-of-them bear-accusative
           'Then they laid the bear on top of them.'

On evidence like this, any OVS claim that was not backed up by detailed syntactic argument would simply be dismissed.

The only explicit remark about order of nominal constituents of the transitive clause that I have so far been able to find in the literature on Algonquian is a passage in Frantz (1966: Paragraph 2.3). He states that, where ambiguity might arise in a sentence in Blackfoot, NPs are usually interpreted on the assumption that their order will reflect the person hierarchy: *speaker > addressee > primary topic > secondary topic > third topic (subordinate to secondary)*. Symbolizing the above by subscripted 1, 2, 3, 4, and 5, he gives the following example from Blackfoot:

(23)    *Ainoyioaiks           ponokaiks ninaiks.*
        they$_{3pl}$-see-them$_{4pl}$ elks       men
        'The elks see the men.' **or** 'The men see the elks.'

Because the assignment of 'elks' and 'men' to categories on the person hierarchy is entirely a matter of narrative structure and style, (23) has two possible

---

relevant reference on Menomini, which I had missed. Bloomfield (1962:442) states: "An actor mostly comes after the verb" and "Objects usually precede the verb . . . ." However, if attention is paid to the rest of the remarks in the same section, it is quite clear that this does not imply basic OVS order when two NPs are present. According to Bloomfield, many types of actor (agent) NPs precede the verb; objects "often follow" the verb; and "If an obviative actor precedes the verb, the object usually follows the verb." See Footnote 11.

translations; but, all else being equal, it is more likely to be understood with *ponokaiks* 'elks' in the 3 (primary topic) role and *ninaiks* 'men' as 4 (secondary topic), which given the verb form in (23) means that 'elks' is semantically the agent. This use of surface order is interesting in the light of a proposal I shall make below about the relation of GR hierarchy position and word order, but in the present context it is irrelevant. It might be noted that the actual structure of the transitive verb is also irrelevant to questions of basic word order, since it can provide no pattern of prefixing and suffixing that could be used to induce a basic constituent order. Far from having any simple subject or object affixes, Blackfoot builds its verbs roughly on this pattern: *1 or 2 person indicator + stem + indicator of rank relation between participants + 1, 2, or unspecified person indicator + plurality indicator + 3 person indicator + 4 person indicator.* Other Algonquian languages have different but equally complicated systems, which similarly show no straightforward subject or object affixes (see Hockett 1966 on Potawatomi, for example). Algonquian languages appear to provide no support at all for any claim that there might be OVS languages.[11]

Finally, there is Rood's (1971) discussion of Wichita (first brought to my attention by Paul Postal): "The object (if there is one) always precedes the verb; the subject may either precede or follow this complex." What this statement suggests, assuming it to be the whole truth about constituent order in Wichita, is that the basic order certainly includes the sequence ... *O V* ..., and that the object NP may be generally identified in superficial structures by its proximity to the verb, but that order between the verb-object complex and the subject is free—NOT fixed in the order OVS. It should be noted that objects are not merely placed adjacent to verbs; very frequently they are incorporated into verbs morphologically. Rood notes (p. 103) that "because the object noun is usually incorporated, the functional load of [the word order] distinction is minimal." However, the data given by Rood suggest one syntactic argument relevant to determining the basic order, if I interpret them correctly. It appears that any absolutive NP (i.e. any NP that is either an intransitive subject or a transitive object; Rood uses the term 'patient' to cover these) can be incorporated into the verb. Thus in the transitive clause (24a), which has the alternative order (24b), the object NP *wi:c* 'man' can be incorporated into the verb as in (24c) and (24d):

(24)         a. *Ka:hi:k'a wi:c ti-        'i:y-s*
                woman     man nonfuture-see-imperfect

             b. *Wi:c ti-        'i:y-s        ka:hi:k'a*
                man nonfuture-see-imperfect woman

             c. *Ka:hi:k'a ti-        wi:c-'i:y-s.*
                woman     nonfuture-man- see-imperfect

---

[11] If there is a basic order for Algonquian languages, I believe it might be VSO, as (23) suggests.

    d. *Ti-*         *wi:c-'i:y-s*        *ka:hi:k'a.*
    nonfuture-man- see-imperfect woman
    'The woman saw the man.'

Note that the object is incorporated into the verb on the same side of the stem as it appears when not incorporated. This is surely not surprising; in fact, we would expect that, when (intransitive) subjects are incorporated, they would appear on the same side of the verb stem as they appear when not incorporated IN BASIC WORD ORDER. In other words, assuming that position relative to the verb stem in incorporated forms gives us a clue to basic word order, we can reasonably guess at the basic order for subjects by looking at an example of subject incorporation. Such an example is given in (25):

(25)                    a. *Wi:c ti-*      *hish.*
                      man   nonfuture-go

                   b. *Ti-*       *hish wi:c.*
                    nonfuture-go   man

                   c. *Ti-*       *wi:c-hish.*
                    nonfuture-man-go
                    'The man went.'

The incorporated form of the free variants (25a) and (25b) is shown in (25c); notice that the subject NP appears TO BE LEFT of the verb stem. I propose that this is because the basic word order is SOV, and both subjects and objects attach to the side of the verb on which they are placed by the linearization rule. This means that (24b), (24d), and (25b) must be regarded as derived via an optional postcyclic rule of rightward subject shift. The linearization rules proper need not allow for OVS ordering in Wichita any more than in any other language.

## IMPLICATIONS

I have argued that the summary of our present knowledge about basic word order in the languages of the world—quoted in (1) from Greenberg—must now be revised. Four basic word orders, not three, are found: SVO, SOV, VSO, and VOS. The other two logically possible orders, OSV and OVS, do not occur at all, contra various allusions in the literature on syntactic typology. In view of the complete absence so far of any success in exhibiting a language that is (even in its surface syntax) as purely ergative-absolutive as English is nominative-accusative, I have maintained that the claim that there is no deep ergativity (espoused by Perlmutter and Postal, 1974 Linguistics Institute lectures, and by George 1974) is probably correct.

This array of facts is in itself sufficient to falsify several previous proposed theories of word order quite decisively. One example is the theory defended by Sanders (1970), referred to in Koutsoudas and Sanders (1974:Footnote 6), in which subject NPs are distinguished by the configuration $_S[NP, _S[X]_S]_S$ and all surface ordering is determined by a set of ordering rules placing constituents in their surface order relative to sister constituents. Sanders will obviously have to allow a rule which places subjects in final position (as in Malagasy). He will also have to permit objects to be placed before verbs (as in Japanese). His theory therefore has no non–ad hoc way of preventing a grammar from being constructed for a language that has both these rules and is thus strict OVS. But there are no such natural languages. The inability of Sanders's framework (which countenances no movement rules whatsoever) to distinguish between LINEARIZATION (as with the final subject placement of Malagasy) from optional postcyclic MOVEMENT (as with the subject postposing of Wichita and probably Tagalog) prevents it from characterizing the class of natural languages correctly.

Another theoretical framework that seems to me to be utterly and irretrievably falsified by the facts so far known is that of Culicover and Wexler (1974). Culicover and Wexler recognize eight types of language because they regard the subject-predicate split as a universal and also countenance (indeed, they lay great stress on the predicted existence of) deep ergative languages. The types they provide for are indicated by the informal deep-structure configurations listed in (26):

(26)                    *(Agent (Predicate-Patient))*
                        *(Agent (Patient-Predicate))*
                        *((Predicate-Patient) Agent)*
                        *((Patient-Predicate) Agent)\**
                        *((Agent-Predicate) Patient)\**
                        *((Predicate-Agent) Patient)\**
                        *(Patient (Predicate-Agent))\**
                        *(Patient (Agent-Predicate))\**

I do not believe that any of the asterisked types represent possible deep structures for human languages. The last four types in (26) represent four types of deep ergative language, and the other asterisked case represents nominative-accusative (i.e. agent as subject) OVS. Missing altogether (because of the insistence on a subject-predicate binary division) is nonergative VSO. For all VSO languages that show no trace of deep ergativity (and there are hundreds), Culicover and Wexler must try to motivate a transformation which derives the VSO order from some deep structure order different from this (SVO, SOV, VOS, or OVS). The theory predicts that all SOV languages have a subject-predicate split, i.e. NP-VP structure, and this seems to be false (Muraki 1971; Hankamer 1971:Section 1.4.6; and Hinds 1974). It also predicts that no SOV language can display ergativity, which is wildly wrong: SOV seems to be the commonest basic order for languages with ergative case marking. What seems to have been accomplished by Culicover and Wexler (apart from a massive tabulation of word order data with a bibliography which, I should point out, I have found useful despite occasional inaccuracies) is a conclusive reductio ad absurdum of the NP-VP universal deep structure proposal adumbrated in Chomsky (1965).[12]

Other theories stand refuted on points of detail and on unclarity in their empirical bases, but nevertheless remain remarkably close to being tenable, at least in broad outline. Among these are the universal VSO deep structure hypothesis of Bach (1971a, 1971b, and 1974: Chapter 11) and the universal SOV deep structure hypothesis discussed by Ross (1973) and Koutsoudas and Sanders (1974). Both proposals have the attractive feature that they can present the construction of a grammar for an OSV or OVS language simply by incorporating a substantive theory of transformational rules that does not allow for an obligatory Object Fronting rule. They gain strength, in other words, from their rigidity in laying down a fixed order of constituents that will not vary unless some transformational rule with its own specific motivation applies to reorder some element.

The fixed deep structure order assumed in these theories is not itself given any explanation; it is merely imposed as a brute fact about deep structures. I would like now to raise the possibility that it is not a brute fact, but that what is correct about the deep structure VSO and SOV theories can be applied to shallow structure linearization rules in relational grammar and can be derived from an independently established part of relational theory.

One of the results that has emerged with clarity from work in Relational Grammar is that there is a hierarchy among the GRs. Perlmutter and Postal give this hierarchy as in (27):

(27)　　　　　　　　　　　GR Hierarchy

$$① > ② > ③ > Ⓝ$$

The relation '>' may be read as 'outranks'. Keenan and Comrie (1975) motivate a more elaborate hierarchy which nevertheless corresponds exactly to this if its last three places are lumped together as belonging to Ⓝ:

(28) Accessibility Hierarchy

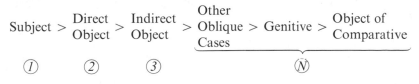

[12] The situation for Culicover and Wexler becomes far worse once indirect objects, etc., are taken into account; their theory predicts various kinds of indirect-object-initial languages and other mythical beasts.

The empirical basis of such a hierarchy derives from the support that has been amassed for a wide range of claims involving relativization, coreferential control, identity deletion, quantifier floating, omissibility, referentiality, dummy insertion, raising rules, case-changing rules, causativization, and many other phenomena. In each case it has been found that the GR hierarchy can be applied to predict degree of syntactic "activeness", accessibility to the operation of various processes, extent of participation in grammatical operations, etc. For some discussion see e.g. Comrie (1973); Keenan (1973); Keenan and Comrie (to appear); Johnson (1974); and Postal (1976).

I wish to propose that linearization, which has not in general been involved in any way in the development and validation of the GR hierarchy, depends upon it in a very direct way. I claim that, although several specific transformational operations obscure it in many languages, the fundamental principle for linearization in natural language is (29):

(29)   *The NP constituents of a clause are linearized in their GR hierarchy order, from left to right.*[13]

This does not have to be stated in the grammar of any particular language. What does have to be stated is, first, the position of the verb relative to the NPs (which is clearly a language-particular matter), and, second, any departure from the basic principle (29) that is to be imposed. With respect to verb placement, there seem to be just three possibilities:

(30)                     *The verb of a clause may be placed in*

        (a) *initial position in all clauses,*
        (b) *second position in all clauses,*

*or*

        (c) *final position in all clauses.*

This does not permit, for example, languages in which the verb must be the third constituent if there are more than three, or languages in which verbs are final in transitive clauses but initial in intransitive clauses.[14] Finally, I believe that one further principle of basic order must be allowed. Besides requiring that (with the possible exception of true free-word-order languages if there are any) all languages have (29) and one of the subcases of (30) governing their basic

---

[13] Cf. the earlier discussion of Blackfoot word order and the person hierarchy. Note also the interesting remarks of Hale (1973) on Navajo and the animateness hierarchy, which suggest a conspiracy (involving apparently cyclic rules) to get animate NPs to precede inanimate NPs in superficial structures.

[14] Note, on the other hand, that, since verb placement refers to the linearization stage, it is not incompatible with the existence of a language in which a postcyclic verb-object interchange rule makes a basically SOV language into one which normally has the verb SECOND TO LAST in the clause. Tai (1973) argues that Chinese is like this.

word order, principle (31) is also available:

(31)   *If placement of the verb by (30) leaves the subject NP noninitial, it*
        *be assigned final position.*

It is, of course, rare to find a language taking up this option. I suspect it has a motivation in (i) the very widespread association "surface subject = theme" and (ii) the universal preference for themes to be in clause-peripheral positions.

The schema I have outlined provides only for the orders listed in (32) as basic word orders in the strict sense; I am claiming that no other linearization rules exist in natural language:

(32)   a. $V$   ①   ②   ③   Ⓝ   *(V/1)*
       b. ①   $V$   ②   ③   Ⓝ   *(V/2)*
       c. ①   ②   ③   Ⓝ   $V$   *(V/F)*
       d. $V$   ②   ③   Ⓝ   ①   *(V/1 + ①/F)*

The implication of this is that no dominant surface orders other than these can be accounted for unless postcyclic movement rules deriving them can be motivated. Such a claim has empirical content, of course, if and only if a substantive theory of possible postcyclic transformations can be developed (in this regard the discussion of Bach 1974: Chapter 11 is highly relevant). Among the postcyclic rules I am assuming must be available (for I believe their effects are not to be attributed to the linearization schema itself, though I could be wrong) are two that are especially important, and these I should mention immediately. One is the rule that floats oblique NPs (③ or Ⓝ) to the right, discussed above in connection with Malagasy. Some languages (e.g. standard Japanese) do not permit this at all, but others do, and orders like ① ② ③ $V$ Ⓝ, $V$ ② ③ ① Ⓝ, ① $V$ ② Ⓝ ③, etc., may occur as a result. The other is the attraction toward a position immediately adjacent to the verb of the direct object. Hankamer (1971) mentions that the immediately preverbal position in Turkish (SOV) is a focus position to which various other constituents may be attracted. Occurrence immediately next to the verb, or even incorporated inside it, is extremely common for the direct object in a wide range of languages.[15] Orders like ① ③ Ⓝ ② $V$ instead of ① ② ③ Ⓝ $V$ are therefore to be expected, I believe (note e.g. Hindi).

There is much that is still missing from this account. One topic not dealt with is whether chômeurs are to be counted among the nonterms for linearization purposes, or whether special provisions must be added to the linearization rules for different languages to place chômeurs correctly. Initial hopes that the principles involved might be very simple, with all chômeurs in a clause placed

---

[15] As mentioned above, Fijian may be an example of this occurring in a verb-initial language; so may Toba Batak.

together in a bunch either before or after all other NPs, no longer seem to be tenable (Pullum and Harlow 1975), and considerable further study may be needed here. Another matter to be dealt with in the future is the variant orders in different clause types displayed by many languages. For instance, as is well known, German is V/F in subordinate clauses but V/2 in main clauses, and Hungarian has SVO order with definite objects but SOV when the object is indefinite. The present study neither solves such problems nor is incompatible with their solution, but merely provides a context in which to attempt their solution. In general, arguments for 'underlying' order of constituents such as those in Tai (1973) and Koster (1975) will be expressible within the framework I propose as arguments for a specific linearization rule. The thesis of McCawley (1970) that English is underlyingly VSO may lose its motivation given a relational theory (Radford 1975a; also Berman 1974, especially Footnote #28), but many other theses do not. Tai's claim that Chinese is SOV, and Koster's that Dutch and German are SOV, seem quite plausible. There is every reason to regard debate over such questions as empirical and meaningful, since both considerations of general typology à la Greenberg and arguments as to the viability of the reordering transformations postulated can be brought to bear on the issues (see e.g. Pullum 1974).

Despite its inadequacies, however, I believe that the outline I have given of the function of linearization rules in a grammar will provide a firm basis for further investigation. To mention just one topic, the framework assumed above may improve greatly our understanding of word order change, since the shallow-structure location of linearization suggests a much more plausible mechanism of change than the restructuring of the formation rules for the underlying structures of the language: Changes in basic word order will occur when a particular postcyclic rule comes into such frequent employment that a new generation of learners makes the assumption that its output is actually a consequence of the linearization rule for the language. Within this framework, there is absolutely no reason to think that restructuring as an explanation of word order change is incompatible with the claim that base rules are essentially universal.

## ACKNOWLEDGMENTS

Through valuable conversation and correspondence, a large number of people have contributed to the work reported in this study. Among them are Stephen R. Anderson, Wayles Browne, Guy Carden, Bernard Comrie, Robert M. W. Dixon, Joseph Greenberg, T. S. T. Henderson, R. A. Hudson, Edward L. Keenan, Anne Mills, Terence Moore, John Payne, Paul Postal, Neil Smith, R. P. Stockwell, and Deirdre Wilson. I have used their contributions exactly as I saw fit, and have often gone against their advice, so none of them is to be blamed for my errors or misinterpretations. Special thanks are due to the Faculty of Arts, University College, London, for a grant that enabled me to learn more about one of the languages examined in the paper; to David Perlmutter and Paul Postal, whose course at the 1974 Linguistics Institute first convinced me that grammatical relations ⌐rimes; and to John Payne for being my guide and interpreter in consulting Russian sources.

# REFERENCES

Aissen, J. (1975) "Presentational-*there* Insertion: A Cyclic Root Transformation," in R. Grossman, L. J. San, and T. J. Vance, eds., *Papers from the Eleventh Regional Meeting of the Chicago Linguistic Society*, University of Chicago, Chicago, Illinois.

Anderson, S. R. (1976) "On the Notion of Subject in Ergative Languages," in C. Li, ed., *Subject and Topic*, Academic Press, New York.

Anderson, S. R. (in preparation). "Ergativity and Linguistic Structure."*

Arms, D. (1974). *Transitivity in Fijian*, unpublished Doctoral dissertation, dissertation, University of Michigan, Ann Arbor, Michigan.*

Bach, E. (1971a) "Questions," *Linguistic Inquiry* 2, 153–166.

Bach, E. (1971b) "Syntax since *Aspects*," Georgetown University Monograph Series on Languages and Linguistics 24, 1–17.

Bach, E. (1974) *Syntactic Theory*, Holt, Rinehart and Winston, New York.

Bell, S. (1974) "Two Consequences of Advancement Rules in Cebuano," in E. Kaisse and J. Hankamer, eds., *Papers from the Fifth Annual Meeting*, North Eastern Linguistic Society, Harvard University, Cambridge, Massachusetts.

Berman, A. (1974) "On the VSO Hypothesis," *Linguistic Inquiry* 5, 1–38.

Bloomfield, L. (1962) *The Menomini Language*, Yale University Press, New Haven, Connecticut.

Breckenridge, J. (1975) "The Post-cyclicity of *es*-insertion in German," in R. Grossman, L. J. San, and T. J. Vance, eds., *Papers from the Eleventh Regional Meeting of the Chicago Linguistic Society*, University of Chicago, Chicago, Illinois.

Browne, W. and Vattuone, B. (1975) "Theme-Rheme Structure and Zenéyze Clitics," *Linguistic Inquiry* 6, 136–140.

Bush, F. W. (1964) *A Grammar of the Hurrian Language*, unpublished Doctoral dissertation, Brandeis University, Waltham, Massachusetts.

Chomsky, N. (1965) *Aspects of the Theory of Syntax*, MIT Press, Cambridge, Massachusetts.

Chung, S. (1976) "An Object-creating Rule in Bahasa Indonesia," *Linguistic Inquiry* 7, 41–87.

Comrie, B. (1973) "Causatives and Universal Grammar," read to the Philological Society [duplicated, King's College Research Centre, Cambridge].

Culicover, P. and K. Wexler (1974) "The Invariance Principle and Universals of Grammar," Social Sciences Working Paper No. 55, University of California, Irvine, California.

Dixon, R. M. W. (1972) *The Dyirbal Language of North Queensland*, Cambridge University Press, Cambridge.

Frachtenberg, L. J. (1913) *Coos Texts* (Columbia University Contributions to Anthropology 1), Columbia University Press, New York, and E. J. Brill, Leyden.

Frachtenberg, L. J. (1914) *Lower Umpqua Texts* (Columbia University Contributions to Anthropology 4), Columbia University Press, New York, and E. J. Brill, Leyden.

Frachtenberg, L. J. (1922a) "Coos," *Handbook of American Indian Languages* 2; U.S. Government Printing Office, Washington, D.C., 297–429.

Frachtenberg, L. J. (1922b) "Siuslaw (Lower Umpqua)," *Handbook of American Indian Languages* 2; U.S. Government Printing Office, Washington, D.C., 431–629.

Frantz, D. G. (1966) "Person Indexing in Blackfoot," *International Journal of American Linguistics* 32, 50–58.

George, L. M. (1974) "Ergativity and Relational Grammar," in E. Kaisse and J. Hankamer, eds., *Papers from the Fifth Regional Meeting*, North Eastern Linguistic Society, Harvard University, Cambridge, Massachusetts.

Greenberg, J. (1963) "Some Universals of Grammar with Particular Reference to the Order of Meaningful Elements," in J. Greenberg, ed., *Universals of Language* MIT Press, Cambridge, Massachusetts. 58–90.

* I have not been able to consult this work personally.

Haiman, J. (1974) *Targets and Syntactic Change*, Mouton, The Hague.
Hale, K. (1973) A Note on Subject Object Inversion in Navajo," in B. Kachru et al., eds., *Issues in Linguistics: Papers in Honor of Henry and Renée Kahane*, University of Illinois Press, Urbana, Illinois.
Hankamer, J. (1971) *Constraints on Deletion in Syntax*, unpublished Doctoral dissertation, Yale University, New Haven, Connecticut.
Hankamer, J. (1974) "On the Non-cyclic Nature of WH-clefting," in M. W. La Galy, R. A. Fox, and A. Bruck, eds., *Papers from the Tenth Regional Meeting of the Chicago Linguistic Society*, University of Chicago, Chicago, Illinois.
Harries, H. (1973) "Coordination Reduction," *Working Papers on Language Universals* 11, Stanford University, Stanford, California, 139–209.
Henry, V. (1879) *Esquisse d'une Grammaire Raisonnée de la Langue Aleoute*, Paris.*
Hinds, J. (1974) "On the Status of the VP Node in Japanese," duplicated, Indiana University Linguistics Club, University of Indiana, Bloomington, Indiana.
Hockett, C. F. (1966) "What Algonquian Is Really Like," *International Journal of American Linguistics* 32, 59–73.
Hudson, G. (1972) "Is Deep Structure Linear? Explorations in Syntactic Theory," in G. Bedell, ed., *UCLA Papers in Syntax* 2, University of California, Los Angeles, California, 51–77.
Johnson, D. E. (1974) *Toward a Theory of Relationally-Based Grammar*, unpublished Doctoral dissertation, University of Illinois, Urbana, Illinois.
Jones, W. (1911) "Algonquian (Fox)," Handbook of American Indian Languages 1, Bureau of American Ethnology, Bulletin 40, U.S. Government Printing Office, Washington, D.C., 1. 735–873.
Keenan, E. L. (1973) "Variation in Universal Grammar," duplicated, King's College Research Centre, Cambridge.
Keenan, E. L. (1976a) "A Universal Definition of 'Subject of '," in C. Li, ed., *Subject and Topic*, Academic Press, New York.
Keenan, E. L. (1976b) "Subject Properties List" [supplement to Keenan 1976a], in C. Li, ed., *Subject and Topic*, Academic Press, New York.
Keenan, E. L. (1976c) "Remarkable Subjects in Malagasy," in C. Li, ed., *Subject and Topic*, Academic Press, New York.
Keenan, E. L. and B. Comrie (to appear) "Noun Phrase Accessibility in Universal Grammar," *Linguistic Inquiry*, in press.
Knorozov, J. V. (1963) *Pis'mennost' Indeytsev Maya*, Akademija Nauk SSSR, Moscow and Leningrad.
Koster, J. (1975) "Dutch as an SOV Language," *Linguistic Analysis* 1, 111–136.
Koutsoudas, A. and G. A. Sanders, (1974) "On the Universality of Rules and Rule-ordering Constraints," duplicated, Indiana University Linguistics Club, Indiana University, Bloomington, Indiana.
McCawley, J. D. (1970) "English as a VSO Language," *Language* 46, 286–299.
Menovščikov, G. A. (1968) "Aleutskij Jazyk," in V. V. Vinogradov et al., eds., *Jazyki Narodov SSSR*, 5, Nauka, Leningrad, 386–406.
Muraki, M. (1970) *Presupposition, Pseudo-clefting and Thematization*, unpublished Doctoral dissertation, University of Texas, Austin, Texas.*
Peterson, T. (1971) "Multi-ordered Base Structures in Generative Grammar," in *Papers from the Seventh Regional Meeting of the Chicago Linguistic Society*, University of Chicago, Chicago, Illinois.
Perlmutter, D. and P. M. Postal (in preparation) *Relational Grammar*.*
Postal, P. M. (1976) "Avoiding Reference to Subject," *Linguistic Inquiry* 7, 151–182.
Pullum, G. K. (1974) "A Note on Coordination Reduction and Word Order in Hindi." *Working Papers on Language Universals* 14, Stanford University, Stanford, California, 95–101.

I have not been able to consult this work personally.

Pullum, G. K. and S. J. Harlow (1975) "Two Problems for Relational Grammar from Mandarin Chinese" [Squibs on Relational Grammar No. 7], unpublished paper, University College, London.

Radford, A. (1975a) "Bidirectionality in Raising," unpublished Doctoral dissertation, University of Cambridge, Cambridge.

Radford, A. (1955b) "Pseudo-relatives and the Unity of Subject Raising," *Archivum Linguisticum* 6, 32–64.

Reichard, G. A. (1933) "Coeur d'Alene," *Handbook of American Indian Languages* 3, 515–707 [J. J. Augustin, Glückstadt, Hamburg, and New York].

Rischel, J. (1970) "Some Characteristics of Noun Phrases in West Greenlandic," *Acta Linguistica Hofniensia* 13, 213–245.

Rood, D. S. (1971) "Agent and Object in Wichita," *Lingua* 28, 100–107.

Ross, J. R. (1970) "Gapping and the Order of Constituents," in M. Bierwish and K. E. Heidolph, eds, *Progress in Linguistics*, Mouton, The Hague.

Ross, J. R. (1973) "The Penthouse Principle and the Order of Constituents," in C. Corum, T. C. Smith-Stark, and A. Weiser, eds., *You Take the High Node and I'll Take the Low Node*, Chicago Linguistic Society, University of Chicago, Chicago, Illinois.

Sampson, G. (1973) "The Irrelevance of Transformational Omnipotence," *Journal of Linguistics* 9, 299–302.

Sanders, G. A. (1970) "Constraints on Constituent Ordering," *Papers in Linguistics* 2, 460–502.

Schultz-Lorentzen, C. W. (1951) *Det grønlanske folk og folkesind*, Statsministeriet, Copenhagen, Denmark.*

Silitonga, M. (1973) *Some Rules Reordering Constituents and Their Constraints in Batak*, unpublished doctoral dissertation.*

Speiser, E. A. (1941) *Introduction to Hurrian* (*Annual of the American Schools of Oriental Research*, 20), American Schools of Oriental Research, New Haven.

Staal, J. F. (1967) *Word Order in Sanskrit and Universal Grammar* (*Foundations of Language Supplementary Series* 5), D. Reidel, Dordrecht, Netherlands.

Tai, J. H-Y. (1973) "Chinese as an SOV Language," in C. Corum, T. C. Smith-Stark, and A. Weiser, eds., *Papers from the Ninth Regional Meeting of the Chicago Linguistic Society*, University of Chicago, Chicago, Illinois.

Ultan, R. (1969) "Some general characteristics of interrogative systems," *Working Papers on Language Universals* 1, Stanford University, Stanford, California.

Underhill, R. and R. Vago (1973) "The OSV Construction in Aleut," paper read at the Annual Meeting of the American Anthropological Association. Mimeographed, University of California at San Diego, La Jolla, California.

Vattuone, B. (1975) "Notes on Genoese Syntax," unpublished paper, University College London.

* I have not been able to consult this work personally.

# REFERENCE-RELATED AND ROLE-RELATED PROPERTIES OF SUBJECTS

*PAUL SCHACHTER*

*University of California, Los Angeles*

## INTRODUCTION

This study is a sequel to one concerned with the problem of identifying a grammatical subject in the sentences of Philippine languages (cf. Schachter 1976a hereafter SPL). At the end of that study, I note some possible implications of the Philippine data for the analysis of subjects in other languages. In the present study I propose to examine these implications in more detail, and to look as well into various other implications for syntactic theory of the Philippine data in question.

As is demonstrated at length in SPL, in Philippine languages there is no single constituent type with a clear preponderance of the syntactic properties that are commonly associated with subjects in other languages. Instead, the set of so-called subject properties (cf. Keenan 1976) is divided into two subsets, each of which is associated with a distinct constituent type—one subset associated with what Philippinists commonly call the TOPIC, the other with what they commonly call the ACTOR. (The semantics of the topic and the actor will be discussed later in this section. Meanwhile, the reader is cautioned that the labels "topic" and "actor" are not necessarily to be taken at face value.)

From the point of view of most other languages, then, Philippine languages appear to divide the syntactic properties of the subject between the topic and the actor. Conversely, from the point of view of Philippine languages, most other languages appear to merge the syntactic properties of the topic and the actor within a single constituent type, the subject. While this latter point of

279

view may be unfamiliar, it is, as I shall try to show, one that has significant insights to offer. For the syntactic properties of the Philippine topic and actor can be shown to follow to an appreciable extent from their SEMANTIC properties. And the syntactic properties of SUBJECTS can be shown to follow from THEIR semantic properties as well, once the set of subject properties is analyzed into its proper components, through use of the convenient prism provided by Philippine languages.

Before this point can be profitably pursued, however, as background for further discussion of the topic and the actor, it will be necessary to introduce the reader to the basic facts of Philippine sentence structure. The structural sketch to be presented (part of which is borrowed verbatim from SPL, as are some subsequent passages) will be limited to what may be called SIMPLE NARRATIVE SENTENCES, and will make use of examples from Tagalog. (Hereafter, all Philippine-language examples not otherwise identified will be Tagalog, and other languages will be cited only when they differ from Tagalog in ways that are of special interest. By and large, the languages of the Philippines appear to be quite similar in their basic structure, so that examples taken from any one language will generally have close parallels in all the others.)

The Tagalog simple narrative sentence consists of a verb followed by a string of (one or more) nominals, one of which is marked as the topic. Formally, the topic is marked either by the use of a topic pronoun form or by a prenominal topic marker. Notionally, the topic is always interpreted as definite. (For further discussion, see below.) Any nontopic nominals that occur in the sentence are marked for case—again, either by the use of a distinctive pronoun form or by a prenominal marker. Unlike topics, case-marked nominals may in general be interpreted as either definite or indefinite. The cases do have some semantic significance, however, and case-marked nominals are commonly given quasi-semantic labels such as actor, goal, direction, etc. There is also a case-marking affix on the verb, which indicates the case role of the topic nominal. Thus there are ACTOR-TOPIC VERBS, GOAL-TOPIC VERBS, DIRECTION-TOPIC VERBS, etc., and the topics that occur with these verbs may be called the ACTOR-TOPIC, the GOAL-TOPIC, etc. Each case role is represented once per simple sentence, so if there is an actor-topic, there is no other actor nominal in the sentence; if there is a goal-topic, there is no other goal nominal; and so on.

Let us look now at some examples. (In the translations that accompany these and subsequent examples, the following abbreviations are used: AT, GT, and DT preceding the translations of verbs indicate that the verbs are marked as, respectively, actor-topic, goal-topic, and direction-topic, and A, G, D, and T preceding the translations of nouns and pronouns indicate that the (pro)nouns are marked as, respectively, actor, goal, direction, and topic.)

(1)             a. *Magbibigay **ang babae**  ng bigas sa bata.*
                AT-will-give T   woman G rice   D child
                'The woman will give some rice to a/the child.'

　　　b. *Ibibigay* 　　　*ng babae* 　**ang bigas** *sa bata.*
　　　　GT-will-give A woman T 　rice 　D child
　　　　'A/the woman will give the rice to a/the child.'

　　　c. *Bibigyan* 　　　*ng babae* 　*ng bigas* **ang bata.**
　　　　DT-will-give A woman G rice 　T 　　child
　　　　'A/the woman will give some rice to the child.'

The three sentences of (1) all express the same event, but differ from one another in the choice of topic. The topic marker for common nouns is *ang*, and the topic nominal of each sentence is indicated by boldface. Also in boldface is the verbal affix that indicates the case role of the topic. Thus in (1a) **mag-** is an actor-topic affix, and **ang babae** is an actor-topic; in (1b)**i-** is a goal-topic affix and **ang bigas** a goal-topic; in (1c) **-an** is a direction-topic affix and **ang bata** a direction-topic. In the English equivalents of these sentences the topic must always be marked as DEFINITE. Thus (1a) requires a translation with 'the woman', (1b) with 'the rice', and (1c) with 'the child'. Nontopic nominals, on the other hand, may or must be translated as INDEFINITE. (Specifically, a nontopic goal in a simple narrative sentence is always indefinite, while in general other nontopic nominals may be either definite or indefinite.) As the examples show, with common nouns the case marker for both a nontopic actor and a nontopic goal is *ng* (pronounced [naŋ]), while that for a nontopic direction is *sa*.

It should be pointed out that, except for the initial position of the verb, the ordering of the constituents in the examples of (1) is arbitrary. That is, any ordering of the actor, goal, and direction nominals is permissible, and the topic may occur in any order in relation to the nontopic phrases. (But, as will be pointed out on p. 295, there are some other Philippine languages in which word order is less free than it is in Tagalog.)

With the above structural sketch as background, let us turn to a discussion of the semantic properties of the topic nominal and the actor nominal in Philippine languages. In the usage of non-Philippinists, the term "topic" often designates the constituent that represents the "center of attention" of the discourse context (cf. Li and Thompson 1976). That this usage is NOT relevant to the Philippine-language topic is clear from examples like the following, in which the discourse context overtly directs attention to a referent which is subsequently represented by a nontopic nominal:

(2) 　　　　　Speaker A : 　*Nasaan ang katulong?*
　　　　　　　　　　　　　where 　T 　maid
　　　　　　　　　　　　　'Where's the maid?'

　　　　　　　Speaker B : 　*Inihahanda niya 　ang pagkain.*
　　　　　　　　　　　　　GT-prepare A-she T 　food
　　　　　　　　　　　　　'She's preparing the food.'

In this example, the center of attention established by the discourse context is the maid, but the pronoun that refers to the maid is the nontopic actor pronoun *niya*, while the sentence topic is *ang pagkain* 'the food'.

The Philippine-language topic does, however, share one characteristic with the constituent identified as the topic in analyses of other languages. As Li and Thompson note, the topic is regularly definite, and this is as true of the Philippine-language topic as it is of the identically labeled constituent of non-Philippine languages. Thus the Philippine topic is regularly translated into English as a definite noun phrase, such as a common noun preceded by *the*, a proper noun, or a personal pronoun.

To say that the topic is regularly definite is to say that it is regularly referential, and, moreover, that its reference is presupposed, in the sense that the speaker assumes that the hearer knows the intended referent. Nontopics, on the other hand, do not regularly have presupposed reference, and thus may be either definite or indefinite. The difference between topics and nontopics in this respect is clearest when, as in the examples of (1), both the topic and the nontopic nominals are headed by common nouns, in which case, as already noted, only the topics are unambiguously definite, while the nontopics may or must be taken to be indefinite. The difference is less clear in cases like (3), where the nontopics are headed by personal pronouns or proper nouns:

(3)         *Ibibigay       niya    ang bigas kay Juan.*
            GT-will-give A-she T    rice   D    Juan
            'She will give the rice to Juan.'

Here it is certainly true that the nontopic nominals *niya* and *kay Juan*, as well as the topic nominal *ang bigas*, are necessarily definite. Note, however, that, in the case of the topic nominal of (3), its necessary definiteness, or presupposed reference, is ATTRIBUTABLE to its being a topic. [A nontopic nominal headed by a common noun like *bigas* 'rice' does not have presupposed reference—cf. (1).] In the case of the nontopic nominals of (3), on the other hand, their presupposed reference is not attributable to their being nontopics (as a comparison with the examples of (1) makes clear), but rather to the fact that they are headed by a personal pronoun and a proper noun. Only the topic nominal, then, carries a guarantee of (presupposed) referentiality, regardless of the type of noun or pronoun that is its head. One can thus say that the topic nominal has REFERENTIAL PROMINENCE vis-à-vis any nontopic nominals in the sentence.

To turn now to the semantic properties of the actor, the following examples show that the label 'actor' should not be taken as equivalent to agent, at least if AGENT is associated with some such role as "the typically animate perceived instigator of the action" (Fillmore 1968:24). [In each of these examples, the actor nominal is in boldface. The examples are presented in pairs, with the actor as topic, and an actor-topic verb, in the (a) example, and with the actor as nontopic, and a goal-topic verb, in the (b) example.]

(4)  a. *Tatanggap*   ***ang bata*** *ng bigas sa babae.*
     AT-will-receive T child G rice D woman
     'The child will receive some rice from a/the woman.'

    b. *Tatanggapin*   ***ng bata*** *ang bigas sa babae.*
     GT-will-receive A child T rice D woman
     'A/the child will receive the rice from a/the woman.'

(5)  a. *Nagtiis*   ***ang babae*** *ng kahirapan.*
     AT-endured T woman G hardship
     'The woman endured some hardship.'

    b. *Tiniis*   ***ng babae*** *ang kahirapan.*
     GT-endured A woman T hardship
     'A/the woman endured the hardship.'

These examples show clearly that the referent of the actor nominal is not necessarily the "perceived instigator of the action." Thus the child is no more an instigator of the action in the sentences of (4) than in the sentences of (1), even though in the case of (4) the child is the actor. In the case of (5), it is not clear that there is any "action" at all, but if there is it was certainly not instigated by the referent of the actor, i.e. the woman.

What, then, CAN be said about the semantic properties of the actor? I believe that a label like PROTAGONIST might be more appropriate than ACTOR in indicating the properties in question (although, in deference to tradition, I shall continue to use "actor"). For as is the case with the protagonist of a drama, the referent of the actor is the individual who is viewed as being at the center of events. Thus what is involved in the choice of the actor is less the particular objective role an individual has played in an event than it is the subjective viewpoint of the speaker with regard to the importance, or interest, of this role and this individual. For instance, the sentences of (1) and those of (4)—like their English equivalents—express essentially the same event, involving the transmittal of rice from a woman to a child, but, in the case of the sentences of (1), the role of the woman is being viewed as central, while, in the case of the sentences of (4), the role of the child is being so viewed. Similar examples might be given involving events that can be expressed either with a verb equivalent to *sell* or with one equivalent to *buy*, or with the equivalent of either *lend* or *borrow*. In each such case, the speaker has a choice of the individual to whose role in the event he wishes to give prominence, and in Philippine languages this individual is in each case expressed by an actor nominal. We can therefore say that the referent of the actor nominal is always given ROLE PROMINENCE vis-à-vis the referents of any nonactor nominals in the sentence.

Thus in Philippine languages we can distinguish two different kinds of semantic prominence associated with constituents: the referential prominence associated with the topic and the role prominence associated with the actor. In the case of sentences with actor-topic verbs [such as (1a), (4a), and (5a)], both kinds of prominence are in fact associated with a single constituent, the actor-topic. This is, however, not a necessary convergence of properties in these languages, since the topic and the actor are often distinct.

In most other languages, on the other hand, it is usual for a single constituent type, the subject, to show both referential prominence and role prominence. With regard to the referential prominence of subjects, Keenan (1976) claims that, in English and in languages in general, the subjects of basic sentences— but not, for example, the direct objects—are "absolutely referential," in the sense that the sentences logically imply that their subjects have referents. Keenan notes that the subject of a basic sentence may be indefinite (as in *a student just called you*), but says that such indefinites are nonetheless referential. For example, the subject of *a student just called you* does in fact purport to refer to a particular student. (Nonsubject indefinites, by contrast, are often nonreferential, as is shown by Keenan's examples *John ordered a beer*, *John painted a pony*, etc.)

The fact that subjects can be indefinite does distinguish them to some extent from Philippine topics. That is, while both subjects and topics are "absolutely referential" in Keenan's sense, only topics have the PRESUPPOSED reference that make them regularly definite. (Apparently, however, the great majority of SUBJECTS are also definite—cf. the statistics given in Givón 1974.) Nonetheless, it is clear that subjects, like topics, are referentially prominent vis-à-vis other nominals in the sentence.

That subjects are like actors with regard to role prominence follows from the fact that the Philippine actor is regularly TRANSLATED by a subject in other languages. (More specifically, the actor in a simple narrative sentence is regularly translated by an ACTIVE subject.) Thus that part of the meaning difference between (1a) and (4a) that is associated with a different choice of actor is, in the English translations of these sentences, associated with a different choice of subject. And if this meaning difference is describable as involving "role prominence" in the one case, it is so describable in the other as well.

To return now to some points made earlier, I have shown (in SPL) that the syntactic properties associated with subjects in other languages represent, from the viewpoint of Philippine languages, a convergence of the syntactic properties associated with the topic and those associated with the actor. I have also suggested—and hope to show in more detail in the present study—that the syntactic properties of topics and actors follow from their semantic properties. More specifically, I suggest that the syntactic properties of topics are REFERENCE-RELATED, and follow from the topic's referential prominence, while the syntactic properties of actors are ROLE-RELATED, and follow from the actor's role prominence. But if, as I have just claimed, the subject represents a convergence of the SEMANTIC properties of the topic and the actor (in that it manifests both referential prominence and role prominence), and if the semantic properties of the topic and the actor condition the syntactic properties, then the observed convergence of the SYNTACTIC properties of the topic and the actor within the subject may also be presumed to have a semantic basis. Thus it may be possible, in the light of the Philippine evidence, to show that the syntactic properties of subjects are not the arbitrary set they might otherwise appear to be, but, rather, are analyzable into a reference-related subset and a role-related subset. It is to this endeavor that I would now like to turn.

## REFERENCE-RELATED PROPERTIES

In the following subsections, I shall discuss three syntactic properties that topics in Philippine languages share with subjects in other languages. In each case I shall try to show that the property in question follows from the fact that the Philippine topic and the subject in other languages are referentially prominent.

### Relativization

The first property to be considered is one that has already been discussed from this point of view in SPL: the property of relativizability. Keenan and Comrie (to appear) have proposed that constraints on the types of sentence constituents that a language allows to be relativized must reflect a universal ACCESSIBILITY HIERARCHY. At the top of the proposed hierarchy, which is supported by data from a wide range of languages, Keenan and Comrie place the subject, claiming that all languages allow subjects to be relativized, and that some languages allow ONLY subjects to be relativized.

In Philippine languages it is clear that only topics can be relativized. Relative clauses in these languages have the form of sentences with deleted topics; the missing topic of the relative clause is always understood as being coreferential with the head of the relative construction. For example, compare the sentences of (6) with the grammatical relative constructions of (7) and the ungrammatical strings of (8). (In the translations of (7) and (8) 'Li' stands for the "linker," -*ng*, that introduces relative clauses.)

(6)                    a. *Bumili     ang babae  ng baro.*
                         AT-bought T   woman G dress
                         'The woman bought a dress.'

                    b. *Binili      ng babae   ang baro.*
                         GT-bought A  woman T   dress
                         'A/the woman bought the dress.'

(7)  a. *Iyon ang babaeng    bumili    ng baro.*
that T   woman-Li AT-bought G dress
'That's the woman who bought a dress.'

b. *Iyon ang barong   binili    ng babae.*
that T   dress-Li GT-bought A woman
'That's the dress that a/the woman bought.'

(8)  a. **Iyon ang barong   bumili    ang babae.*
that T   dress-Li AT-bought T   woman

b. **Iyon ang babaeng    binili    ang baro.*
that T   woman-Li GT-bought T   dress

Given sentence (6a), in which there is an actor-topic verb and a nontopic goal, it is possible to relativize the actor-topic but not the goal [compare (7a) and (8a)]. On the other hand, given sentence (6b), in which there is a goal-topic verb and a nontopic actor, it is possible to relativize the goal-topic but not the actor [compare (7b) and (8b)].

Now, as was explained in the introduction, the topic is referentially prominent, in the sense that it is the only nominal in a simple narrative sentence that regularly has a presupposed referent. But note that a RELATIVIZED nominal also regularly has a presupposed referent, since the referent of such a nominal is always identical to that of the head of the relative construction. [For example, the referents of the relativized nominals of (7a) and (7b)—i.e. the referents of the missing topics of the relative clauses—are necessarily identical to the referents of the head nouns *babae* 'woman' and *baro* 'dress', respectively.] It therefore seems very reasonable that the topic should be chosen as the relativizable category in Philippine languages.

Similarly, if subjects are "absolutely referential," and are more likely than nonsubjects to have presupposed referents, it is reasonable for subjects always to be at least as relativizable as any other syntactic category within a language, which is in accord with the cross-linguistic observations of Keenan and Comrie. Thus the accessibility of subjects to relativization, like the accessibility of topics in Philippine languages, is explainable on the basis of what I have called referential prominence.

## Floating Quantifiers

According to Bell (1974), it has been claimed within the framework of the theory of Relational Grammar being developed by David Perlmutter and Paul Postal that only "terms of grammatical relations"—i.e. subjects, objects, and indirect objects—may "launch floating quantifiers," where a 'floating quantifier' is one that has been permitted "to leave its NP, as in 'The men were all surprised' from 'All the men were surprised'." Moreover, terms are ranked in a hierarchy

(*I. subject, II. direct object, III. indirect object*), and "structure-dependent" rules such as Quantifier Float can be restricted to apply to just part of the hierarchy: "For example, quantifier float applies only to subjects in English, to subjects and direct objects in Japanese, and to all three terms in French" (Bell 1974).

The Tagalog quantifier *lahat* 'all' usually occurs within a noun phrase, as in:

(9)        a.    *Bumabasa ang lahat ng mga bata  ng mga libro.*[1]
               AT-read  T  all    Li Pl   child G Pl   book
               {'All the children are reading (some) books.'
               {'All children read (some) books.'

        b.    *Binabasa ng lahat ng mga bata  ang mga libro.*
               GT-read A all    Li Pl   child T   Pl   book
               {'All the children are reading the books.'
               {'All children read the books.'

        c.    *Binabasa ng mga bata  ang lahat ng mga libro.*
               GT-read A Pl   child T   all    Li Pl   book
               'The/some children are reading all the books.'

However, as was noted in SPL, there is also a construction in which *lahat* follows the sentence-initial verb (cf. Schachter and Otanes 1972: 147–148 for details). In this construction *lahat* is always understood as referring to the topic, as the following examples illustrate:

(10)       a.    *Bumabasa lahat ang mga bata  ng mga libro.*
               AT-read    all    T  Pl   child G Pl   book
               {'All the children are reading (some) books.'
               {'All children read (some) books.'

        b.    *Binabasa lahat ng mga bata  ang mga libro.*
               GT-read all    A Pl   child T   Pl   book
               'The/some children are reading all the books.'

In (10a) *lahat* can only be understood as referring to the actor-topic, in (10b) to the goal-topic. It thus appears that only the Tagalog topic can "launch" *lahat*, just as—according to Bell—only the English subject can launch its translation equivalent *all*.

In seeking an explanation for the facts just summarized, we may note, first of all, that, when *lahat* occurs within a noun phrase of the type illustrated in the examples of (9), this noun phrase is always referential, and, moreover, its reference is always presupposed: i.e. the speaker always assumes that the hearer

---

[1] The *ng* [naŋ] that follows *lahat* in this sentence may be analyzed as a type of linker. *Mga* [maŋa] is a pluralizing particle.

knows the intended referent of the phrase. (Often the *lahat* phrase is ambiguously specific or generic—note the two readings of *lahat ng mga bata* in (9a) and (9b), the specific 'all the children' and the generic 'all children'; but, whether specific or generic, the phrase conveys a meaning of presupposed reference or definiteness, and this is equally true whether the phrase is used as a topic [as in (9a) and (9c)] or as a nontopic [as in (9b)].)

Now, as was previously noted, topic nominals (with or without *lahat*) also convey a meaning of presupposed reference or definiteness.[2] Thus, when *lahat* is allowed to "float" away from a topic nominal, the presupposition associated with the quantifier is still expressed by the nominal to which the quantifier refers. On the other hand, if *lahat* were allowed to float away from a nontopic nominal—such as the actor phrase in (9b)—this phrase in itself would no longer convey a meaning of presupposed reference or definiteness, and there would be a potential conflict between the presuppositionality of the quantifier and the nonpresuppositionality of the phrase to which it refers.

To extrapolate from the Tagalog situation to the situation found in other languages, it seems to be the case across languages that only certain quantifiers that are associated with a meaning of presupposed reference (such as Tagalog *lahat* and English *all*) are allowed to float. This being the case, it is reasonable to expect that floating quantifiers should be most easily "launched" by the nominal constituent type that is itself the most likely to be referential. Since in most languages this constituent type is the subject, it makes sense that the subject should have the privileged status that it apparently does have with regard to launching floating quantifiers.

## Existentials

In Clark (1970), the translation equivalents of sentences (11a) and (11b) in some thirty-odd languages are examined:

(11)             a. *The book is on the table.*
                 b. *There is a book on the table.*

While (11a) and (11b) appear to be similar in meaning, and might be described as differing semantically only with regard to the definiteness or indefiniteness of the referent of *book*,[3] their syntactic structures are obviously quite different.

---

[2] It was not previously noted, but is nonetheless true, that topics without *lahat* may show the same specific-generic ambiguity as *lahat* phrases. Compare the two readings of the following sentence with those of (9a):

> *Bumabasa ang mga bata  ng mga libro.*
> AT-read  T  Pl   child G Pl   book
> {'The children are reading (some) books.'}
> {'Children read (some) books.'}

[3] I shall argue on pp. 296–298, however, that such a description would be incorrect.

Clark finds, moreover, that the use of different syntactic structures for LOCATIVES [e.g. (11a)] and EXISTENTIALS [e.g. (11b)] is very common cross-linguistically, and in fact characterizes the majority of the languages examined.[4]

Analyzing (11a) and (11b), we find that one difference between them is that in the locative sentence the entity being located (*the book*) is expressed by the subject, while in the existential sentence, the "existent" (*a book*) is expressed as part of the predicate. And just this same type of difference appears to hold for all of the twenty-four languages examined by Clark that use different syntactic structures for locatives and existentials (cf. Clark 1970:Table 3). That is, in all twenty-four of these languages, the equivalent of *the book* in (11a) is expressed by a nominal in sentence-initial position, which appears to be the usual subject position in each of the languages. And in all twenty-four languages the equivalent of *a book* in (11b) is expressed not by a sentence-initial nominal, or subject, but, rather, as what appears to be part of the predicate.

Looking further into the structure of existential sentences in the twenty-four languages under discussion, we find that it is possible to make another generalization about them: all twenty-four languages appear to use either a SUBJECTLESS construction (twenty-one languages) or a DUMMY SUBJECT construction (three languages) for existential sentences. (That is, existential sentence either do not have a sentence-initial nominal, or have a semantically empty proform such as English *there* or French *il* in sentence-initial position.) The absence of ordinary subjects from the existential sentences of a wide range of languages is unlikely to be a coincidence, and can in fact, in the light of the evidence provided by Philippine languages, be understood as a reasonable consequence of the referential prominence of subjects.

The Tagalog equivalents of (11a) and (11b) are (12a) and (12b), respectively:

(12)             a. *Nasa mesa ang libro.*
                    on    table T   book
                    'The book is on the table.'

                 b. *May libro sa mesa.*
                    E/P  book on table
                    'There is a book on the table.'

Sentence (12a) conforms to the general pattern found in SIMPLE NONNARRATIVE SENTENCES in Philippine languages, and consists of a predicate followed by a topic. This general pattern, which is further illustrated in (13), is used for sentences with predicate nominals [e.g. (13a)], predicate adjectives [e.g. (13b)], and

---

[4] According to Clark's Table 3 (p. 12), twenty-four of thirty-one languages use different structures for locatives and existentials. Moreover, one of the seven languages Clark lists as using the SAME structure for locatives and existentials is Tagalog, and this is, as we shall see, incorrect.

predicate phrases introduced by particles or prepositions of various types
[e.g. (12a) and (13c)]:

(13)                              a. *Nobela ang libro.*
                                     novel   T   book
                                     'The book is a novel.'

                                  b. *Mahal     ang libro.*
                                     expensive T   book
                                     'The book is expensive.'

                                  c. *Para-sa iyo  ang libro.*
                                     for      you T   book
                                     'The book is for you.'

Sentence (12b), on the other hand, is topicless, and consists of a predicate (*may
libro*) followed by a prepositional phrase (*sa mesa*).[5]

   The fact that existential sentences in Philippine languages are topicless follows
very naturally from the fact that topics are regularly definite, i.e. regularly have
a presupposed referent. For the meaning of an existential sentence requires that
the existent be indefinite, and it would thus be inappropriate to represent the
existent by means of the referentially prominent topic. Similarly, in languages
with well-defined subjects, since the subject is referentially prominent vis-à-vis
other nominals, it would be an unlikely candidate for representing the existent—
hence the widely attested absence of ordinary subjects from existential sentences.


## ROLE-RELATED PROPERTIES

   We have now looked at three properties that subjects in other languages share
with Philippine topics—relativizability, the ability to launch floating quantifiers,
and nonoccurrence in existential sentences—and have seen that the properties
in question can plausibly be attributed to the referential prominence common
to subjects and topics. Let us turn now to look at some properties that subjects
in other languages share with "actor" nominals in Philippine languages. As was

---

   [5] The translation 'E/P' under *may* in (12b) is intended to represent the two functions of this
particle: the existential function illustrated in (12b), and the possessive function illustrated in a
sentence like:

                          *May libro ang bata.*
                          E/P  book T   child
                          'The child has a book.'

The relation between these two functions is an intriguing matter for speculation, but is left unexplored here.
   The phrase *sa mesa* in (12b) is the nonpredicate counterpart of the locative prepositional phrase
*nasa mesa* found in (12a).

noted in the introduction, the actor nominal represents the individual whose role in the event the speaker views as central—the protagonist, as it were. The actor nominal can therefore be described as having role prominence vis-à-vis other nominals in the sentence, and this is a characteristic that the actor shares with the subject nominals of other languages that are its usual translation equivalents. In the following subsections, I shall discuss four syntactic properties common to actors and subjects, and in each case try to show that the property in question is attributable to the role prominence of these constituents.

## Imperatives

Keenan (1976) has claimed that "subjects normally express the addressee phrase of imperatives." Putting this claim somewhat differently (and ignoring the possibility of first- or third-person "imperatives"—i.e. hortatives or optatives), one might suggest as an apparently valid generalization that the only subjects tolerated in imperative sentences are second-person pronouns. If we turn now to Philippine languages, we see that ACTORS normally express the addressee phrase of imperatives (whether or not the actor is also the topic), and that the only ACTORS tolerated in imperative sentences are second-person pronouns. The following Tagalog examples illustrate these facts:

(14)          a. *Magbigay ka     sa kaniya ng kape.*
               AT-give   T-you D him    G coffee
               'Give him some coffee.'

          b. *Bigyan mo    siya   ng kape.*
               DT-give A-you T-him G coffee
               'Give him some coffee.'

          c. *Ibigay  mo    sa kaniya ang kape.*
               GT-give A-you D him   T   coffee
               'Give him the coffee.'

The special status of the actor in imperative sentences in Philippine languages follows very naturally from the actor's role prominence: i.e. from the fact that the actor expresses the individual whose role in the event the speaker views as central. In the case of the event expressed in an imperative sentence, the occurrence or nonoccurrence of this event is entirely contingent upon whether or not the addressee complies with the speaker's wishes. It is therefore quite appropriate that the addressee should be expressible by the constituent regularly associated with a meaning of role prominence, the actor, and that the only actor allowed should be one that represents the addressee. Mutatis mutandis, the special status of the SUBJECT in imperative sentences in other languages is also explicable on the basis of role prominence.

## Reflexivization

In languages with well-defined subjects, one syntactic property that is regularly associated with the subject is control over reflexivization. More specifically, there are many languages with reflexive nonsubjects that are interpreted as anaphors of subjects, but there do not appear to be any languages with reflexive subjects that are interpreted as anaphors of nonsubjects. No doubt one important factor in this situation is word order. That is, subjects precede nonsubjects in the great majority of languages (cf. Keenan 1976), and "precedes" is one of the "primacy relations" relevant to the control of anaphora (cf. Langacker 1969). Now I shall argue below that the ordering of subjects before nonsubjects is in fact a reflex of the subject's role prominence, so that one might describe the subject's control over reflexivization as role-related on this indirect basis. I believe, however, that there is also a more direct connection that can be established between the reflexivization facts and role prominence.

As the following Tagalog examples indicate, in Philippine languages the actor—whether or not it is also the topic—can control reflexivization [cf. sentences (15a) and (15b)], but cannot itself be reflexivized [cf. the ungrammatical strings (16a) and (16b)]. (Tagalog reflexives are formed with a possessive pronoun and the nominal **sarili** 'self'.)

(15)   a. *Nag-aalala ang lolo          sa kaniyang sarili.*
          AT-worry  T   grandfather D his          self
          'Grandfather worries about himself.'

       b. *Inaalala    ng lolo          ang kaniyang sarili.*
          DT-worry A grandfather T    his          self
          'Grandfather worries about himself.'

(16)   a. **Nag-aalala sa lolo          ang kaniyang sarili.*
          AT-worry  D grandfather T    his          self

       b. **Inaalala    ang lolo          ng kaniyang sarili.*
          DT-worry T grandfather A his          self

In other words, it is the actor in Philippine languages that possesses the subject properties with regard to reflexivization. How is this fact explained?

If we consider the meanings of sentences like those of (15), it is clear, first of all, that such sentences contain two nominals that refer to the same individual: the actor nominal and the reflexive nominal. Secondly, it is clear that the individual referred to by these two nominals is viewed by the speaker as central to the event expressed by the sentence (there being, in fact, no other individual involved). And finally, it is clear that, of the two nominals that refer to this central individual, only one, the actor, refers INDEPENDENTLY, actually IDENTI-

FYING the individual in question; the other, the reflexive, refers to the central individual only by virtue of being coreferential with the actor.[6]

Now since, as noted earlier, it is the actor that regularly identifies the central individual in the sentences of Philippine languages, it is not surprising for the actor to have this function in sentences involving reflexives, such as (15a) and (15b). By the same token, it is not surprising for strings like (16a) and (16b) to be disallowed, since in these strings the putative actor does not actually identify the central individual but merely refers one to another nominal that does.

Similarly, in languages in which it is the subject that identifies the central individual, it seems reasonable that this identification should be as straightforward as possible, and hence that the subject should be capable of controlling reflexivization but should not itself be reflexivizable. Thus the properties that actors and subjects share with regard to reflexivization can reasonably be viewed as a consequence of the role prominence of these constituents.

### Elliptical Complements

There is some disagreement among contemporary grammarians about the correct analysis of sentences with subjectless infinitival complements, such as *John wanted to leave* (compare, for example, the analyses of Postal 1970 and Jackendoff 1972). There is no room for disagreement, however, about the elliptical character of the complements in such sentences—i.e. about the absence of an overt complement subject—or about the fact that these complements are understood as having the same subject as the matrix verb.

In Philippine languages the elliptical construction that corresponds to the subjectless infinitival complement is an ACTORLESS infinitival complement. This construction is illustrated in the examples of (17):

(17)    a. *Nag-atubili  siyang  humiram    ng pera   sa bangko.*
               AT-hesitated T-he-Li AT-borrow G money D bank
               'He hesitated to borrow money from a/the bank.'

        b. *Nag-atubili  siyang  hiramin    ang pera   sa bangko.*
               AT-hesitated T-he-Li GT-borrow T    money D bank
               'He hesitated to borrow the money from a/the bank.'

---

[6] Thus the reference of the actor is not changed if the reflexive is replaced by some other nominal, but the reference of the reflexive IS changed by a change in the actor, as is shown by a comparison of (15b) with the following two sentences:

(i)    *Inaalala   ng lolo       ang tatay.*
      DT-worry A grandfather T   father
      'Grandfather worries about father.'

(ii)   *Inaalala   ng tatay  ang kaniyang sarili.*
      DT-worry A father T   his      self
      'Father worries about himself.'

c. *Nag-atubili    siyang   hiraman      ng pera    ang bangko.*
AT-hesitated T-he-Li DT-borrow G money T    bank
'He hesitated to borrow money from the bank.'

If we compare these sentences with those of (18), we see that in each case the complement in (17) is formed by omitting the actor (whether or not the actor is also the topic) from the corresponding sentence of (18) and replacing the finite verb form of (18) with the corresponding infinitive:[7]

(18)                        a. *Humiram      siya ng pera    sa bangko.*
AT-borrowed T-he G money D bank
'He borrowed money from a/the bank.'

b. *Hiniram        niya ang pera    sa bangko.*
GT-borrowed A-he T    money D bank
'He borrowed the money from a/the bank.'

c. *Hiniraman      niya ng pera      ang bangko.*
DT-borrowed A-he G money T    bank
'He borrowed money from the bank.'

As was argued in SPL, the absence of an actor nominal from the complements of sentences like those of (17) can be viewed as a reasonable consequence of the role prominence of the actor. For in such sentences the central role in the event expressed by the complement is overtly attributed to the referent of a nominal in the MATRIX sentence: e.g. in (17) the central role is attributed to the referent of the matrix nominal *siya* 'he'. It thus seems appropriate to exclude from the complement itself the nominal that would, if present, be interpreted in this same way. And, again, since subjects share with actors the semantic property of role prominence, one can expect them to share as well the syntactic properties that are correlated with role prominence, such as the ellipsis property under discussion.

There are, however, certain English subjectless complement constructions that might appear to provide counterevidence to the claims made above. These are the PASSIVE complement constructions of sentences like:

(19)                 *John wants to be examined by the doctor.*

According to the usual account of passives in transformational grammars, the passive subject is derived from an underlying object. And according to the usual assumptions about the relation between syntax and semantics, only the UNDER-LYING function of a nominal is semantically relevant.[8] It might therefore seem

---

[7] In the case of the actor-topic verb *humiram* [cf. (17a) and (18a)], the finite (perfective) and infinitive forms happen to be homophonous.

[8] This is, of course, necessarily the case within the framework of the Standard Theory of transformational grammar, where the only level of syntactic structure that is assigned semantic relevance

questionable to attribute the lack of a complement subject in a sentence like (19) to the general semantic 'role prominence' of subjects.

Interestingly, Philippine languages do not have any constructions that are comparable to (19). To express the approximate equivalent of (19) in Tagalog, for example, one would use (20a), in which there is no ellipsis within the complement, rather than the ungrammatical (20b):

(20)    a. *Gusto    ni Juang    suriin    siya ng doktor.*
           GT-want A Juan-Li GT-examine T-he A  doctor
           'Juan wants the doctor to examine him.'

       b. *\*Gusto    ni Juang    suriin    ng doktor.*
           GT-want A Juan-Li GT-examine A  doctor

The ungrammaticality of (20b) is consistent with the claim made above that only the role-prominent nominal, the actor, may be omitted to form an elliptical complement. What has been omitted from the complement of (20b) is not an actor, but a goal-topic [cf. (20a)]—hence the ungrammaticality of the result.

On the other hand, the grammaticality of (19) seems, as already noted, to be inconsistent with the claimed relation between ellipsis and role prominence, IF one accepts the usual transformational account of the passive. I shall, however, suggest in a later section (pp. 298–301) that this account of the passive is in fact incorrect, and that the passive subject is as much an underlying subject as is the active subject. If this suggestion is correct, then sentences like (19) do not provide counterevidence to the claimed role-relatedness of ellipsis in complements.

## Word Order

As was noted in the introduction, in simple narrative sentences in Tagalog only the verb occurs in a fixed position (i.e. initial position), while in general the ordering of the nominals in the sentence is quite free. There are other Philippine languages, however, in which nominals occur in a fixed order after the sentence-initial verb. And in these languages the actor manifests subjectlike ordering characteristics.

As far as I know, in all Philippine languages in which the ordering of nominals is fixed, the actor, whether or not it is also the topic, is always the FIRST nominal in the sentence. This is, for example, the case in Cebuano (cf. Bell 1974), Kalagan (cf. Collins 1970), and Pangasinan (cf. Benton 1971).[9] Now it is generally true of fixed-word-order languages with well-defined subjects that the subject

---

is the level of deep, or underlying, structure. But even within the framework of the Extended Standard Theory of Chomsky (1972), in which certain aspects of meaning are identified with the syntactic surface structure, it is still claimed that "insofar as grammatical relations [such as subject-of] play a role in determining meaning, it is the grammatical relations of the deep structure that are relevant" (p. 134).

[9] In Kalagan, but not in the other languages cited, the topic is also relevant to word order, in that a nonactor topic in this language immediately follows the actor.

precedes any other nominal in the sentence. In fact Keenan (1976), although he notes that there are some exceptions, proposes "leftmost" NP position as one of his universal subject properties. It thus seems clear that the actor in Philippine languages is subjectlike with regard to ordering, both by virtue of being RELEVANT to ordering and by virtue of its actual POSITION in relation to other nominals.

The positioning of the actor before any nonactors in a sentence would seem to follow naturally enough from the actor's role prominence. Since the actor expresses the individual whose role in an event the speaker views as central, it seems appropriate that this individual should be identified as early in the sentence as possible. A similar account can be given of the ordering of subjects before nonsubjects. Thus it seems that the ordering properties that subjects share with actors, like the previously noted properties relating to imperatives, reflexivization, and elliptical complements, can plausibly be correlated with the fact that subjects and actors share the semantic property of role prominence.

## OTHER IMPLICATIONS

I hope to have shown above that Philippine languages, even though they lack a syntactic category that can be uniformly identified with the subject category of other languages, offer some insights into why the subjects of other languages have the syntactic properties they do. In the remainder of this paper I propose to look into certain other consequences of the Philippine-language facts for the syntactic analysis of other languages and for general syntactic theory. In particular, I want to consider the implications of the Philippine data for the analysis of existentials (pp. 296–298), the analysis of 'derived subjects' (pp. 298–301), and the status of SUBJECT in universal grammar (pp. 301–305).

### The Analysis of Existentials

On p. 289, it was noted that the equivalents in Philippine languages of existential sentences such as:

(11)                              b. *There is a book on the table.*

do not have topics, and it was argued that this syntactic fact has a semantic basis: viz., a topic regularly has presupposed reference, and this presupposed reference is incompatible with the meaning of an existential sentence. It was also noted that, in the majority of languages with well-defined subjects, existential sentences in fact lack ordinary subjects and either are subjectless or have semantically empty subjects, such as English *there*. This fact too, it was claimed, has a semantic basis, since subjects, like topics, are referentially prominent.

Now in the usual accounts that grammarians—both pregenerative and generative—have given of English existentials such as (11b) or:

(21)                    *There is a solution to the energy problem.*

it is claimed that the subject proper or underlying subject is the nominal that follows *be* in the surface structure [e.g. *a solution to the energy problem* in (21)], and that the *there* that occurs before *be* is a quasi-subject or surface subject.[10,11] The displacement of the deep subject and the insertion of *there* are, in generative grammars, accounted for by a transformational rule of *there*-insertion (see, for example, Bach 1974: 143–145). This rule, which moves the underlying subject into predicate-nominal position and inserts *there* into subject position, appears to be simply an arbitrary rule of English syntax. Thus one would have no reason to expect to find parallel rules in other, unrelated languages.

Yet, as noted on p. 289, Clark (1970) has found that existential sentences in most other languages are like English existentials in representing the existent as part of the predicate (although relatively few are like English in using a semantically empty morpheme in the usual subject position). Thus, if English has an arbitrary rule moving the underlying subject of an existential sentence into predicate-nominal position, presumably most other languages must also have an arbitrary rule with this same effect—surely an odd coincidence.

What I would like to suggest is that the syntactic structure of existential sentences is not so arbitrary as the generative account summarized above suggests, but is, rather, a reasonable reflex of the meaning of such sentences. In my view the existential sentence (21) is both semantically and syntactically rather similar to the nonexistential identificational sentence (22):

(22)        *Conservation is a solution to the energy problem.*

In both (21) and (22) there is a syntactic predicate, *is a solution to the energy problem*, which expresses a property (the property of being a solution to the energy problem) as being predicable of some entity. Where (21) and (22) differ semantically is in whether some entity is actually identified as having the property in question. In the case of (22) there is such an entity (i.e. conservation), while in the case of (21) there is not; and the syntactic correlate of this difference is the occurrence of an ordinary definite-nominal subject (more precisely, a generic-nominal subject) in (22) and the absence of such a subject in (21).[12]

In my view, then, the underlying and surface structures of English existential sentences, such as (21), are essentially identical—a view which differs sharply from that reflected in the usual generative analysis. According to the usual

---

[10] "Subject proper" and "quasi-subject" are Jespersen's terms (1949:109–110), while "underlying subject" and "surface subject" are the corresponding terms used in the transformational literature.

[11] It should be noted that there is at least one generative account of existential sentences that does NOT identify the nominal that follows *be* as an underlying subject. This analysis, which is similar to the analysis advocated below, is to be found in Jenkins (1972).

[12] I assume that the occurrence of the "empty subject" *there*, rather than of no subject at all, in English existentials reflects the fact that in English there is a general prohibition against syntactically subjectless nonimperative sentences. Thus English also requires a syntactic subject in *it's raining*, *it's hot today*, etc., while many other languages do not.

analysis, as already indicated, (21) would be derived from an underlying structure closer to:

(23)                           *A solution to the energy problem is.

and *a solution to the energy problem* would thus be identified not as an underlying predicate nominal but as an underlying subject. While some syntactic arguments have been offered in favor of such an analysis (arguments that I hope to be able to deal with in a subsequent study), there are also some syntactic arguments that can be offered against it.[13] And, semantically, a derivation of (21) from (23) suggests that *a solution to the energy problem* in (21) should, like other subjects, be referential, and this does not seem to me to be a correct account of the semantic facts. Moreover, while the usual account, as already noted, fails to make sense of the cross-linguistic evidence, the account proposed above does not fail in this way. According to the proposed account, most languages express the existent as a SYNTACTIC predicate because it identifies a SEMANTIC predicate. And existential sentences in languages with well-defined subjects are subjectless (or have semantically empty subjects) for the same reason that existential sentences in Philippine languages are topicless: subjects, like topics, are referentially prominent, and this referential prominence is incompatible with the meaning of existential sentences.

## The Analysis of "Derived Subjects"

On pp. 290–296 above, it was claimed that certain syntactic properties of actor nominals in Philippine languages can reasonably be viewed as following from the actor's semantic role prominence. It was also claimed that in languages like English, where the syntactic properties in question are associated with subject nominals, the same kind of syntax-semantics correlation can appropriately be posited.

One possible objection to the latter claim was mentioned in the section dealing with elliptical complement constructions. As was noted in that section, examples like:

(19)                     *John wants to be examined by the doctor.*

[13] For example, if (21) is to be derived from (23), then obviously the base component must generate structures of the general form $NP + be$. In cases like (23), where the "underlying subject" NP is indefinite, *there* insertion is presumably obligatory, so ungrammatical strings like (23) do not actually surface. But what if the underlying subject is DEFINITE? Since one does not wish to generate strings like:

*The solution to the energy problem is.

and since there is no obligatory transformation that can be applied to make them grammatical, they must apparently be "filtered out" in some ad hoc fashion—an unappealing consequence of the usual generative analysis of existential sentences that does not arise under the analysis advocated in this paper.

show that in English ellipsis from an infinitival verb complement is a property not just of active, but also of passive, subjects. Since transformational grammars commonly derive English passive subjects from underlying objects, and since only the UNDERLYING role of a nominal is commonly assigned semantic relevance, it might be argued that the ellipsis property shared by active and passive subjects cannot be semantically based.

Similar arguments against the putative syntax-semantics correlation can be built upon examples like the following:[14]

(24)   a. *Don't you be fooled by him.*
       b. *McGovern wasn't defeated by Nixon; he was defeated by **himself**.*

(25)   a. *Don't you be too easy to please.*
       b. *John appeared to himself to be the obvious choice.*
       c. *John doesn't want to appear to be overconfident.*

The examples of (24) show that ellipsis from complements is not the only putatively role-related subject property that passive subjects share with active subjects: (24a) illustrates that the addressee phrase of an imperative can be expressed by a passive subject (cf. p. 291) while (24b) illustrates that a passive subject can control reflexivization (cf. p. 292). And the examples of (25) show that, like passive subjects, certain other surface subjects that are commonly analyzed as transformationally derived show putatively role-related subject properties. Thus the surface subject of (25a) corresponds, according to a common transformational account (cf. Postal 1974), to an underlying embedded object, while the surface subject of (25b) corresponds to an underlying EMBEDDED subject that presumably has no semantic relation to the matrix verb. Similarly, in (25c), the missing subject of the complement of *want* is, according to this account, not the underlying subject of *appear*, but, rather, the underlying subject embedded UNDER *appear*. Yet in each case the surface subject in question shows one of the subject properties that I have claimed are role-related: the imperative-subject property in the case of (25a); the reflexivization property in the case of (25b), and the elliptical-complement property in the case of (25c). And, of course, all of the surface subjects in the examples of (24) and (25) occur in subject POSITION, which I have also claimed (p. 296) to be a role-related subject property.

Now it seems to me that, whatever the derivation of passive subjects and the raised subjects illustrated in the examples of (24) and (25), these subjects do in fact share with the subjects of simple active sentences the semantic property

---

[14] I recognize that some of these examples involve construction types that are often classified as syntactically deviant, e.g. the passive reflexive illustrated in (24b). My own view is that these construction types are syntactically well formed, although sentences involving them are often SEMANTICALLY odd. At any rate, the general point being made does not depend crucially upon the grammaticality of all of the construction types illustrated.

of role prominence. That is, the referent of the subject is in each case the individual that the speaker views as having the central role in the relevant event. Indeed, in the case of the passive, I believe that it is THE major function of this construction to assign role prominence to the patient at the expense of the agent. (It is interesting to note, in this connection, that in passive sentences only the patient is obligatorily expressed, while expression of the agent is optional.) Thus I would claim that there is a semantic difference between (26a) and (26b)—and of course between (26a) and (26c)—that can be explained in part on the basis of the prominence the speaker is assigning to the referent of *McGovern*:

(26)          a. *Nixon defeated McGovern in 1972.*
              b. *McGovern was defeated by Nixon in 1972.*
              c. *McGovern was defeated in 1972.*

Similar claims can be—and have been—made with regard to the semantic prominence of raised subjects vis-à-vis their unraised counterparts. Thus Partee (1971), in discussing the following examples:

(27)          a. *It appears that John is shooting at Bill.*
              b. *John appears to be shooting at Bill.*

notes a semantic difference between them which she characterizes as follows: "The difference here seems to be a difference in point of view of the speaker—in *a* he is taking in the whole situation, in *b* . . . focusing on John" (pp. 17–18). The "focusing on John" that is found in (27b) is, I suggest, the usual role prominence that is assigned to the referent of the subject of a sentence. I would claim, then, that passive subjects and raised subjects share the semantic prominence of subjects in general, and that this shared semantic property underlies the shared SYNTACTIC properties noted above. But, if this claim is correct, then something must be wrong either with the way that transformationalists have derived the constructions in question or with the account that they have given of the relation between syntax and semantics—or possibly with both. For transformationalists have commonly claimed that passive subjects, etc., are DERIVED subjects, and at the same time they have claimed that only UNDERLYING syntactic relations have semantic relevance (cf. footnote 8). Obviously it is not possible to maintain both of these claims if one also wishes to maintain the claim made above with regard to the semantic similarity of passive and raised subjects to subjects of other types.

One way out of this dilemma—and a way which has, I believe, a good deal of independent motivation—is to reject the common transformational account of passives and of constructions involving raising in favor of an account in which the surface subject that occurs in these constructions is also the underlying subject: i.e. an account in which the passive and raising transformations are eliminated from the grammar. With regard to the passive, Shopen (1972) and

Freidin (1975) have presented a variety of arguments in favor of a nontrans-formational analysis, and some additional arguments are to be found in Schachter (1976b: Section 4.2). As for constructions involving raising, Lasnik and Fiengo (1974), among others, argue in favor of a derivation of so-called Tough Movement sentences (e.g. *John is easy to please*) in such a way that the underlying and surface subjects are identical, and it is not hard to find arguments in favor of a similarly direct derivation for the surface subjects of the other relevant type of raising construction (e.g. *John appears to be shooting at Bill*)—cf. Schachter (1976b: Section 4.2).

Another way out would be to retain the passive and raising transformations and to modify the account that is given of the relation between syntax and semantics so that it becomes possible to assign semantic prominence to derived subjects. At any rate, the recognition that there are role-related subject proper-ties, and that these role-related properties are shared by certain types of subjects that have been thought to be transformationally derived, has far-reaching consequences.

## The Status of "Subject" in Universal Grammar

Perhaps the most interesting implication of the Philippine-language facts with which we have been concerned has to do with the status of "subject" in universal grammar. For if in Philippine languages there is no single constituent type that corresponds to the subject in other languages, but instead there are two con-stituent types—the topic and the actor—that divide the set of subject properties between them, then the common assumption of the universality of subjects apparently cannot be correct. While I have already made this point in SPL, it seems to me to be worth pursuing further, since if it is well taken, it could invalidate a great many claims about language that are based on the presumed universality of subjects—including, for example, the various claims of this kind that (as I understand it) characterize the theory of Relational Grammar. In this connection, I should like in particular to consider the possibility (suggested to me by Paul Postal, personal communication) of analyzing Philippine lan-guages so that the topic and the actor are BOTH identified as subjects, but as subjects at different levels of syntactic analysis.

According to the proposal in question, the actor would be identified as an "initial subject" (or underlying subject), while the topic would be identified as a "cyclic subject" (i.e. the subject after application of all transformations that apply within the domain of the lowest dominating S-node). Sentences with actor topics would thus have a status similar to that of ordinary active sentences in English, in which the initial subject is also the cyclic subject, while sentences with nonactor topics would have a status similar to English passives, in which the initial subject and the cyclic subject are said to be distinct. (In this section, I shall, for the sake of argument, accept the assumption that passive subjects are transformationally derived, although, as is clear from the preceding section, I think that there is good reason to doubt this assumption.) Thus it would not be the case that in Philippine languages the set of subject properties is divided between two constituent types, neither of which is a subject, but rather that this set of properties is divided between initial subjects and cyclic subjects.

There are, however, a number of arguments that can be offered against this proposal. (Some of these arguments have already been presented in SPL, but I repeat them here for the sake of completeness.) The first argument, which I owe to Bell (1974), presupposes the correctness of certain syntactic universals that have been proposed within the framework of Relational Grammar: first, that certain grammatical properties are associated uniquely with so-called terms of grammatical relations, i.e. subjects, objects, and indirect objects; and, second, that the following Relational Annihilation Law holds:

(28)  RELATIONAL ANNIHILATION LAW: *If an* $NP_i$ *assumes a grammatical relation previously borne by* $NP_j$, *then* $NP_j$ *ceases to bear any grammatical relation; it becomes a* CHÔMEUR (French for 'unemployed person').

According to the Relational Annihilation Law, then, if an initial subject is transformationally replaced by a derived cyclic subject, the initial subject should become a CHÔMEUR, and no longer have those properties that are associated uniquely with terms.

Now one of the syntactic properties that are said to be unique to terms is control over reflexivization, and in Philippine languages, as we have already seen, control over reflexivization is vested in the actor, whether or not the actor is also the topic—cf. the examples repeated below:

(15)        a. *Nag-aalala ang lolo          sa kaniyang sarili.*
               AT-worry  T   grandfather D his       self
               'Grandfather worries about himself.'

            b. *Inaalala    ng lolo          ang kaniyang sarili.*
               DT-worry  A  grandfather T   his       self
               'Grandfather worries about himself.'

But according to the analysis that we are considering, in which the actor is an initial subject and the topic a cyclic subject, a nontopic actor must be a subject whose original role has been assumed by the topic. Thus, according to the Relational Annihilation Law (28), the nontopic actor should be a chômeur, and should not be able to control reflexivization, as it does in (15b). Therefore, if the Relational Annihilation Law is valid, the analysis under consideration must be wrong: the actor cannot be an initial subject because a nontopic actor is clearly not a chômeur.[15]

---

[15] This argument is somewhat weakened, however, by the fact that the data in question could be accounted for by rule ordering: i.e. let the actor be the initial subject and let the topic be the cyclic

A second argument against the proposal that actors are initial subjects and topics cyclic subjects can be based on the fact that, in those Philippine languages that show fixed word order, it is in general the actor, rather than the topic, that is relevant to word order and shows subjectlike ordering characteristics (cf. p. 295). This is certainly not the situation that one tends to expect if the proposal in question is correct, since in languages with well-defined subjects, such as English, word order is always defined on putative CYCLIC subjects and not on putative INITIAL subjects. For example, in English passives, subject position is occupied not by the agent (which Relational Grammar would analyze as an initial subject) but by the passive subject (which Relational Grammar would analyze as an initial object that has become a cyclic subject). Philippine languages that show fixed word order would thus differ curiously from other fixed-word-order languages in that the rules that putatively change syntactic relations would in general leave the underlying constituent order intact.

A third argument against the proposal in question depends upon the correctness of the claims made in the preceding section concerning the semantic similarity between the Philippine actor and the SURFACE subjects of other languages. What was claimed in that section was that the "role prominence" that is associated with the actor in Philippine languages is, in other languages, typically associated with the surface subject, WHETHER OR NOT this surface subject is one that is ordinarily analyzed as corresponding to an underlying—or initial—subject. Thus it was claimed that passive subjects and subjects that are ordinarily thought to have been raised into subject position from embedded sentences show the same role prominence as ordinary active subjects.

But now note that, if the proposal being discussed is correct, then the actor in Philippine languages is an initial subject, but not necessarily a surface subject. And one must then account for the puzzling fact that semantic role prominence, which is associated with surface subjects in languages for which the identification of the subject is not problematic, is associated only with initial subjects in Philippine languages.

A final argument against the proposal being discussed is based upon the fact that, given this proposal, all non–actor-topic verbal constructions must be derived from underlying constructions in which the actor is the subject, so that, if no term-changing rule applies, an actor-topic sentence is the result. Now, as noted in SPL, there are in Tagalog (and, I believe, in other Philippine languages) a good many actor-topic transitive verbs that are distributionally more restricted than their goal-topic counterparts. While the goal-topic forms of these verbs

---

subject, but let reflexivization be ordered before the rule that derives nonactor topics. Under this proposal, in the derivation of (15b) the actor is still a subject at the time that reflexivization applies, so the Relational Annihilation Law does not come into play. But, according to Bell (1974), this proposal would violate a general ordering principle of relational grammar, to the effect that term-creating rules always precede feature-changing rules. Clearly the rule that derives the nonactor topic ( = "cyclic subject") in (15b) must be a term-creating rule, but it would, under the rule-ordering proposal, have to FOLLOW the feature-changing reflexivization rule.

may occur as predicates of simple narrative sentences, the actor-topic forms may not; the latter are found only in relative clauses and certain nominalizations. (The nominalizations in question appear to be analyzable as headless relative clauses.) The following examples illustrate these distributional properties:

(29)  a. *Tinakot       ng lalaki ang bata.*
          GT-frightened A man   T   child
          'A/the man frightened the child.'

      b. **Tumakot*      ang lalaki ng bata.*
          AT-frightened T    man   G child

      c. *Nasaan ang lalaking tumakot       ng bata?*
          where   T    man-Li AT-frightened G child
          'Where is the man who frightened a child?'

      d. *Nasaan ang tumakot        ng bata?*
          where   T    AT-frightened G child
          'Where is the one who frightened a child?'

As these examples show, the goal-topic verb *tinakot* occurs as the predicate of a simple narrative sentence [cf. (29a)], but the corresponding actor-topic verb *tumakot* fails to occur in such a sentence [cf. (29b)], although it may occur in a relative clause [(29c)] or in a nominalization [(29d)].

How could this distribution be accounted for in an analysis in which the actor is always the initial subject, and a "goal-subject" (i.e. goal-topic) is derived only transformationally? Presumably the verbs in question would have to be marked with a lexical feature that would have the effect of making the goal-subject rule apply obligatorily in just the right cases—i.e. in main clauses but not in relative clauses, etc. While such a lexical marking is no doubt possible, it is unappealing, requiring as it does an otherwise unneeded formal device of considerable power. On the other hand, if goal-topic constructions are not transformationally derived, all that is needed to account for the distribution reflected in examples like those of (29) is a contextual feature on certain actor-topic verbs, constraining their insertion to the appropriate contexts.

The above arguments seem to me to show that, if an analysis of Philippine languages that treats the actor as an initial subject and the topic as a cyclic subject is not strictly impossible, it is almost certainly misguided. For, in order to maintain this analysis, one must be willing to give up various otherwise valid generalizations about subjects, based upon languages for which the identification of the subject is straightforward, and one must also be willing to settle for a rather ad hoc account of the Philippine facts themselves. Since I know of no more successful analysis of Philippine languages that analyzes them as having subjects, and since the languages CAN be analyzed quite satisfactorily as NOT having subjects, I conclude that the assumption of the universality of subjects is, in the case of Philippine languages, something of a Procrustean bed, and see nothing to be gained by forcing the languages into this bed. On the contrary, I see real advantages to continuing to analyze Philippine languages as having, instead of subjects, two nonsubject constituent types that manifest subjectlike properties. And not the least of these advantages is—as I hope to have shown in this study—that analyzing Philippine languages in this way can shed some unexpected light on just why it is that the well-defined subjects of other languages have the properties they do.

## REFERENCES

Bach, E. (1974) *Syntactic Theory*, Holt, Rinehart and Winston, New York.
Bell, S. (1974) "Some Notes on Cebuano and Relational Grammar," unpublished paper.
Benton, R. (1971) *Pangasinan Reference Grammar*, University of Hawaii Press, Honolulu, Hawaii.
Chomsky, N. (1972) "Some Empirical Issues in the Theory of Transformational Grammar," in *Studies on Semantics in Generative Grammar*. Mouton, The Hague.
Clark, E. V. (1970) "Locationals: A Study of the Relations between 'Existential', 'Locative', and 'Possessive' Constructions," in *Working Papers on Language Universals* 3, Stanford University, Stanford, California, 1–36.
Collins, G. C. (1970) *Two Views of Kalagan Grammar*, unpublished Doctoral dissertation, Indiana University, Bloomington, Indiana.
Fillmore, C. J. (1968) "The Case for Case," in E. Bach and R. Harms, eds., *Universals in Linguistic Theory*, Holt, Rinehart and Winston, New York.
Freidin, R. (1975) "The Analysis of Passives," *Language* 51, 384–405.
Givón, T. (1974) "Toward a Discourse Definition of Syntax," unpublished paper.
Jackendoff, R. (1972) *Semantic Interpretation in Generative Grammar*, M.I.T. Press, Cambridge, Massachusetts.
Jenkins, L. (1972) *Modality in English Syntax*, unpublished Doctoral dissertation, M.I.T., Cambridge, Massachusetts. [Available in mimeographed form from the Indiana University Linguistics Club, University of Indiana, Bloomington, Indiana.]
Jespersen, O. (1949) *A Modern English Grammar on Historical Principles*, part VII, George Allen and Unwin, London.
Keenan, E. L. (1976) "Toward a Universal Definition of 'Subject'," in C. N. Li, ed., *Subject and Topic*, Academic Press, New York.
Keenan, E. L. and B. Comrie (to appear) "Noun Phrase Accessibility and Universal Grammar," *Linguistic Inquiry*.
Langacker, R. W. (1969) "On Pronominalization and the Chain of Command," in D. Reibel and S. Schane, eds., *Modern Studies in English*, Prentice-Hall, Englewood Cliffs, New Jersey.
Lasnik, H. and R. Fiengo (1974) "Complement Object Deletion," *Linguistic Inquiry* 5, 535–571.
Li, C. N. and S. A. Thompson (1976) "Subject and Topic: A New Typology of Language," in C. N. Li, ed., *Subject and Topic*, Academic Press, New York.
Partee, B. H. (1971) "On the Requirement that Transformations Preserve Meaning," in C. Fillmore and D. T. Langendoen, eds., *Studies in Linguistic Semantics*, Holt, Rinehart and Winston, New York.
Postal, P. (1970) "On Coreferential Complement Subject Deletion," *Linguistic Inquiry* 1, 439–500.
Postal, P. (1974) *On Raising*, M.I.T. Press, Cambridge, Massachusetts.
Schachter, P. (1976a) "The Subject in Philippine Languages: Topic, Actor, Actor-Topic, or None of the Above," in C. N. Li, ed., *Subject and Topic*, Academic Press, New York.
Schachter, P. (1976b) "A Nontransformational Account of Gerundive Nominals in English," *Linguistic Inquiry* 7, 205–241.

Schachter, P. and F. T. Otanes (1972) *A Tagalog Reference Grammar*, University of California Press, Berkeley, California.

Shopen, T. (1972) *A Generative Theory of Ellipsis*, unpublished Doctoral dissertation, University of California, Los Angeles, California. [Available in mimeographed form from the Indiana University Linguistics Club, University of Indiana, Bloomington, Indiana.]

# GREENLANDIC ESKIMO, ERGATIVITY, AND RELATIONAL GRAMMAR

*ANTHONY C. WOODBURY*

*University of California, Berkeley*

## BACKGROUND

Within the theory of Relational Grammar as developed by David Perlmutter and Paul Postal (Summer Institute, Linguistic Society of America, 1974), by Johnson (1974), and others, the notions 'subject of,' 'object of,' and 'indirect object of' are the primitives on which derivations in the transformational component are based.[1] This immediately raises questions about so-called ergative languages, where at least some of the transformations and surface morphology point to the use of relational primitives where transitive objects ($O_t$) and intransitive subjects ($S_i$) are grouped together (ABSOLUTIVE), and transitive subjects ($S_t$) make up a separate relation (ERGATIVE). In this chapter, I will give a relational grammatical analysis for some aspects of the transformational component of Greenlandic Eskimo. I will consider not only the general question

---

[1] My sources of data on Greenlandic are Kleinschmidt (1851) (abbreviated Kl in references for citations of data); Schultz-Lorentzen (1927 and 1945) (abbreviated SL:1927 and SL:1945, respectively); Swadesh (1944); and Bergsland (1955) (abbreviated Bg.).

The transcription is autonomous phonemic. /g/ represents a voiced velar approximant, /r/ a voiced uvular approximant, and /v/ a voiced bilabial fricative. All other symbols have their standard value.

The following abbreviations are used in morpheme-by-morpheme translations: ABL = ablative; ABS = absolutive; AL = allative; APAS = antipassive; CONJ = conjunctive; ERG = ergative; IMP AG = impersonal agent; IND = indicative; INF = infinitive; IP = intransitive participle; INST = instrumental; LOC = locative; POSS = possessive; and TP = transitive participle.

of ergativity, but also miscellaneous problems which arise from this type of analysis. I will then review the proposals made by Perlmutter and Postal for the treatment of ergativity, showing that they are in some points ad hoc, and that they unnecessarily increase the class of possible grammars which the theory describes. In the final section I will suggest a mechanism for deriving ergativity and accusativity from a neutral substratum based on markedness, and discuss ways of restricting where ergativity (or accusativity) can be assigned, drawing on the data from Greenlandic and on previous work in the literature along these lines.

Perlmutter and Postal's conception of Relational Grammar[2] can be sketched as follows: First, all rules affecting grammatical relations are claimed to be included within the cycle. Cyclic mappings between levels of structure make reference EXCLUSIVELY to grammatical relations: that is, there is. no crucial notion of order or of dominance within the clause at this stage. At the end of each cycle, a template indicating unmarked word order is imposed on the clause, which is subject to modification only by the application of postcyclic transformations. All derivations and grammars of particular languages, as well as formal properties of the theory itself, are constrained and governed by an exterior body of laws, which in turn makes formal and substantive claims about the notion 'possible grammar of a natural language'. Most of the significant details of the theory, which I will unfold as they become germane to this discussion, find expression in this body of laws. Now, some terminology. Perlmutter and Postal posit the following hierarchy of grammatical relations:

$$
(1) \qquad
\begin{array}{l}
primaries \left\{ \begin{array}{l} subject\ (I) \\ object\ (II) \end{array} \right. \\
nonprimaries \left\{ \begin{array}{l} indirect\ object\ (III) \\ other \end{array} \right.
\end{array}
\left. \begin{array}{c} \\ \\ \end{array} \right\} terms \\
\qquad\qquad\qquad\qquad\qquad\qquad\qquad\qquad\qquad\quad \} nonterms
$$

If a term has ceased to bear any grammatical relation to the verb through the operation of a transformation, it is called a CHÔMEUR. For example, the subject, which in English is displaced by the object by the application of Passive, appearing optionally in a *by*-phrase, is a chômeur.

Greenlandic is a polysynthetic, SOXV suffixing language. Left- and right-branching are equally possible at the clause level, while central embedding is rather rare. Aside from the fact that adjectives and relative clauses follow their heads, Greenlandic is in accordance with most of Greenberg's (1963) claims about SOV languages.

The verb consists of a single root, followed by (theoretically) any number of derivational and adverbial suffixes, a mood suffix, subject and object agree-

---

[2] For a published account, more detailed than I can give here, of a similar version of Relational Grammar, I refer the reader to Johnson (1974).

ment markers, and finally optional enclitic conjunctions and adverbials, for example:

(2) [Bg:16]  *silar  -luk -ka      -u -ssi    -qa -lu -ni -lu*
outside-bad-strongly-be-become-have-INF-4sg-and
'and it becoming very apt to be bad weather'

Most often, the agreement suffixes are phonologically fused to such a degree that it is impossible to tell whether they work on a nominative-accusative basis or on an absolutive-ergative basis. In the infinitive mood, however, where only one argument, $S_i$ or $O_t$, is permitted, we find that the same agreement marker is used for either function, given any specific person and number combination. This argues for an absolutive and an ergative agreement suffix, as opposed to a nominative and an accusative suffix (hence cycle-final agreement rules would be of an absolutive-ergative nature). The verbal moods are of two kinds, INDEPENDENT and DEPENDENT. Independent moods are used in the main clause of a sentence, and they indicate illocutionary force. They are: the INDICATIVE (marked with *-p(u)-* ∼ *-v(u)-*); the INTERROGATIVE (*-pa-* ∼ *-va-*); the OPTATIVE (*-li-* ∼ *-la-*); and the IMPERATIVE (*-∅-* ∼ *-git-*). Dependent moods are used in subordinate clauses, including relative clauses, complement clauses, and adverbial clauses of various kinds. They divide into three subcategories: PARTICIPIAL, OBLIQUE, and INFINITIVE. The participial moods consist of the INTRANSITIVE PARTICIPLE (*-tu-* ∼ *-su-*)—for intransitive relative and object complement clauses; the TRANSITIVE PARTICIPLE (*-ki-* ∼ *-gi-*)—for transitive versions of same; and the PASSIVE PARTICIPLE (*-(g)aq-*) and ACTIVE PARTICIPLE (*-ti-*)—for nominalizations with $O_t$ and $S_t$ heads, respectively. The oblique moods are the CONJUNCTIVE (*-(m)m-*)—which complementizes clauses which describe something anterior to a realized event expressed in the matrix clause (e.g. *because*-clauses); and the SUBJECTIVE (*-(p)p-*)—which complementizes clauses which describe something anterior to a unrealized, or irreal, event expressed in the matrix clause (e.g. conditionals). The INFINITIVE mood complementizes clauses describing events occuring at least in part concurrently with what is described in the matrix clause; thus, it complementizes certain object complement clauses, and also such adverbial clauses as *as*- and *while*-clauses.

The noun consists of an obligatory root, any number of derivational suffixes, a case suffix, a possessive agreement marker indicating the person and number of the possessor if there is one, and finally enclitic suffixes, for example:

(3) [Bg:28]       a. $\sqrt{}$*inalua-miniŋ-ŋuil  -∅      -lu*
gut   -piece -small-ABS:sg-and
'and small gut piece'

b.  $\sqrt{nini}$ -miŋ        -nik
    share-POSS:4sg-INST:pl
    'with their own shares'

Note the parallels in structure between nouns and verbs.

There are two purely grammatical cases, the ABSOLUTE (-$\emptyset$-), for $O_t$'s and $S_i$'s, and the ERGATIVE (-$(u)p$-), for $S_t$'s and possessors. There are also five oblique cases, in all but one instance suffixed to the $p$ of the ergative marker, which is thereby nasalized to $m$ by a more or less regular alternation. These cases are: the LOCATIVE (-mi-), the PERLATIVE (-kut-) (i.e. 'through', 'on', etc.), the ABLATIVE (-mit-), the ALLATIVE (-mut-), and the INSTRUMENTAL (-mik-). Only the last three of these cases can receive chômeurs. In the oblique cases, the plural (-$(i)t$-) neutralizes the absolutive/ergative morphological opposition, and its corresponding nasal $n$ replaces the nasalized ergative marker.

Pronominalization of absolutive and ergative NPs is accomplished by deleting the full NP, while leaving its agreement marker on the verb intact, as in (4a–c) for $S_i$, $S_t$, and $O_t$, respectively:

(4) [Swadesh:45]

   a. *Aŋut-$\emptyset$    sana -vuq.*      ⇒ *Sanavuq.*
      man -ABS work-IND:3sg
      'The man works.'                'He works.'

   b. *Tigiania-p      iglu  -$\emptyset$    taku-vaa.*      ⇒ *Iglu taku-vaa.*
      fox      -ERG house-ABS see  -IND:3sg,3sg
      'The fox sees the house.'                          'He sees the house.'

   c. *Tigianiap iglu takuvaa.*  ⇒ *Tigianiap takuvaa.*
      'The fox sees the house'    'The fox sees it'

The same is the case for possessive constructions:

(5) [Swadesh:45]  *tigiania-p      iglu  -$\emptyset$    -a*        ⇒ *iglua*
                  fox      -ERG house-ABSsg-POSS:3sg
                  'the fox's house'                      'his house'

For the expression of pronouns (of all persons) in oblique cases, there are pronominal roots onto which the appropriate case markers can be suffixed.

## SOME APPLICATIONS OF RELATIONAL GRAMMAR TO GREENLANDIC ESKIMO

### The Cycle-final Word-order Template

Based on the foregoing, we posit the following cycle-final word-order template for Greenlandic:

(6)                        *(erg) abs (III) (nonterms) verb*

Now, it has been argued by Perlmutter and Postal that a word-order template for an ergative language could just as easily be stated in nominative-accusative terms. However, Edward Keenan (personal communication) has pointed out that the vast majority of languages displaying ergative case-marking and agreement rules are verb-final, and that all the others of which he is aware are verb-initial. If, in fact, there exist no verb-medial ergative languages, and if we assume the Chômeur Segregation Law,[3] then there can be no empirical proof for the claim that the word order of these languages works on a nominative-accusative basis, since both (7a) and (7b) make exactly the same claim:

(7)  a. *(erg) abs verb*
     b. *I (II) verb*

Proof of a universal nominative-accusative basis would consist of surface word order in verb-medial ergative languages, as in (8a), and proof of an ergative-absolutive basis would consist of surface word order in these languages, as in (8b):

(8)  a. *transitive: erg verb abs*
        *intransitive: abs verb*
     b. *(erg) verb abs*

I am using the ergative-based template in (6), rather than something along the lines of (7b), because we need ergative relations to trigger the correct configurations of agreement suffixes in the verb.

## The Cycle

In this section we will consider some cyclic rules in Greenlandic and formulate them in relational grammatical terms. We will take them in the order that they occur in the cycle, as far as I have been able to determine.

### RULES OF COMPLEMENTATION

We will look first at rules which merge a clause and its complement into a single surface clause.

*Clause Union.*  Consider the following sentences:

(9) [SL:1927:293]  a. *Iŋi    -rqu-vai.*
                      sit down-tell-IND:3sg,3pl
                      'He ordered them to sit down.'

---

[3] Full statements of the laws from Perlmutter and Postal will be found in the appendix to this chapter.

b. *Uvav-nut    taman-na     sana -rqu-vaa*
me -ALsg this   -ABSsg work-tell-IND: 3sg,3sg
*inu -at       -a.*
man-ERGsg-POSS: 3sg

'His man ordered me to work on this one.'

(10) [K1: 55]    a. *Pi  -n    -i        inun  -nut   taku-rqu-vai.*
thing-ABSpl-POSS: 4sg person-ALpl see  -tell-IND: 3sg,3pl
'He told the people to watch his things.'

b. *Takurquvai.*
He ordered that they be watched.'

(11) [K1: 159]         *Unig    -taili  -vaa.*
stand still-hinder-IND: 3sg,3sg
'He hindered him from standing still.'

*-rqu-* and *-taili-* belong to a class of verbal suffixes in Greenlandic called DOUBLE
TRANSITIVE by Kleinschmidt (1851), most of which have some kind of causative
meaning and correspond semantically quite closely to the English class of verbs
triggering Subject-to-Object Raising. We can derive sentences with double
transitive verbal suffixes [for example, (9a–b)] from structures like (12a–b),
respectively:

(12)                    a. *(he)* $[_{abs}[_s(they)$ *iŋi-*$]_s]_{abs}$-*rqu-*
erg          abs

b. *inuata* $[_{abs}[_s$*uvav- taman- sana-*$]_s]_{abs}$-*rqu-*
erg          erg     abs

by an obligatory rule of Clause Union:

(13)   *Join a clause and its complement to form a simplex clause.*
Condition: *The matrix verb is of the class of double transitive verbal*
   *suffixes.*
Side effects:

(a) $erg_{subord.\ cl.}$ $\Rightarrow$ $chômeur_{matrix\ cl.}$

(b) $abs_{subord.\ cl.}$ $\Rightarrow$ $abs_{matrix\ cl.}$

(c) *The verb of the subordinate clause is adjoined to the left of the*
   *verb of the matrix clause.*

(d) *The matrix clause chômeur is marked with the allative case suffix.*

*Equi Subject Deletion.*   We would derive sentences like:

(14)          a. *Nalag-sinnau-vaa.*
                 obey -can    -IND: 3sg,3sg
                 'He can obey him'

              b. *Ajuliri        -artu           -lir   -puq.*
                 became feeble-more and more-begin-IND: 3sg
                 'She began to become more and more feeble.'

from structures like (15a) and (15b), respectively:

(15)                     a. $(he_i)[_{II}[_S(he_i)\ (him_j)\ nalag-]_S]_{II}$-*sinnau-*
                            $\phantom{.}$I$\phantom{xxx}$I$\phantom{xxxx}$II

                         b. $(she_i)[_{II}[_S(she_i)\ ajuliriartu-]_S]_{II}$-*lir-*
                            $\phantom{.}$I$\phantom{xxx}$I

To do this, we will need an obligatory rule of Equi Subject Deletion:

(16)    *Join a clause and its complement to form a simplex clause.*
        Conditions:

        (a) $I_{subord.\ cl.}$ *is coreferent with* $I_{matrix\ cl}$ .
        (b) *The verb of the matrix clause is an equi subject verb.*

        Side effects:

        (a) $I_{subord\ cl} \Rightarrow \emptyset$

        (b) $II_{subord.\ cl.} \Rightarrow II_{matrix\ cl}$ .

        (c) *The verb of the subordinate clause is adjoined to the left of the
            verb of the matrix clause.*

To prove that there is actually a merger taking place, I will show that side
effect (b) is indeed the case:

(17) [Bg: 36]
     *Tamak-ku      tigu -niq                 ajur -na      -qa -ut.*
     this     -ACCpl take-abstract nominal cannot-IMP AG-very-IND: 3pl
     'These are impossible to take.'

The subject of *tigu-* has been deleted (the subject of *ajur-*, with which it was
coreferent, is suppressed by Impersonal Agent, cf. below), and *tamakku* is now
the object of the matrix verb, evidenced by the plural agreement marker *-ut*.[4]

---

[4] *Ku-* marks $O_i$'s exclusively in plural demonstratives (singular demonstratives have absolutive–
ergative-type marking). VERB + *niq* functions here as the infinitive does in English; it is triggered
automatically by a small class of equi subject verbs which are roots rather than suffixes. *Ajur-* is
one of these verbs.

Condition (b) of rule (16) appears ad hoc. But the class of verbs which trigger rule (16) has an interesting independent motivation, namely, all of its members require the Like-Subject Constraint (discussed in Perlmutter 1971); that is, they select only complement subjects which are coreferential with their own subjects, such as *try*, *begin*, and *can* in English. In Greenlandic there are, therefore, no syntactic minimal pairs with equi subject verbs like (18a) versus (18b) in English:

(18)                      a. *Ben wants to buy a Cadillac.*
                          b. *Ben wants Lorraine to buy a Cadillac.*

Equi subject verbs must be contrasted with semantically equivalent double transitive verbs to make pairs of this kind:[5]

(19) [Bugge 1960:689]     a. *Ani-nia-lir   -puq.*
                             go -try-begin-IND:3sg
                             'He wants to get going.'

                          b. *Ani-rqu-viŋa?*
                             go -tell-INTERROG:2sg,1sg
                             'Do you want me to go?'

We have seen, then, two distinct processes of clause merger, and have shown not only that they differ on semantic grounds, but also that they differ in that one process, Clause Union, refers crucially to ergative-type relational primitives, and the other, Equi Subject Deletion, to accusative-type relational primitives.

Let us now turn to rules of complementation where clauses remain separate. Recall from the beginning of this chapter that there is an elaborate system of complementizers in Greenlandic, called dependent moods, which serve to keep clauses separate.

*Object Complement Clause.*   The following I will take to be the basic form for object complement clauses:

(20) [Bg:forthcoming:1]
        *Ipaksar  -nit    sukanirut-lutik    malug-aa.*
        day before-ABLpl faster    -INF:4pl notice-IND:3sg,3sg
        'He noticed that they were going faster than the day before.'

In this example *malugaa* is transitive, with the third-person-singular absolutive agreement marker cross-referencing the entire complement clause. Hence the

---

[5] Of course, reflexive versions of double transitive verbs contrast with nonreflexive versions in this way—there is simply a privative syntactic opposition between the two types of verbs as to coreference restrictions.

complement clause is a primary. But Kleinschmidt gives examples where the subject (i.e. $S_i$ or $S_t$) of the complement clause is copied into absolutive position in the matrix clause, and Bergsland (1955) gives examples where the direct object of the complement clause is copied (thus spoiling this rule's candidacy for ergative OR accusative status):

(21) [Bg:50]   a. *Tusar-pakka*          *qavaniit*    *-tut.*
                  hear -IND:1sg,3pl in the south-IP:3pl
                  'I hear (of them) that they are in the south.' (Kl:99)

            b. *Ilisima -vaaŋa*          *urni -ssa  -giga.*
                  know of-IND:3sg,1sg come-FUT-TP:1sg,3sg
                  'He knows (of me), that I will come to him.' (Kl:76)

            c. *iglu  -∅    -ni        tammar-tuq    ujar   -ini*
                  cousin-ABSsg-POSS:4sg lost     -IP:3sg look for-TP:4sg,3sg
                  *unnir-lugu*
                  say  -INF:3sg
                  '. . . saying (of his$_i$ cousin$_j$) who was lost that he$_i$ was looking for him$_j$'

The optional copying rule suggested by (21) will take the form of an ascension rule, that is, in the words of Perlmutter and Postal, "a rule where a subconstituent of an NP becomes a term":

(22)   *Ascend and copy a primary from a II host clause.*
       Side effect: *The ascendee becomes the II of the matrix clause by the Relational Succession Law, thereby displacing the host clause and causing it to become a chômeur.*

That this is a copying and not a raising rule is evidenced by (21c), where *igluni tammartuq* is a full NP which is the object of *ujarini*, the lower verb. Rule (22) interacts with a rule involving reflexive constructions. Consider the following:

(23) [Bg:34]   a. *Kunuk-∅    iŋmi-nik    tai-  -vuq.*
                     -ABS self -INSTsg name-IND:3sg
                  'Kunuk named himself said his name'

            b. *Kunuk taivuq.*
                  'Kunuk named himself, was named.'

(24) [Kl:54]       a. *Iŋmi-nut    tuqup-puq.*
                       self -ALsg kill  -IND:3sg
                  'He killed himself.'

b. *Tuquppuq.*
'He killed himself, was killed.'

Although I have no examples, both Bergsland and Kleinschmidt agree that
there are also uses of the reflexive particle *iŋmi-* 'self' in all of the oblique cases,
where they refer to underlying oblique case NPs: there are no ergative and
absolutive forms for this particle. From (23)–(24) we can see that, in reflexive
constructions involving coreferent primaries, the verb is formally intransitive,
and that there is optional expression of the reflexive particle as a chômeur in
the instrumental (23) or in the allative (24). (The case here seems to vary by
dialect when replacing primaries, but the use of the allative is becoming
standard.) We know that these are chômeurs because, in addition to bearing
no grammatical relation to the verb, they are optional, and they vacillate
dialectally between the two typical cases for chômeurs—allative and instrumental—insensitive to the semantic value of these cases. Finally, note that the
(b) forms of (23) and (24) are isomorphic with the output of a certain passive
construction (cf. below), as evidenced by the two-part glosses for these sentences. In formulating a reflexivization transformation, we realize that there is
no way to determine empirically whether an underlying $S_t$ or an underlying $O_t$
is converted to *iŋmi-* or to $\emptyset$. That is to say, we cannot determine whether this
process is ergative or accusative.[6] I will by fiat assume it is the $S_t$, which
becomes *iŋmi-* and refrain from drawing conclusions about ergativity based on
that in the following (obligatory) reflexivization transformation:

(25)   $NP_1 \Rightarrow$ **iŋmi-**
      Condition: *There is an $NP_2$ such that $NP_2$ is a primary;*
         *$NP_2$ outranks $NP_1$ on an abs > erg > III > non-term hierarchy;*
         *$NP_2$ and $NP_1$ are coreferent; and $NP_2$ and $NP_1$ are clausemates.*

$$\begin{matrix} \textbf{iŋmi-} \\ [+primary] \end{matrix} \Rightarrow \left\{ \begin{matrix} chomeur \\ \emptyset \end{matrix} \right\}$$

      Side effect: *The chomeur is marked with the instrumental or the*
         *allative case marker.*

(25b) is a suppression transformation; it is in violation of the Motivated
Chomage Law and the Reranking Law. Later we will see more evidence for
rules suppressing grammatical relations without concomitant advancement.

   Returning to Copying, we see that it feeds Reflexivization, and must therefore
be ordered before it:

(26) [K1:76]   a. *Nappar -simav -luni      misig -lir   -puq.*
                  sickness-PERF-INF:4sg realize-begin-IND:3sg
                  'He began to realize (of himself) that he was sick.'

---

[6] I owe this observation to Stephen Anderson.

    b. *Tuni-umar-lugit*     *unnir-puq.*
       give -want-INF:3pl say  -IND:3sg
       'He said (of himself) that he wanted to give them something.'

After Copying takes place in (26a–b), the transitive matrix clause with the copied element as object is obligatorily made intransitive by Reflexivization, since the copied element is coreferential with the ergative argument of the matrix clause.

*Infinitives.*   Consider the following infinitive mood constructions:

(27)    a. [Kl:89] *qiviag-luŋa*     *taku-vara*
                back -INF:1sg see  -IND:1sg,3sg
                'turning around, I saw him'

    b. [Bg:58] *aŋuti-rujug-šuaq-∅*    *silig -tu -rujug-šuaq-∅*
                man -very -big  -ABS broad-IP-very -big -ABS
                *aavir -šuaq-∅*    *uniar-lugu*    *tiki -lir  -suq*
                whale-big -ABS trail -INF:3sg come-begin-IP:3sg
                'the huge, broad man who began to come, trailing
                the big whale'

In (27a) the $S_i$ of *ilaga-*, the lower verb, is coreferential with the $S_t$ of *autlar-*, the matrix verb. In (27b) the lower verb, *uniar-*, is underlyingly transitive. However, only *aaviršuaq* agrees with *uniar-*, and it is read as an $O_t$. It is not coreferent with *aŋutirujugšuaq siligturujugšuaq*, the $S_i$ of the matrix clause. The UNDERSTOOD subject of the lower verb in this sentence is coreferent with the $S_i$ of the matrix clause. From this we isolate two properties of infinitive constructions: first, subject-subject coreference between clauses, and, second, *abs + verb* structure in the lower clause, with no possibility of an ergative case argument. In the case of transitive lower clauses, we posit a deletion of the subject in the ergative case. (27b), a centrally empedded construction, shows us that it is the coreferent NP in the lower rather than the matrix clause that is deleted: otherwise, *aŋutirujugšuaq siligturujugšuaq* would appear in the ergative case. An optional rule of Infinitive Assignment can be formulated as follows:

(28)    a. *Assign infinitive mood.*
    b. $erg_{subord.\ cl.} \Rightarrow \emptyset$

    Conditions:

      (i)   *The two clauses express events which are at least partially*
           *concurrent.*
     (ii)  *Parts (a) and (b) are conjunctively ordered.*
    (iii)  $I_{subord.\ cl.}$ *is coreferent with* $I_{matrix\ cl.}$

Side effect:

*The subordinate verb takes the infinitive mood suffix -lu-.*

Infinitive Assignment interacts with Copying and Reflexivization, as can be seen in (26a–b). From (26b), it is apparent that Copying must preceed Infinitive, since Infinitive deletes the original lower clause occurrence of the copied element.

*Fourth Person.*   Third-person agreement markers in possessive suffixes and in verb agreement suffixes in the dependent moods are of two kinds: One, called the FOURTH PERSON, cross-references NPs coreferent with the $S_t$ or $S_i$ of the verb of the same clause for possessives, and of the verb of the next higher clause for primaries in subordinate clauses; the other, called the THIRD PERSON, cross-references all other nonfirst- and nonsecond-person NPs.

Let us consider first the case of possessives:

(29) [K1:29]      a. *Arq -∅     -i           tai -vaa.*
                         name-ABSsg-POSS:4sg say-IND:3sg,3sg
                         'He$_i$ said his$_i$ name.'

                     b. *Arq-∅-a              taivaa.*
                             -POSS:3sg
                         'He$_i$ said his$_j$ name.'

In (29a) the subject and the possessor are coreferential; hence -*i*, the fourth-person agreement suffix, appears. In (29b) the subject and the possessor are noncoreferential, and the possessor is cross-referenced by -*a*, the third-person agreement suffix.

(30) illustrates the use of the fourth-person marker for subordinate constructions [cf. also (20) and (21c)]:

(30) [K1:91]   *Kivv   -at      -a           urniŋ   -mani*
                   servant-ERGsg-POSS:3sg come to-CONJ:3sg,4sg
                   *isi      -rqu-ŋŋil  -aa.*
                   come in-tell-NEG-IND:3sg,3sg
                   'When his$_i$ servant$_j$ came to him$_i$, he$_i$ ordered him$_j$
                   not to come in.'

Here, the entire NP *kivvata*, marked with the ergative case suffix, is the subject of *urniŋ-*, and therefore the possessor of *kivv-* cannot be coreferent with that which it possesses, its 'possessum'. Accordingly, the possessive suffix is third person. However, the object of *urniŋ-* is coreferential with the subject of *isirquŋŋil-*, the matrix verb, and thus the lower object is cross-referenced in the lower verb, *urniŋ-*, by the fourth-person absolutive agreement suffix.

To integrate the possessive and subordinate clause uses of the fourth-person marker, we can make use of a frequent proposal in the literature on Eskimo— put forth most recently by Mey (1969) and by Rischel (1971)—which makes the claim that possessive constructions are derived from underlying transitive sentences. In terms of Relational Grammar, then, possessive constructions would look something like (31) in underlying structure:

(31) $\qquad NP_i[_{NP}[_S \quad NP_i \qquad NP_j \quad verb]_S]_{NP}$
$$\qquad\qquad\qquad (possessor)\,(possessum)$$
$$\qquad rel_k\ rel_k \qquad I \qquad\quad II \qquad\quad rel_k$$
$$\qquad (\text{where } rel_k \text{ is any term or nonterm})$$

Among the arguments in favor of such an analysis are that the appearence of the possessor in the ergative case, and also the morphological similarity between possessive endings and verbal agreement suffixes, are thereby explained. Furthermore, this allows us to say that fourth-person marking is assigned to NPs coreferential with the subject of the next higher clause up, an important generalization in light of the operation of the fourth person in subordinate clauses, discussed above. We can now formulate a rule assigning the fourth-person marker (obligatory when the sentence contains more than one third-person term, optional otherwise), as follows:

(32)    *Assign fourth person to a primary in the third person in a subordinate clause.*
        Conditions:

    (a) *The affected primary is coreferent with the subject of the matrix clause.*

    (b) *The controller and the affected primary are separated by exactly one clause boundary.*

    (c) *The subordinate verb is not complementized by the IP.*

I pointed out at the beginning of this chapter that verbs in the infinitive mood are marked with the same agreement suffix, regardless of whether the single primary in the absolutive is an $S_i$ or an $O_t$. Yet, if the primary (or primaries) in the lower clause is in the third person, as in (20) and (27b), this appears to be contradicted. In (27b), the infinitive has a third-person suffix, cross-referencing a direct object, while in (20) it has a fourth-person suffix, cross-referencing a subject. Now, Kleinschmidt's paradigm of the infinitive mood (p. 48) is defective for third-person intransitive suffixes and fourth-person transitive suffixes. What is happening here is predicted by our formulations of Infinitive Assignment and Fourth Person Assignment. Since both rules are triggered by a subject (i.e. $S_i$ or $S_t$) in the matrix clause, they conspire to give this surface patterning. Thus, with intransitives, in order for there to be Infinitive Assignment, the subjects of the matrix and lower clauses must be coreferential, and, this then being the case, the subject of the lower clause must be assigned the fourth-person marker. For transitives, though, the subject of the lower clause is ergative (by definition), and, if Infinitive Assignment applies, it is deleted. Thus the only condition under which the fourth person is assigned to a transitive lower clause in the infinitive mood is when the remaining absolutive in the clause is coreferential with the subject of the matrix clause. But, if it were coreferential with the subject of the matrix clause, then it would also have had to have been coreferent with the ergative NP which was deleted by Infinitive Assignment under coreference with the subject of the matrix clause. If that were the case, then the clause would not have been transitive when Infinitive Assignment applied: It would have been reflexive (= intransitive, morphologically), since Reflexivization applied to it obligatorily on the previous cycle. In effect, then, the surface outcome is as follows: on nonfirst-, nonsecond-person absolutive arguments of verbs in the infinitive mood, the fourth person redundantly marks underlying intransitivity of the verb, and the third person marks underlying transitivity of the verb. Thus, we maintain the generalization on which we based our arguments for ergative-type agreement rules, namely, that infinitive mood clauses have only one primary argument, an absolutive.

## Advancements and Suppressions

In this section we will touch on some one-story transformations which affect grammatical relations.

*Impersonal Agent Constructions.* The Greenlandic impersonal agent construction is very similar semantically to German *man* constructions such as:

(33)            a.  *Man sieht die Frau.*
                    $\left\{ \begin{array}{l} \text{'I} \\ \text{'Someone} \end{array} \right\}$ see(s) the woman.'

                b.  *Man fährt ab.*
                    $\left\{ \begin{array}{l} \text{'I} \\ \text{'Someone} \end{array} \right\}$ depart(s).'

Like *man*, the Greenlandic impersonal agent expresses either an indefinite subject or a deferential first-person subject:

(34) [K1:157]   a. *Aŋut-∅     autlar   -puq*        ⇒
                   man -ABS go away-IND:3sg
                   'The man went away.'

b. *Autlar-nar*     *-puq.*
        -IMP AG-
$\left\{ \begin{array}{c} \text{'I} \\ \text{'Someone} \end{array} \right\}$ went away.'

(35) [Kl:56]      a. *Taku-vaa.*      $\Rightarrow$
              see  -IND:3sg,3sg
              'He sees him.'

              b. *Taku-nar*      *-puq.*
                  -IMP AG-IND:3sg
              $\left\{ \begin{array}{c} \text{'I} \\ \text{'Someone} \end{array} \right\}$ see(s) him.'

(36) [SL:1927:271]
           a. *Usur*       *-aatit*      $\Rightarrow$
             call happy-IND:3sg,2sg
             'He calls you happy.'

         b. *Usur-nar*      *-pusi.*
             -IMP AG-IND:2sg
             'Someone calls you happy.' = 'You are (said to be) happy.'

But a definite $S_t$ can be expressed as an allative chômeur:

(37) [Kl:56]      *taman-nuı*    *taku-nar*      *-puq.*
                  all    -ALsg see  -IMP AG-IND:3sg
                  'All have seen it.'

Clearly what is happening in (34)–(36) is that the subject of the verb is being suppressed, and the verb agrees with the remaining $O_t$ if there is one [recall now (17), where the verb agrees with an accusative case object only], and takes unmarked agreement (third-person singular) if there is neither a subject nor an object left for it to agree with. We can formulate this (optional) Impersonal Agent process as follows:

(38)    I $\Rightarrow$ $\left\{ \begin{array}{c} \textit{chômeur} \\ \emptyset \end{array} \right\}$

       Condition: *For a chômeur to result, the **I** must also be a full NP bearing the erg relation. Otherwise, the **I** must be either first person or pro.*

Side effects:

(a) *If there is no abs argument in the output for the verb to agree
with, the verb takes the 3sg agreement marker ($\emptyset$).*

(b) *The verb is marked with the IMP AG suffix, -nar-.*

(c) *The chômeur is marked with the allative case suffix.*

As mentioned earlier, suppression rules are at odds with Perlmutter and
Postal's conception of relational grammar. But consider the two possible
strategies for avoiding a suppression rule, instead treating the demotion as an
automatic side effect in accordance with the Motivated Chômage Law. This
can be formulated as an advancement transformation, as in (39):

(39)
$$
\begin{array}{c}
II \Rightarrow II \\
\left( I \Rightarrow \left\{ \begin{array}{c} ch\hat{o}meur \\ \emptyset \end{array} \right\} \right)
\end{array}
$$

This would explain the verb agreement in the case of transitives [but not the
accusative in (17)], but it would leave us with nothing to move into subject
position in the case of intransitives. This must be rejected.[7] Now, since we do
not have anything real to move into subject position with intransitives, we could
call this a dummy insertion rule, where a covert dummy, realized as $\emptyset$ and
signalled by *-nar-*, is inserted into subject position. Technically this will work,
since, according to the Dummy Agreement Law, dummies may trigger no agreement at all, and in these constructions intransitives display no agreement and
transitives agree with the object only. But this is clearly a notational varient of
the suppression formulation, and since there is no linguistic evidence for a
dummy here, the dummy insertion analysis is ad hoc, motivated only by theoretical considerations. Moreover, it turns our attention away from the fact that
spontaneous suppressions really seem to exist in natural languages.[8]

*Antipassive.* Consider the following sentences:

(40) [SL:1945:94]    a. *Miirqa-t        paar       -ai*        $\Rightarrow$
                        child-(ABS)pl take care of-IND:3sg,3pl
                        'She takes care of the children.'

---

[7] We could attempt to treat the transitive and intransitive cases as separate rules. But this would
miss a generalization in terms of morphology (i.e. *-nar-* occurs in transitive and intransitive constructions), and it would describe neither the pragmatic function of these constructions (to de-
ferentially indicate a first-person subject) nor their semantic function (to code sentences with
pro subjects).

[8] We are left, then, with two cases of suppression, Reflexivization and Impersonal Agent. This
admission increases the power of the theory, since it says that NPs can go *en chômage* spontaneously
and without motivation. Therefore, we must permit suppressions only where there is no other
choice. Eventually, though, we must examine all of the known cases of genuine suppressions so that
this class of transformations can be characterized and restricted.

b. *Miirqu-nik      paar-ši    -vuq.*
   -INSTpl     -APAS-IND:3sg
   'She takes care of children.'

(41) [SL:1945:94]
  a. *Nakuras-p     taku-vaa          piniartu-p    qiŋmiq-∅*
     doctor -ERG see -IND:3sg,3sg hunter -ERG dog    -ABS
     *unatar-aa            ⇒*
     beat   -TP:3sg,3sg
     'The doctor saw that the hunter beat the dog.'

  b. *Nakursap takuvaa piniartuq-∅     qiŋmi-mik    unata-i      -šuq.*
                                -ABS        -INST      -APAS-IP:3sg
     'The doctor saw that the hunter beat a dog.'

The (b) forms both contain an antipassive (APAS) suffix in the verb and an instrumental argument which is often glossed as an indefinite direct object. Now, we could easily formulate this antipassive rule as a direct-object suppression rule, leaving the subject unaffected (just as we could easily formulate English Passive as an ergative suppression rule, leaving the absolutive unaffected). Since suppression is a less constrained notion, however, and an advancement formulation is feasible here, we will consider antipassive to be an optionally applying advancement process,

(42)  *erg → abs*
      Side effects:

   (a) *The verb is marked with the antipassive suffix (variously -i, -si, -ši, -ŋŋiɣ, -llir, or -∅, depending on the verb stem).*

   (b) *The old abs becomes an instrumental case chômeur, or else it is deleted.*

Note that in (41) Antipassive applies to the lower clause, giving evidence that it is a cyclic process.

*Passive.* The Greenlandic passive can be built on the passive participle plus copula, *-(g)a + u-*, or else on the abstract nominalizer plus suffix meaning 'have', that is, *-niq + qar-*:[9]

(43)    a. *Aŋut-ip    arnaq- ∅    taku-vaa              ⇒*
           man -ERG woman-ABS see -IND:3sg,3sg
           'The man saw the woman'

_____

[9] These examples were elicited by Jerrold Sadock; they are used here for purposes of brevity. All of the constructions represented by the various alternatives in brackets are attested in Bergsland (1955).

b. *Arnaq-* $\emptyset$ $\left(a\eta uti\text{-}\begin{Bmatrix}mit\\mut\\mik\end{Bmatrix}\right)$ $taku\text{-}\begin{Bmatrix}tau\\niqar\end{Bmatrix}$ *puq.*

woman-ABS man $-\begin{Bmatrix}\text{ABLsg}\\\text{ALsg}\\\text{INSTsg}\end{Bmatrix}$ see- PAS    -IND:3sg

'The woman was seen (by the man).'

Passive, then, converts forms like (43a) to forms like (43b). The case of the demoted subject varies by dialect. Passive can be (optionally) formulated as in (44):

(44)   $II \Rightarrow I$
       Side effects:

   (a) *The verb takes the passive suffix, -(g)au- or -niqar-.*

   (b) *The displaced I may become a chomeur in the ablative, allative,*
       *or instrumental, according to dialect, but is most often deleted.*

The passive construction, according to Kleinschmidt, is used much less frequently in Greenlandic than it is in German. The reason for this is, I conjecture, that the $S_t$ in an active indicative sentence already has a relatively oblique position with respect to the verb, since it appears in the ergative case. Thus the purpose of a passive is fulfilled in part. This also explains why the demoted subject is only very rarely preserved as a chômeur. Kleinschmidt points out further that, when the speaker wants to suppress the subject of a transitive, he is more likely simply to delete it than he is to form a passive and then delete the chômeur [cf. also (23)–(24)]:

(45) [Swadesh:45]    a. *Tigianaq-$\emptyset$     taku-vaa.*
                        fox       -ABS see  -IND:3sg,3sg
                        'He sees the fox.'

                     b. *Tigianaq-$\emptyset$ taku-vuq.*
                                                IND:3sg
                        'The fox was seen.'


It would be premature to say that this deletion passive is entirely productive. The absolutive argument of the intransitive forms of some verbs must be derived from the subject—rather than the object—of the corresponding transitive expression:

(46) [Kl:55]                      a. *Sana-vaa.*
                                     work-IND:3sg,3sg
                                     'He worked on it.'

b. *Sana-vuq.*
-IND:3sg
'He worked.'

If (45b) and (46b) are derived transformationally from the corresponding (a) forms, they appear to be the results of advancements with obligatory chômeur deletion, along the lines of passive for (45b), and of antipassive for (46b). Derived or not, the same relationships hold between (47a) and (47b) (active–passive) and between (48a) and (48b) (active–antipassive):

(47)                        a. *Fritz sank the cruiser.*
                            b. *The cruiser sank.*

(48)                        a. *Grace ate the rabbit.*
                            b. *Grace ate.*

Thus in English and Greenlandic we find semantically parallel but morphologically opposite processes. To account for these processes, we have several options open to us. We can invoke the Subject Persistence Law, and say that (45b) and (47b) result from a Deletion Passive, and that (46b) and (48b) result from Direct Object Deletion. Or, we could say that (45b) and (47b) result from Ergative Deletion, and that (46b) and (48b) result from a Deletion Antipassive, thereby invoking an Absolutive Persistence Law. The first solution seems rather ad hoc for Greenlandic, while the second seems ad hoc for English. The parallels between the two languages in this respect, and between the relationships of morphology and semantics in both languages, can be captured if we admit both Subject and Absolutive Persistence laws, the former applying to accusative rules, the latter to ergative rules. In doing this, we will not have to do damage to our ideas of 'subject' and 'absolutive' by calling (46b) the result of Accusative Deletion and (47b) the result of Ergative Deletion.

ARGUMENTS FOR INCLUDING THE PRECEDING RULES IN THE CYCLE

The Cyclicity Law states that a rule is in the cycle if its application affects term structure. But neither Fourth Person Assignment nor Infinitive Assignment (when applied to intransitive lower clauses,) affect term structure. Even though this is the case, I will show that these rules must be ordered in the cycle, because they may feed Passive. This suggests that we broaden the wording of the Cyclicity Law to include rules simply REFERRING to term structure. Now, sentences like (49a) and (50a) indicate that Passive follows Infinitive Assignment and Fourth Person Assignment, while sentences like (49b) and (50b) indicate that Passive precedes Infinitive Assignment and Fourth Person Assignment:

(49) [K1:92] a. *Tuni-niqar-puq        pi   -qa   -ŋaa-rqu-lugu.*
                give- PAS -IND:3sg thing-have-alot-tell-INF:3sg
                'To him$_j$ was given [by him$_i$], [he$_i$] wanting him$_j$ to have a lot.'

b. *Piqaŋaa-raluar        -luni        tuniniqarpuq.*
    -even though-INF:4sg
    'Even though he<sub>j</sub> has a lot, he<sub>j</sub> was given to even more [by him<sub>i</sub>].'

(50) [K1:92] a. *Sinig-tit    -lugu      tuqut-tau- vuq.*
                sleep-cause-INF:3sg kill  -PAS-IND:3sg
                '[He<sub>i</sub>] allowing him<sub>j</sub> to sleep, he<sub>j</sub> was killed [by him<sub>i</sub>]'

          b. *Sinig-luni        tuquttauvuq.*
                -INF:4sg
                'He<sub>j</sub> was killed [by him<sub>i</sub>] while sleeping.'

In the (a) forms, Infinitive Assignment applies, deleting the lower subject be-
cause it is coreferential with the subject of the matrix clause. Then Passive
applies, and the former subject of the matrix clause is deleted. Were Fourth
Person Assignment ordered after Passive here, the verb of the lower clause
would have a fourth- and not a third-person agreement suffix. Ordered before
Passive, the lower verb's environment for application is eclipsed by Infinitive
Assignment, since it is transitive. In the (b) forms, however, it is evident that
Infinitive Assignment and Fourth Person Assignment could have applied only
AFTER Passive, since only the derived subject produced by Passive is coreferential
with the subject of the subordinate clause. Kleinschmidt (p. 92) claims that
Passive applies first when a lower clause in the infinitive is transitive, and that
Infinitive Assignment and Fourth Person Assignment apply first when a lower
clause in the infinitive is intransitive. I know of no evidence contradicting this,
and it is theoretically interesting. The most striking example I have found
bearing out Kleinschmidt's claim is the following:

(51) [Bg:60] *Killisaat        -∅      sani-mut piŋisuuv-luni*
                platform edge-ABSg side-ALsg be three-INF:4sg

                *naammak-kajug    -puq        issia-vigi -ssa  -vlugu.*
                sufficient -be apt to-IND:3sg sit   -LOC-FUT-INF:3sg
                'Since the edge of the platform is three-sided, it is
                    sufficient to sit on.'

In transitive form, *naammakkajugpaa*, the main verb, means 'he considers it
sufficient'. Thus, the matrix verb must have started out as transitive; then
Infinitive Assignment applied down to *issiavigissav-*, deleting its subject, co-
referential with the subject of *naammakkajugpaa*, hence blocking Fourth
Person Assignment. Then, Deletion Passive applied to *naammakkajugpaa*,
making it intransitive. At that point, Infinitive Assignment and Fourth Person
Assignment applied again, down to *piNasuuv-*. This proves that it is Infinitive
Assignment and Fourth Person Assignment—not Passive—which change their

ordering. Whether Kleinschmidt is correct or not, sentences like (49a) and (50a) provide evidence that Infinitive Assignment and Fourth Person Assignment must be included within the cycle, along with the rules which actually affect, rather than simply refer to, term structure.

## TOWARD A TREATMENT OF ERGATIVITY IN RELATIONAL GRAMMAR

Perlmutter and Postal point out that most previous theories of ergativity make the (incorrect) assumptions in (52):

(52)    a. *Ergativity appears only in case marking and agreement.*
        b. *Languages can be classified as ergative or nonergative.*

That (52a) is false is made clear in this chapter by the demonstration of the fact that many rules in Greenlandic aside from Case Marking and Agreement refer crucially to ergative relational categories (e.g. Antipassive, Clause Union, and Infinitive Assignment). (52b) is also false: a great many so-called ergative languages are in fact SPLIT ERGATIVE: that is, they make use of both ergative and accusative categories, according to specific parameters. Examples of this are Georgian, which splits according to tense, exhibiting ergative case marking in the aorist and accusative elsewhere; Dyirbal, Walbiri, Chinook, and Washo, which split according to person and number, as well as 'inherent lexical content' of pronouns and full NPs; 'active' or 'agentive' languages (e.g. Dakota, Tlingit, Onondaga, and Guarani), which make the split according to activity/stativity (roughly) of the verb; and, finally, Greenlandic, where, as we have seen, some rules apply on an ergative basis while others apply on an accusative basis.

Perlmutter and Postal have proposed that the absolutive be considered the lowest ranking primary, and, if I understand correctly, that there be a separate secondary term hierarchy [shown in (53)] for use in formulating the ergative rules (if any) found in a language:

(53)                    *abs*
                        *erg*
                        *III*
                        *nonterms*

Above we have seen that such a hierarchy is necessary; nevertheless, this does not mean that the existence of two hierarchies is crucial at all times. An example of this would be a rule like Copying, which refers to primaries as functioning categories, rather than as subjects or absolutives. Note also that the behavior of the categories 'absolutive' and 'ergative' in ergative rules is parallel, respectively, to that of the categories 'subject' and 'direct object' in accusative rules. Thus, for example, a Greenlandic clause may not contain an ergative argument, but it must always contain an absolutive argument (except in the case of suppressions), because of the ergative nature of the case-marking and agreement rules. This leads us to conclude that the laws which apply to subjects can also apply to absolutives, and that the laws which apply to direct objects can also apply to ergatives, a measure independently necessary if we are to constrain the set of possible ergative rules.

Given, then, two NP hierarchies, each with its own parallel set of laws, we must see whether it is the case that ergative relational categories are defined derivatively in terms of accusative relational primitives, OR that accusative relational categories are defined derivatively in terms of ergative relational primitives, OR that both ergative and accusative relational categories are derivative, and defined in terms of some neutral, more general set of primitive grammatical relations.

### Ergativity, Accusativity, and Markedness

I am going to argue that ergative and accusative relational categories must be defined in terms of a neutral set of grammatical relations. To do this, I will give evidence that ergativity and accusativity are relatively surface phenomena, and show that there are strong parallels between the two systems which indicate that they operate according to the same principles. The neutral set of primitives, then, will express what the two systems have in common, and it should be possible to project onto them the various groupings of $S_i$, $S_t$ and $O_t$ found in nautral languages.

This is shown from an historical perspective by Kuryłowicz (1949), who argues against the 'stage development' theory of N. I. Marr and others. This theory claims that accusative languages represent a higher stage of social development, and that all present-day accusative languages come at some point from ergative languages. Kuryłowicz demonstrates that ergativity may equally well grow out of accusativity; he shows a mirror-image parallelism between the two types, using the voice distinctions active/passive and active/antipassive as the ground for comparison. He provides the following diagram, which I have altered to fit our terminology:

(54)    a. accusative                          b. ergative

       (i) *active indicative*           (i) *active indicative*
           *transitive*                *transitive*
     (ii) *passive with demoted*    (ii) *antipassive with demoted*
           $S_t$ *deleted*              $O_t$ *deleted*
    (iii) *passive with demoted*   (iii) *antipassive with demoted*
           $S_t$ *as chômeur*          $O_t$ *as chômeur*

Where for any language, $\exists(iii) \Vdash \exists(ii) \Vdash \exists(i)$.

Now, the (ii) and (iii) forms are elaborations, and are therefore synchronically and diachronically less basic than the (i) forms. Even if a language with all three forms of (54a) lost (aii) and (aiii), it would be an accusative language, but would lack an opposition of voice. If it lost (ai) alone, however, it would have to be reinterpreted as being ergative, containing only (bi), and the former oblique would become the ergative. But the reverse may equally well occur: An ergative language with all three forms of (b), if it lost (bii) and (biii), would be an ergative language lacking a category of voice. If it lost (bi) alone, it would be reinterpreted as being accusative, containing only (ai), and the former absolutive would become the nominative, the former oblique the accusative. According to Kuryłowicz, this is just what happened in Indo-Iranian to produce ergative constructions in the perfective. I might point out that in the Hudson Bay dialects of Eskimo[10] the antipassive is not marked in the verb as it is in Greenlandic, and what is known to scholars of Greenlandic as the instrumental case functions as an accusative in those dialects. This is complementary to Kuryłowicz's Indo-Iranian example.

Such a simple historical process governing "typological change" hardly bespeaks treatment of these "types" as important elements of deep grammar. Rather, it shows that ergativity is a parallel and equally viable surface means of expressing synchronic oppositions of voice and transitivity. But Kuryłowicz provides no detailed demonstrations using linguistic data. His claim that ergativity may develop out of accusitivity—and as a relatively quick and superficial process at that—is supported and elaborated in Silverstein (1974). In that paper, Silverstein internally reconstructs an earlier, accusative stage from the now ergative possessive and pronominal system of Chinook. The mechanism he gives comes in two parts. The first consists of two transformations—for which there is independent historical evidence—which create ergatives out of datives for some (rigorously defined) parts of the pronominal paradigm. The second part, which occurred later, is the analogical spread of certain morphemes to the rest of the pronominal system, making it completely ergative. This mechanism accounts for the rather bewildering present-day pronominal paradigm, and indicates that the switch from an accusative system was a relatively superficial phenomenon.

Thus, from an historical perspective, we have evidence that the two systems are not so far apart. The existence of split ergativity also points in that direction. The use of neutral grammatical relations captures this fact, and has the added advantage of allowing us to collapase our parallel sets of laws governing the behavior of ergative and accusative categories into a single, unified set. Furthermore, it permits us to state certain transformational types with ergative and accusative analogues (such as Passive and Antipassive, as Kuryłowicz has shown us) just once, using the neutral relations. To determine the correct set of neutral grammatical relations, we must extract the properties which parallel

[10] Cf. Spalding (1960).

elements in the two NP hierarchies in (55) have in common:

(55)                a. *I*              $\longleftrightarrow$      b. *abs*
                       *II*             $\longleftrightarrow$         *erg*
                       *III*            $\longleftrightarrow$         *III*
                       *nonterms*       $\longleftrightarrow$         *nonterms*

The notions 'subject', 'object', etc., are defined by their behavior in the derivation, and this behavior is formally stated in the corpus of laws. Now that we
have expanded the laws to apply to an ergative hierarchy when a rule is ergative,
we have, in effect, given the same definition to subject and absolutive, direct
object and ergative. In fact, the behavior delineated in the set of laws for the
elements in the NP hierarchies is remarkably similar to, though more explicit
than, the Praguian theory of markedness. For example, the Reranking Law
defines a tropism toward subject status: A term can only decrease in markedness as the result of a rule and still remain a term. There is a Subject Persistence
Law, making the subject the only obligatory, and therefore unmarked, relation.
The hierarchy in (55a) is similar to Keenan and Comrie's (1972) NP Accessibility Hierarchy, which also can be construed as a functional syntactic markedness hierarchy.[11] In Relational Grammar nonterms are defined as being unable
to undergo or trigger many syntactic processes, which is characteristic of marked
elements. Finally, in almost all languages, the direct object, or else the ergative,
is the morphologically marked relation (unless grammatical relations are
signalled by order-class only), as opposed to the subject or the absolutive. Based
on this, then, we can posit (56) as our neutral NP hierarchy:[12]

(56)                            $\begin{Bmatrix} \textit{unmarked relation} \\ \vdots \\ \textit{marked relation} \end{Bmatrix} \textit{primaries}$
                       terms $\begin{cases} & \\ & \\ & \\ \textit{III} \\ \textit{nonterms} \end{cases}$

We now only need to formulate the corpus of laws once, in terms of (56) (e.g.
there would be an UNMARKED TERM PERSISTENCE LAW rather than a Subject
Persistance Law or an Absolutive Persistence Law). Furthermore, rules with
ergative and accusative varients can be stated using these neutral relations: for
example, Passive and the Antipassive can be collapsed as follows:

(57)    *marked relation* $\Rightarrow$ *unmarked relation*/Conditions $_{1,2,\ldots,n}$
        Side effect: *unmarked relation* $\Rightarrow$ *chômeur, by the Relational
        Annihilation Law*

[11] An NP Accessibility Hierarchy for Greenlandic like (55b) is argued for in Woodbury (1975).
[12] Even though markedness applies to the entire hierarchy, it would be beyond the scope of this
paper to apply it to more than primaries. For example, it is not at all obvious to me how indirect
objects would fit in.

Finally, rules such as Reflexivization [cf. (25)], about which we must make unwarrented assumptions as to ergativity or accusativity if we are committed to one hierarchy or the other, can be stated with a vagueness commensurate with the empirical claims we are able (or unable) to make. Thus, we would substitute the hierarchy in (56) for the hierarchy mentioned as condition of the Reflexivization rule as formulated in (25).

A crucial test for the claims made by (56) is to look at languages which are neither accusative nor ergative—for example, Takelma, where there are three cases for primaries, one for $S_i$'s, one for $S_t$'s and one for $O_t$'s. If the categories of primaries in languages like Takelma do not conform to a markedness hierarchy as in (56), obeying the neutral laws stated in terms of (56), then my proposal is falsified.

## Constraining the Assignment of Ergativity and Accusativity

A proposal such as I have outlined, or indeed any admission that there must be anything beyond (55a), points up a more general problem for universal grammar: That is, is there any definable regularity in the languages of the world as to where and to what degree ergativity (or accusativity) can occur? If there is, it should be possible to make explicit the following:

(58)   a.   *A function which projects all of the groupings of $S_i$, $S_t$, and $O_t$ possible in natural languages[13] onto the hierarchy in (56) (thereby interpreting these groupings in terms of markedness).*

       b.   *A class of rules in the grammars of particular languages which determine where to project a given set of groupings [e.g, in Georgian, a rule would specify that ergative-type groupings are projected onto (56) in the environment of the aorist, accusative-type groupings elsewhere].*

       c.   *Laws defining what is a possible member of the class described in (58b) (i.e. so that the theory does not predict that there will be languages which are, e.g. accusative in sentences where the main verb begins with a consonant cluster, and ergative elsewhere).*

---

[13] Not all groupings of these three grammatical functions are relevant, at least in surface NP marking. For example, there is no language which does not differentiate between $S_t$'s and $O_t$'s in some way. Perhaps the groupings which get projected onto the markedness hierarchy (56) should be derived from an ordered triplet, as in (i):

(i)                        $\langle S_t, S_i, O_t \rangle$

by means of a function that would draw a line (two lines for languages like Takelma) between two members such that everything to the left of the line has NP marking (or treatment in rules) *i*, and everything to the right has NP marking *j*. The advantage of this is that, by insisting that at least one line be drawn, groupings of $S_t$ and $O_t$ together are ruled out.

The tasks described in (58a–c) have been undertaken with astonishing success in Silverstein (1973) with regard to splits according to person and number of NPs: The end result of this study is a universal account which serves to cut down vastly the class of full NP and pronominal paradigmatic splits predicted by the theory. Silverstein constructs first a hierarchy of full and pronominal NPs based on Benveniste's (1966a and 1966b) feature system for pronouns according to strict principles of classical markedness theory, using as features $[\pm tu]$, $[\pm ego]$, $[\pm plural]$, and $[\pm restricted]$ (i.e. to distinguish the dual), and, for third-person and full NPs, adding features of 'inherent lexical content', such as gender and animateness. This gives a hierarchy, crudely, *full NPs > third person > first person > second person > inclusive*, from unmarked to marked. Silverstein then shows how certain rules, including Case Marking, when calibrated according to this feature hierarchy, can account for the split ergativity in Chinook and Dyirbal. The claim is, then, that for some rules a language will cut the hierarchy at a given point: Everything on the more marked end of the cut will be accusative, and everything on the less marked end will be ergative. Furthermore, if in a language where, say, only second persons are accusative, there is a Direct Object Deletion rule, into which the feature value $[+tu]$ is incorporated, thus blocking deletion of absolutive $O_t$'s. The virtue of such a system is that it greatly restricts the class of possible split-ergative pronominal and full-NP case paradigms, so that the only thing not predicted is exactly where a language will cut the hierarchy. Silverstein's insights can be readily incorporated into the Relational Grammatical treatment for ergativity we have been developing here: the hierarchy and the line-drawing mechanism would stand among the laws discussed in (58c), and the specifications as to where the cut would be made in a particular language would be stated as a rule of the class described in (58b).

Silverstein's analysis meshes nicely with considerations of semantic markedness. As he points out, the $S_t$ is the grammatical function most likely to code agents, and the $O_t$ is the function most likely to code patients. $S_i$'s tend to be neutral in this respect, depending often on considerations like activity/stativity of the verb. Now, unlike the third person, the second and first persons are almost always human; hence, they are more likely to be agents. Therefore it is not surprising that in the languages of the world the agent is more likely to fall into the UNMARKED case for agents (nominative) rather than the MARKED case for agents (ergative) in the first and second persons than it is in the third person. If this is correct, then it provides us with a semantically motivated means of determining the markedness of the derivative categories of primaries, a task which the function described in (58a) must carry out.

Let us now return to the data on Greenlandic, and consider the question of rule ergativity. Four different situations may arise: (i) a language may have a rule $R$ in accusative terms only; (ii) a language may have $R$ in ergative terms only; (iii) a language may have $R$ in both accusative and ergative terms (e.g. Greenlandic has both Passive and Antipassive); and (iv) a language may not have $R$ at all. This precludes the possibility of setting up a simple line-drawing implicational hierarchy such that, if a language has a certain rule as ergative, then everything below that rule on the hierarchy would be predicted to be ergative for that language. We must look for principles which govern whether a rule will be ergative or accusative, both on the language-particular and the language-independent levels.

Now, there is a striking regularity in the patterning of ergative and accusative rules in Greenlandic, which in turn suggests a pair of rules of the type outlined in (58b):

(59)  a.  *Project accusative-type relations on rules making crucial use of referential indices, referring to grammatical relations.*

      b.  *Project ergative-type relations onto rules that govern elements of surface morphology (e.g. case-marking and agreement rules).*

(59a) is supported by our formulations of Equi Subject Deletion, Fourth Person Assignment, and the referential part of Infinitive Assignment [i.e. condition (iii) on the formulation in (28)]; (59b) is supported by the case marking and agreement rules. But we must ask why Infinitive deletes only ergatives. This can be understood when we realize that Equi Subject Deletion is a rule wherein a clause merger takes place. That is, it is not necessary for the lower clause to obey the surface morphological rules governing what constitutes permissible clause structure, since it is incorporated into the matrix clause. In infinitive constructions, on the other hand, no merger of the matrix and lower clauses takes place; hence, the infinitive clause must obey regular rules of clause structure. Since clauses normally have absolutive arguments, the $S_i$ is preserved from deletion when Infinitive Assignment applies, while the $S_t$ is not. We must therefore add to our statement of (59a–b) the following:

(59)  c.  *When (59a) comes in conflict with (59b), (59b) takes precedence.*

That is to say, the ergative nature of the surface morphology prevents the deletion of an accusative-type category on the surface, even when such a deletion is in keeping with the general tenet that reference rules (such as Infinitive Assignment) are by nature accusative.

In turning to universal questions of rule ergativity, brought up by the need for laws of the kind outlined in (58c), we must realize of course that data from Greenlandic alone will not be sufficient. Rather, rule typologies from a variety of languages must be compared to determine the content of these laws empirically. We can, however, begin to tie what we have already in with Silverstein's analysis for the assignment of markedness to derived categories of primaries according to semantic criteria: This will permit us to make some universal predictions, and also to test Silverstein's assertions.

Consider, for example, Impersonal Agent. As we have seen, this is a suppression transformation, and frequently it has the force of a deferential first-person subject. It is not surprising, therefore, that subjects, rather than absolutives, ergatives, or direct objects, are suppressed: Subjects are most often semantic agents, while absolutives and accusatives exclude, for example, the very active class of causers, and ergatives exclude subjects of nonstative intransitives. Now, the need for deference is most acute when the speaker is the semantic agent, especially in expressions of volition, desires, etc; hence, a SUBJECT suppression is ideal. On a universal level, then, we would predict that it is extremely unlikely for transformations with this pragmatic function to turn up in other languages with an ergative formulation.

To attack this problem from the other direction, we note that ergatively working clause unions are common in accusative languages (e.g. French, Turkish, and Japanese) as well as in ergative languages. Using Silverstein's analysis, we would predict from this fact that the patient of the lower verb is semantically central, and unmarked in these constructions.

One final example is in order. To my knowledge, relationships between transitive and intransitive versions of certain verbs—for example, *sink* in (47a–b)—are universal. They are often said to be mediated semantically by an abstract predicate CAUSE, and they may well be called ergative, since they equate $O_t$'s and $S_i$'s. In pairs of this kind the patient relation is central; it would not be, however, if there were equivalent pairs mediated by a predicate like SUFFER, as in (60):

(60)          a. *The cruiser **suffered a sinking by** Fritz.*
              b. *The cruiser **sank**.*

where the boldface portions in both sentences are replaced by a single imaginery surface verb, transitive in (60a), intransitive in (60b). Hence the semantic coding of ergativity and accusativity can be linked to the question of why SUFFER is a less productive abstract predicate than is CAUSE.

By this example, and the examples provided by Impersonal Agent and clause unions, I mean to show that among 'ergative' and 'accusative' languages—although there is a certain range of variation on some points as to what is coded ergatively and what is coded accusatively—there are other points where coding one way or the other is uniform, indicating that both are viable and stable patterns in natural language. Because of this, and because of its possible implications for universal semantics, a renewed importance is lent to the task of discovering and characterizing the range and extent of ergativity and of accusativity. But at this point such a task ceases to be a problem for Relational Grammar specifically, and becomes a matter of concern for any theory of language.

## ACKNOWLEDGMENTS

My views about ergativity are due significantly to the work of Michael Silverstein, who conducted a seminar on that subject at the University of Chicago during the spring of 1974. The analysis of Greenlandic found in this paper is presented and justified more fully in Woodbury (1975); it is based in part on work by Jerrold Sadock which he presented in a course on the structure of Greenlandic at the University of Chicago during the fall of 1973. I am very indebted to him for what he has taught me about Greenlandic and, more importantly, for the stimulus which his acute sensitivity toward language has provided me with during many conversations, related and not-so-related to the subject matter of this chapter. I would also like to thank Paul Postal for his provocative comments on an earlier version of this chapter. Needless to say, none of the above may be blamed for anything in this study; all errors are my own responsibility.

# APPENDIX

Laws from Perlmutter and Postal cited in this paper:

RELATIONAL SUCCESSION LAW: *An NP promoted by an ascension rule assumes the grammatical relation (GR) borne by the host out of which it ascends.*

RELATIONAL ANNIHILATION LAW: *If an NP assumes a GR to a verb, then the NP that previously bore that GR to the verb ceases to bear any GR whatsoever, i.e. it becomes a chômeur.*

MOTIVATED CHÔMAGE LAW: *Chômeurs can only come as a result of the Relational Annihilation Law.*

CYCLICITY LAW: *A rule which affects term structure is cyclic.*

RERANKING LAW: *A rule that alters the status of an NP with respect to termhood must increase the rank of that NP.*

CHÔMEUR SEGREGATION LAW: *The only rules which fix the order of chômeurs with respect to terms are the following: (i) chômeurs precede all terms, and (ii) chômeurs follow all terms.*

SUBJECT PERSISTENCE LAW: *At every state of the derivation through the end of the cycle defined by verb$_i$, verb$_i$ must have a subject.*

DUMMY AGREEMENT LAW: *A verb whose cyclic subject is a dummy either does not agree at all or else agrees with its cyclic subject's brother-in-law.*

# REFERENCES

Benveniste, E. (1966a) "Structure des Relations de Personne dans le Verbe," in E. Benveniste, *Problemes de Linguistique Générale*, Gallimard, Paris.

Benveniste, E. (1966b) "La Nature des Pronoms," in Benveniste (1966a).

Bergsland, K. (1955) *A Grammatical Outline of the Eskimo Language of West Greenland*, Doctoral dissertation, University of Oslo, Micro-Editions, Inter-Documentation Company, AG, Zug.

Bergsland, K. (forthcoming) "Some Questions of Subordination in Eskimo and Aleut," in E. Hamp, ed., *Papers from the Chicago Conference on Eskimo Linguistics*, Chicago Linguistic Society, University of Chicago, Chicago, Illinois.

Bugge, A., et al., (1960) *Dansk-Grønlandsk Ordbog*, Ministeriet for Grønland, Copenhagen.

Greenberg, J. H. (1963) "Some Universals of Grammar with Particular Reference to the Order of Meaningful Elements," in J. H. Greenberg, ed., *Universals of Language*, M.I.T. Press, Cambridge, Massachusetts.

Johnson, D. (1974) On the Role of Grammatical Relations in Linguistic Theory, in M. La Galy, R. A. Fox, and A. Bruck, eds., *Papers from the Tenth Regional Meeting of the Chicago Linguistic Society*, University of Chicago, Chicago, Illinois.

Keenan, E. L., and B. Comrie (1972) "Noun Phrase Accessibility and Universal Grammar," presented at the Annual Meeting of the Linguistic Society of America.

Kleinschmidt, S. (1851) *Grammatik der Grönländischen Sprache*, Georg Olms, Hildesheim.

Kurylowicz, J. (1949) "La Contruction Ergative et le Dévelopment 'stadial' du Language," *Annali della Scuola Normale Superiore di Pisa* 18, 84–92.

Mey, J. (1969) "Possessive and Transitive in Eskimo," *Journal of Linguistics* 6, 47–56.

Perlmutter, D. M. (1971) *Deep and Surface Structure Constraints in Syntax*, Holt, Reinhart and Winston, New York.

Rischel, J. (1971) "Some Characteristics of Noun Phrases in West Greenlandic," *Acta Linguistica Hafniensia*, 13.2.

Schultz-Lorentzen, C. W. (1927) *Dictionary of the West Greenland Eskimo Language*, Meddelelser om Grønland, LXIX, Copenhagen.

Schultz-Lorentzen, C. W. (1945) *A Grammar of the West Greenland Language*, Meddelelser om Grønland, CXXIX, 3, Copenhagen.

Silverstein, M. (1973) "Hierarchy of Features and Ergativity," presented at the January 1973 meeting of the Chicago Linguistic Society, University of Chicago, Chicago, Illinois.

Silverstein, M. (1974) "Person, Number, and Gender in Chinook: Syntactic Rule and Morphological Analogy," presented at meetings of the American Anthropological Association and the Linguistic Society of America.

Spalding, A. E. (1960) *A Grammar of the East and West Coasts of Hudson Bay*, Queen's Printers, Ottawa.

Swadesh, M. (1944) "South Greenlandic (Eskimo)," in *Viking Fund Publications in Anthropology* 6, New York.

Woodbury, A. C. (1975) *Ergativity of Grammatical Processes: A Study of Greenlandic Eskimo*, unpublished Master's essay, University of Chicago, Chicago, Illinois.

# INDEX

## A

Abasheikh, M, 180, 183, 188, *218*

Abdication, *see* Demotion

Absolutive construction, 259, 264, 307, 310, 327–328, 330

Absolutive-ergative pattern, *see* Ergative-absolutive construction

Absolutive persistence law, 330

Ac, *see* Achenese

Accessibility approach, 27–45
  noun-phrase hierarchy in, *see* Accessibility hierarchy
  relative clause formation in, 157
  for subjects and nonsubjects compared, 172

Accessibility hierarchy, 29, 157–158, 330, *see also* Hierarchy; Relational hierarchy
  representation of, 271
  for specific languages, 84–85

Accusative-infinitive complement, 121–136

Accusative language systems, ergative development in, 329

Accusative rules, regularity of, in Greenlandic, 333

Accusativity pattern, 328–329, 333

Achenese (Ac) 99, 168, 211, 220–223, 224–244

AcI, *see* Accusative-infinitive constructions

Actorless infinitive complement, 293–294

Actor nominals, 279–305, *see also* Actor role

Actor role, 282, 283, 284, 290–296

Actor topics, as subjects, 301

Actor-topic verbs, 284, 301

Adjacency, of causative end-embedded verbs, 142

Adjectives, noun agreement of, in CM, 181

Adsessive case, 144

Advancee laziness law, 164n
  language types generated by, 174–175

Advancee tenure laws, 113, 114, 117

Advancement, 156, *see also* Promotion
  to direct-object chaining constraint, 164
  to subject chaining constraint, 159

Agency for change, in case determination, 77

Agent, 50, 61, 66, 69, 72, 143–144, 259, 260, 282, 321–322, 332

Agent-instrument distinction, 71

Agentive constructions, 264

Agentive languages, 327

Agentivity, concept of, 270

Agreement law, 157
  in passivization and fronting, 233

Agreement morphemes, in Achenese, 239–244

Agreement prefixes, of nouns in CM, 181

*Ah*, *see* Exclamation Ah

AH, *see* Accessibility hierarchy

Aissen, J., 122, 123, 124, 136–137, 142–143, 148, *149*, 257, *275*

Akkadian, mentioned, 262

Aleut, as OSV language, 259, 264

Algonquian, 265–268

*A*-marking, in Breton, 14–17

Ambiguous sentences, case structure in, 63, 64

Anaphora, 292, *see also* Reflexivization

Anderson, John, 71, *80*